reflections on the
recreation
and park movement

reflections on the recreation and park movement

A BOOK OF READINGS

DAVID GRAY
California State University, Long Beach

DONALD A. PELEGRINO
California State University, Northridge

 WM. C. BROWN COMPANY PUBLISHERS

Copyright © 1973 by Wm. C. Brown Company Publishers

Library of Congress Catalog Card Number: 72-92051

ISBN 0—697—07378—5

  Third Printing, 1976

Printed in the United States of America

Contents

Preface

In the selection of these articles there has been no attempt to maintain a consistent point of view. Many of the articles present antagonistic theses. This exposition of differing views is essential to an understanding of the recreation and park movement as it is developing in the latter half of the twentieth century. Nevertheless, the selection has not been entirely at random. We have tried to select articles which represent a point of view that may be important to the further development of the recreation and park movement. Our choices have been motivated by the belief that this movement has a significant contribution to make to American life and that our services should be guided by a social conscience.

The articles have been chosen from a wide range of sources published in the last ten years. Collectively they provide a perspective on some of the significant ideas circulating in park and recreation agencies but they are not a representative sample of our literature. They do not, for example, reflect the broad interest in recreation activities or the design of urban parks; rather they represent some other aspects of the movement and the cultural environment in which it works. This field has changed substantially in the last ten years and until now reports of these developments have been extremely diffused. This book brings together many of these significant contributions to the movement.

We are indebted to many professional associates who assisted in developing our evolving understanding of the recreation and park movement—what it is and what it might be, to the authors who permitted us to reprint their work, to Audrey Perritt who helped with the literature search, and to Barbara Lloyd who coordinated the many details of obtaining reprint permissions and preparation of the final manuscript. We gratefully acknowledge all of these contributions and extend our thanks and appreciation.

Leisure and Recreation

Long Beach Recreation Department
270 East Seaside Boulevard
Long Beach, California 90802

DAVID E. GRAY "This Alien Thing Called Leisure"

Leisure-Society-Politics: "The Political Environment of Parks and Recreation" *Proceedings* 1971, Park and Recreation Administrators Institute, University of California, Davis, 1972.

JOSEPH H. KRAUSE "Observations on Art in Our Time"

Leisure-Society Politics: "The Political Environment of Parks and Recreation" *Proceedings* 1971, Park and Recreation Administrators Institute, University of California, Davis, 1972.

"Too Much Is Too Little"

Time, The Weekly Magazine, August 1969.

WALTER L. STONE "Recreative Use of Leisure"

Parks and Recreation, National Recreation and Park Association, April 1967.

JAMES S. COLEMAN "Introduction: In Defense of Games"

The American Behavioral Scientist, Sage Publications, Inc., October 1966.

EVELYN BROWNE "An Ethological Theory of Play"

Journal of Health, Physical Education, and Recreation, AAHPER, September 1968.

GARY SMITH "Violence & Sport"

Canadian Association for Health, Physical Education and Recreation, CAHPER Journal, July/August 1970.

WALTER L. STONE "Recreation and Leisure: Their Impact on American Living Today"

Parks and Recreation, National Recreation and Park Association, February 1962.

RICHARD KRAUS "The Economics of Recreation Today"

Parks and Recreation, National Recreation and Park Association, June 1970.

GORDON K. DOUGLASS "The Economics of Leisure: How Much? What Kind? How Soon?"

A conference paper on Leisure and the Quality of Life.

IRA J. HUTCHISON, JR. "Promoting Functional Play Patterns"

Parks and Recreation, National Recreation and Park Association, September 1967.

"Charter for Leisure"

International Recreation Association JOHPER, February, 1971.

Leisure and Recreation

As a people we are seldom free of the work ethic. We are fundamentally a nation of workers. We carry over into time off the job the same pace and the same values we exercise on the job. "The worthy use of leisure time" requires us to work at the pursuits of leisure. For most Americans who are employed there are more "worthy" uses of leisure than there is leisure, and we are in a constant time bind that makes time scarce. The result is a high transience in leisure activities, high mobility, and a rapid tempo of life off the job as well as on it.

George Bernard Shaw once said ". . . a perpetual holiday is a good working definition of hell." Many Americans avoid this bond of hell by overscheduling and maintaining a hectic pace. This revolving round of task-oriented busyness takes one's mind off the business of living. If one's job and the tasks surrounding the

"Talk of the leisure oriented society and the decline of the Protestant Ethic has obscured the basic fact of the matter: modern populations on the average remain busy . . ."

home do not absorb all of the time, it is easy to invent a round of activities to augment the other requirements. In the end no leisure in the classical sense need be faced.

There are a great number of myths about the quantity of free time available to Americans. We clearly do not have all the time free of compulsion that advocates of the current economic system would lead us to believe. There seems to be some evidence that we have a small gain in the order of three to four hours weekly when commuting, working wives, sharing of household duties, and other developments taken into account. What time off the job is available is unevenly distributed. There have been two dramatic changes in this regard. The first change is the increase in retired leisure among elderly people. We have 20,000,000 retirees and we appear to be headed for 50,000,000. For them leisure is the core of life. The other major change is in children. There was a time when children were a leisured class. They are no longer. The demands of extended school years, extended school days, summer school, homework, lessons, commuting, and other activities have created for many young people a schedule only a computer could love. The leisurely, carefree days of the young are gone.

"The skilled urban worker has now achieved the position of his 13th century counterpart, whose long workday, seasonally varied, was offset by many holidays, rest periods and long vacations; annual hours of work now, as then, remain in the range of 19,000 to 25,000."

We think we can now see a technological efficiency that will free men from the necessity of producing goods to the extent that there will be an abundance of leisure, but there is no agreement on how much work there will be, nor how much leisure, nor how soon the technological revolution and the redeployment of the work force implied in the vision will be accomplished.

We have in the world a growing accessibility to more goods, services, and information, and a worldwide movement that results in changing values, traditions, and attitudes. All of these factors deeply influence leisure and its uses. What will people need and want beyond maintenance? In the pursuits of leisure, aspirations not necessities will count.

"Leisure hours are a period of freedom, when man is able to enhance his value as a human being and as a productive member of his society."

The benefits of leisure are the benefits of cultivating the free mind. Leisure offers opportunity for creativity. The activities of leisure are inner-directed; the opportunity to follow one's own inclination is there, whether one's bent matches the norm or not. Since the pursuits of leisure are the product of free choice, what is done is an expression of values. In making the choices of leisure one employs a value system that helps discriminate between what is helpful or harmful, good or bad, right or wrong. The leisure life offers not only a means of shaping values but also of expressing values.

A case can be made for the influence leisure has on the development of ethics. One cannot develop his ethics on the basis of decisions made by another, they must be based on the decisions he makes for himself. Since most free choices are made in leisure, the ethics one develops are based in leisure pursuits. In an important sense leisure is existential because it involves the exercise of free will—an important concept in existentialism. Everyone must make his own choices in leisure. Opportunity for fulfillment can be offered by others but fulfillment can only be accomplished by oneself.

From one point of view the pursuits of leisure are great social levelers. Relationships of work are conditioned by status and role, seniority and graded expertise, but in leisure activities these conditions are not so strong. In ideal situations they may be totally inoperative. In leisure there is the possibility that relationships can be based on shared interest without all the artificial constraints of social role. Most of the ills of our society are "time intensive" rather than "goods intensive." By that we mean that improvement requires greater investment of time rather than investment

"There are those who believe the use of leisure is a final test of a civilization and that when man has reasonable security and leisure he can seek cultural and spiritual values that he could not in a toil oriented world."

of goods. In our time-scarce economy we have not made the investment of time in ghetto schools, for example, which would improve the quality of education. We have not created a school system that can stand alone without substantial time support from the home and the community. In the ghetto this support is not provided from outside the school and the result is unsatisfactory. If ghetto education is to be improved, our time commitment must be increased, if not from the home and the community then at public expense within the schools themselves.

Leisure is nonutilitarian. The great use of leisure, as we understand leisure in our society, is play. This self-generated and often self-regulated activity is an attempt at self-fulfillment. For the child it is the ultimate reality. It can be carried to the limits of exhaustion with no motivation except its own. Play is the primary developmental activity in the life of the young child.

Leisure is the central fact of life for growing millions of the earth's population. Increased vacation and earlier retirement extend the amount of free time available to Americans. The growing trend to a four-day work week and the five annual three-day weekends now common in the United States increase the size of the increments of time off the job. Meeting the demands for goods and services in this "leisure boom" has created a 105 billion dollar industry, and the demands are still growing. There is impressive evidence that meeting the desires of the American people for leisure oriented activities is a growth operation with few parallels anywhere. In this field, as in many others, the United States may be leading the world.

Social movements like individuals are the prisoners of their successes. They tend to repeat the acts that have brought success in the past. We found success in the promotion of recreation activities and we have repeated that act throughout the history of the recreation movement. We should have discovered long ago the nature of the business we are in, but we have not. Only now are we beginning to evaluate recreation. In the emerging view it is not activities or facilities or programs that are central, it is what happens to people. Recreation is not a specific event, a point in time or a place in space; it is a dimension in life; it is a state of being.

"one of the greatest problems in recreation is the education of the public to the need for a philosophy of play"

It is only today that industries are becoming aware of the various kinds of business they are in. When IBM discovered it was not in the business of making office equipment or business machines but it was in the business of processing information, it began to conduct its affairs with a much clearer vision of what it is about, and the corporation became amazingly successful. This reassessment of the nature of the work generated great changes and released enormous energy.

Recreation is not an activity; it is the result of an activity. We constantly pair the word recreation with an activity and in this way we have come to interpret the word recreation in terms of an activity. But recreation as a psychological response is independent of activity. The fundamental error of equating recreation with activities has focused attention of nearly everyone in the recreation movement on activities. This obsession with activity has prevented formulation and adoption of a truer definition of recreation. Lacking such a definition we have been content to define our goals and limit our services to the provision of activities with little regard for the influence such activities have on the participants. The activity is the medium; it is not the message.

We must give more attention to the recreation concept and improve our definition of it. Current definitions ignore or give little attention to the psychological implications of recreation. They are activity-centered. Definition in terms of activities is unsatisfactory because a given activity may provide recreation for one individual and not for another; worse yet, it may provide recreation for a person at one time but not at another. Current definitions work within a time frame—leisure—but recreation may occur at any time. They hold out for inherent reward, but many recreation responses are dependent on feedback from others. It is not clear why acceptance of material reward invalidates the experience. Some mandate social acceptability; a little introspection will reveal the absurdity of that criterion.

I propose the following definition: Recreation is an emotional condition within an individual human being that flows from a feeling of well-being and self-satisfaction. It is characterized by feelings of mastery, achievement, exhilaration, acceptance, success, personal worth and pleasure. It reinforces a positive self-image. Recreation is a response to esthetic experience, achievement of personal goals or positive feedback from others. It is independent of activity, leisure, or social acceptance.

Adoption of this definition will change many of the things we do in recreation agencies. Although recreation may involve mass activity and mass participation, in the sense that many people are active in the same place at the same time, those who are participating are not having mass recreation. There is no such thing as mass recreation. Recreation is the internal, individual, pleasurable response of the organism. It may occur in the company of masses of people; it may even be stimulated by the presence of large numbers of others engaged in the same activity, but it cannot be said that there is a mass response that is recreation.

"The key concepts in the community role are engagement and participation—engagement in the great problems and issues of our time and participation in the lives of our communities."

This Alien Thing Called Leisure

David E. Gray

INTRODUCTION

"Leisure is the best of all possessions."
Socrates

". . . I've no doubt that the relationship between leisure and hypochondria is taken for granted, but I imagine it is only taken for granted in a society in which work is considered moral and leisure is looked upon with suspicion."
Russell Lynes

"Tell me what you do when you are free to do as you wish and I will tell you what kind of a person you are."
Charles Brightbill

"The leisure problem is fundamental. Having to decide what we shall do with our leisure is inevitably forcing us to reexamine the purpose of human existence, and to ask what fulfillment really means . . ."
Julian Huxley

"To be able to fill leisure intelligently is the best product of civilization."
Bertrand Russell

"Leisure is the mother of philosophy."
James Hobbes

". . . a perpetual holiday is a good working definition of hell."
George Bernard Shaw

These quotes and the hundreds of others that could be cited are emblematic of the enormous interest in leisure through the centuries, but interest does not equal understanding. For all the attention given leisure, we do not know much about it. Depending on your value system and life style, you might agree with any one of these quotes. If you are a typical American, you probably would not agree with any of them. Most Americans respond to a different definition of leisure than these quotes assume. There has been much confusion in our consideration of leisure. This confusion stems, in part, from our lack of any

Reprinted with permission from David E. Gray, Vice President for Administration, California State University, Long Beach.

generally accepted definition of the term. Perhaps that is the place to begin.

The central thesis of the remainder of this paper is that in the large volume of literature written about leisure in recent years at least three general approaches to a model of leisure can be identified. Once these distinctions are made, the interrelationships of leisure with work, time, and values become a little clearer.

TOWARD WORKING MODELS OF LEISURE I, LEISURE II, AND LEISURE III

The first model is the economic and discretionary time concept advocated by Marion Clawson, of *Resources for the Future*, and many others. This concept holds leisure is the portion of time which remains when time for work and the basic requirements for existence have been satisfied. What remains is discretionary time which parallels the economic concept of discretionary money. Ott Romney suggested in 1934 that leisure is "choosing time" free of attention to the necessities of living and available for use according to one's wish. This definition divides time into three great classes: time for existence—sleeping, eating, sanitation and the like; time for subsistence—working on one's job; and leisure which was the time left over when at least a minimum level of existence and subsistence had been accomplished. This definition of leisure has been widely adopted. It is the most widely accepted concept of leisure in America, embraced by Madison Avenue, the mass media, and most of the people of the nation. This concept is reenforced by Webster's dictionary which defines leisure as "... freedom or spare time provided by cessation of activities ... free time as a result of temporary exemption from work or duties ... time at one's command that is free of engage-

ments or responsibilities ... a period of unemployed time ..." I have labeled this model Leisure I.

The second view, based on the Greek concept of leisure has been forcefully articulated by Sebastian de Grazia in *Of Time, Work and Leisure* and others. The origin of the word leisure is the Greek word for school. For the Greeks, leisure was not vacant time, it was time spent in the exercise of one's intellectual powers and moral character for the benefit of one's community and one's self. Leisure, in the classical sense, is an activity which involves pursuit of truth and self-understanding. It is an act of aesthetic, psychological, religious and philosophical contemplation.

Robert Lee in *Religion and Leisure in America* has suggested:

> "To be at leisure is not to be on vacation from reality. Leisure is the time for discovery. It is the freeing of the mind from immediate habitual concerns to a consideration of ultimate concern. It is a time for rediscovering the meaning and purpose of life, for seeing the pursuit of living in its wholeness. Leisure is the occasion for the development of broader and deeper perspective and for renewal of body, mind, and spirit. Leisure is the growing time of the human spirit ... the occasion for learning and freedom, for growth and expression, for rest and restoration, for rediscovering life in its entirety."

This concept of leisure argues that leisure is expressed as the contemplative life. It is a mind set and a life style which is free of work or time. It is a state of being. I have labeled this model Leisure II.

The third concept of leisure apparent in our current popular literature is the anti-utilitarian view which has been recently articulated by Walter Kerr, the former drama critic for the *New York Times*, in an attractive and provocative book called *The Decline of Pleasure.* Kerr takes as his central thesis a denial of the idea that only utilitarian activity has value. This concept rejects the position that every investment of human energy must produce a useful result. It rejects the work ethic as the only source of value and permits the investment of self in pursuits that promise no more than the expression of self. This concept accepts joy and seeks pleasure. It suggests leisure is a state of mind that is a worthy end in itself. I have labeled this model Leisure III.

These three models: Leisure I, which embraces the concept of discretionary time, Leisure II, which adopts the classical sense of a contemplative state of being, and Leisure III, which accents joy, encourages self-expression, and denies utilitarianism as the only source of value, are central to the rest of this paper. In the following pages some interrelationships of these three models with work, time and values will be explored.

RELATIONSHIP WITH WORK

The great promise of the industrial revolution and of the technological revolution that followed it was that it would make leisure a universal possession. True to that promise those who speak loudest for our "American way of life" have taught us that Americans have the greatest amount of leisure ever enjoyed by a nation in the history of the world. From some perspectives that view is a myth. The best that can be claimed is that our current society has afforded an increased measure of Leisure I—discretionary time. There are those, and Sebastian de Grazia, who made a landmark study of this matter, is among them who would deny that the industrial and technological revolutions have added appreciably even to Leisure I. In the contemplative life style demanded by Leisure II and the

nonutilitarian demands of Leisure III, the industrial and technological revolutions have been an antagonistic influence.

The necessity and desirability of work has been a central ethic of Christian teaching. The biblical admonition declares ". . . this we command you, that if any would not work neither should he eat." In the unnecessary but prevalent dichotomy drawn between work and leisure this "protestant ethic" is a formidable roadblock in the path to enjoyment of leisure. This tendency to draw a dichotomy between leisure and work and to ascribe good characteristics to work and bad characteristics to leisure is a false dichotomy. If one subscribes to the "protestant ethic" leisure is impossible. A pervading sense of guilt permeates any experience that even approximates leisure.

To permit some response to the desire for leisure and the promise of leisure held out by our economic system we have developed an elaborate rationalization that holds that leisure is a respite from work that provides rest and relaxation. It is recuperative in nature. It restores our powers and makes each individual ready to work again. That is its purpose, its meaning, and its justification. This view of leisure demands only the discretionary time of Leisure I; it is ambivalent or antagonistic to Leisure II and Leisure III.

With the development of automation there has been a lot of speculation on replacement of the role of work as central to our culture. The replacement may be leisure, or recreation, or education depending on the orientation of the individual doing the speculating. For the foreseeable future this appears to be nonsense. The nature of work may change, but whatever forms the central core of our lives, is going to look like work. We cannot adjust to a life without work, or to a life in which work has a minor role, in the space of one or two generations even if we want to and we don't want to.

The vision of a world in which machines do all the work and men do everything else has some other flaws in it. This vision is the result of extrapolating increases of productivity in the manufacture of goods. It does not take into account redeployment of our work force into the service field where the demands are less predictable and the inefficiencies are much greater. It does not recognize the tremendous need for social work either. If only a small part of the necessary domestic programs are undertaken, there will be enough work to go around for a long time.

RELATIONSHIPS TO TIME

Our vision of time is a never ending stream passing by, second by second and minute by minute. Flowing in from an unknown future and disappearing into the void of the past. Time is a straight line, linear entity rushing around and through us silently and inexorably. Time cannot be captured, stored or expanded. It is beyond our understanding and control. A minute lost is gone forever.

There was an era when man's view of time was different. Observing the ebb and flow of the tide, the waxing and waning of the moon, and the coming and going of the seasons man conceived of time as circular. The tide that ebbed would again flow, the moon that waned would return to full, the summer that trailed off into fall would return again. There was a rhythm to time and to life that was repetitive. In such a view the pace was slower. A minute lost would be around again. In such a time man could pause to listen to his soul.

The most obvious relationship between leisure and time is seen in Leisure

I where the concept of discretionary time is central. Somehow the distinctions inherent in calculation of Leisure I make time scarce. Most of us are in a time famine. In our time the "rat race" is a kind of escape. This revolving round of task oriented busyness takes one's mind off the business of living. If one's job and the tasks surrounding the home do not absorb all the time, it is easy to invent a round of activities to augment the other requirements. In the end the contemplation of Leisure II and the anti-utilitarian approach of Leisure III need not be faced.

Some of our young people today are making choices in the time-work dichotomy that do not square with 300 years of American tradition. Given the choice of more work to buy more goods or time off the job, they are choosing time off. This violates the "Protestant ethic" and is a cause of wonder and distress to their parents. It also increases Leisure I and may even lead to Leisure II or III.

Some young people have begun to pursue Leisure II. For a few members of the counter culture, Leisure II has become a central focus of their lives. They have abandoned the busyness cycle of the straight society, settled for a bare subsistence, adopted a more leisurely pace, and begun to act out some of the philosophical themes they are contemplating. The number that may ultimately be drawn to this life style, the length of their commitment, and the impact they may have on the larger society are yet to be tested. But the attitude of the larger society is clear. They think behavior of this type should be punished.

The schedule and tempo of a mechanized and urbanized society have in recent decades largely governed our existence. The demands of industry have dictated our divisions of time and the pace of contemporary life. The needs of our industrial machine have been the great rigidity around which our other uses for time have been scheduled.

The school calendar with its relatively short school day and long summer vacation was adopted to fit the casual labor needs of an agrarian economy. In spite of this, the industrial schedule for work and the agrarian schedule for school have been reasonably compatible. When adjustment was necessary, the school schedule usually gave a little to permit scheduling of family leisure activities.

As the new pattern of our industrial society emerges and the traditional school calendar is projected into the future, conflicts are apparent, and as pressures for academic accomplishment increase, the demands of school become even more rigid. If the school calendar is not altered, it may become the governing factor in development of family leisure activities. If it is, much of the potential for family response to Leisure I will be lost. The relatively new but rapidly spreading movement toward the four days-forty hours work week will throw the industrial and school calendars even further out of balance.

For those who are fully prepared for leisure, the availability of time may be a greater limitation on our activities than availability of income. Economic growth can increase real income, but it cannot add to total time and may easily increase the demands on what time is available.

Time, unlike purchasing power, cannot be expanded or accumulated. It is permanently and irretrievably fixed at 168 hours per week per person. Time can be reallocated among uses, but even here the limits are narrow. Time then can become more and more scarce compared to goods. Thus the "price" of time can rise faster than the price of goods. The housewife who lines her oven with aluminum foil is spending goods to save the time cleaning the oven requires.

One of the outcomes of the dynamic relationship between time and goods may be that we will seek things to buy with rising income, that take little time to enjoy and maintain. As time becomes more scarce and goods become more plentiful, there is a tendency to invest in the activities which involve the purchase and consumption of goods in place of activities which involve the commitment of time. Thus activities like eating out, racing cars, or water skiing, which are high consumption activities with relatively low time requirements take precedence over low consumption, high time commitment activities like contemplation, writing, or sculpture. As long as goods can be substituted for time, people have reason to want more income. But goods cannot be substituted for time indefinitely. Eventually it will be impossible to raise the level of well being of society by improving the level of consumption. Where that point is, we have not yet decided. For many Americans we may have already reached it.

The distribution of Leisure I and the size of its increments condition the uses that can be made of it. The length of leisure periods and frequency of their occurrence are matters of considerable interest. Leisure I can occur on a daily, weekly, annual or other basis. Currently our daily leisure is broken up into rather small segments—perhaps a little before work and a little at lunch time, but most is available in the late afternoon or early evening, after work and before bed. The total number of leisure hours per day— usually about four—is broken up into small increments. This limits its uses. Our weekly leisure is weekend leisure. We normally think of this as two whole days, but all of this time is not leisure. Regular personal chores reduce the time available and often jobs undone during the week are allowed to pile up on the weekend. Nevertheless, the longer period of time and the more flexible schedule which mark the weekend permit activities which would be impossible during the remainder of the week. Other Leisure I is vacation time. This longer period—frequently one to three weeks—will allow activities which cannot be undertaken at other times—particularly travel.

CONSTRAINTS AND INHIBITIONS

It will be the work of the young among us to develop an environment in which Leisures I, II, and III can mature. The next two or three decades will be years of transition. During these years, Americans will be evolving some kind of adjustment to the radically different society automation and other forces are now creating. Hopefully, in the latter years of this century we will generally have a substantial amount of leisure and a value system and enough security to permit us to enjoy it. In the interim, however, we do not have the traditions, or the philosophy, or the skills to deal with it. It appears likely that the attitudes of the present adult population will not adapt quickly to the demands of the society now forming. One of the difficulties we shall encounter is formation of attitudes and values in keeping with changed patterns of life. This has enormous implications for public planning and programs where it is easy to so far outrun public opinion that programs lack public support.

There has been a growing tendency for a good many people to become spectators in life. Jay Nash struck out at this tendency a good many years ago when he attacked "spectatoritis." We know now this state of affairs had not reached full flower when he was expressing concern, because the first generation baby sat by TV has not reached maturity. They are now in college and we are amazed to learn that the typical high school graduate today has had 18,000 hours in school and 22,000 hours before the television set.

There is nothing intrinsically wrong with watching spectator events or TV, of course, but watching, at best, is living second hand. When watching absorbs more time than school, one wonders whether the rewards merit the investment.

The spectator lives life at arms length; he lacks involvement and his life has an antiseptic quality about it. Emotions induced from outside stimuli somehow don't seem genuine. The business of living is acted out in symbolic terms and life becomes an abstraction. Watching the events of our time is an important and rewarding facet of living, but when watching becomes central, the price is sacrifice of living experiences which are necessary to fulfillment.

Somehow Madison Avenue has gotten across the idea that leisure and sales are synonymous and the dimensions of the good life are rung up on the cash register. Madison Avenue, of course, is interested in mass sales so it pictures the good life as one of mass spectatorship or mass consumption. That is the vision that rings the cash register. Such an image is misleading. It may promote Leisure I and perhaps Leisure III, but it is extremely antagonistic to Leisure II.

One of the constraints on expression of self in leisure activities is the reluctance of the adult to demonstrate lack of skill. It is important to start lifetime pursuits early in life. Up to a point, the young don't mind being taught, but adults resent being a beginner. Study after study confirms the thesis that comparatively few recreational interests not initiated in the teens or earlier, are pursued as adults. We need to get over these inhibitions. The world changes;

people change; if we become all we can become, the joys of boyhood cannot sustain the man.

Until recently philosophy was the province of a small group of scholars working on highly esoteric specialties. But the rapid dissemination of existential thought has brought philosophy out of the libraries and into the streets. Philosophical questions are now being discussed by a wide variety of people, including particularly the young. They realize the continuing questions like what is the meaning of life?; what is the meaning of death?; what does it mean to be human?; what is the good life? are the great unyielding mysteries of the human condition and they want to make their own judgments. The greatest minds in the history of western philosophy have made only hesitant, tentative statements about these matters, but their effort has produced the values we try to act out in our daily lives.

Contemplation of these matters is a product of Leisure II. Not many of us are capable of a sustained effort of this kind. To deal with leisure as the Greeks conceived it, one must have a kind of serenity that is rare in our time. (It may have been rare in any time including the golden age of Greece when the concept was postulated.) It is an unusual individual that can contemplate the mysteries of the human condition for long periods. To be able to live with one's self on such intimate terms, one must have an inner harmony. Introspection is the most hazardous of all occupations. To be truly contemplative, one must have inner resources. It is often a lonely state. One does not contemplate much in the midst

of a cocktail party or a hockey match.

Leisure III is nonutilitarian. The great use of leisure, as we understand leisure in our society, is play. This self-generated and often self-regulated activity is an attempt at self-fulfillment. For the child it is the ultimate reality. It can be carried to the limits of exhaustion with no motivation but its own, and it affords great benefits in learning, self-expression, and social interaction. We grudgingly sanction play for children, but our society does not really approve of play for adults.

CONCLUSION

Vast numbers of people can be induced to conform to a stereotype life style by convention, but somehow the individual personality will assert itself. For most people in our society, the expression of the individual personality comes during leisure. Leisure is amoral. It is the uses that are made of it that cast it as moral or immoral. To be really comfortable in a life with large segments of leisure we will have to revise our whole concept of the nature of mankind and his place in the universe. To reap the enormous benefits leisure potentially affords, we must stop treating it as an alien thing and nurture it whether it comes as Leisure I, II, or III. Society has always exercised a substantial amount of control over the uses of leisure. Undoubtedly, our society will continue to influence the uses that are made of it. But we must exert such controls with caution. The mind that guides must not be given the power to direct.

Observations on Art in Our Time

Joseph H. Krause

Although I agreed to speak to the topic of Recreation and The Arts, time, distance and considerable thought have caused me to more specifically define my topic as: "Observations on Art in Our Time, The Relation of The Arts to Recreation and Entertainment Is More Than You Think It Is." These are the three major ideas which formed the basis for the new approach to Recreation and The Arts that are responsible for this restatement of the topic:

I. My belief that most of us who have been responsible for teaching about the arts have painfully misjudged the role they play in modern Western culture;

II. My belief that the form the arts have taken relative to leisure and recreation have been far more successful as entertainment than they have as art by almost all definitions; and

III. My belief that the most significant value of both the arts and most so-called recreational activities, exists primarily in their ability to entertain us.

I would now like to expand on these ideas and offer support for my arguments beginning with the function of art in modern society:

I. The definitions of art which have been developed in Western culture and which are a part of the current art mystique are based on a theory which although relating back to the ideas of Plato were rectified, simplified and given wide circulation during the nineteenth and early twentieth centuries, not as theory but as fact. This was the concept, for it is as yet unproved, that art was the revelation of an absolute value related to the nature of beauty which, in turn, was hypothesized to be an absolute form, namely; "truth visually revealed." This occurred regardless of the media or form involved. This idea or its counterpart was evidenced in music, the dance, painting, sculpture and as new art forms were evolved the idea tagged along.

With this as a starting point those who sought to bring enlightenment to the masses via the arts—an activity that was as highly popular with numbers of "cultured" Victorian ladies as was that of bestowing charity on "the deserving poor"—postulated, with the help of a number of nineteenth century estheticians, that the self-evident qualities of truth and thus beauty via the arts, had only to be recognized and

Reprinted with permission from Joseph H. Krause, Professor of Art, California State University, Long Beach.

appreciated to be effective. And, since truth would make men free and freedom was, and remains, an ultimate personal value in Western culture—exposure to the truth visually revealed was to be, and is, highly desirable.

There were, however, several serious problems, problems which I must add are still quite with us. First, that exposure to truth, as revealed by beauty presented through the arts, didn't seem to make much difference in either people's attitudes or actions. For regardless of the amount or depth of the exposure to art while good men remained good, evil men continued to be evil, the poor and destitute remained poor and destitute and life for members of the middle class was still filled with all those problems unique to the middle class and the state of the world seemed to get but more confused and difficult. Secondly, that even when the museums, concert halls and other institutions which were held responsible for the care and maintenance of the arts in our culture were opened freely to the public and the various arts were made an integral part of public education an overwhelming majority of the people simply weren't interested in either their potential or the problems of their support. Proof of this is to be seen in the difficulty encountered by those who have tried to convince voters of the advantages that could be gained by voting bond issues by which the arts would be supported. No one seemed to argue that art was bad, it was just that other things were more important. And thirdly, the sources, public and private, that have traditionally supplied the money necessary to support the arts and bring their benefits to the people never seemed to fully understand the importance of the arts as a civilizing influence. This, in spite of the fact that they themselves were for the most part usually well-educated and cultured men and women who when elected or appointed were so on the premise that they would represent not only the best interests of the arts but also those of their constituents.

Recognition of the arts as truth revealed, to be sure, depended upon what can only be defined as a mystic force communicated to those capable of receiving it. This is an idea that is still current not only among many laymen but also among those educated in the arts and members of the critical art press. William Wilson, art critic for the Los Angeles Times in a recent review (September 13, 1971) of the Los Angeles County Art Museum's Survey of Oriental Ceramics noted in his lead paragraph that:

> "An object that has become a work of art has a distinctive thing about it. It seems to kind of hum."

Unfortunately, or perhaps fortunately, not everyone is able to perceive this "kind of hum." But granted that art objects do emit something that can be sensed by people sensitive enough to receive the transmission there are still a number of questions that must be raised. Foremost among these is "Why is it that what is transmitted can be received by so few and that the majority of the people have to be told it occurs?" And secondly, "Were those who are able to hear the "kind of hum" referred to born with this ability, was it the result of a revelatory phenomenon, education or training?"

The art critics and art teachers of the late nineteenth and twentieth centuries almost unanimously agreed that the reason most of us were unable to recognize art and thus unable to benefit by "truth revealed" was that:

A. we weren't sensitive enough; a state that could be overcome only by exposure to "the finer things in life," education and exercise of our intellect and/or emotions. Or, it was suggested that:

B. our true and innate response was inhibited by our early relationships with one or the other of our parents—father or mother as the case may be; our brothers or sisters—in which case it was referred to as a case of sibling rivalry; or by members of our peer group or our society in general with special attention currently being given to our membership in minority ethnic groups. In any case, however, our inhibitions could be overcome by some form of exposure or education and in the more stubborn cases some form of personal or group therapy was helpful.

But still granting that some type of real sensory phenomenon does occur when one is exposed to an art object I would like to suggest that still other questions have to be raised. For example, how do we know that what occurs is not a self-induced hallucinatory response based upon prior learning or conditioning; a not impossible probability especially in light of the observation that even among the art critics and art scholars of equally highly respected reputations there is some disagreement as to the "artness" of specific objects and that some objects which have elicited the highest praise for their clearly established esthetic values have, upon being exposed as fakes, been declared by the same experts that praised them to be of little or no esthetic value, the value, I assume, being one that is determined, to some degree, by the recognition of the "distinctive thing about it" or the occurrence of the "kind of a hum" noted earlier.

Without suggesting that this is not all possible it does seem clear to me that art as it is currently defined or justified by most of the recognized leaders in the arts is a relatively recent construct created by an extremely esoteric segment of Western culture. Therefore, I would like to suggest that art in our culture exists by definition alone and that responses to "art," on this level, are the result of learning or value recognition.

To prove the first of these points one need only examine:

A. the evolution of the word art and its counterpart in the Indo-European language group and the original function and value of the majority of so-called "art objects" housed or displayed in our museums dedicated to the preservation of traditional art values and forms. (and)

B. the languages of those cultures, of which there are many, that have neither a word for art as we understand it, nor combinations of words by which our concept of art can be expressed.

This is not to imply that men of all ages and cultures have not made objects considered special in their class to which special values have been attached or that concepts of beauty do not occur universally. It is merely to point out that art and beauty as we understand them, are the results of specific rather than universal value judgments and that like all value judgments they are subject, not only to the forces which bring about changes in all value systems but, in fact, have changed and do continue to change with the continuing shift in the social values we have all been able to observe.

To prove the second point one need only examine the changing patterns of what even our most conservative agencies charged with the development and protection of the arts; *i.e.* schools and museums, have identified as art. An examination of their storage vaults and/ or the records of what they have sold or traded will reveal that works which were at one time considered important in their collections, have at another time been determined to be of so little value that they have either been stored or disposed of. To be sure some of them are rediscovered at a later date to have merit and brought back at the expense of some other work currently judged less artistically or esthetically valuable.

But the art to which I have been referring is obviously only one of the two major artistic traditions with which our modern culture is involved. The other, with its roots in the emergence of mass society in the eighteenth century, is what is referred to as the Popular Arts. This was the culture of the middle and lower classes that emerged as the dominant segment of Western population in the nineteenth century. Prior to this, art was a much more singular phenomenon consisting of the works commissioned by wealthy patrons, including the church, produced by skilled craftsmen and used to demonstrate the highest level of praise or cultural attainment possible. It was an elitist art produced by artists working within a defined esthetic context, its content and form dictated by the existence of standards recognized and agreed to by both the artist and his patron. Prior to the existence of the popular arts the great masses of the people had only their folk tradition from which to draw any type of artistic involvement which was, of course, in no way competitive with that of the elite.

At different times in history the product of the elite arts has served different purposes. A large part of what we term art today was, in fact, created for religious or ritual purposes. Religious paintings and statues were either votive or iconographic; secular forms were either portrayals of specific people or events with honorific intentions or were simply decorative. Music, dance and drama were also originally tied to religious or ritual performance, however, by the time the Renaissance reached its height a number of these forms had been shifted from ritual form to that of entertainment. Music was performed to be enjoyed, drama to engage and amuse, paintings were painted to depict the wonder of the landscape and strange foreign places. The arts had shifted and I would suggest that with the shift entertainment became one of its major functions. In the eighteenth century with the growth of increasingly large popular audiences a number of artists (including dramatists, novelists and painters) were finding their patronage not in the wealth of single patrons but in the subscription of a popular audience. The new patron-audience was catered to. The artists produced, as they always have until most recently, not what satisfied them but what satisfied their patrons.

During the nineteenth century the audience for the popular arts increased mightily while the audience for the elite arts, now called fine arts to distinguish them from the commercial or less fine, decreased mightily. But not, I must add without making it very clear that theirs was the road to truth. And they told it loud and clear and everyone believed them especially those middle-class strainers who rather thought of themselves as potential aristocrats. And a lot of them became ministers and others became school teachers and a well developed network of salesmen for the genteel tradition went to work. The popular arts had to be allowed only because they couldn't be stopped. However, because it was believed that an appreciation of the fine arts by the masses would have a beneficial effect on our society fine arts appreciation was introduced to some degree by the twentieth century on all levels, though certainly not in all categories, of education and churches regularly sponsored poetry readings, moral dramas, concerts, etc. By the middle decades of the twentieth century there were few, if any, general education or liberal arts programs that did not include some exposure to the arts via required course work in literature or arts appreciation classes of some type. For a number of years the vogue was for large freshman classes of "Man and Civilization" in which the alleged civilizing quality of the arts was demonstrated.

II. There as a carry over and when it was realized that recreation was more than organized games there was some effort made to introduce the arts, albeit in altered forms, into programmed recreation. As far as the concepts of the fine arts were concerned the resultant programs and the products they spawned were disastrous and for many years supporters of the fine arts have considered them in such poor esteem as to be beneath the dignity of recognition. But, I would suggest that as bad as the wares produced were the programs were highly successful because of what has to be considered as their primary function, that of recreation. Countless people of all age groups responded positively to the one or two hours a week they spent painting plaster, messing in clay, folk dancing or putting on amateur theatrical evenings.

I'm not sure, however, that any of the art educators dedicated to the spread of the elite taste recognized that there was little, if any, connection between what they conceived art to be and what was taking place on the playgrounds and recreation facilities of America.

Those art educators who did see the relationship were those mainly charged with teacher preparation and while a few classes with titles like "art for recreation leaders" were offered their major efforts were in educating elementary teachers who knew something about art and secondary art teachers who knew not much more. The confusion arose because once again there was an unresolved conflict between opposing theories. This time it was the elitest concept of absolute standards in art and the educationally oriented theory that the value of the arts was in the creative process involved in *all* types of manipulative hand production. This idea formed the cornerstone of public school art education. It was, and still is, the official position of both the National Art Education Association and their regional art education organizations.

Art appreciation which had once been achieved by exposure, lecture and/or discussion was now to be achieved by encouraging students to make art. The rationale was the argument that experiencing the creative act was a more direct and significant means of understanding art than exposure to objects whose esthetic values had been determined by others. The quality of what was produced, that is being capable of being judged as good as, or better than other forms of the same class, was not a factor which was taken into consideration. When this was joined by the concept that creativity was an inherited characteristic of every child that could be developed by accepting all that the child created, the result was the production of objects of which the only critical judgment raised was the rather timid question, "What does this mean?" Any answer was sufficient to grant the object identification as art, although it might bear no relationship either to the standards of the fine arts or to those of the popular or folk forms. These ideas gained some stature at a time when most recreation programs considered their responsibilities met if some facilities were provided for organized play, some facilities were provided for general picnicking and some provision made for those who wanted to commune with nature. But it was also a time when the pressures on recreational facilities to expand, not only in the number of facilities available but also in what was to be included in the programs, were increasing.

Thus the concept of art by doing appeared attractive in light of several factors, not least of which was the idea that art was a cultural phenomenon that would bring an increased awareness to those who were exposed to it. Other factors were, of course, the limits of the budgetary allocations and the limits of personnel available. Programs that could attract and engage the attention, time and energy of fairly large groups of children or adults that cost relatively little in terms of equipment, material or personnel were indeed attractive. With materials more often than not the financial responsibility of the participants, only limited work space available and teachers whose lack of experience in the arts—fine or popular—which could command only the lowest salaries, low budget programs could be launched and carried on.

With budgets for materials and equipment limited and the personnel consisting primarily of art students and enthusiastic amateurs they were forced to turn to the lesser crafts that demanded as little in material expenditure as they did in skill development. And thus to a degree they failed. Not that the program did not offer some constructive use of leisure time but that it frustrated the potential involvement of those who were soon bored with such limited means of expression and potential for extended self-involvement. With more highly trained personnel in the arts and greater budgetary expenditures they could have created an expanding program geared to a higher degree of client involvement and professionalism rather than being forced into programs dependent upon a continual inflow of clients.

The situation in art departments where the elitest concepts of a superior order of the arts still held forth was made more difficult to defend with the spill over of the do-your-own-thing philosophy that developed in the decades following the Second World War. Whereas this philosophy may have some validity in the education of young children or as a form of therapy it fails to provide the intellectual and emotional stimulus that is demanded by the arts if they are to continue to serve human needs.

And here lies the failure of the arts, in and out of recreation, for what began as an attempt to define "truth" by means of physical form according to the collective beliefs of the social group—however false or misdirected these beliefs may have been—they served as a means of social cohesion; whereas today with the arts fostering "truth" as a completely individualistic phenomenon, this belief serves only to destroy our ability to compromise for the maintenance of our social fabric. Proof of the failure of the elite arts in our time should be apparent from the ever increasing demand for subsidies needed to keep them functioning. If the values that we have not been smart enough to make them evident or else we have been expecting far more than they could provide on the level of mass consumption. For, after all, we have been injecting massive doses of art into a position where public exposure has been almost guaranteed. While I have no way of currently assessing the number of our citizens who have enjoyed exposure to the arts via publicly supported programs I do know that the number of people participating in programs sponsored by the schools and museums of America has steadily increased in the last three decades. Although we have read that we are still in the midst of a culture boom with more people involved in the arts than ever before it has still apparently not been significant enough to bring about any sensitive change in the quality of life led by most Americans in most American cities.

Neither, I might add, has the boom in recreation been seemingly adequate to stem the tide of a deteriorating life pattern. Although more people want to use the beaches and mountains we are so rapidly despoiling our meager resources that the time is not far off when we will have to have tickets and wait our turn. With more people having more leisure what should have turned out to be an historic triumph for the middle and lower classes has turned out to be a time increasingly fraught with tension and anxiety.

In the recently released report (September ——, 1971) of the "Commission on the Cities in the '70s" established by the National Urban Coalition to discover what changes, if any, have occurred in our American cities within the last three years relative to the Kerner Commission report that racism and the harshness of city life was tearing the nation apart, it was made patently clear that the quality of life in American cities was still declining. And, remember, the percentage of the population living in large urban centers has never been as large as it is currently, with no significant signs of any decline on the horizon. It's true that these reports were the results of investigations aimed at a consideration of the life style of inner city ghettoization but

don't think for one minute that there are not serious implications here for the rest of us. For the spill over and interaction has also had its effect on those who live in the seemingly protected enclaves called suburbia. We need only look at the personal alienation expressed and the social disintegration occurring within an increasingly large segment of our middle-class population to realize that these are people whose lives are increasingly threatened by growing fears and hostility.

III. If it is true then that the arts and recreation have not fulfilled the potential they seemingly offered those of us who believed in working toward a better world—one in which the life style was to have been enriched by the arts and our leisure time was to be meaningfully used—perhaps it is justified to suggest that we have, in misdefining the arts, successfully blocked them from the very function where they would be most valuable to modern society. For stripped of their false mystique, the false demands that they be considered in terms of morality and their value as a commercial product, the arts still provide one of the primary forms of entertainment available to modern man. Doubly valuable because man cannot only be involved on the level of personal production but also on the level of critical examination and appreciation. It is the arts which provide us with the opportunity to wonder at the marvelous things men are able to create.

I know that for those of you who consider art a frill, at best, and a waste of time more often than not the idea of linking art with entertainment may be nothing to get excited about, because you always were a bit suspicious that art wasn't all that it was supposed to be—especially modern art which seemed like a lot of fuss over things that could allegedly be made by any three year old. Furthermore, you've always known that artists were an immoral lot, what with their interest in naked bodies, the fact that they don't have what everyone else considers a regular job; and besides everyone knows that artists wore their hair long before it became a contemporary fad and that they have irregular sex lives, are in all probability involved with narcotics and currently have become bigger troublemakers than ever before. Yes, it's easy to see that people who carry on like this are probably engaged in nothing more important than entertainment. But not so, the clean cut, short haired All-American representative of the world of professional recreation, you'd argue. Everyone knows, from an equally prejudiced point of view, that recreation can't be linked to entertainment—for after all, recreation is an essential part of life—besides which it builds character, it makes honest and constructive use of leisure time and builds healthy bodies and minds.

Or you might argue that the arts and recreation aside, entertainment is really only show business which is a tawdry affair, at best, what with its loose living and underworld connections. Or, perhaps you feel that entertainment fails because it is such a passive phenomenon and only active participation can lead to the desired goals of personal involvement for the good life.

Ladies and gentlemen, if you've entertained any of these myths you're missing the point, not only about art but also about recreation. And, at this time I'd like to suggest we recognize entertainment for the positive phenomenon it is in the sense of being that activity or nonactivity capable of engaging and holding our attention for a personally meaningful time span in such a way that time passes pleasantly and rewardingly. What is entertaining is that which is

capable of diverting us from the incessant demands of our day to day lives. Entertainment is a source of meaningful diversion which is an essential element of life itself. It has been demonstrated over and over again that diversion is an essential component of the healthy life.

But remember, diversion is *any* activity that is capable of engaging our attention and occupying it in a manner that leaves us feeling rested and refreshed and ready to once more face the tensions and traumas of modern life. This means that the essential quality of diversion is to be found in variation and contrast, meaningfully recognized. Without diversion, which is the primary element of entertainment, we would become vegetables or, at best robots.

In my own field, which is art, this means we must ease the distinction between the "cultural arts" and the "popular arts" and realize that they are both but examples of what different segments of our society consider entertaining. We must recognize entertainment as a legitimate function of all the arts in the twentieth century. After all—at one time much that we consider within the realm of the "cultural arts" today were but examples of what different segments of our society consider entertaining. We must recognize entertainment as a legitimate function of all the arts in the twentieth century. After all—at one time much that we consider within the realm of the "cultural arts" today were but examples of popular entertainment including the plays of Shakespeare, Kabuki Theatre, Grand Opera and the lithographs of Daumier and the woodcuts of Winslow Homer to name a few. Today, far too many people launch themselves into the arts because they feel the arts are good for them and/or because they feel their participation in or support of the arts label them as superior human beings. But to do this,

I would suggest, destroys the only valid function of the arts left to us—that of enjoying them!

If art and recreation are to function for the benefits of human culture, in this the last few decades of the twentieth century, they must do so on the level of building social cohesion which will be determined only by our ability to perceive our belonging, the ability to perceive that we share with other members of the race common values, commonly expressed. The arts based on doing-your-own-thing are fine but only if they are conceived of as production that exists within the framework of common values that maintain the doer's sense of belonging to his social group. Doing-your-own-thing, however, fails when it is conceived of in terms of absolute values that place the doer outside of his social group. Conceived of like this it can only be destructive to the individual doer and the society he lives in.

With the increased demands for the filling of our leisure time we have, of course, destroyed the original concept of leisure. What we have created in its place is a seemingly frantic effort to organize unused time into nonleisure time. As a result of this, the problems which face those who have accepted responsibility of providing the pleasurable means by which we gain our recreation only grow larger.

Certainly the problem is not simple or easy but I would further suggest that perhaps a part of the solution lies in redefining the nature of our recreational activities to include a broader range of human involvement and noninvolvement than we currently consider; in making people more responsible for their own recreational activities and in ridding ourselves of the competitive and elitest attitudes which have so long been attached to the fine arts and certain aspects of the more traditional forms of recreation.

Too Much Is Too Little

I hope succeeding generations will be able to be idle. I hope that nine-tenths of their time will be leisure time; that they may enjoy their days, and the earth, and the beauty of this beautiful world; that they may rest by the sea and dream; that they may dance and sing, eat and drink.

—Novelist Richard Jefferies
(1848-1887)

From John Stuart Mill to John Maynard Keynes, economists, as well as authors and politicians, have cherished such a utopian vision of the abundant life. The millennium, it was always assumed, would arrive when full employment combined with high productivity to supply mankind with everything it needed, as well as the leisure time to enjoy it. If any problem existed, it would be finding enough to do. But things are not working out that way. So, at least, argues Staffan Burenstam Linder, 38, a professor at the Stockholm School of Economics who has taught at Yale and Columbia. He states his case in *The Harried Leisure Class*, a book that has already ruffled Swedish composure, and will be published in English this December by the Columbia University Press. "I find it paradoxical," says its author, "that as income rises, we are all running like hell."

Linder's socio-economic put-down is based on the assumption that the rarest element on earth is time. Time cannot be stored or saved, or consumed at a rate faster than it is produced. The rich man has no more of it than the pauper—and no less. Previous economic theory, says Linder, fails to take into sufficient account that leisure time must be consumed, either by doing something or doing nothing. For a society both affluent and leisured, and anxious to put every moment to good use, there are simply too many things to do. Overwhelmed by a burgeoning store of goods and services designed for pleasure, the would-be consumer, trying to do everything at once, succumbs to a malady that Linder calls "pleasure blindness."

"If I keep a cow," Ralph Waldo Emerson said, "that cow milks me." Linder argues that the same holds true of the commodity time, and that as one result, people become slaves of the possessions and services that compete to fill their leisure hours. "One may possibly *buy* more of everything," he writes, "but one cannot conceivably *do* more of everything." To belong to a golf club as well as a sailing club is to spend half one's time going from one to the other, the other half observing all the social amenities that they entail.

The arguments that Linder offers are gently satirical. A mischievous streak rises irrepressibly in his book. Some of his more trenchant diagnoses:

On Being On Time: Punctuality has become a virtue that we demand of those around us. Waiting is a squandering of time that angers people in rich countries. Only personal mismanagement, or the inconsiderate behavior of others, will create brief—and highly irritating—periods of involuntary idleness.

On Eating: Actual cooking is a time-consuming process, and has been abandoned for thawing and heating, which is not an unqualified advance. Since there is a limit—for most people a fairly low one—to how far the pleasures of sitting at table can be enhanced by increasing the amount and quality of the food, it is probable that eating will become an inferior pursuit.

On Love: Love takes time. To court and love someone in a satisfactory manner is a game with many and time-consuming phases. Modern love affairs are reminiscent, according to Sebastian de Grazia, of business agreements: "No frills, no flowers, no time wasted on elaborate compliments, verses and lengthy seductions, no complications, and no scenes, please." Those who complain that girls these days are "easy" fail to understand that in a hectic age girls must accelerate to save time for both themselves and their male friends. People have not stopped making love any more than they have stopped eating. But—to extend the surprisingly adequate parallel with the joys of gastronomy—less time is devoted to both preparation and savoring.

No Time

Lines from a favorite contemporary poem of Linder's, by Abbe Michel Quoist, quoted in *The Harried Leisure Class:*

Good-bye, Sir, excuse me, I haven't time.
I'll come back, I can't wait, I haven't time.
I must end this letter—I haven't time.
I'd love to help you, but I haven't time.
I can't accept, having no time.
I can't think, I can't read, I'm swamped, I haven't time.
I'd like to pray, but I haven't time.

On Marriage: On the whole, it is probable that conjugal fidelity is increasing, if not in thought, at least in practice. It takes too much time to establish new contacts as compared with relaxation in the home. For the same reason, perhaps, young and energetic people tend to marry early and cut down on the time-consuming process of search.

On Experience: A tourist need no longer content himself with enjoying what he sees. He can give himself a feeling of really using his time by taking pictures. It is easy to understand why love is so vulnerable to competition if we reflect that we are spending time on only one person and cannot even take photographs of the occasion.

On Parties: People have a surprising liking for large banquets, conventions and cocktail parties. One explanation for this may be that it seems a highly efficient way of exploiting the time allocated to social intercourse. One devotes oneself to the simultaneous consumption of food and people. To be the only guests to dinner is normally considered less flattering than to be invited with many others, perhaps because it suggests that your time is at such a low price that you are content to meet a couple of people at a time.

Economist Linder offers no solutions. But his own life can stand as a kind of example for the harried leisure class. He does not own a swimming pool, a boat or a summer cottage and frowns on watching television while eating dinner, reading the newspaper or making love. His way of using consumption time—Linderese for leisure—is to take a walk somewhere. This month he and his 9-year-old son Goran will leave for a hike through the mountains of Dalarna in central Sweden.

Like the very poor, who are forced to be passive because they have no choice, the well-to-do Linder family actively fills many a leisure hour in the pursuit of idleness—and in those vanishing arts of reading, thinking, enjoying the earth and—the TV dinner notwithstanding—eating and talking with friends.

Recreative Use of Leisure

Walter L. Stone, PH.D.

The world in the last half of this century is becoming an increasingly turbulent place in which to live, due to the explosions in population, knowledge, freedom, technology, leisure, communication and international relations.

Value systems and institutions are being subjected to unbelievable strains. In this country we are emerging from an economy of scarcity, toil and exertion as a way of life to produce "goods" to an economy of abundance, freedom from toil as a way of life in which we consume "goods."

The world of yesteryear was characterized by hard work on farm and factory, a small amount of earned leisure, comparative isolation from the rest of the world, individual entreprenury, a simple morality, nationalism, little government control, small towns and cities and a production oriented economy.

Today we live in a situation characterized by labor saving machines, more and more leisure forced on us, more income for less work, world leadership in a shrinking world, advancing science, corporations and big business, big government, big cities and suburbia, and an economy that is consumption oriented.

Tomorrow it has been predicted that we will live in a society that is leisure oriented, in which toil as a means of subsistence has been eliminated and an economic system in which all men are guaranteed an income from shares of industry, government bonds, part time employment in tending the machines and in "service" industries.

Leisure is not a new phenomena in the life of man, but freedom from toil to make a living, where the curse of Adam has been removed, is. In the past most people had to work to earn leisure, but in this phenomena of Western civilization, they are now confronted with having leisure thrust upon them. The situation described by Aristotle, "work is a means of subsistence in order that man can pursue leisure activities" has changed. The size of the leisure class is exploding also.

Leisure of course is whatever people say it is. The word leisure is derived from the Latin "licere" to be free, from the Greek "scola" school and from the French "loisir," to be permitted. The essence of leisure seems to be freedom. Freedom of time and attitude. As time it is that period of life not spent in making a living or in self-maintenance. As an attitude it is related to free will, lack of compulsion, and choice.

Reprinted with permission from National Recreation and Park Association. Official publication *Parks and Recreation*, April, 1967.

Leisure does not mean that many will no longer work, for as Dr. Cabot has pointed out, work is one of the four things men live by, the others being play, love and worship. Dr. Alexander Reid Martin[1] has said in this connection, "In our way of life we are rightly expressing the need for work, struggle and exertion, but we are inclined to overlook, neglect and ignore the indispensable part that leisure and relaxation play in the creative process. True leisure is not the opposite of work in the sense of being opposed to work. In work there is a narrowing, a focussing, a contraction of faculties, a concentration and an acuteness of consciousness. During true leisure there is a widening of consciousness, an unfocussing, a broadening and expanding, a greater diffusion of the consciousness."

The opportunities afforded by the change in the time habits of people are unlimited. The problem is that the good in time has too often been lost in our work oriented world. We blind ourselves to life as we bind ourselves to the clock and feel that leisure time is something to be filled and everywhere there are frenzied efforts to do just that. The good in time is only possible for those who can free themselves from the time machine as they have been freed from the necessity of toil to make a living.

Leisure time provides the opportunity for the mind to dwell in order that it can create. Leisure cannot be equated with idleness. Leisure is a positive attitude, idleness is a negative one. J.T. Fraser[2] points out, "Time must and should occupy the center of man's intellectual and emotive interest. The essence of time like that of man's existence is only a permission to partake creatively in a world whose contents and properties we may experience, contemplate and share, but never completely describe or precisely formulate."

There are many patterns of leisure time: week ends, shorter work weeks, longer vacations, early retirement and no work at all for an increasing number of people. Automation—the machine—cybernetics has removed toil from work, jobs for subsistence, and has taken over many of man's mental functions as well as replacing his muscles and has increased leisure time for everyone.

This situation has raised many questions and problems; how make routine tasks bearable, how prevent people from dying from boredom? How can leisure be used for fullness of life? How secure self-realization in a world of leisure rather than alienation? How can the boon of life be both conferred by the facilities and programs for the worthy use of leisure on people and by the people on the facilities and programs?

There are those who believe that the use of leisure is a final test of civilization and that when man has reasonable security and leisure he can seek cultural and spiritual values that he could not in a toil oriented world.

Leisure time rather than work time has become the arena for self-preservation and self-realization. Leisure not necessity is the mother of invention. Countries where the necessity for food is primary do not have the time or energy for basic invention.

Leisure time means more time for travel, for education, for entertainment, for cultural activities, for community service, for neighborliness.

Leisure time means time to practice the arts of leisure, which have been described by Marjorie Barstow Greenbie[3] in a book by that title as first, the arts of solitude which includes such things as reading, going places, seeing things, meditation. Second the arts of social life including manners, being sociable, letter writing, playing with children, courtship and the high art of loving. Third the arts of civilization as song, exercise, self-improvement, dialogue, making believe, making things, growing things, doing good. Leisure is anything not packaged and sold by advertising.

Gracious and happy living is the objective of these arts. Gracious living has to do with human relations and values. Happy living has to do with meaningful activity and in the pursuit of significance which results in growth in outlooks and insights, attitudes and appreciations and means of control both personal and social.

Leisure activities include both work and play, but the play element is the most important. Play is universal and found in all societies. It has been called the source of civilization by Johann Huizinga.[4] It may well become the conserver of civilization. Work and play complement each other. Play increases life's meaning. Play is voluntary, not compulsory.

Play is enjoyable, relaxing, refreshing and creative. The creative urge is what distinguishes man from the animal. Poems have been written, pictures painted, machines invented, movements and organizations started, rules and regulations invented and religions developed because of this quality in man. The basis of the creative urge is imagination, the essential ingredient in play. All of man's inventions, poems, paintings, organizations required work, but the most rewarding results were obtained when the spirit of play was present.

Aristotle noted long ago that in play the emotions become purified of a great deal of dangerous and distasteful properties which adhere to them. When the spirit of play is present an activity does not become a blazing fire which burns and consumes, but is rather like firelight on the wall which enlightens but does not consume.

The distinguishing characteristic of recreation is play, and the unique contribution that recreation can make to life in a leisure oriented world is play.

Recreation is both a means to an end and an end in itself. It is used as a means to an end in industry, in hospitals, in churches, in schools and colleges. As an end in itself it has to do with education, culture and the good life.

The fundamental needs of people that recreation has always been concerned with are: "the exercise of both the larger and smaller muscle systems, the sharpening of sense perceptions, the manipulation of varieties of materials, neuromuscular coordination, enjoyment of discovery, cooperation and collaboration with others, and activity that is intellectually and emotionally satisfying, that is conducive to quiet contemplation and the opportunity for self-improvement."[5]

Recreation is education that uses the skill of opening up the universe from a single interest. "The universe is a unit and one can begin at any point and move over, around and under it. Tennyson's 'Flower in the crannied wall, I pluck you out of the crannies . . . if I could understand what you are root and all and all in all, I would know what God and man is' expresses the idea of the recreation use of leisure time for education."[6]

Recreation is concerned with the good life for all, and it is not a charity. Life is not good when social relationships leave us unrefreshed, when as we get closer together physically we get farther apart spiritually. Recreation is concerned with the re-creative use of time that results in fullness of life for all regardless of social class, nationality or color.

Any recreative use of leisure must be a sharing and participant use and not an alienated one which too often exists in the acquisition and consumption of commodities as the major employment of leisure time.

This problem has been pointed out by

Eric Fromm[7] in these words, "How can man make use of his leisure time in an active and meaningful way, if there is no general relatedness to what he is doing. He will always remain the passive and alienated consumer. He consumes ball games, books, lectures, social gatherings, natural scenery in an alienated and an abstractified way. He does not participate actively, but wants to 'take in' all there is to be had and get as much pleasure, culture and what not as possible. His taste is manipulated. The value of fun is determined by its success on the market.

"In any productive and spontaneous activity something happens within myself while I am looking, reading, talking to friends, I am not the same as I was before. In an alienated form of pleasure nothing happens to me. I have consumed this or that but nothing is changed within myself and all that is left is memories of what I have done."

"Fullness of life through leisure"[8] can be a reality or an empty dream. Leisure time is not a luxury, not time to kill but a challenge and an opportunity. If man can construct machines that make leisure possible, it may be he can construct creative and recreative ways of behaving in a leisure oriented world.

The recreative use of leisure could also strengthen democracy as an idea and as a way of life for both recreation and democracy demand freedom of choice, both are compatible with the scientific laws of relativity and diversity, both require continuous reformulation, because there is no final perfection in either. Both cherish the differences in people and both strive for control with people, not over them, through sharing and dialogue that can lead to new and better ways of behaving.

Notes

1. Alexander Reid Martin, M.D. "Leisure and the Creative Process." Address Hanover College Convocation. April 9, 1959.
2. J.T. Fraser. *The Voices of Time* (New York: Braziller, 1965).
3. Marjorie Barstow Greenbie, *The Arts of Leisure* (McGraw-Hill Book Co., 1935).
4. Johann Huizinga. *Homo Ludens* (Beacon Press, 1950).
5. Walter L. and Charles G. Stone. *Recreation Leadership* (William Frederick Press, 1952).
6. *Ibid.*
7. Eric Fromm, *The Sane Society* (Harpers, 1955).
8. John Collier, "Fullness of Life Through Leisure" (New York: University Press, 1930).

Introduction: In Defense of Games

James S. Coleman

The fascination of games is a curious matter. It must arise in part from the arbitrary setting aside of the vaguely defined but complex and deadly serious rules which govern everyday life, and substitution of a set of explicit and simple rules whose consequences vanish when the game is over. But if I were to attempt to explain this fascination in general terms I should never succeed. I will instead introspect, and ask what it is that fascinates me, not as a player in a game but rather as a sociologist in constructing them. For in this there is certainly something to be explained. Why should self-respecting sociologists, who could be working in research directions that would gain far more recognition from colleagues, instead toy with games in a field—educational sociology—that has long languished in the cellar of the discipline?

Let us even take as given, for the sake of argument, that games have remarkable potentials for learning—that they could transform the techniques by which children learn in schools and thus transform children that schools presently leave untouched or mildly "educated." Important as such effects are, they are no reason for the sociologist to excite himself about games, no reason to leave his other work for the fascination of constructing and testing games. The sociologist is not, after all, educator; his task instead is to study, and hope to better understand, society and social organization.

What is it then that fascinates me and the other students of social organization whose papers constitute this issue? What makes us abandon the proper behavior of sociologists and fix instead on games that may induce learning in children?

To come to an answer requires first a closer look at the very notion of games and the peculiar relations they bear to social life. A game—nearly any game, not merely those termed "simulation games"—constitutes a kind of caricature of social life. It is a magnification of some aspect of social interaction excluding all else, tearing this aspect of social interaction from its social context and giving it a special context of its own. Even those games that are farthest from those described in this issue exemplify this. A boxing or wrestling match abstracts from its context the direct physical violence that resides in social life and recreates this violence under a set of explicit rules. When I was a boy in

"Introduction: In Defense of Games" by James S. Coleman, reprinted from *American Behavioral Scientist*, Vol. 10, No. 2 (October, 1966) pp. 3-4, by permission of James S. Coleman and of the Publisher, Sage Publications, Inc.

the midwest cornhusking contests abstracted one activity from the life of farmers, established a set of rules, and gave this activity a temporary but central position for the participants.

This unique relation of games to life can be seen even better in other ways. The informal games of young children appear to be crucial means for learning about life and experimenting with life. One of the most perceptive students of the social and intellectual development of young children, Jean Piaget, has observed this development in the simple games children play, such as the game of marbles. It appears that for children, games are more than a caricature of life; they are an introduction to life—an introduction to the idea of rules, which are imposed on all alike, an introduction to the idea of playing under different sets of rules, that is, the idea of different roles, an introduction to the idea of aiding another person and of knowing that one can expect aid from another, an introduction to the idea of working toward a collective goal and investing one's self in a collectivity larger than himself. It appears that games serve, for the young child, all these functions as an introduction of life.

Still another aspect of this special linkage between games and life is provided by a recent development in psychiatry—a turn from the emphasis on traumatic events in the patient's life, on oedipal complexes and mysterious fixations, toward an emphasis on the often destructive behavior strategies that adults use toward others. I refer principally to the book *Games People Play*, by Eric Berne. While Berne's use of the term "games" to describe these strategies extend the meaning beyond that used in these pages, the very use of the term indicates the close liaison between explicit games and the behavior people engage in as part of everyday life.

All these illustrations are intended to convey the intimate connections between games and social life. If there is such an intimate relation, and a few sociologists are wagering their professional lives that there is, then games themselves in all their forms become of great potential interest for the sociologist. It may be that he, just as the young child, can gain insight into the functioning of social life through the construction and use of games.

But beyond this there are certain special characteristics to the games described in this issue, and to the games that sociologists find of particular interest. Some games involve the interaction of a player with his physical environment, for example a maze or a jig-saw puzzle, or block puzzles, or a cornhusking contest, or a pole vault. These games abstract from life either certain physical skills or certain intellectual skills of inference from physical evidence. Other games such as number puzzles or crossword puzzles involve interaction with a symbolic environment, in these two instances an environment of numbers and an environment of language.

Such abstractions of activities from life hold some interest for the sociologist, but much less interest than another class of games which abstract from life some elements of social relations or social organization. Many games incorporate some aspects of such relations, but a few games incorporate enough such relations that a special term has been used to describe them: social simulation games. Such games pluck out of social life generally (including economic, political and business life) a circumscribed arena, and attempt to reconstruct the principal rules by which behavior in this arena is governed and the principal rewards that it holds for the participants. Such a game both in its construction and in its playing then becomes of extreme interest to the student of social organization. For from it he may learn about those problems of social relations that are his central concern. The game may provide for him that degree of abstraction from life and simplification of life that allows him to understand better certain fundamentals of social organization.

It is this, then, that makes the sociologist fascinated with a certain kind of game—the possibility of learning from this caricature of social relations about those social relations themselves.

But the question immediately arises, how possibly could a professional sociologist and a sixth or twelfth grade child learn about social life from the same game? My answer is that it is precisely appropriate that this be so. For children have too long been taught things that are "known," and have too seldom been allowed to discover for themselves the principles governing a situation. It may well be in the physical sciences that the young student and the professional scientist cannot learn from the same environment. (Yet Einstein, in a paper he wrote to explain the meandering of streams, mentioned that although the mechanical principles involved were well-known and simple in application to the problem, he had met very few physicists who understood these principles well enough to use them in the

simple application. I suspect that a perceptive high school student would suffer no serious disadvantage relative to a professional physicist.) But it is certainly the case that the professional sociologist and the young student can learn from a single game.

It is also true that what is meant by learning is quite different for the sixth grader and the professional sociologist. The sixth grader is learning to incorporate this experience into his own life, learning to recognize the dominant aspects of this social environment so that he can respond appropriately to them when he meets such an environment in his own life. The professional sociologist is learning how to describe in general terms the functioning of this system of relations, learning to fit the system of relations to an abstract conceptual scheme.

This, then, is the fascination of the sociologist with social simulation games—the opportunity to learn about social organization by forming a caricature of such organization and then observing this caricature. This is supplemented by his fascination in seeing young children learn as much about such environments as he himself can know how to transmit through the construction of the game.

An Ethological Theory of Play

Evelyn Browne

For a number of years I have been puzzling over what appears to me a curious dichotomy between the world of our profession, built on a complex of educational stilts, and the real-life, slam-bang, heart-stopping world of sports and athletics. It would seem that there are only two happenings in our culture today that can even begin to challenge our national obsession for sporting events. One is the awesome ritual and pageantry surrounding the death of a national hero; the other is war.

We of this profession know that the culture of sports is by no means unique to the United States in the twentieth century. With all the peoples of the world, communication through sports transcends language barriers. The sport may be soccer not baseball, rugby not football, field hockey for men not for women or dance not calisthenics, but the human need behind this variety of expression is not confined by territorial boundaries or geographical limitations. In our world today it is universal.

This universal need is also boundless in time. Pluck a first century Roman citizen out of his seat in the Colosseum and transport him in time, change his clothes, and pop him into a seat to watch a professional football game in any of our twentieth century American coliseums and my guess is that he would feel quite at home. He might miss the animals and the sand surface for absorbing blood of his home town sport center, but other than that, the violence and ritual would appeal to him and come close to his favorite sport at home, the gladiatorial combats.

My question is simple: What is it that links the Brazilian soccer fan to the Boston Red Sox fan? What links the wine drinking, wild-eyed spectator in Rome 2,000 years ago as he roars his disapproval and turns "thumbs down" on some unfortunate gladiator and the beer drinking, disheveled baseball fan leaping to his feet and, along with thousands who share his feelings, shouting at the top of his hoarse voice "Murder the bum!"?

I would like to suggest that the link both to the present and the past is generic. I believe that its roots may be found in a study of the relatively new science of ethology, the precise study of animal behavior. I believe that man's ageless and universal passion for sports is based on

Reprinted with permission from the American Association for Health, Physical Education, and Recreation *Journal*, AAHPER, September, 1968.

instincts which we have inherited from our animal ancestry. Certainly the layers of civilized veneer, applied during the centuries, have failed to tame the sports fan. Whether he be a Christian martyr fan or a Cassius Clay fan, he remains a unique, violent, and primitive reminder of our ancient origins.

To this end, I am proposing an ethological theory of play. My reasons for this proposal are based on the premises outlined below.

In the controversial book, *African Genesis*, by Robert Ardrey, three major theories are presented which form the basis for this discussion.[1]

1. *Territory*. Ardrey, through a series of well-documented "case studies" in the realms of animal, bird, and fish worlds, makes the point that the drive for territory comes first and the sex drive is of secondary importance and is aroused only when the male has secured his "territory." In his second book, *The Territorial Imperative*, Ardrey further expands his thesis that man is indeed a territorial animal. One of his most persuasive arguments is his brilliant analogy of the production *West Side Story*, in which the rumble between teenage gangs is compared to the law of the jungle ("One Tiger to a Hill"). One also thinks of Alexander the Great, the Peloponnesian wars, the Roman Empire, and Adolph Hitler's fanatic scream for *Liebensraum*. Today one thinks of the conflict in the middle east, the war in Vietnam, and the civil rights issues in this country.

2. *The Pecking Order*. Within each species, according to authorities, groups within the species establish a hierarchy of rank from the lowliest member of the group to the proud leader. This is a well-established ethological principle in regard to such bird colonies as

ravens or chickens in a barnyard—hence the name "pecking order." But this ranking order is true of primates, such as a colony of gorillas in a natural state, and many other species of animals. In essence, it is nature's way of maintaining order and discipline and, as a result, the survival of the group as a whole. The pecking order is the competitive basis of survival in the animal world. There are many examples of this "social" process in our society today. Perhaps the best example is our military hierarchy from general down to the lowly buck private. But there are other less obvious examples: the jungle of the world of Madison Avenue, the Greek system in colleges and universities, Riesman's *Lonely Crowd*, Maslow's self-actualized man, India's caste system, and the presidential primaries in this election year.

3. *Weaponry*. This theory is based on the discoveries of Raymond Dart. In 1955 Dr. Dart submitted a report to the Smithsonian Institution regarding his discovery of the fossil of the skull of a human being which lived one million years ago near the present Kalahari Desert in South Africa. He named our earliest known ancestor, the Australopithecus (Southern Ape) man. This skull was that of a young male and his death had been caused by a blow to his face by a weapon which was probably the business end of an ante-

1. The author would like to acknowledge her indebtedness, primarily, to Robert Ardrey, whose book, *African Genesis*, started her thinking along ethological paths and whose latest book, *The Territorial Imperative*, served to increase the excitement of the quest for primary origins of human behavior. The author would further like to acknowledge the contribution to this theory of Lonrad Lorenz in his books, *King Solomon's Ring* and *On Aggression*.

lope's humerus bone. The implications of this discovery are tremendous. Ardrey has suggested on the basis of this evidence that man is not just a tool maker as so many scientific works insist, but primarily a *weapon maker*. He further makes the heretical suggestion that man's one million year old passion for making and manipulating weapons created man's renowned and revered "big brain," not the other way around, as our religions would have us believe. Further, the remains of the million year old Australopithecus boy indicate that he was killed deliberately, murdered by one of his own kind. Why? The paleontological evidence gives rise to the haunting thought that we are descendants of murderers and cannibals, Cain not Abel.

If one thinks *weapons* and takes a look into the past, scenes will jump to mind: David slinging his stone at Goliath; the horse-drawn chariots of the pharaohs of Egypt; the horse as a new dimension of hunting and warfare; Leonardo da Vinci's plans for battering rams; the glorious armor and finely chaced weapons of the age of chivalry; the long bows of England at Agincourt; and, of course, the eventual fruits of evolution, gunpowder, cannons, tanks, battleships, submarines, our airborne arsenal, and finally—the ultimate weapon—the nuclear bomb. Such a view of our past lends persuasive evidence in support of the theory that weapons played a major role in the evolution of Homo sapiens and the society in which he lives in the twentieth century today.

With this information serving as a brief and all too flimsy background, I would like to propose the following hypothesis:

- that all animals including man play.
- that play for any species at whatever age level involves the principles of territory and the pecking order.
- that play for primates and Homo sapiens also includes the use of weapons.
- that, through the process of evolution, man today gives expression to these genetic instincts through our social institutions of war, play, and pageantry.
- that, in the areas of play and pageantry (and in the absence of uninhibited warfare), these events are carried out strictly according to rules.
- that the rules of the game and the protocol of pageantry are the ethological counterparts of the inhibitory mechanisms that exist throughout the animal kingdom for the purpose of preventing intra-species murder.
- that play at all levels and for all participants consists of practice in an artificial but deadly serious arena, for entrance into an adult world which reflects its ancient origins through the quest for territory, status, and weaponry, all of which exist in many forms in our world today.
- that the closer every particular activity comes to clearly containing the elements of territory, the pecking order, and weaponry, the more successful that activity will be as a tool to teach our youth to know themselves and their relation to the real world they are about to enter.

TERRITORY, COMPETITION, WEAPONRY

To substantiate this theory I would like to point out that no form of play exists today that does not in some way include the concepts of territory, competition, and weaponry. There follows some examples from our own field.

Territory

Childrens' games are a good place to begin. Without benefit of adult supervision and wisdom any number of games burst into being according to the season of the year. "I Am the King of the Castle." (Young gorillas play this game.) Prisoner's Base. Hide-and-Go-Seek and its victory call: "Home Free." Hop Scotch. Red Light. The list of games could go on and on.

It is interesting that in the area of movement education, the concept of choosing and exploring an area of space is in essence a territorial concept. But perhaps the best example of the role of territory in sports in this country is football. In this game the object of territorial aggrandizement is spelled out in clear and unmistakable terms— yardage. The need to gain 10 yards of territory in four tries is what keeps the tribe alive. Implicit in the territorial theory is the principle that animals will fight hardest to defend their territory the closer the enemy comes to the heart of their territorial homeland. The aggressor, on the other hand, tends to lose his aggression the further he is from his own territory and the deeper he penetrates another's territory. Hence the fabled phenomenon of the "goal line stand" in football by the defensive team. To defend the team's heartland or goal is their raison d'etre. The odds are with them both in the animal world and on the playing fields. The odds also favor the team playing on its home ground.

The Pecking Order

The pecking order in sports is almost as obvious as it is in a military hierarchy. Competition is the soul of all sporting contests. All over the country youth are competing for a place on a team and a renewed reason for living and being a person. Can you remember back to the days when you waited while two well-established leaders briskly took turns choosing individuals to play on their teams in the neighborhood softball contest about to commence? If you were small and skinny and the youngest you know what its like to be at the bottom of the pecking-order. It's almost as bad as being cut from the pro roster and either dismissed or sent back to the farm system.

Once the team is chosen and the season under way, competition intensifies under the glaring light of publicity and the assiduous compiling of statistics. The goal now becomes winning the league championship and ultimately the national championship whether it is in Little League, the Santa Claus Bowl, the Rose Bowl, or the World Series in the professional world of sports. Today, as in ancient Greece, to become an Olympic champion is truly the epitome of standing at the top of the athletic hierarchy. Perhaps this is one reason for the aura and magic surrounding this greatest of all athletic events.

Weaponry

Many of our sports today consist of the use of weapons important in the warfare of our past: the javelin (spear), the discus, the shot-put, bows and arrows, fencing foils, and even rifles. Many sports use obvious weapons or weapon substitutes. Take a look at some sports: golf, baseball, hockey—clubs, bats, and sticks; cricket, hurley, and polo—bats, sticks, and mallets; badminton, tennis, and squash—rackets.

And let's not underestimate the power of the ball. The ball is the pitcher's weapon in baseball. If he can hurl it skillfully through the enemy's territory, he can eliminate his adversary and give his team a measure of security. The batter, defending his territory with his weapon, can knock the pitcher's weapon into the third row of the stands. Thus the pitcher and his team are rendered weaponless and helpless while the batter trots around the bases securing four outposts of the defending teams territory: first base, second base, third base, and home plate. Symbolically he has conquered the diamond.

The ball in football is equally important. No man can be stabbed without a weapon similar to a knife; no soldier can be shot without a bullet; in football no territory can be gained without the ball. The ball becomes the key to the combat whether passed, carried, or intercepted. The ball is football's weapon. The use of weapons is as true of women's sports as it is for the man's world. (The March 1968 *Journal* cover is a reminder of this fact.)

In applying Ardrey's theories to the world of sports, it is difficult if not impossible to pick out one sport as an illustration of just one of these concepts. In one way or another, all three theories seem involved in all sports. Further, all sports have rules and a group of well-trained, although often much maligned, officials to enforce them. This point is important! It is analagous to the animal world. Evolution has equipped all species with a built-in inhibitory mechanism which prevents intra-species murder. On the human scale intra-species murder is what war is all about. With the exception of the one enormous and vital area of sports, man seems to have lost his animal inhibitory mechanisms while retaining all his territorial avarice, obsession with weapons, and excessive preoccupation with world dominance on the ladder of the international pecking order.

I believe this ethological approach to our field may well give a new dimension and impetus to all of us involved in the profession. I have used some of these theories in teaching a principles course in physical education to major and minor students and athletes. They seem to like this approach; they become enthusiastic. They tell me that in pro-football circles the players are reading *African Genesis.* Students from other disciplines are also interested. Ardrey has greatly helped in closing a generation gap inside and outside the classroom. For almost the same reasons that Ardrey's theories interest professional athletes, experts in movement education at the elementary school level might wish to examine these concepts further. In any area throughout the world, a person who has actual contact with children and men and women playing, whether as coach, teacher, or Peace Corps volunteer, can gain a new insight as to what they are doing if they place the day's events against this ethological background.

This ethological approach could become a cross-disciplinary approach involving all the humanities. Our field, biologically oriented, might well get a new lease on life with some cross-fertilization from the fields of sociology, psychology, and the new generation of the behaviorial scientists. I can also envision a closer alignment of our physical education programs with the exciting, real-life competitive world of secondary school, college, and professional athletics.

I invite all disciplines to participate in a quest, but I would suggest that we travel light. Leave behind all cerebral baggage. Remember, theorists and researchers, how that "big brain" of yours evolved! I invite further inquiry into the animal origins of our wonderful, wide, and wild world of sports.

Violence & Sport

Gary Smith

Part of the rationale behind the promotion of sport in our society is that it supposedly contributes to character development and aids in forming ethical behavior. One begins to wonder, however, after viewing the contemporary sports scene, if these claims are not somewhat anti-quated. Today's sport appears to reflect society's fast-moving, tense, up-tight, violent mood.

There are many instances where the once revered values of sportsmanship and fair play are given only lip service or completely ignored in the all-out striving for victory. This lack of sportsmanship and ethical behavior on the part of athletes, coaches, and spectators most often manifests itself in the form of overt aggressiveness or violent behavior. Verification of this fact is as close as the nearest newspaper, where in past months there have appeared items involving both athletes and spectators which amply demonstrate that the virtue of sportsmanship is in a moribund state.

Incidents involving player violence which received national publicity are noted, viz:

> During the 1968 Stanley Cup playoffs a player was suspended for four games and fined $1,500 as a result of his actions in a brawl on the ice.
> The 1968 junior hockey finals ended prematurely when the St. Thomas team withdrew from their series with Flin Flon claiming that the excessive brutality on the ice was potentially injurious to their players. The St. Thomas coach felt that in fairness to his players and their parents, he could no longer expose his team to the violence that had pockmarked the first few games of the series.
> During the 1969 football season there was the famous "Sonny Wade incident." The exasperated Montreal quarterback, after having a pass intercepted, tackled the interceptor, then after the whistle in a fit of utter frustration, proceeded to stomp on the man's head. This atrocious lack of discipline was then repeated again and again on instant replay in front of a national audience.

Players have by no means been alone in this trend toward mayhem under the guise of sport. Spectators can lose their composure just as easily and are just as prone to hostile behavior. Sheed notes that riots at soccer matches in Great Britain are the rule rather than the exception. In Turkey, four people were killed last year in a soccer riot, but perhaps the ultimate in immature behavior was seen in the Latin American countries of Honduras and Guatemala where a soccer match caused a war. Soccer is perhaps best known for its violent eruptions amongst

Reprinted with permission from the Canadian Association for Health, Physical Education and Recreation, *CAHPER Journal*, Vol. 36 #6, July/August 1970.

spectators but hockey is not far behind, as fan disturbances (and especially in playoffs) occur with regularity.

What is behind this proclivity toward violence in contemporary sport?

This question can only be answered by examining the reasons for the prevalence of violence in today's society at large. Farina feels that this is the key to understanding violence in modern day sport. In his insightful account of violence in sport, Farina states:

> Perhaps the blood lust of the spectator is a true reflection of the values of society . . . a true representation of a socially immature population struggling to achieve self-realization in a technically sophisticated society.

Denney supports the above statement when he notes that "the sports public often responds with an ugly eagerness to the promotion of sports sadism and masochism." Denney also states that this condition will not likely improve unless there is a change of heart in the public itself.

Sociologists list many reasons which attempt to explain the phenomenon of violent behavior. One of the most prominent of these is the ever increasing tendency toward societal disorganization. When social controls break down a violent eruption usually follows. For example, one of the places where societal disorganization is most pronounced is in the ghettos of our larger cities. Not unexpectedly, crimes of violence, and crime in general, are increasing rapidly in these locations.

SOCIAL DISORGANIZATION AND DEHUMANIZATION

Societal disorganization is most visible in the slums, but it is evident in the middle and upper class neighborhoods as well, particularly in the suburbs of the larger cities. The disorganization is due largely to the transitory existence of the people who live there, the average family moving once every two years. As a consequence, there are no deep roots, people do not have a stake in the community. The final result is a breakdown in social control and eventually some form of violent behavior.

It is also noted that violence is most prevalent in the 18-22 year old age group. Societal disorganization affects people more in this age group than in any other. People at this age are unsettled; they are neither adults nor adolescents; they are on the brink of maturity yet still prone to immature acts. Witness the numerous campus rebellions in North America and Europe in the past few years.

A second major reason for the high incidence of violence in our society is the ever growing trend toward dehumanization. As West notes, "we have entered the age of aliens . . . an age that induces terror, disorder, violence, quackery and fanaticism." Machines are taking over. People exist merely as numbers in a computer; they are treated as if they were inanimate objects, devoid of feeling.

This impersonality often leads to estrangement from society, which in turn leads to frustration. People have difficulty in justifying their existence. This feeling of uselessness and rejection is reinforced in work-alienating jobs and in culturally deprived, stifling home lives. When this kind of situation occurs, and it occurs often, there is a frequent tendency to resort to violence as a means of adding zest to a life that is largely meaningless and unfulfilled.

Where does sport fit into this picture? Can it be of any help as a vehicle for channeling aggression and violent behavior? Previously, it was mentioned that some of the violence that is present in society is spilling over and contaminating sport. Despite this trend, sport is still recognized as being the healthiest, most socially acceptable outlet for purging one's emotions.

Some philosophers and historians go so far as to suggest sport as an alternative to war. The rationale for this theory is based on the assumption that man is innately competitive and aggressive. Rather than having this competition take the form of warfare with the ensuing loss of life, why not substitute sport for war and have the competing teams release their aggressions without the carnage and bloodshed?

This is being done to some extent through international competitions such as the Olympics, British Commonwealth, and Pan American Games. Another competition between international powers is the space race. Some government officials feel that the space race and the Olympics are two major reasons why the cold war has not turned hot.

Aside from the rather grandiose hypothesis that sport may be an alternative to war, sport has many attributes which make it an ideal way of reducing or curbing violent behavior.

SPORT IS A FORM OF SOCIAL CONTROL

Sport is a form of social organization, as opposed to the societal disorganization that is shown to breed violence. Because it is a form of social control, sport has the power to eradicate violence. In most sports this is done. The game of football is a good example; five referees closely control the game and players are expelled for fighting. Violence is inherent in the game but it is closely supervised. On the other hand, hockey, which is not as violent a sport as

football, frequently breaks down into fighting and disorganization. Fighting persists in hockey, according to Clarence Campbell, president of the NHL, because: "fighting on the ice is a safety valve; stop it and players would no doubt develop more subtle forms of viciousness." As a result, violence continues. It could be severely cut back if more stringent rules were put in, or even if the present rules were enforced more uniformly. Perhaps the major reason that this has not been done is that the fans like the fighting and would likely stay away if it were eliminated.

This social control aspect of sport is also seen as an effective way of combating and reducing juvenile delinquency. Most coaches require strict adherence to certain behavioral rules. Most athletes conform to these rules and also exert pressure on the other athletes to conform. These influences are also supported outside the school community, where training rules are fairly well-known and the athletes' behavior is under surveillance. In short, participation in athletics is one of the best ways to avoid becoming a juvenile delinquent.

EXERCISE IS NATURE'S TRANQUILIZER

Another way in which sport is influential in reducing violence is through physical exertion. Strenuous exercise is nature's tranquilizer. When an individual is operating under stress he often becomes anxious and hypertense. One useful remedy for this situation is a heavy bout of physical exercise, which can restore the body to a state of physiological and psychological equilibrium. If the individual does not release this excess energy through a healthy outlet such as sport, it could be stored up and expressed later as hostile or violent behavior.

Sport is also frequently used as a form

of mental escape, whereby the involvement in the activity takes the individual's mind off the anxieties and frustrations that may be afflicting him. Very often the type of sport that fits this category is one that is predicated on curbing aggression rather than expressing it. For example, much of the value of golf and bowling lies in the concentration required to play your best. If you are absorbed in the game, you are forgetting the reasons (at least temporarily) for your frustration. In sports like golf and bowling there is usually no strenuous physical exertion taking place, and no aggressive behavior, but just as effectively there is a reduction of tension and proneness to hostility.

Sport is effective as a means of controlling or curbing violence but it is by no means a panacea. For example, in the case mentioned above involving a sport such as golf, tension reduction is likely to occur only if an individual is playing well or if he has no great concern for his score. If the individual is playing poorly, there could easily be an increase in frustration and a resulting tendency toward aggressive behavior. Golf lore is replete with instances of club throwing, tree smashing, and green gouging, all of which invariably stem from a poor performance.

In the same vein, team sports are often tension reducing and calming for the winners, but very often the losers are left more frustrated and depressed than when they started. This is seen often in team sports, as many of the fights break out late in the game when one team is hopelessly behind in the score. For example, the near riot in the 1969 Toronto-Boston Stanley Cup semi-final game started with Boston ahead in the game 10-0.

Another of the shibboleths surrounding the topic of violence and sport has been contested recently by Stone. Stone found when examining aggression in football players that playing football and expressing overt aggression in the game does not appreciably diminish fantasy aggression. Stone feels that "the hypothesis that football helps boys let off steam has to be restated." It is probably more accurate to say that football only channels aggression rather than reduces it.

TECHNIQUES FOR
REDUCING VIOLENCE

Recognizing the above weaknesses, how can sport be used more effectively as a means of diminishing violence? The conditions which lead to the reduction of violence through sport have not been tested definitely. There has been some speculation and conjecture as to what these ideal conditions might be. Some of the commonly mentioned possibilities are listed below.

1. People should attempt to establish some kind of a regular exercise routine. This hopefully would accomplish two purposes: (a) it would take their minds off their problems; (b) their aggressive tendencies would be dissipated in a socially acceptable manner.
2. If people adopt this work-out habit, many more facilities will have to be made available. Most schools are locked on nights, weekends, and holidays. These facilities are rarely taken advantage of. There are not enough outlets for people to work off their excess energies. This is most evident in the midtown slum areas, where lack of proper sport facilities often twists the activity urge into some form of deviant behavior.
3. Perhaps in our society there should be less emphasis on winning and excelling and more emphasis on just playing the game. The "compulsion to win"

syndrome creates frustration and anxiety and can be traumatic for the loser.

4. Finally, in the popular contact sports, there should be more stringent enforcement of the rules. This should start at the professional level, as these are the people who are emulated by the country's youth. Perhaps if this example were started at the top, it would filter down through the whole system.

Hopefully, these are some ways in which sport can reduce violence and make a greater contribution to our society.

Recreation and Leisure:
Their Impact on American Living Today

Dr. Walter L. Stone

Man lives in time and space and groups. Students of society and human nature as formed by society study the interaction of these three factors on culture, society, and personality.

Leisure TIME is the time one has free from making a living and from time spent on self maintenance. Today the world of leisure in point of time is larger than the world of work. Average leisure time increases from year to year as a by product of gain in productivity with less and less man hours of labor.

The changing ratio of work (toil and labor) to leisure is a twentieth century phenomena and a controlling factor in human relations, social organization and cultural development. Leisure time is not only an attribute of modern life, it is a pervasive force in shaping it. The impact of leisure on human behavior and values the last half of this century will be greater than the impact of science on religion and the resulting values of the first half.

As leisure time increases, population is also increasing and SPACE for both living room and enjoyment of leisure decreases. The growth of suburbia and exurbia, the replacing of rural living by urban living indicates the way man is adapting to space for living. In the competition for space for the outdoor use of leisure on the one hand and for industrial expansion on the other we see a conflict which industry up to the present time generally wins. Increased leisure time and increasing population has brought pressures for more schools, more recreation areas and facilities, more family activities and space.

The place and function of GROUPS change and rearrange themselves under the impact of increased leisure time, increasing population and decreasing space. We have today leisure for the masses (earned leisure) as well as a leisure class who know nothing of toil and live in leisure. We also have rising unemployment, one in every 33 workers were jobless in 1953 and one in every 16 workers jobless in the fall of 1960.

Unemployment will have to be dealt with in terms of the uses of leisure time.

Commercial recreation is our third largest economic force, exceeded only by manufacturing and agriculture.

In education a mixture of work and play for youth and for the aging with emphasis on work for youth and play for the aging might well be explored in the world of leisure.

Reprinted with permission from National Recreation and Park Association. Official publication *Parks and Recreation*, February, 1962.

Leisure for the masses (mass leisure) has brought about a Mass Culture.

Serious concern about leisure or free time and how it can be used for increased production, national achievement, and fullness of life is basic to the continued growth of our industrial democracy.

Leisure (free time) is not merely free from work, but is free for the pursuit of things we enjoy in off-the-job-life. The true use of leisure makes one want to go on living. The true use of leisure is an art which Marjorie Greebie classifies as the arts of solitude, the arts of social life, and the arts of civilization.

Leisure time activity includes Recreation, Voluntary Services and Citizenship participation regardless of whether it is earned leisure, inherited leisure, or unwanted leisure. One of the major uses of leisure is Recreation. Not all leisure time activity is recreative some activity is decreative. Great wealth, unemployment and leisure without organized recreation which provides facilities and leadership for something to do, to think about and to enjoy is a dangerous situation for any society.

WHAT IS RECREATION?

Recreation is both work and play. "Toil and pleasure in their nature opposite are yet linked together in a kind of necessary connection."—Livey. Recreation is diversification of occupation that is voluntary, non-compulsive, re-creative pursuit of happiness carried on in leisure time.

Recreation as the pursuit of happiness may be the pursuit of significance in terms of meaning, understanding and appreciation of people and things or it may be the pursuit of satisfaction in terms of skills, participation, and health.

All recreation is play in the following sense:

"I am tired; I play to relax.
I am bored; I play to be amused.
I am sad; I play to be happy.
I am weak; I play to grow strong.
I am shallow; I play to increase life's meaning."

It is possible that the other activities of leisure: Voluntary Services and Citizenship participation can be recreation if they meet for the individual the criteria of diversification, non-compulsive, recreative pursuit of significance and play. If not they can be either work or decreative experience. What is recreation for one may be work for another. Pleasure for one may be poison for another.

The forces and needs of man that organized recreation is concerned with are:

The need for—

1. Exercise of both larger and smaller muscle system.
2. Sharpening of the sense perceptions.
3. Manipulation of varieties of materials.
4. Neuro-Muscular coordination.
5. Enjoyment of discovery.
6. Collaboration and cooperation with others.
7. Activity that is intellectually and emotionally satisfying.
8. Activity that is conducive to quiet contemplation.
9. Opportunity for self-fulfillness.
10. Developing independence and responsibility.
11. Growing—not just conforming.
    Create—not simply adjusting.
    Object—not just agreeing.
    Select—not just accepting.
12. Belonging—of being wanted, and the feeling of security that comes with it.

Recreation is a universal need, on a par with health, education, and social security. Its values are fullness of life including rest and stimulation, relaxation and creativity, physical and mental health.

Organized recreation's place and function in society is that of a satisfying and creative force and its place and function in personal life is a re-creative experience.

Organized recreation under qualified leadership is:

A crusade against the commonplace.
A pursuit of happiness.
A program of physical and mental health.
A service that is as important as formal education, housing, sanitation, and social work.

GOALS OF RECREATION

The goals of organized recreation in the world of leisure are:

1. Providing facilities and opportunities and leadership that will meet the needs of people in society today.
2. Pioneering in learning that "easy does it" and that leisure can be enjoyed.
3. Developing a balance between—
   Togetherness and Solitude
   Conformity and Individuality
   Work and Recreation
4. Extending recreational opportunities to all groups where for economic, social, physical, or health reasons, opportunities are scarce.
5. Working for beauty rather than ugliness in Urban Development and redevelopment.
6. Providing opportunity for citizens, young and old, to plan and conduct, and be responsible for recreation programs, community affairs, participation and responsibility.
7. Activity to promote all cultural arts.
8. Utilize all resources and cooperatively plan with all organized recreation agencies, and services.
9. Providing opportunity for understanding and appreciation of what recreation is, and when it is recreative.

Recreation is re-creative when:

It is interesting and artificial motivation is not necessary to arouse interest.

It is fun and can be carried on throughout most of our life.
It is refreshing to the body, mind and spirit.
It is engaged in for its own sake and not some extraneous reward.
It releases energy, tension and emotion.
It provides for human association, recognition, response, and understanding.
It leads on to other interests and the pursuit of significance of any interest.
It does not exploit or harm anyone else.
It maintains man's dignity and status as a man.
It provides opportunity for personal quiet contemplation.
It leads to social sensitiveness and cooperation.
It makes life meaningful and well rounded.
It lets one be oneself; idling without concern, walking to get nowhere, thinking that solves nothing, making things that can not be sold.
It is its own exceeding great reward.

The essentials for planning the recreational use of leisure time for a democratic people are:

To understand the meaning of leisure in the Western world.
To appreciate the place and function of recreation in American life.
To study and understand our local communities: their needs, resources, and their possibilities.
To make use of all existing facilities: schools, churches, libraries, parks and playgrounds, museums, associations, and clubs, etc.
To bring about community planning and responsibility and community action to provide for all ages, classes and groups through adequate budget and leadership for both tax supported and voluntary supported agencies.
To provide trained professional leadership to develop high grade volunteer leadership that is ingratiating, ingenious and inspirational.
To develop in local areas cooperation between agencies, public, private, and commercial and coordination of services that prevents both overlapping of services and overlooking of needs.

The Economics of Recreation Today

Richard Kraus

Over the past two decades spending on leisure in the United States has become recognized as one of the bulwarks of the national economy. In the mid-1960's, the financial columnist, Sylvia Porter, wrote of recreation as "a big, booming professional business—dazzling even the most optimistic projections of a few years ago . . . ." More recently, in the January 1970 National Economic Review of *The New York Times*, it was stated:

> At the dawning of the seventies, leisure has become an essential part of American life, with a pattern of growth significantly greater than that of the economy. The varied groups in the highly diversified leisure "industry" expect therefore continued expansion of their revenues . . . as the market for their products and services broadens.

While the growth of recreation spending is widely recognized, there is considerable disagreement as to its actual extent in the United States today. Some recent estimates have placed the annual figure at $150 or $200 billion. More conservatively, the *Statistical Abstract of the United States*, annually published by the U.S. Department of Labor, reported in 1969 that the total amount of "personal consumption expenditure for recreation" in the most recent year for which statistics were available, 1967, was $30.6 billion. Obviously, there is a disparity between these estimates.

What is the correct sum? How much do we actually spend on recreation in the United States, and in what ways? First it should be made clear that the *Statistical Abstract of the United States*—authoritative as it may be in other areas—has always underestimated the amount of leisure spending in the United States. For example, in 1959 the *Statistical Abstract* reported consumer expenditure on leisure as $16 billion. Yet in the same year, *Fortune Magazine*, a leading financial publication, reported that its economic studies found that the annual sum spent on recreation was $41 billion.

What accounts for this disparity?

In part, the problem is one of defining recreation itself. Should all activities carried on voluntarily within leisure time for pleasure or self-enrichment be regarded as recreation—regardless of their moral desirability or social purpose? If so, spending for such items as liquor (which the *Statistical Abstract* does not include, but which is obviously used

Reprinted with permission from National Recreation and Park Association. Official publication *Parks and Recreation*, June, 1970.

recreationally by the bulk of the population) must be included in an analysis of leisure spending. Another problem is the difficulty in determining what portion of a given activity represents recreation. For example, domestic travel in the United States represents a $39 billion industry, not including short local trips. It would appear difficult to determine what portion of this should be regarded as recreation, in the sense of being "vacation" or "pleasure" travel. Yet, economic studies have yielded formulas that make it possible to assign portions of such multipurpose forms of activity to recreation.

ANNUAL SPENDING ON RECREATION

Generally, the *Statistical Abstract* has dealt with an extremely narrow range of recreational involvements. A more comprehensive statement of annual spending on recreation in the United States follows. It draws on statistics reported

---

TABLE I
Annual Consumer Spending on Recreation
in the United States in the Late 1960's*

1. Books, maps, magazines, newspapers, and sheet music	$ 5.6
2. Nondurable toys and sports supplies	3.9
3. Wheel goods, durable toys, sports equipment, pleasure aircraft, and boats	3.4
4. Radio and television receivers, records and musical instruments	7.4
5. Radio and television repair	1.2
6. Camping equipment and supplies	5.0
7. Swimming pools and accessories	1.0
8. Equipment and supplies for home "do-it-yourself" activities	12.0
9. Motion picture houses, gross receipts	1.9
10. Admissions to legitimate theaters and opera, and entertainment of nonprofit institutions	.6
11. Spectator sports admissions	.4
12. Gross receipts, including dues and fees, of clubs and fraternal organizations (luncheon, athletic and social clubs, and school fraternities)	.9
13. Commercial participant amusements, including billiard parlors; bowling alleys; dancing, riding, skating, shooting, and swimming places; amusement devices and parks, etc.	1.6
14. Other purchases and fees, including photography, dogs and other pets, collectors' and other hobbies' expenses, camping fees, etc.	2.4
15. Pari-mutuel betting on thoroughbred and trotting horse racing	5.4
16. Domestic pleasure travel	32.0
17. Foreign pleasure travel	5.0
18. Home entertaining	7.0
19. Purchase of alcoholic beverages	14.5
20. Purchase of tobacco and smoking supplies	9.2
21. Hunting and fishing licenses, equipment and related expenses	4.0
22. Lawn and garden supplies and equipment	2.0
Total	$125.9

*Stated in billions of dollars.

chiefly in 1968 and 1969, but to some degree earlier in the 1960's, by the following sources: a) the Securities Research Division of Merrill, Lynch, Pierce, Fenner and Smith, a leading stockbrokerage firm; b) *Forbes Magazine*, a respected financial publication; c) the financial section of *U.S. News and World Report;* d) the annual National Economic Review of *The New York Times;* e) studies of leisure spending reported by *Life Magazine* and *Fortune Magazine;* f) the *Statistical Abstract of the United States;* and g) various other trade association or industrial reports which have appeared in the press.

It should be made clear that this is a conservative estimate of leisure spending. In a number of cases, the figure cited is clearly a low one. For example:

1. Item 3, taken from the *Statistical Abstract*, includes boating as one of its sub-items that add up to a total of $3.4 billion. However, other sources indicate that pleasure boating alone involved an annual expenditure of $3.1 billion in the late 1960's. Obviously, the total sum should be far higher.
2. Item 14, also taken from the *Statistical Abstract* and including photography as a sub-item, adds up to $2.4 billion. However, other economic reports indicate that photography alone involves a total annual expenditure of $3.0 billion.
3. Item 15 reports only the amount of money legally gambled on horse racing. However, authorities have estimated that the total amount of *all* gambling in the United States is $50 billion a year. The Mafia alone is reported to do a $20 billion business annually on illegal betting on sports events and racing.

No attempt has been made to assess spending on narcotics, commercialized vice, or the sale of pornographic materials (books, magazines, pictures, or film). The latter item alone has been estimated to run as high as $2 billion a year in the United States today. Each of these may be regarded as voluntary, pleasure-seeking uses of leisure, although they clearly would not be acceptable forms of community-sponsored recreation activity.

Nor does this report take into account the great number of vacation homes which Americans are building today for clearly recreation purposes. It does not include the recreation facilities being built by apartment or private home developers, such as community swimming pools, tennis courts, saunas, lounges, clubs, or golf courses, which are generally paid for in rents, the purchase price of homes, or special fees. It does not include the vast amount of commercial spending on recreation development to support such recent ventures as the Astrodome complex in Houston, Texas (over $70 million), the new Madison Square Garden in New York City ($150 million), or the new Disney World being planned for Florida ($160 million). Nor does it include the rapidly increased spending on artistic and cultural activities, except for the figures on admissions to legitimate theaters and opera. It has been calculated that spending on cultural activities alone would comprise a $7 billion expenditure by the early 1970's.

Moreover, this figure does not include other major aspects of recreation expenditures, such as government or voluntary agency programs. These are extremely difficult to calculate, and appear in no economic or professional report or yearbook. However, they may be estimated on the basis of known facts.

FEDERAL EXPENDITURES ON RECREATION

A major area of federal spending on recreation is in the provision of outdoor recreation facilities and services. Based on total recorded visitor days in 1968 of the United States Forest Service, the National Park Service, the United States Army Corps of Engineers, the Tennessee Valley Authority, the Bureau of Reclamation, and the Bureau of Land Management, and using a cost per visitor-day unit based on the National Park Service operation (an annual budget of $125.5 million to serve 150.8 million visitors), total federal expenditure on outdoor recreation is estimated at $450 million.

Federal spending on Armed Forces recreation appears in no report or publication. However, it is known that U.S. Army Special Services employs over 13,000 full-time and 200,000 part-time military and civilian employees, and operates over 1,800 major recreation facilities throughout the world. Similarly, the Air Force, Navy, and Marine Corps operate extensive recreation programs; the total cost of armed forces recreation is estimated here as no less than $300 million. Other federal costs for recreation, including the provision of therapeutic recreation services in Veterans' Administration and National Institutes of Health Hospitals, support by the Office of Economic Opportunity and the Department of Health, Education and Welfare of local programs, planning funds and facilities subsidies by Housing and Urban Development and the Model Cities programs, and funds provided by the Land and Water Conservation Act program, would appear to comprise at least $500 million.

Adding all these programs, federal recreation spending comes to at least one-and-a-quarter billion dollars annually.

STATE EXPENDITURES ON RECREATION

According to National Conference on State Parks statistics, state park and recreation agencies spent $295 million in 1967. With rapidly accelerating programs of land acquisition and major bond programs for outdoor recreation, conservation, and antipollution efforts in the late 1960's, it would appear that state expenditures for recreation are now in the neighborhood of $400 million per year. Other state recreation programs, including the provision of special services in homes and schools for the retarded, hospitals for the mentally ill, grants to local communities for youth and Golden Age recreation programs, and school-sponsored programs, and the support of professional education in recreation, must add up to at least $100 million per year.

Thus, state spending on recreation is conservatively estimated at a half-billion dollars per year.

LOCAL GOVERNMENT EXPENDITURES ON RECREATION

Spending by local recreation and park agencies rose from $567 million in 1960 to $905 million in 1965. Assuming that this trend has continued, which appears justified by the overall growth of municipal and county facilities and programs, the figure for 1970 is $1.4 billion. This, however, does not include many other forms of recreation programs which are sponsored by departments of welfare, municipal housing agencies, police departments, municipal hospitals, museums, libraries, social service and youth boards, and similar bodies. In New York City, for example, there are at least 10 important public departments which offer recreation programs, of which only three are reported in the *Recreation and*

Park Yearbook. The total sum spent for local recreation and parks is probably close to $2 billion.

Based on these calculations, all government spending on recreation in the United States is estimated at $3.75 billion per year.

VOLUNTARY AGENCIES EXPENDITURES ON RECREATION

It is equally difficult to estimate spending for recreation by voluntary agencies throughout the United States. There are hundreds of national organizations and thousands of local groups that provide recreation for their membership, or promote recreational activities by offering facilities or leadership to the public at large. No attempt has yet been made to assess the expenditure of religious agencies, nonprofit community centers and settlement houses, youth organizations, agencies serving the ill and disabled, special interest organizations, and similar voluntary groups. However, some statistics are available through annual reports. For example, the Boy Scouts of America had a national operating budget of $8.6 million and spent $60.3 million through local councils in 1967. The annual operating budget of the Boys Clubs of America in the same year was $28.9 million. The Young Men's Christian Association had an income of about $234 million in 1968, of which a sizable portion must have been spent to support athletic, cultural, and social programs. Considering the number and diversity of similar organizations throughout the United States, it seems reasonable to assume that they spend at least a billion dollars a year on recreation activities and facilities.

Finally, it was reported in the late 1960's that American industries and business concerns were spending a billion-and-a-half dollars a year for employee recreation programs and services.

Putting all these figures together, one arrives at the total of $132.15 billion being spent each year for recreation in the United States today. This figure is supported by comparison with a regional study reported by the Southern California Research Council in 1968, which found that in the Southern California region, serving a total population of 12.3 million persons, $9.89 billion was spent annually on recreation. Extrapolating this to the total population of the United States (slightly over 200 million persons in the late 1960's) would mean the nation as a whole spent about $160 billion a year for recreation. However, since the Southern California climate is generally more favorable for recreation and the population more affluent (although it includes sizable numbers of retired older persons on small incomes), it would seem reasonable to reduce the overall figure by approximately 15 percent. This would yield a national figure of $137 billion—extremely close to the total of $132 billion arrived at earlier.

This sum can be appreciated by comparing it to the national expenditure on all forms of education, public and private, which consisted of $58.5 billion in 1968. What do these statistics mean? First, they reflect growth of the national economy during the 1960's. In this period, the Gross National Product rose from $589 billion in 1963 to $861 billion in 1968 and, despite the effects of inflation, the spendable per capita income of the average American rose by one third. The growing use of discretionary income to satisfy leisure interests demonstrates the increased value placed on recreation in modern society. Yet, it also illustrates that Americans are accustomed to spending much greater sums privately for recreation than they are to supporting essential public programs and services. The imbalance between private spending on recreation ($125.9 billion) and public, voluntary agency or employee program spending ($6.25 billion) has meant that many recreation and park operations serving the public at large have been starved for financial support.

CITIES CAUGHT IN FINANCIAL SQUEEZE

A number of the larger cities of the nation have been caught in a traumatic financial squeeze by declining tax bases and the need to provide ever more costly welfare, educational, law-enforcement, housing, transportation, and environmental services. In such cities, recreation and parks have been placed in a precarious position on the budgetary totem pole. As a single example, in New York City during the spring of 1969, budget cuts were announced that slashed recreation and park and school-sponsored programs by several millions of dollars. Important summer and year-round activities were eliminated, hiring "freezes" placed into effect, and museums, libraries, and botanical gardens compelled to reduce their visiting hours or to impose a new visitor fees.

On the federal level, there has been a comparable lack of adequate financial support. The Land and Water Conservation Fund has not had, since its inception in 1965, the amount of money for recreation resource development envisioned in the original legislation. The National Park Service was compelled by the Revenue and Expenditure Control Act of June 1968 to carry out a drastic personnel rollback which resulted in sharply curtailing park and recreation area seasons and operations. In the light of a recent economic study which showed that travel to the National Parks generates $6.4 billion in overall expenditures each year, contributing $5.7 billion to the Gross National Product and $4.7 billion in personal income, this kind of shortsighted economy is sheer idiocy.

In a number of other areas the federal

government has been equally penurious. Each year, Congress has provided funds for the National Endowment on the Arts, to assist cultural programs throughout the nation, that are actually less than the money provided by some European cities to support municipal opera companies or symphony orchestras. Today, with a number of major American symphony orchestras in danger of imminent bankruptcy because of rapidly rising costs, the need for increased government subsidy is crucial. As another example, the total budget of the President's Council on Physical Fitness and Sport in 1969 was only $317,000—a ridiculously small sum compared to the amounts spent by other nations to promote fitness and sport. In February 1970, it was announced that the Office of Economic Opportunity would no longer fund special community recreation programs although it had, over the past several years, provided substantial sums for recreation and cultural activities in disadvantaged urban neighborhoods.

Generally, park and recreation administrators have responded to such financial strictures by moving in the direction of "pay-as-you-go" resource and program development. More and more new facilities are being developed in municipal and county programs with the expectation that their costs will be substantially met by fees and charges. If all citizens could afford to pay the generally reasonable fees attached to such facilities or programs, this might be a logical solution for the problem.

However, even within today's affluent society, it has been estimated that 25.4 million persons have family incomes below the minimum subsistence level. Such families, living at the bare edge of necessity, with less than $3,500 or $3,600 for an urban family of four, cannot possibly afford to use the kinds of commercial recreation opportunities cited earlier in this article. They are largely dependent on the network of recreation and park facilities and programs provided by public agencies for constructive leisure opportunities. To permit such programs to depend increasingly upon fees and charges to support capital development and current operations will mean, more and more, that poor people will be excluded from all but the most minimal and barren facilities.

The President's Advisory Commission on Civil Disorder documented the necessity of providing adequate recreation and park facilities in our cities. If this is to be done, without excluding the economically disadvantaged, it will be necessary for us to rethink our priorities as a nation to insure that a fuller portion of the huge sums which today are spent on recreation are used to support vitally needed public and voluntary programs and facilities.

While we may be impressed by the fact that Americans today spend over $132 billion each year to meet leisure needs, this does not mean very much in impoverished neighborhoods in our cities and towns, where the only recreation opportunities are likely to be limited to a poorly equipped, littered, and unattended playground—or to the corner bar. Our public and private expenditures on recreation need to be placed more nearly in balance.

Planning for the
New Free Time
William R. Ewald, Jr.

WHAT LEISURE?

This regional conference is examining leisure—the primary focus of the future society. We think we can now foresee that technological efficiency will produce free time for people in abundance. We cannot foresee the date of that sweeping change, but at least we can recognize 50,000,000 people over 55 in retirement by the year 2000 will be a new phenomenon in this direction in its own right. Perhaps retirees will man the proving ground for the greatest shift we have yet to take as humans—from life centered on work to living centered on leisure.

Robert Theobold has predicted either mass unemployment, the dole, or make work jobs for tens of millions within the next 10 years. Herman Kahn says it will take hundreds of years to reach that stage. Carl Oglesby says if the New Left's revolution is won there will be recognition of so much to be done on behalf of humans all over the world that we will be working 12-14-16 hours a day seven days a week. Resources for Future, Inc. in *Resources of American Future* (John Hopkins, 1963) put the work picture this way (per worker, including moonlighting).

	1955	1970	1985	2000
Hours per year	2070	1950	1860	1790
Weeks per year	49.6	49.2	48.9	48.6
Hours per week	41.8	39.6	38.0	36.8

Kahn and Weiner, in *The Year 2000* (Macmillan, 1967) put the work hours in the year 2000 at 1600, with average weekly hours (for 52 weeks) declining to 31. The National Planning Association in their 1967 *National Economic Projection Series* Report 67-N-1 put average weekly hours in the year 2000 at 31. (It's not exactly clear if moonlighting is accounted for in these latter projections.)

Meanwhile, back in the market research room of major corporations, in the fertile minds of ad men, and in the worried heads of government bureaus, the vision of the great new free time dances like sugarplums. We are already gearing up for the great new "Leisure World" and, indeed, a few have already been built and inhabited—by retirees. *That* may be the point to make.

Reprinted with permission of William R. Ewald, Jr.

The New Free Time—whenever it does come, will be derived from leisure, retirement or idleness. Forced idleness, underemployment or unemployment or sickness is not a free choice. Is it really, then, free time? De Grazia was strong on this discussion in his paper for the American Institute of Planning 50th Year Consultation "The Problems and Promise of Leisure" in *Environment and Policy, The Next Fifty Years* (Indiana Press, 1968). Maybe forced idleness is *not* free time until somehow we free it from the dominance of the word "forced." Maybe the same holds true of retirement (particularly forced retirement at age 55—with the vigor of a 45 year old extended to age 90-100). Until we ourselves perceive that retirement as desired—is it really free time?

So we come to leisure. Leisure is described by Webster as "time free from employment," or "time free from engagement." Robert Hutchins pointed out at the AIP 50th year conference in Washington that

> "the origin for our word for leisure is the Greek word for school. Leisure for the Greeks was not free time. It was not vacant time. It was not spent riding around the country in second-hand Fords trying to get glimpses of the countryside between the billboards. It was not spent in moderate or excessive alcoholism, though that was not unknown. Leisure was distinguished from vacant time by the exercise of one's intellectual powers and moral character for the benefit of one's community and one's self. And the question is whether all the free time that we are going to have can be turned into leisure. I think that it can if one of the first steps toward it is taken through universal, and I mean literally universal liberal education."

De Grazia, at the same conference, ridiculed the "precise" vision of the year 2000 future forecasters with projections like "our standard of living will be three

to seven times higher than 1965 and in tune with this increase will be the increase in leisure time." Yet he seemed to be willing to accept that more free time, more leisure was inevitable and a "disbanding of the labor force."

Finally, there is a different perspective on the prospect for leisure in *Fortune* (March 1970) in "The Myth of a Leisure Society" by Gilbert Burck. The argument there is that to project past productivity-per-man increases into the future ignores the shift of employment growth from manufacturing (and its susceptibility to rational, efficient process) to the vagaries and inefficiencies of the service industries.

> "Contrary to all predictions that automation will throw millions out of work, the scarcest of all resources will be manpower. By 1980 the economy will be able to draw on some 200 million man-hours a year, up from 165 million today. But 200 million man-hours will suffice only if they are employed with increasing efficiency. Meantime the prospect of greatly reducing the hours on life's treadmill remains mainly a prospect. For a long time we'll probably have to work as hard as ever."

To try to get a hold on the subject of how we go about Planning for the New Free Time—leisure, retirement and idleness—suppose we arbitrarily say all of the views given above have a bit of the "eternal truth" in them. How then do we react now to planning for the new leisure? If we are not to have as much leisure as the ad men say, but we do have more than we have now. If Oglesby's revolution is not won but we somehow move at least part way from a low morale to a high morale society and recognize the huge effort (and huge number of man-hours) we need to put into making men, the community, the nation and the world "a success" (synergistically, a la Buckminster Fuller). If there is at least wider acceptance as national purpose in the stated thrust of the AIP 50th Year Consultation

"To assure the primary importance of the individual, his freedom, his widest possible choice, his access to joy and opportunity, his impetus to self-development, his responsible relation to his society, the growth of his inner life and his capacity to love." (See Introduction, *Environment and Change, The Next Fifty Years*, [Indiana Press 1968]).

If *Fortune* is partially correct that there won't be as much leisure as we think, but it's partially wrong in its estimate of how unlikely it is that "efficiency" can be brought to the growing service sector. If all of these "ifs," rewritten if you like, refine current projections of free time—we are still left with more of it—and in any case we have the 20-50 million retirees—and we need to plan. But how?

WHAT IS LEISURE?

Maybe now we need to look more closely into what free time or leisure really are. The expert on this is De Grazia. He is worth quoting at length from his statement at the AIP conference (see also his chapter in *Environment and Policy, The Next Fifty Years* [Indiana Press 1968]).

"Free time leads to recreation. It is leisure which bears directly on creation. Most Americans when they use the word leisure, have free time in mind. True leisure, however, is different. It's a state of doing, of doing free from everyday necessity. Distinct from free time, it requires freedom from time and work. Not hourly or daily or monthly freedom, but freedom from the necessity to work, preferably over a lifetime. By contrast, the present American free time is one-half of a pendulum: job time, free time. First you work, then you rest and recreate yourself.

Leisure has no particular activities. Men in a leisure condition may do anything. Much of what they do an outsider may consider suspiciously like work .... And creative work ought not to be called work. Not having anything to do, these men do something. Often they may turn to religious ritual, music, wining and dining, friends, poetry, but most notably to the play of ideas and theory, in a phrase, to the theoretical life.

With the lack in America of a strong tradition of leisure, it is not surprising that we must ask, 'What can leisure do for us?' The benefits of leisure, simply put, are the benefits of cultivating the free mind. If persons have been brought up with a liberal education and have no need to work at anything except what they choose, they enjoy a freedom that lays the condition for the greatest objectivity, for example in science; the greatest beauty, for example in art; and the greatest creativeness, for example in politics. The founding fathers of this country had leisure.

'Leisure,' said Hobbes, 'is the mother of philosophy.' If such are its benefits, and we need them sorely, can we increase leisure? Now, this is difficult. It is not contained, as is free time, by time off work, and space for recreation. To increase free time it is usually enough to send a man, any man, home early from work. For his recreation it is usually enough to give him some space to play in. But how to provide leisure? All steps that can be taken by the government through legislation and institutions, by business organizations, schools and churches ... have a limited value even for free time, but much less value for leisure.

There are some traces of the leisure ideal in the recent attempts by government and universities to provide in centers and institutes a creative setting, especially for scientists. These efforts and others can help only inasmuch as they, through teaching an example, diffuse an appreciative climate. Much more than this cannot be directly done. For, you know, there are two important limits to face. First, not everyone has the temperament for leisure. For most people leisure lacks sufficient guidance and sense of purpose. The leisure life is too hard. Those who have the toughness, or psychological security for it are not many. Second, since leisure will have nothing to do with work, except that freely chosen, which by definition should not be called work, it involves having means of support. In modern terms this means that whoever is to lead a life of leisure should have some form of economic independence.

The objectives in creating more leisure should be these: First, to allow the greatest number of those who have the temperament for it to develop to their fullest extent; second to allow them to secure the means of existence without work, and then to create an atmosphere more kindly than hostile in which they may lead their kind of life. A number of the developments we have already discussed do affect these objectives. For example, a liberal education is almost a *sine qua non* for the growth of the leisure temperament. Universal education today may see to it that almost all will have a college education. On the negative side, however, that education is not being freely chosen. Military service is the alternative. Education, moreover, has and will continue to decline in quality because of the great numbers of students in compulsory attendance and because of the nursery climate of the college as a place to put grown up children while the adults go to work.

Also, forced free time will not have to expand much to reach a net separation of income and work. Recent proposals for a guaranteed annual wage or salary intimate the separation already. Should this happen, the wherewithal for a life of leisure will be there for all who think they have the temperament. Many will try, many will drop out. Among the survivors, the right few will be found.

The last thing I mentioned, the last prerequisite: an atmosphere friendly to leisure, may be brought about by the increase in free time whether forced or not. If the worker-consumer model which we have today breaks down, if more free time is not only forced upon men, but, in time, also sought and taken the accompanying change in

attitude may well be receptive to true leisure. A more relaxed pace to life may bring about a more favorable view of the whole idea, as well as more reflection, more refinement and less ambitious political, military and economic projects. Play, in man's free time, is a taste of leisure. In turn the ideal and practice of leisure creates standards for the enjoyment of free time. Indeed without leisure the outlook for the resolution of the problems of hidden unemployment and forced free time seem desperate: hedonism, disintegration of social and political ties, crises of law and order, a cynical and callous foreign policy. There is both promise and threat then in the future. Leisure for the few, free time for the many—that is what appears to be coming. A not unpleasant prospect. Spoiled only by the introduction in free time of the adjective forced."

It becomes clear that we have to provide adequate income before there is free time (the form for this, certainly not the amount, may be in the Nixon-Moynihan-Finch guaranteed annual income). And it becomes clear also *forced* free time has to be understood, accepted and wanted before it *is* free time and the guaranteed income more than a dole. Only then do we have the stuff from which leisure can grow—and then only for those who themselves are adequately prepared. Free time or leisure time, there is no reason to castigate one or the other. The distinction made here is that one is creative and one is not. Both must be planned for and tested by pioneers, both can add to community, national and world development as well as to self development. The distinctions, as made by De Grazia are worth pondering.

Part of the answer to how to plan for the future leisure and free time might be found in for whom. Who, for certain, will have the most free time? We might quickly, perhaps much too quickly, say the young (in school). That may be too quick an answer if you understand the disgust for our system of education that is growing in the young in school, both those who should be there and those who shouldn't be (in universities). If we now understand that both leisure and free time are crippled by being forced—we must admit we have some serious changes to make with the student years, to say nothing of the preparation there to maximize the future opportunity for leisure.

As for the working—young, middle aged and senior—while still at work they will most likely be having more free time. But we probably need to accept with De Grazia that time off the job is, for most, recreating and not leisure. Besides this is a horrendous conglomeration of people to plan for or with. This leaves us with retirees as experimenters. At present people retire at age 62-65 but this is said to be headed to age 55.

Can we consider for a moment that those over 55-65 may be our pioneers into the new society of the future—the leisure society? Here may be more of a discernible block of people to work and plan with than any other. Already a third of them have a guaranteed annual income. And here is *full time* leisure and free time for 20 millions now—going to 50 millions by the year 2000—of all incomes, life styles, experience, intellect. It would seem that just as the black man has soul, style, compassion and faith to contribute to American society (as Whitney Young put it at the AIP Minneapolis Regional Conference in November 1968)—perhaps the older in age have a living example of how to be free and thrive. This is an inspiration we badly need now. Perhaps in our over-zealous concentration on children we are overlooking the greatest experiment of our day on behalf of a day to come: how to shift from a work economy to a pleasure economy.

In his "Moral Equivalent of War" (1917) William James may have said it all: "The transition to a pleasure economy may be fatal. If we speak of fear of emancipation from the fear regime we put the whole situation in a single phrase—fear regarding ourselves now taking the place of the ancient fear of the enemy." Maybe this transcendental thought can be thought through first in practice by older minds, and not children, youth or the harassed middle aged.

So here we are continuing to try to arrive at how we plan for leisure and mainly, so far, we have said that maybe it is with *whom* we arrive—the retirees—that may be critical to this venture. They have the time, they have the need, they can be identified, and maybe they have the inclination. Maybe they are nearer to admitting than any that human life is not a totally rational matter—that it should not and must not be. Maybe they can see more readily than the rest of us, with a self-serving perspective that may also serve us all, that efficiency is not the goal. (Many of them are no longer considered efficient enough to be employed by society so maybe they do have this perspective.) Yet they may understand more than others how "patience rewards," what "practical" means, and that perhaps God is Dead as a phrase is a great purge for religiosity but has nothing to do with the reality of Spirit.

THE CONTEXT FOR LEISURE

Having attempted to lodge this claim for a great living adventure into the future with our present older population let me say that the following must be taken into account:

1. We are into an epic time measured in the truest sense of human history, but we don't accept that.
2. Our present decision making institutions, public and private, are failing us.

3. Our middle aged, preoccupied with the present, are failing us.
4. Radical youth's total preoccupation with the present is failing us.
5. Our singular faith in specialization and efficiency is failing us.
6. Technology and population (both its growth and its concentration) are the driving force of our epic time, changing the meaning of space, time and our expectations.
7. Man is rational, irrational and extrarational all at one time, but we seem disappointed that he is not totally rational. (A thing)

To plan for leisure and free time we need a recognition that:

1. Great amounts of leisure, except for the retirees is in the distant future but that doesn't mean leisure shouldn't be experimented with or planned for now—the opposite. How, sensibly, can there be "crisis planning" for leisure?
2. We have alternatives in addition to reforming ourselves, joining the party of our choice or creating ways for private enterprise to bring its expertise to bear. Instead of merely decrying the short term criteria used by public and private institutions in making decisions, perhaps we should recognize them as they are—amelioratable at a slow pace—and get on with inventing whatever new institutions and programs we may need for whatever it is we want of the future leisure and free time.
3. Our decisions must *simultaneously* accommodate as accurate an understanding as possible of a) technological change, b) population change, c) various functions at different geographic scales (room, house, neighborhood, or out to the nation, world), d) increments of time (the minute, day, week, month, year, out

to 5-10-50-100 years); and e) how knowledge or misunderstanding of all this can and will change people's expectations.

What a challenge for pioneers age 50+! What they have failed to do in their work life is now up to *them* to formulate in their leisure life.

PLANNING FOR THE NEW FREE TIME

Primary requirements before free time, as described in this paper, to be truly free would seem to be that it must be:

1. (and foremost) individually sought
2. financially self-sustaining
3. without social stigma
4. enjoyed at a high level of wellness.

If these are indeed primary requirements it follows that planning for the New Free Time-Leisure, Retirement, Idleness, Recreation is first of all a social and economic matter (incorporating political and cultural matters into those terms). There is obviously some serious work to be done to "free" free time for all ages. For most this free time will be time off from work for recreation. For those idled there is education, retraining, useful community jobs of last resort (if we are really to implement the Full Employment Act of 1946), recreation and to a certain extent, leisure. For the retired the problem and opportunity is much greater. Their new free time is full time, forever. As such it may be more of a sample of the future leisure society than the others.

There will be physical expressions of social and economic plans. Planning for physical things is what most people understand to be the planning for free time. Perhaps that's because to most people, when we get to building things, it's more comprehensible, and to them that's when we get "practical." What they may mean is that at some point the philosophies and priorities of society move from the metaphysical world and become physical entities—"real." Visible expressions of societies' and individuals' values are made in how they go about developing beaches, parks and playgrounds, ski lodges, care centers, golf courses, swimming pools, libraries, craft centers, learning centers, etc. The design, number and location of these facilities determine their accessibility, utility and are in themselves expressions of how society understands its philosophy and priorities.

The attempt to quantify these facilities for serving; people's free time is already the business of planning, recreation, health and education departments of government and certain private enterprises. But physical planning for free time is about as far as the planned retirement communities have gone. Recognizing the skill and funds required for this part of the planning and building for free time is clearly not enough. The attitudes and organizations as well as the resources are of primary moment, all taken into account within the context of free time as previously described.

But let us get down to the planning for leisure—the creative essence of free time. Whereas leisure can be part time for a few, and full time for even fewer who really enjoy and create in their life's work, it is potentially much more likely to be found in those who have retired. To realize the opportunity of the retirees, and for the sake of an ongoing experiment into the future leisure society, we need first of all to satisfy our primary requirements for free time (individual acceptance, financial support, societies' acceptance and high level wellness). To that, for free time to become leisure, must be added the reviving and/or nourishing of the very special frame of mind that frees people to innovate and create.

On our *own* behalf then, to plan for leisure is to open the challenge and provide the basis for retirees to experiment with the future leisure (and free time) society. Seen this way the model is not simply to concentrate on large, efficient housing projects for the elderly. On the contrary, to discover the process for achieving unity with diversity for the leisure world would be the purpose— attempting to take full account of existing and pending technology (especially in communication, transportation, education and health). This is probably a multi-disciplinary effort beyond the scope of present government and private enterprise. It has moral, synergistic, technological, humanistic, motivational, and ecological overtones. The first need may be to invent the organization, the process—and the money—to develop such experiments in leisure—with the explicit understanding that they are not to be for baby sitting grandma but to experiment for the kind of attitudes and style of leisure life we might all like to move to. Because we all may someday, I suspect the largest part of it will be to avoid building a totally efficient "perfect" community, to learn how to make things work while planning for serendipity—in order for leisure to be truly free.

Promoting Functional Play Patterns

Ira J. Hutchison, Jr.

In a seemingly magical fashion a blending of physiological and psychological phenomena seems to take place within all children that catapults them into a special world of fun and games; . . . a world that is partly their own creation and partly a legacy of socially imposed play patterns inherited from the society into which they are born.

Many theorists in the field of recreation assert that the child can gain from his play activity a special kind of functional orientation that will enable him to cope with the transition from childhood to full maturity. The laymen seems to accept the simpler explanation that play is a natural human activity and part of the gestalt of childhood growth and development. These particular points of view do have a reasonable degree of validity. Unfortunately, within some communities there are other attitudes and practices toward play that are severely limiting its effectiveness as an aid in the social and physical growth of the individual. It is these, the negative aspects, that must be exposed, and means found to reduce their effects.

Play is an integral part of childhood; and its most important contribution during this period is the influential role it assumes in the acquisition of socio-recreative skills and habits by the child. For the most part, participation in normal play activity offers the youngster a number of opportunities to form and reinforce such habits and skills which later become a part of his adult pattern of living.

In many instances we find that adults are making a strange kind of pilgrimage into the play-world of the child. Where this happens, there will also be a corresponding distortion of the normal patterns of voluntary selection and involvement, both being vital elements in the composition of a total play experience. Adult needs and values are often vicariously met by placing an emphasis on winning, on skill, and on personal achievement as opposed to recognizing and protecting the right of children to participate in an activity at his own pace and for his own reasons.

Play is most beneficial as a form of activity for the participant when he is basically self-motivated to become involved. Unless the importance of external factors is minimized, and the effects of such factors controlled, the participant is apt to receive less than the full value of the play experience. This does not mean that the necessity is lessened

Reprinted with permission from National Recreation and Park Association. Official publication *Parks and Recreation*, September, 1967.

for adult supervision to protect the child from physical or emotional strain. It does mean, however, that adults, while exercising this responsibility, should not overlook the possibility that the child might be involved in an autonomous process that is an essential aspect of his growth and development.

It is difficult to believe that in our enlightened society many still regard play as basically a waste of human energy. Within many locales there are still punitive vestiges of puritanical attitudes toward play. It is still possible for a child to raise the ire of the communities' elders by showing a preference for play to the point of equating it with work in his personal value system. He is likely to be emphatically reminded that the "sweat of the brow" is the major ingredient in the formula for success. The discouraging aspect of this state of affairs is that we, as a cultural group, have not been able to separate the image of play from this archaic frame of reference. A number of domiciliary agencies and treatment facilities are providing large scale remedial treatment services for persons who have been psychologically crippled by this attitude.

Fortunately, it now appears that many communities are beginning to gain a new perspective of play. One reason for this might be the mushrooming efforts of government and private agencies to improve the socio-economic patterns in which large groups of people now exist. Many social investigators, while attempting to identify those elements that can bring about a more ideal state of existence, have come to recognize play as an essential aspect of the life experience and are advocating programs that include the use of the play-experience as a socio-economic therapeutic tool.

In spite of the beginning of positive changes in community attitudes and ideals regarding play, much remains to be accomplished in this area if we are to keep pace with the economic and social factors in our society that affect the well-being of the citizen in the community.

There is every reason to believe that in the near future a 30-hour work week will be the rule rather than the exception. As a result, individuals in many communities will have much leisure time at their disposal. It is this probable abundance of leisure that bids to become a major social problem of the future and makes the acquisition and use of meaningful leisure time habits and skills of such critical importance.

If the transition from our present work-oriented society to one characterized by leisure and plentitude is to be successful, it must be accompanied by a vigorous program of education and preparation for the wise use of leisure. In the past, other professional groups have led the way in anticipating, studying, and attempting to meet the sociological needs that arise within our society. These same groups are now giving the problem of leisure time illiteracy serious consideration. It will take time for such groups to propose and implement effective solutions. Sociologists will need time to compile new statistical data that can be used as a guide in making the adjustments to changing community structures and altered patterns of living. Psychologist and psychiatrist cannot be rushed into providing us with the kind of information that will give us a workable awareness of the psychic state of the public in relation to the use of leisure time. Whether these, or any other constructive measures, can do the job is a question that can only be answered by the social scientist of the future.

In the meantime what can be done? More specifically, what can be done by the recreation profession that will significantly increase the capacity to provide profitable leisure time experiences?

Why shouldn't a resourceful recreation specialist be able to implant the seeds of quality adult leisure time interest and pursuit in the framework of a planned activity program? Why can't he, with a concentrated effort, influence the mothers, the fathers, the teachers, and other persons in the community to accept the essentiality of proper play and socio-recreative experiences? Within any community establishing this kind of leadership and support, the resulting integrated action will lead that community toward the maximum utilization of play-activity as a means of furthering the leisure-time aptitude of its members.

It would seem quite appropriate to begin as early as possible to structure the play-patterns of the individual. Sooner or later the child finds out that playing in a "sand-pile," or riding his tricycle is just the beginning of the limitless play-experiences that are available to him. As he grows older other activities become attractive and the focal point of his leisure-time interest. With the wise and firm guidance of a recreation specialist, the child can be led to understand and appreciate the total spectrum of physical and social recreative activities.

The number of physical activities in which an individual can successfully participate decreases as he grows older and there is a corresponding increase in the skill level required. In early playground and school play experiences, the number of participants is limited only by physical facilities available and the willingness of the individual to wait his turn. A few years later there are teams to make, squad cuts to avoid, and the task of meeting specific standards of performance.

On the other hand, the broad socio-recreative needs of the individual remain constant or even increase with age and responsibility. It is a significant obligation of the recreation specialist to interject this kind of meaning into the variety and order of his program planning.

Direct or formal contact with the individual is not the only avenue that the recreation specialist might constructively use to furnish recreative learning experiences. There are many civic-oriented groups that have the potential organizational structure and philosophy for becoming involved in the programing of the recreation or leisure-time agency. Many of these groups are currently presenting organized play opportunities for both adults and young people. Other groups can be encouraged to go beyond the realm of discussion and sponsor or present a program of activities that meet the criteria for socio-recreative development. Somehow everyone that becomes interested or involved in community service in the area of recreative activity must be convinced that "Little League Baseball" and "Midget Football" are not the only activities that build character.

Recreation specialists can no longer afford to be affected or even intimidated by individuals and groups that insist on a flashy program of major sports and popular social activity. Those individuals who plan and supervise community centers must not let the popularity of an activity be the major criterion for its inclusion in their programs. Who is to say what particular activity has the greater facility for providing a maximum degree of socio-recreative orientation? The activity most applicable to the psychological needs and the socio-economic environment of the individuals involved should take precedence in program planning.

There are many reasons why we should play. However, none is more important than those that involve the relationship between the individual's play-experiences and his emotional and physical development. If the adult population can learn to recognize the value of play as a valuable aspect of everyday living, it is possible to garner their full support in the efforts that must be made to prepare future generations for the economic and social changes of the future.

Charter for Leisure

PREFACE

Leisure time is that period of time at the complete disposal of an individual, after he has completed his work and fulfilled his other obligations. The uses of this time are of vital importance.

Leisure and recreation create a basis for compensating for many of the demands placed upon man by today's way of life. More important, they present a possibility of enriching life through participation in physical relaxation and sports, through an enjoyment of art, science, and nature. Leisure is important in all spheres of life, both urban and rural. Leisure pursuits offer man the chance of activating his essential gifts (a free development of the will, intelligence, sense of responsibility and creative faculty). Leisure hours are a period of freedom, when man is able to enhance his value as a human being and as a productive member of his society.

Recreation and leisure activities play an important part in establishing good relations between peoples and nations of the world.

Article 1

Every man has a right to leisure time. This right comprises reasonable working hours, regular paid holidays, favourable travelling conditions and suitable social planning, including reasonable access to leisure facilities, areas and equipment in order to enhance the advantages of leisure time.

Article 2

The right to enjoy leisure time with complete freedom is absolute. The prerequisites for undertaking individual leisure pursuits should be safeguarded to the same extent as those for collective enjoyment of leisure time.

Article 3

Every man has a right to easy access to recreational facilities open to the public, and to nature reserves by lakes, seas, wooded areas, in the mountains and to open spaces in general. These areas, their fauna and flora, must be protected and conserved.

Reprinted with permission from the International Recreation Association, JOHPER, February, 1971.

Article 4

Every man has a right to participate in and be introduced to all types of recreation during leisure time, such as sports and games, open-air living, travel, theatre, dancing, pictorial art, music, science and handicrafts, irrespective of age, sex, or level of education.

Article 5

Leisure time should be unorganized in the sense that official authorities, urban planners, architects and private groups of individuals do not decide how others are to use their leisure time. The above-mentioned should create or assist in the planning of the leisure opportunities, aesthetic environments and recreation facilities required to enable man to exercise individual choice in the use of his leisure, according to his personal tastes and under his own responsibility.

Article 6

Every man has a right to the opportunity for learning how to enjoy his leisure time. Family, school, and community should instruct him in the art of exploiting his leisure time in the most sensible fashion. In schools, classes, and courses of instruction, children, adolescents, and adults must be given the opportunity to develop the skills, attitudes, and understandings essential for leisure literacy.

Article 7

The responsibility for education for leisure is still divided among a large number of disciplines and institutions. In the interests of everyone and in order to utilize purposefully all the funds and assistance available in the various administrative levels, this responsibility should be fully coordinated among all public and private bodies concerned with leisure. The goal should be for a community of leisure. In countries, where feasible, special schools for recreational studies should be established. These schools would train leaders to help promote recreational programs and assist individuals and groups during their leisure hours, in so far as they can without restricting freedom of choice. Such service is worthy of the finest creative efforts of man.

ORIGIN OF THE CHARTER

In 1967, at the Geneva Symposium of some 16 agencies operating internationally in the field of play, recreation and leisure, the International Recreation Association was requested to develop a **Charter for Leisure**. A committee consisting of the following was appointed:

Norman P. Miller, Chairman
International Recreation Association (IRA)

Drummond W. Abernethy
International Playground Association (IPA)

Julien Falize
International Council for Health, Physical Education & Recreation (ICHPER)

Eugene-Marcel Guiton
International Center for the Study of Leisure (CIEL)

Friedrich Roskam
International Working Group on Sports Facilities (IAKS)

After 2½ years of work, it was completed at a final meeting in Geneva on June 1, 1970 and its announcement was made. It is now available in four languages: English, French, German and Spanish. IRA believes this **Charter for Leisure** can be an important tool for use by authorities responsible for planning for leadership and facilities for play, recreation and leisure-time services for all age groups.

We hope the Charter will soon be translated into many other languages, so that authorities may have it as an aid to extending recreation services throughout the world.

The Social Environment of Recreation and Parks

GENEVIEVE W. CARTER "Social Trends and Recreation Planning"
Parks and Recreation, National Recreation and Park Association, October 1965.

EVA SCHINDLER-RAINMAN "Recreation's Changing Role"
Parks and Recreation, National Recreation and Park Association, January 1965.

DAN W. DODSON "The Dynamics of Programing"
Parks and Recreation, National Recreation and Park Association, November 1961.

KENNETH W. KINDELSPERGER "Recreation and Delinquency"
Parks and Recreation, National Recreation and Park Association, April 1960.

URIE BRONFENBRENNER "The Split-Level American Family"
Reprinted with permission from Professor Urie Bronfenbrenner, Cornell University, and Saturday Review, Inc.

EDWARD STAINBROOK "Behavior of Man in the Cities of Man"
Reprinted with permission from Edward Stainbrook, Ph.D., M.D., University of Southern California.

WARREN G. BENNIS "The Temporary Society"
Reprinted with permission from Warren G. Bennis, President, University of Cincinnati.

The Social Environment of Recreation and Parks

The world will never again be as it was; it will never again be as it is for the forces of social and technological change remake it day by day. Great changes are coming in America not because we have deliberately willed them but because they will be compelled by events.

It is in this rapidly changing social environment that the recreation and park movement must operate. The magnitude of social change is so great it defies description; it may defy comprehension until it is seen in the framework of history. But some trends can already be seen as highly influential. Among them the changing pattern of family relationships, deterioration of the sense of neighborhood, the development of an urban man, altered conditions of work, the changing role of women in society, race relations, sorting of society on the basis of age, and revolutionary changes in our system of values appear to be highly significant. There is no accurate way to measure change. From one point of view nothing is static; everything is in process. Change, therefore, is relative. It is also uneven. With respect to human beings, biological change is slow and cultural and social change is very rapid. We know very little about the effects of extremely rapid rates of change on people. We can see some of them, however. Among them are stimulation, creativity, innovation, conflict, alienation, and disorientation. There is enormous acceleration without and within. The pace of life puts substantial stress on the human organism.

"While the family still has the primary moral and legal responsibility for developing character in children, the power or opportunity to do the job is often lacking in the home, primarily because parents and children no longer spend enough time together in those situations in which training is possible."

No one knows where the limit is but there must be a limit. Important new machines alter not only the physical environment but also the way man thinks of himself and the world, and, therefore, they alter the social and cultural sphere as much as the physical. Change fueled by technology has three phases—the creative idea, the practical application, and diffusion through society. The time required for each of these phases is shortening. In the torrent of change we are now experiencing, the rate of change is perhaps more important than the directions of change. It is relatively easy to exceed the adaptability of our people. Adaptability is more closely related to speed than it is to direction. The disorientation created by accelerated social change is painful. We are

"... people understand that individual human development and maturation are slow processes, yet nevertheless expect human groups to develop into cohesive units in quick time. Groups, however, have a maturing process of their own; their slow pace, if left unaltered, could accentuate the stresses of the Temporary Society."

developing a whole new pharmacopoeia for treatment of this malady. Among them the prescriptions which suggest, "If I ignore it, maybe it will go away." and "We have always had change; this is no different than the past." rank high. Many otherwise sophisticated people find the idea of change so threatening, they deny its existence.

The fundamental fact of our contemporary psychology is transience. One cannot grope for an understanding of modern man until he credits the feeling of transience as the central fact. From this fact flows doubt, insecurity, fear, disorientation, progress, change, alienation, even despair. The relationships of each individual woman and man to other women and men, to society and to the world of ideas, are somehow changed.

We have recently witnessed a great outpouring of nostalgia for the nineteen thirties. This return to an earlier era, which has made a cheap tin Coca Cola tray a treasure, is an attempt to go back to what seems from the perspective of forty years a simpler, happier time. People with good memories who lived through the depression of the thirties do not share the impressions that depict that time as trouble free, but if one takes that era as a base line and measures social change from it, the increasing complexity of the social environment as it relates to the park and recreation movement is apparent.

"... bureaucracy tends to routinize jobs of those in both public and private employ, so that the trend is away from seeking the fulfillment of self from the job. Increasingly, the job is followed for a livelihood, and in the remainder of otherwise unoccupied time, the individual must look for the self-realizations which will lead to filled, full lives."

The changing character of work has enormous implications for recreation. There is great and growing evidence that many people do not find satisfaction on their jobs. We have known that for a long time, but we are only now beginning to recognize the symptoms of the psychological distress which unmet personal needs can generate. A pattern of behavior that includes increasing anger against the system, chronic disgruntlement, gradual withdrawal, preoccupation with pay, and redirection of energies into some other field, is common in industries that provide limited job satisfaction. If there is no other outlet for persons trapped in narrow inhuman jobs, the physical and emotional tension developed can lead to neurotic and psychosomatic illness. This type of illness is behind many of our social problems.

Patterns of human interaction are based on kinship, friendship, neighborhood, job association, joint membership in organizations, and service relationships. Among these, park and recreation agencies have an enormous potential for aiding human association in membership and service organizations. When old friendships have been broken by mobility, helping create an environment where new associations are possible is an important social service.

One reads and hears a great deal about cities these days and much of it is negative. Cities are not all bad. The best of life and the worst of life occur in cities. The defects of our cities have been amply cataloged but we have not been so articulate about their virtues. From some perspectives the city is one of the most important and dramatic inventions of mankind. No other environment can match it for stimulation and excitement. It is in many respects our most effective educational institution. Its primary characteristic is the interaction of thousands of people carrying on the tasks of daily living in a relatively confined space. Its great strength is that it permits formation of groups based on shared interest and personal compatability. As long as we were a frontier society living in a sparsely settled country, human association was based primarily on kinship or physical proximity. With the growth of the city, however, the improved opportunity for communication made other kinds of groups possible and shared interest became a strong adhesive. At first the interests were primarily economic but in the last fifty years recreational interests have often become the basis for human association. Whether one is interested in stamps or soaring, politics or painting, films or football, the city can turn up others who share that interest. This little recognized fact has given a whole new meaning to the concept of community. In the decade ahead, world wide communities based on a common recreational interest will be feasible on a scale we have never before known. If they are alert, recreation and park agencies may have a significant role in their development.

In the typical suburban neighborhood today there is no commons—no public meeting place—where the people of the neighborhood can interact. The predilection of the city planner for sorting land use out by functions and putting all like uses together has segregated residential areas into compounds which include only houses. These sterile areas often do not provide even a corner store where one might pass the time of day with a neighbor. Social exchange, if there is any, is apt to be by invitation only. This formalizes the occasion, restricts it to scheduled events, and creates a host and guest relationship. The result is a transformation of neighborhood life that

"There is a new era for the direction of recreation as a vehicle for reaching the isolated or withdrawn and bringing them back into the mainstream of society."

moves it from the informal front porch discussion of the day's events to the invitational Sunday barbeque in the fenced-in backyard.

Recreation activities operate *within* the social environment and *form a part* of the total social environment of the community and the nation. In many communities they are a conspicuous part of the pattern of social interaction. In areas where the neighborhood has lost its social significance as an organizing device for human association, recreation activities are the primary arena beyond work and kinship. In communities with high rates of mobility, recreation may be more effective as a social nucleus than kinship. Open space is social space. In the great urban parks of the nation a daily open house takes place that brings together people of the neighborhood in a no-host social event.

"A recreation program does not have to be defended in terms of its ability to prevent delinquency. It has a legitimate and intrinsic function in its own right in the general welfare of the community."

There are at least three main schools of thought in American psychology. One school is behaviorism which embraces a mechanistic view of man that has no room for such concepts as "will," "mind," "conscience," and "imagination." All behavior is explained as a function of the way people have been conditioned to respond to the stimuli around them.

The second school is psychoanalysis with its view of the pervasive influence of sexuality in human behavior. Psychoanalysis sees human behavior conditioned by psychosexual experiences of the individual, particularly those experiences that occur early in life.

". . . the density of people in the urban environment has a great deal to do with the constant burden upon our attention which must scan and react suitably to very frequent person encounters. Part of the way this task is handled in the city is by learning not to scan or not to respond to a great number of people. This leads to a learned indifference to others as a protection against the density of the human encounter."

The "third force" in American psychology maintains both behaviorism and psychoanalysis were in error when they attempted to understand human behavior entirely in terms of external influences. This view of psychology sees the internal self-concept of the individual as the most significant element that determines behavior. Proponents of this school maintain that each individual finding contradictions within himself moves to attain internal self-consistency and this is the source of human motivations. It is an important concept which has been highly significant in the contemporary world. For a growing number of people, park and recreation experience is a valuable homeostatic device which helps them maintain their internal self-consistency. In the busyness cycle that marks most contemporary relationships, many contacts are task-motivated and task-oriented. Such relationships tend to be shallow. The task regulates the frequency, duration, and the number of meetings. It sets the pattern and depth of the human interaction. It sets the limits of involvement. The involvement is vastly different if one has as a task completing an application for employment or climbing Mount Everest. In today's world there are many more applications than there are expeditions to conquer Everest. There are risks in the

". . . if present-day knowledge of child development tells us anything at all, it tells us that the child develops psychologically as a function of reciprocal interaction with those who love him. This reciprocal interaction need be only of the most ordinary kind—caresses, looks, sounds, talking, singing, playing, reading stories . . ."

contemporary social environment. Alienation, in which the individual lacks a relationship to something external to him when such a relationship is considered to be both natural and desirable, has been amply documented in the written and visual literature of our time. The theme of this thesis is alienation of man and God, of man and man, of man and woman, of man and the earth, and of man and his institutions. As population increases the psychological distance between people seems to increase also. The most sensitive individuals among us complain of the lack of meaningful relationships with others, particularly with people whose life experiences have been different. The rate of technologi-

"More people are now trying to live a good and gratifying life in the city at the very time that cities are failing to provide the social organization that is necessary to keep people in effective committed relationship to other people and to the values and directives that maintain the sense of community, common cause and common goals."

cal and social change is so rapid that two generations do not have enough congruence in their life experience to understand each other readily. The government and other institutions seem impersonal and remote. Our affairs are so complex, the media play such an important part and decisions are made so rapidly and events occur so quickly, the problems seem too big to be managed by human beings. Disillusionment is greater when people feel they have no means of influencing events.

There is a dynamic relationship between social change and the lengthening life of a single man. There was a time when the values and life style one learned as a youth were reasonably congruent throughout a lifetime. Today with the accelerated rate of social change and the dramatic increase in the life span of many people, the values and life-style one learns as a youth may be little more than a memory before one reaches middle age. There are many kinds of revolution; several are at work in our world today, but the most prominent and perhaps the most pervasive is at its root a moral revolution. It involves a rigorous

"Cannot society go beyond its anger at youths' acts of rebellion and hear the cry such young people are making for more space for themselves and all men to live in, for the setting of new rules, new limits."

critique of religions, ideological, and moral philosophies that tend to inhibit expression of the most human qualities of mankind. It is an attempt to recover the human aspects of life lost to a past industrial society.

In the old morality our moral traditions were accepted as absolutes beyond critical inquiry. In the new morality nothing is beyond reappraisal and modification if the demands of modern life demand it. This critique is producing a moral reformation that promises moral ideals that will serve us better in the modern world. A central concept of the new morality is that achievement of human potential is a worthy and necessary goal. It sees restraints on human development and expression as immoral. The new morality reserves its greatest criticism for dehumanizing and depersonalizing aspects of technology. It depicts huge, insensitive, unyielding bureaucracies as antihuman.

The moral codes now developing stress equal rights. Under the banner of "participative democracy" they hold that each individual should have the right to participate in the decisions that affect his life. These principles have been extended beyond the political arena to all kinds of institutions throughout the society. As applied in each setting it is becoming a vital moral principle that holds that participation in social institutions is essential to a high quality life experience and to avoid alienation. The age of reason has become the age of emotions. The young, witnessing the state of the world and the human condition after nearly three hundred years in which rationality has been held up as the highest expression of being

". . . the only meaningful reference group a person has today is his peers."

human, have begun to embrace emotionality. Many deny that man and the world can be explained in rational terms. It is a profound change in the thought of Western man.

"Hostility gives way when groups pull together to achieve overriding goals which are real and compelling for all concerned."

There is a broad and growing humanistic ethic permeating America. It sees the great need of our nation in human terms. It would not rank improved technology or an improved economy as central needs in our national life. It would see the primary social needs as human development, improved processes of human interaction and protection, and restoration of our environment as central. It is precisely in these fields that the recreation and park movement must operate. It is in these fields the movement finds its mission and identity.

Observers of the social scene point out the difference in mood and perspective in the seventies. The sixties dismantled moral conventions, challenged life styles previously thought normative, and questioned national goals. By comparison the seventies thus far have been contemplative, meditative, ritualistic. Youths, who are always highly influential in national life, have led the way to a style of life that is far more introspective and concerned with human development and human relationships. This new approach to life has led to new communities, experimental sexual combinations, new politics, and a general turning inward of the national conscience. Elements of these interests show up as concern for the fragile world ecology, rejection of old patterns of race relations, interest in metaphysics, experiments in new forms of human relationships, the peace movement, revival of early Christian teachings, in popular music that is less worldly and more intimate and personal, and in revised concepts of morality. The list is illustrative, not exhaustive. It points up a new turn in the national psyche.

We must begin with the positive assumption that things can be better. We must continue with the assumption that it is preferable and possible to shape the processes of change. We must work in the world as it is—not as we wish it to be.

Social Trends and Recreation Planning

Genevieve W. Carter

No field of organized services to people has such a broad spectrum for potential research as recreation. The subjects of needed research may range from preservation of wilderness-type sites, varieties of grasses for golf courses, durability and safety of equipment, and land use, to life-saving techniques and physical fitness. The other end of the research spectrum would include practices in recreation therapy, group-work methods, informal education, camping, low-organization activities, leadership functions, as well as the developmental life cycle of leisure-time needs and resources. An examination of relevant social trends and their implications for recreation planning leads into program questions which, in turn, point toward public policy issues.

Social trend data are available from all sorts of surprising sources. There are also changing forces and social conditions which are recognized but for which there are limited data. When several significant social or economic trends converge, social problems are likely to emerge. For example, urban poverty emerges more clearly when the current trends in the changing occupational structure are observed, when the unskilled and poorly educated migrate from the Southern rural areas to the cities, and when, at the same time, the middle-class population of the city moves to the suburbs.

These social forces are interrelated, and a chain process is initiated which results in a new type of disadvantaged people in the central core of our cities. This is not only a concern of the community's social welfare agencies but should also be an interest of the recreation and parks department. Three current issues have importance for recreation planning: the notion of increased leisure time, the changing economy and the occupational structure, and recreation's role and the social problem of poverty.

One of the significant social trends frequently mentioned in recreation planning is the increased leisure time made available by technology, cybernation, and automation. Workweek trends show gains in leisure time when plotted over the last half century; the sixty- and the fifty-hour week is down to a forty-hour week.

When the pace of this change is examined, we find that the workweek has stabilized over the past five or six years. There is no indication of increasing leisure for the head of the household or for his wife. In

Reprinted with permission from National Recreation and Park Association. Official publication *Parks and Recreation*, October, 1965.

fact, the changes over the last decade would indicate less time for leisure but more money to spend for recreation. This trend is not true for the older population, the over-65 group, which is increasing in numbers and in retirement years.

Family income has been increased by higher wages, by more persons with two jobs, and by an increased number of working wives. For example, when trends indicating persons with two jobs are analyzed, the data show that professionals and farmers continue to have high rates of multiple-job holding, between seven and eight percent. This past year, for the first time, equally high or higher rates were found among carpenters, other construction craftsmen, drivers and deliverymen and sales workers (not retail); men who were elementary- and high-school teachers (18.7 percent), and firemen, policemen, and the other protective services (14.2 percent). The lowest rate in multiple-job holding for men was for managers, officials, and proprietors, most of whom already work long hours on their primary jobs. When the trends for average weekly hours of production workers are examined, the prospects for increased leisure also appear to be less or stabilized.

Another trend which belongs in the leisure-time picture is the ever-increasing number of working wives. If families were counted by the husband's income alone, the numbers of families with incomes over $10,000 would be cut by almost half, from seven million to less than four million. The higher the family income, the greater the likelihood that the wife was employed. The greatest increase among married women was among the forty-five and over group, with no children under eighteen.

More leisure evidently is not as important as more income for recreation. As personal wealth increases, most families find they have more each year to spend for pleasure. This is illustrated by the fact that participant sports figures rose from $197,000,000 in 1940 to over $1,000,000,000 in 1961. Spectator sports captured $904,000,000 of their 1940 dollars but over $2,000,000,000 of their 1961 dollars. They bought $500,000,000 worth of radio and TV sets, records, and musical instruments in 1940 and $3,800,000,000 worth in 1961. Very expensive items such as boats and airplanes could be enjoyed by more people. Along with other sports equipment, these expenditures rose from $254,000,000 in 1940 to $2,200,000,000 in 1961.

The implications for recreation planning are interesting. There is less leisure because of more working hours per family, but there is more money to enjoy the benefits. The families with unemployed youth and adults, and the aged who are generally also at the low-income level, have the leisure but not the money.

Projections indicate that the shift to occupations requiring higher levels of education, training, and skill will continue. Concurrent with this shift is an emphasis from goods-producing to service-producing industries, insurance, transportation, and personal services, such as medical and health services. The chief occupational trends in labor force projections to 1970 and 1975 are:

• A relatively rapid growth of white-collar occupations, especially in technical and professional fields.

• A slower growth in blue-collar occupations, with skilled craftsmen experiencing the most rapid gains, but no increase at all for laborers.

• A rapid growth in service worker employment.

• A steep decline in the number of farmers and farm laborers.

Now what effect would these trends have on people in general or recreation in particular? Although the unemployment rate among all age groups rose from 4.0 percent in May 1957 to 4.7 percent in May 1964, or an increase of 17.5 percent, in this same period it rose 56.2 percent in the 14- to 19-age group, from 16.9 percent in 1957 to 26.4 percent in the same month of 1964. Our postwar baby boom has now hit the labor force marketplace full blast!

What does a highly developed society do when its lower-level jobs disappear and when millions of people are not prepared for occupations requiring a high level of education? In our society we believe work is a virtue and although the Gross National Product soars to $600,000,000,000, each able-bodied adult should exchange his services on the free market for income. When, as the trends indicate, there will not be occupational openings for the low skilled, partially educated person which would yield income for family subsistence, what is the answer? There is no indication of a vigorous movement to create or develop a sufficient number of new jobs requiring only marginal skills.

What would be the public attitudes and reaction of recreation or constructive use of leisure were provided for able-bodied youth and adults who have no place in the free market of an employment picture? This same question might be phrased to include all families and children and adults who receive their subsistence through transfer payments rather than from exchange of income through work.

The reason this sounds so strange is because recreation, like other good things, is generally considered to be a reward for worthy work and thrift. The problem ahead is either to create new jobs for this low-skill group or to find a socially acceptable purpose for the use of this leisure. The Youth Corps holds promise for a part of the youth. A role for certain purposive types of recreation is not impossible as one of the alternatives.

The following is a very brief review of the social factors which describe poverty in an affluent society:

• Of the 47,000,000 families in the United States in 1962, some 9,300,000, or more than a fifth of these families, had total money income below $3,000. Eleven million of these people were children.

• Poverty-linked characteristics can be described according to risk or vulnerability. Being nonwhite, a female head of family, over 65 years of age, having four or more children, or living in a rural area increases the chances of being poor. Low educational achievement, having a low level of employable skills, or being young in the labor force with marginal entry skills, plus family, makes for a greater risk of poverty.

• Economic growth in itself does not eliminate poverty, since an analysis of the composition of poor families shows many have no members available for the labor force and thus are unaffected by fluctuations in the business cycle and corresponding changes in employment levels. The recent growth of metropolitan areas has resulted in a new mass of the poor. Urban renewal and redevelopment has brought further attention to these conditions which were formerly hidden in the sections of the city unknown to the majority population.

Now, for the concern of recreation. The concerted-services approach is more than a new cliche. The impoverished are no longer a problem for the economists, the social worker, the sociologists, the educators, or any one profession or agency. The problem is viewed in its totality where a number of social forces convene on certain vulnerable groups. The current demonstrations on delinquency prevention and reduction, supported by the U.S. office of Juvenile Delinquency and Youth Crime of the Welfare Administration, have opened new approaches to cooperative efforts by local communities. These programs have challenged the traditional, institutionalized programs in their services to groups who do not readily utilize the usual organized programs.

In a number of cities where concerted services are organized for a target area, the recreation agency as the city or county unit has participated. These instances are perhaps too few in number to allow for a statement which would describe the stance of recreation and the poverty problem. The question is one which challenges the responsibility of government in the field of recreation. With a national recognition of the problem of poverty, what role does organized recreation have?

The recent report of the President's Appalachian Regional Commission calls for new highways and recreation development which will bring recreation seekers into the depressed areas. This is viewed as economic development or a means of stimulating a low economy. It constitutes one type of legitimate responsibility for recreation. The question before us is what other responsibility does the field of recreation have in making its contribution to the social problems of poverty? The answer must come from the recreation field. Some of the potentials, however, are exciting and challenging. Here are some considerations for recreation planning as an active participant in the intensified attack on poverty:

● Recreation departments have, by necessity of staff limitations, developed leadership in neighborhoods for help in conducting special events or in their

baseball leagues, tennis championships, swim meets, et cetera. Now, we may label this activity as increased emphasis on indigenous nonprofessional services. It really means doing more of what you have been doing in city slum recreation programs to bring in local participants who can direct the recreational activities of others.

● Recreation programs have often stressed their ability to reach underprivileged youth who could excel in sports and physical activities but who might be failures in the academic line. Leading a muscle-building group or a baseball team into a literacy program where reading and arithmetic has real meaning for achieving immediate goals is not impossible. The trained group worker on the playground could be the best go-between for getting the interest of youth into channels for the education needed for today's changing labor market.

● The local swimming pool controversy and the regional facility where a program must serve a broader area is the testing ground for civil rights. There is no question about the relationship of equal opportunities in the use of public facilities and other kinds of equal opportunities for jobs or education which in turn are directly tied to poverty and income.

Public recreation of all kinds is theoretically for all of the people. Studies are available which indicate the utilization of public recreation resources by income levels. A conservative guesstimate would be that ninety percent of the utilization would fall between the $7,000 family income per year to $15,000 income per year for all types of tax-supported recreation programs and developed resources.

Most recreation outdoor and indoor is geared toward the so-called broad middle class. Although public recreation is a general welfare service, it preserves much from the model of gentry leisure now within reach of a larger population. In the harsh terms of our society's value beliefs, access to recreation must be deserved or used for protection of the larger society or to keep idle youth constructively occupied. This is, of course, a simplification of public attitudes, but it serves to make the point.

The national distribution of recreation resources, particularly those under tax support, will more likely follow the pattern of income distribution and therefore may have no viable part in an attack on poverty. There are no statistics on the proportion of all recreation resources utilized by the 17,000,000 of our nation's families with incomes under $3,000.

Organized recreation in urban areas has a first-line opportunity to engage the disadvantaged in its programs. Many good recreation programs have no barriers which hold off the uneasy underprivileged. No membership card is required; there are opportunities to watch before the courage for participation is needed; you can leave, or come and go, which is not permitted in highly organized activities, and you can select or test out your own choice of activity without fear of getting the full curriculum. The "low-organization" philosophy of recreation has a reaching out power for the poor whose unpredictable lives are full of daily crises and problems.

Recreation could offer a first experience in purpose for those who have become submerged and apathetic. The feeling of powerlessness is often used to describe the poor and disadvantaged. There are several routes to finding self worth, something to achieve, an aspiration before one is strong enough for literacy training, retraining for employment, or for work experience leading to a job.

There is a new era for the direction of recreation as a vehicle for reaching the isolated or withdrawn and bringing them back into the mainstream of society. Recreation with good leadership is not stuffy or pedantic and, by planning ways to involve more people in social activities, recreation could develop new powers and skills for these people who need them so much.

Recreation's Changing Role

Eva Schindler-Rainman

Singular and significant social changes are affecting every person in the United States, with far-reaching implications for the recreation field. We are seeing not only the increase in the movement of people from one place to another, but the change of composition in communities and neighborhoods. This change of composition involves not only racial groups moving into areas where they have not been able to live before, but also the mixing in some neighborhoods of different social strata. This means that the professional person and the well-paid vocational person like the plumber may live in the same neighborhood. This change is coming about because of the equalization of wages between the professional and some of the labor groups. We often think of change of community composition only as racial mixture.

We are seeing emigration of people from all over the United States and from other countries, and this is changing the composition of communities. In Los Angeles, we have many foreign students living with American families and adding a new element to community life. These different and changing compositions at the center of a community affect the recreation system. The implication here is clearly that planning for recreation must encompass knowledge about the changing community and its everchanging needs.

An upheaval in employment potential is affecting all communities, whether they are upper, middle or lower class. We see an increase of employment in some areas, such as the space field, and a decrease in other specialties, particularly where automation has taken over. One of the groups having difficulty in employment are civil and mechanical engineers, who heretofore could find jobs all over the map at good rates of pay. Now it is very difficult to find steady employment since most engineering firms are dependent upon government contracts, and, when these are cancelled or completed, engineers are laid off. They must have tremendous mobility or they find themselves out of a job entirely. Recreation must serve a shifting population.

There are different groups of people out of work, ranging from the unskilled to the highly specialized. We see in this picture a great effort to retrain people who can no longer find a job in their particular area of competence, but this is a big question: "Retraining for what?" The implication for recreation is clear. We must educate people to spend

Reprinted with permission from National Recreation and Park Association. Official publication *Parks and Recreation*, January, 1965.

their leisure in successful and satisfying ways. Not only will the work week be shorter, but unemployment may increase, giving people more time even if they do not want it.

Changes in the American family are an important aspect of change in general. Subsummed under this might be the whole area of many more women working. This includes women who do not have to work, but who are no longer satisfied with staying at home. Some find work available whether it is in their professional field, such as teaching, nursing, social work, law, or whether it is in clerical or sales work. With fewer mothers at home, there are more children available for recreation opportunities.

Women are having more children sooner, and therefore have a longer period of work life ahead of them. The nuclear family is very different from the extended family of several generations ago. Early marriage and independent family units all have implications from program. We need to develop programs for young mothers who find it difficult to raise children in new communities and who are very responsive to mothers' groups where they can meet others who have similar experiences and problems. Nonworking mothers are independent of younger children sooner and need to seek recreation outlets other than at home. And, again, the recreation system becomes an important part of the possibility for those outlets.

It is not normal in the 1960's for young families to be dependent on their parents except perhaps financially for a short period of time. Therefore, they must seek their outlets in other areas. Furthermore, life expectancy is on the increase, and therefore there is a larger range of customers; that is, the very young, the middle-aged, and the very old can be considered as potential patrons of a recreation system. The question I would like to raise here is: "Do we really have programs that meet the needs of all of these kinds of people, or do we still have programs that we think worked ten years ago and therefore no change is necessary?"

Another change that is not often discussed but certainly is extant is the change in institutional services that we are seeing all the way across the United States. Historically it was the private agencies that did the experimenting with new programs; today, it is the public agency, whether recreation, public welfare, public health, or others which have the money from the federal government to do the experimenting. Increasingly, federal monies are available for all kinds of programs, and the emphasis is on using federal monies to develop new local programs. Has recreation availed itself of this opportunity and, if not, why not?

Certainly we are also living at a time of social revolution. There is increasing emphasis on serving the poor, on giving opportunity to the culturally deprived, and building on the strengths of these people to help them meet the needs and problems of their communities and to develop programs that will serve them best. One of the things that recreation might look into is, "How can you help people in underserved neighborhoods know what opportunities are available?" The civil rights struggle is another part of this revolution and means that we have to look increasingly to see whether we are serving equally all segments of the population.

An increased emphasis on education, regardless of socioeconomic background, is another change we are seeing. It is part of the social revolution also. Might recreation centers take part in this new emphasis in interest by developing study dens where youngsters who do not have the kind of home where a quiet room is available might avail themselves of one or two rooms in the center for the purpose of doing their homework? Might it not be possible to develop volunteers who could tutor and help these youngsters?

There is also increasing interest in the world of arts, and the implications here for recreation programs are manifold. These changes have additional implications for recreation; they may already be happening; and some we need to be aware of and taking part in.

Since change is all around us, are recreation programs changing too? *To what degree? In what way?* Increased services to the poor must be developed. This implies, in turn, that perhaps the professional person who serves in recreation centers needs to have additional formal education or some specialized in service training.

Increasing cooperation will be necessary between community agencies so that a total service may be given to the people rather than overlapping or underlapping services. It seems imperative that professional people—committees, advisory boards, whatever—need to examine a total neighborhood or a total community and together plan how to serve that community best. Recreation needs to be included, or needs to include itself, in such a planning group. The neighborhood must be represented on such a planning group by the patrons or clients who live in the area. After all, it is they who are going to be affected by the decisions made and the services rendered.

Increasing study of the communities by the professionals and by the advisory committees is necessary, because it will be very important that programs be tailored to the needs of the people in the community. This may mean that what happens at one recreation center may be quite different from what happens at another. For instance, there might be neighborhoods where sports need to be increased and crafts and arts decreased; or where a fine-arts program is needed most because someone else is taking care of the athletic activities.

Increasing involvement of citizens in planning programs and as volunteers in giving services is needed. Increasing use of volunteers on all levels would certainly help extend and enlarge recreation programs, and would involve in a different way some of the citizens who live in the community. For some people it is very recreational to be a volunteer, helping with an activity rather than participating in it.

A larger range of program needs to be envisioned, whether this is in the area of sports, arts, study dens, tutorial programs, discussion groups, or whatever area. There is really no beginning or ending to what comprises recreation for people.

As recreation professionals we have to sharpen our skills in working with people. We need to know a great deal more about what makes people behave as they do; what are the differences between various groups in our society; and what is their value system and life style and to what extent can we tailor programs in relation to these.

More programs for single men are needed. In welfare programs there is no place for him. In many of the structured organizations there is no place for him. The churches have been in the forefront of offering some program for single men, but recreation centers, too, have a responsibility in this area. Since it is not the most acceptable middle-class social habit to be single and male, this means that we have really not integrated this group into our programs. This group includes the young adult and the middle-aged single man as well as the senior citizen.

Development of a series of activities and programs to enhance man's creativity and ability to depend on himself rather than on others is necessary. New creative ideas and ways of involving people must be developed if recreation is to play the important part it can in the years ahead when there will be much less time to work and much more leisure time.

The Dynamics of Programing

Dan W. Dodson

Dynamic programing in today's agencies depends upon an understanding of the dynamics of the era in which we live. We are overdue for a new look at the leisure-recreation concept as we have known it. There are perhaps three reasons why this is necessary:

First, the nature of the workweek has changed. Man now has seventy-two waking hours of leisure and forty of work, whereas he formerly had seventy hours of work and forty of leisure. Stated another way, one hundred years ago the average American workman had just a little more than thirty minutes of leisure for each work hour. Now he has almost has two hours leisure for each hour of work. The question now is, "How much recreation does modern man need?" Obviously, leisure has far outstripped the recreation needs to which it was so completely devoted in the past.

A second reason is implicit in the nature of the change of work itself. In the past work was the principal way through which most people achieved their self-realization. It was thought that people had special aptitudes or "bents" and that these, if discovered and followed, would lead the individual to his self-fulfillment. John Dewey would have contended that these talents were not "natural"; that they were brought out by the interaction of the person with his groups, but that a total life would be integrated "in terms of a calling, a vocation." Many felt that one was called to his vocation in the same way that the priesthood was called, and that service through work was as virtuous as service through any of the helping professions. One famous layman's formula for a self-fulfilled life was, "Make all you can, Save all you can, Give all you can."

Today, this concept of work is rapidly passing. For the vast body of labor in America, work is no longer self-fulfilling. One reason is that status has changed from being vested in skill and excellence of artisanship to status being based on capacity to consume. A second reason for work no longer being a vehicle for self-fulfillment is the changed nature of production. Robot production has relegated man to the sideline. He sees the machines deprive him of that which gave life meaning and purpose; namely, work.

The third reason for the new look at the leisure-recreation problem is closely allied with automation. It is the growing pattern of bureaucrat-

Reprinted with permission from National Recreation and Park Association. Official publication *Parks and Recreation*, November, 1961.

ization which structures the work life of so many in the helping professions and service trades. Giantism in production, which is probably necessary if we are to continue to have the standard of living we now enjoy, produces giantism in labor and in government. In order to administer such a structure there has appeared a vast army of bureaucrats. These are persons whose jobs are carefully prescribed in fine print in manuals; whose promotion is more dependent upon seniority than upon performance; whose perogatives and responsibilities are those of the office, rather than the person; and they relate to each other in a chain of command which pyramids to the top administrator. Increasingly, community service is provided by such persons who have no part in making the policies which guide them, and whose aspirations are limited by the knowledge that their upward progress is ordered and often circumscribed. The narrow training to do one specific job leads to lack of integration of perspective and over-conformity. Above all else, bureaucracy tends to routinize jobs of those in both public and private employ, so that the trend is away from seeking the fulfillment of self from the job. Increasingly the job is followed for a livelihood, and in the remainder of otherwise unoccupied time, the individual must look for the self-realizations which will lead to filled, full lives.

Thus, there has combined the shortening of the work week, so that leisure as a time for *re*-creation is oversubscribed, and the change in the pattern of work, making it necessary for increasingly large numbers of people to find in sources other than work the opportunity to develop those "bents" which are uniquely theirs. Hence, the professional leadership needed to serve this newly developed aspect of American life must possess competencies which are not by

any means entirely re-creational in nature—although the undue emphasis still placed on athletic activities indicates that too, too many of our program designers have not recognized this profound change which leadership is called upon to meet. Dynamic programing will, of necessity, continue to meet the very real need of assisting people to find those outlets from work which will provide in a part of their leisure time the recreation of body and soul in the varied assortment of activities which meet their interests. On the other hand, a program which concentrated solely upon recreation objectives would miss the point of this transformation of the life of America.

A real challenge to programing comes from the changes in group living. Since World War II there has been a tremendous movement toward homogeneity in group living. A few of these trends are:

Residential Living. A major number of the residences created since the war have been in projects large enough to have an identity of their own, built to attract a homogeneous population. Fundamentally, they have been of two types; on the one hand, suburban developments erected on a mass scale; or urban-renewal projects within the inner cities, built, again, sufficiently large to have an identity of their own and be homogeneous in nature. An illustration of the suburban pattern in the New York area would include Levittown on Long Island where six-and-a-half square miles of potato fields in 1947 were transformed by 1954 into fifteen thousand houses for forty-five thousand people. All were beginning families, all of a narrow segment of income. This community is where young couples with modest incomes go to make their start. Once the family is on the way, a third bedroom is needed, and, if the expected promotions come through, the family moves to the next type of specialized neighborhood—the project with the three bedrooms, most often of split-level architecture. Here is a community again with homogeneous age and family status peoples, that has an entity all its own.

In the inner city a comparable thing happens. New York City is the extreme example, but its pattern indicates the trend elsewhere. Practically all urban renewal is of a project nature, large enough to be identified as a neighborhood of its own, designed to serve a homogeneous population. Whether it is Stuyvesant Town, built by Metropolitan Life Insurance Company to serve thirty-five thousand middle-income people; Penn Station South, designed to serve ten thousand low-middle-income people as a cooperative; or Grant Houses, erected to serve seventy-two hundred low-income people, who must move as soon as their income improves—the story is the same. The agencies which provide services of a neighborhood nature are faced with dealing with a homogeneous population.

Increased segregation on a faith basis. Even where peoples are brought together as neighbors, there is no guarantee that they will associate with each other except where they are members of the same faith. Churches are rapidly becoming community centers for the flock. Too many are becoming places where upwardly mobile people find a safe, respectable association which is endlessly involved in meetings of the brotherhoods, sisterhoods, and church suppers, but seems to serve only the same exclusive clientele. Instead of churches being places where dedicated people meet to marshall resources and deepen commitment to move out to change life, they seem to be becoming a sanctuary from life.

Will Herberg has pointed out that now since it is also respectable in America to be Catholic or Jew as well as Protestant, we are moving toward a triadic culture in which we make a tri-faith approach to community life, instead of an interorganizational or interpersonal one. Dynamic programing in the years ahead will have to learn to deal sensitively with these pressures. In the name of "moral and spiritual values," "God and country" and other slogans, we foster faith differences by marching Catholic and Protestant children in one direction at meals and Jewish children in another at many camps. On Sundays we divide them up and march each faith in a different direction to worship in many of our modern recreation facilities. Religion is a basis of grouping in American life, and any dynamic programing had better be sensitive to it.

Grouping On a Racial Basis. The great migration of Negroes and Spanish-speaking peoples to the larger cities of America has accentuated segregation. In spite of a Supreme Court decision in 1954 desegregating public education and most other facilities, the *defacto* segregation is more pronounced perhaps than at any other time in America. In part, this stems from segregation in neighborhood living; in part, it grows out of other patterns of homogeneous grouping which makes associations across lines of racial identity difficult. The great challenge to leaders dealing with use of leisure time will be to learn how to provide intelligent leadership in communities torn by tension, those deadlocked in power fights between the groups, and those which are mandated by public policy, including law, to desegregate against the wishes of the dominant power groups of the local community.

Age is another significant aspect of homogeneous grouping. Reisman and Whyte have written tellingly of the passing of inner direction as a part of American character, and its being replaced by "outer" or "peer group" direction. One author seems to think this is due to the age change of the population, and the attendant passing over to a consumer society. The other thinks it is in no small part because of the passing of the Protestant ethic. I doubt if either are correct.

I believe the reason for "peer group" domination is because of the "peer grouping" which has dominated practically every aspect of American life in the past fifty years. For instance, when I went to my first school in the backwoods of Northeast Texas we had only one teacher for the thirty pupils. This teacher taught all the community's children from the first grade as far as the student wanted to go, which was usually the seventh grade. While she did not teach as much content as do modern schools, she would, by comparison, not come off too badly—especially if she were compared to teachers in some of the changing inner city neighborhoods.

Today, a teacher claims she can't teach unless the children are homogeneously grouped on achievement tests and she has the "bluebird" section—leaving the "peckerwoods" to someone else. I never cease to be amazed that the older boys in my neighborhood take the younger ones in tow when they are quite young, and teach them how to figure baseball percentages before the teachers can teach them to do simple multiplication. We have so homogenized in grouping that the only meaningful reference group a person has today is his peers.

Another dimension of this problem relates to the impact upon personality because such grouping tends to sever the thread of historical continuity between the generations. A Levittown makes no provision for uncles, aunts, grandfathers, and grandmothers. This contact with the generations is shortened and in many instances severed. Family, in the larger sense, is weakened. Hence the controls are those of the peers, rather than of family tradition.

Dynamic programing faces no more serious issue than this of grouping in its many ramifications. Sensitivity to the trends, and intelligence in dealing with them may be one of the major tasks facing those whose job in the years ahead is that of assisting America use this growing amount of leisure time to achieve more fulfilled lives.

Recreation and Delinquency

Kenneth W. Kindelsperger

Next to the international situation and the constant interest in the latest political developments, there is perhaps no other issue that attracts more discussion, more Sunday supplement stories, more editorials than the question of juvenile delinquency in the United States.

While there may be a rare variation, the general picture these statements, editorials, television programs, and word-of-mouth discussions present is a discouraging, depressing image of the young people of America rapidly degenerating into a mob of unruly, violent, disorderly teen-agers. A peculiar emotion seems to develop whenever adults take to the soapbox or editorial page to discuss juvenile delinquency. Nothing seems to irritate adults more than irreverent or disrespectful adolescents. Words like "teen-age mobsters," "hoodlums," "ferocious wolf packs," and other similarly endearing terms have become standard copy in most accounts of juvenile misbehavior.

The role of recreation in preventing, or alleviating, juvenile delinquency is and has been questionable. The pros and cons are violently opposed. There has been a general assumption that providing adequate recreation facilities for youth is, in its broadest sense, preventive in keeping youngsters out of trouble. Many community programs have been deliberately trying to "prevent juvenile delinquency." This has been a mistake. Recreation should be an end in itself. The entire community should have the opportunity for good recreation experiences for the joy and satisfaction they bring. These activities do not have to be coupled with a vague generalization that they might "prevent juvenile delinquency." There is no objective evidence that a playground or recreation program in itself has prevented any great amount of juvenile misbehavior. But first let me supply some background for this discussion.

In the midst of all this barrage of statements about the present juvenile members of society, it is truly amazing how little is actually known about the real extent of the problem, the nature of its origin, or the ways in which it seems to persist in our society. Everyone seems to have an answer to the problem of juvenile delinquency. The police "don't crack down enough," "the do-gooders" are too soft on "hoodlums"—these and other statements flow from the lips of citizens in all walks of life. This is part of the problem: everyone has an opinion

Reprinted with permission from National Recreation and Park Association. Official publication *Parks and Recreation*, April, 1960.

about the problem of delinquency but has very little concrete idea what's involved in doing something about it.

An increasing number of social scientists and others have studied or are studying the problem, and the information gathered shows a certain degree of consistency. We know a great deal about this phenomenon, but we still do not have one single theory, which has been tested and proved, to explain satisfactorily all those types of juvenile behavior called delinquencies.

The problem is made more complex because delinquency is a complex of both individual behavior on the part of young people and the amount of community tolerance or acceptance on the part of adults in the community. The same act, such as breaking windows, may be tolerated in one community, where the child's family will make restitution. In another, this act might mean calling police and charging the child with juvenile delinquency.

Most scholars in the field who have studied the problem of juvenile behavior in recent years, generally agree upon certain facts. In the first place, there is a marked difference between boys and girls in the extent to which they get into difficulty with the law. Approximately five times as many boys as girls come to the attention of local police systems for various acts of misbehavior. We also know that, although some children begin to show delinquent behavior at an early age, it remains relatively rare until the ages of thirteen through seventeen. Several studies indicate the peak of behavior difficulties, in terms of apprehension by police, occurs somewhere between the fourteenth and fifteenth year. Most offenders appearing before police officers seem to overcome their difficulties and do not reappear.

We also know that there is a higher proportion of children living in cities or concentrated urban areas who get into difficulty than those who come from suburban and rural settings. Some studies have indicated an increase in the suburban and rural types of delinquent behavior, but this is still only a small proportion of total youngsters in difficulty. There are also quite marked differences in the types of offenses committed by youngsters living in suburban or semirural areas than those living in concentrated urban areas. The city's size also seems to have some relationship, the larger cities having a higher concentration of organized gangs than medium-sized smaller cities. Not too many studies have been made of delinquency rates in relation to city size, but there seems to be some evidence that the rate tends to diminish correspondingly to the decrease in city size.

Even within the city itself, there are marked differences in certain areas. Some census tracts will have a rate ten or fifteen times higher in proportion to youth population than other tracts. Depressed areas consistently produce an inordinately higher rate of delinquency than areas of a higher socio-economic status. Whichever racial or nationality group occupies the lower socio-economic rung at any particular time seems to produce a greater number of children who get into difficulty with the law.

Even the above information suffers from the fact that it is based upon a system of reporting by various law enforcement groups, with a consequent high degree of unreliability. Delinquency rates can be influenced by a number of factors, primarily the attitude of the community or of the police enforcement agencies. At any given time, when an order for a crackdown comes, juvenile delinquency rates increase. If there is more tolerance of deviant behavior, the rate goes down.

Many departments of recreation have

become increasingly concerned about the role they might play in helping to reduce troublesome behavior in their community in a prescribed and organized fashion. This is not something to be entered into casually or with any assumption that mere extension of existing services will meet the particular needs of the more troublesome youth. Sometimes, the continuation of traditional recreation activities in difficult areas can actually increase the opportunity for youngsters to participate in delinquent activities. In a great many ways delinquency *is* recreation (the wrong kind), but certain other concrete procedures have to be adopted if a recreation program is to meet a particular community's need in reducing troublesome behavior.

In the first place, any recreation program particularly geared to this type of area must be free to adapt its program to meet the needs of these youngsters. In a large urban center this implies working with street gangs in nontraditional settings. It calls for small group activities, with decreased emphasis on mass activities. It means experimental use of different types of recreation activities, such as programs involving automobiles and participation in work-camp experiences. Many of these activities must be carried on away from the traditional community center or recreation facility.

In the second place, there has to be distinct consideration given to special leadership. Workers going into high-delinquency areas need additional training in understanding group process, handling aggressive behavior, and an ability to function in potentially dangerous situations. These abilities are more closely related to the kinds of training received by social workers. Training in itself, however, is not the whole answer. Personalities who can operate effectively in these settings must also be very carefully selected.

Finally, this kind of recreation program has to be carefully integrated into the total community services, on a planned basis. This involves frequent consultation with such groups as police officers, social workers, and neighborhood organizations. This also implies some conscious plan of interagency cooperation so that emergencies may be handled in a constructive way. A planned program of recreation services in a highly delinquent area must involve a large degree of this kind of cooperation.

All this adds up to the rather blunt statement that if a recreation department or agency wants to get involved in a serious program related to the specific problem of reducing troublesome and delinquent behavior, it should do it with its eyes open and with a realization of the difficulties involved. A fuzzy-minded approach with rather general goals often does more harm than good. A recreation program does not have to be defended in terms of its ability to prevent delinquency. It has a legitimate and intrinsic function in its own right in the general welfare of the community. When it does specifically focus on high-delinquency areas, however, recreation can be a very significant part of the total community approach to this problem, if some of the safeguards mentioned above are built into the program.

One final comment seems appropriate. Our knowledge about the forces that propel young people into deviant or delinquent behavior is rapidly increasing. There still is a lot we do not know. Any organized community program specifically geared to the reduction of delinquent behavior has a responsibility to build into its function a dedication to research and scientific inquiry.

We can achieve this only through

organized research involving the use of social scientists as participating team members in our efforts. Critical evaluation may prove disastrous to some of our traditional assumptions in the recreation field, particularly in this area of working with the more troublesome and delinquent youngsters. But in the long pull, careful programing, with honest appraisal of what we do while we are doing it, will give us a much firmer base from which to deal with future problems. We may never eliminate the problem of juvenile delinquency, but we can make some substantial strides in reducing the amount of delinquency.

The Split-Level American Family

Urie Bronfenbrenner

Children used to be brought up by their parents. It may seem presumptuous to put that statement in the past tense. Yet it belongs to the past. Why? Because de facto responsibility for upbringing has shifted away from the family to other settings in the society, where the task is not always recognized or accepted. While the family still has the primary moral and legal responsibility for developing character in children, the power or opportunity to do the job is often lacking in the home, primarily because parents and children no longer spend enough time together in those situations in which such training is possible. This is not because parents don't want to spend time with their children. It is simply that conditions of life have changed.

To begin with, families used to be bigger—not in terms of more children so much as adults—grandparents, uncles, aunts, cousins. Those relatives who didn't live with you lived nearby. You often went to their houses. They came as often to yours, and stayed for dinner. You knew them all—the old folks, the middle-aged, the older cousins. And they knew you. This had its good sides and its bad sides.

On the good side, some of these relatives were interesting people, or so you thought at the time. Uncle Charlie had been to China. Aunt Sue made the best penuche fudge on the block. Cousin Bill could read people's minds (according to him). And all these relatives gave you Christmas presents.

But there was the other side. You had to give Christmas presents to all your relatives. And they all minded your business throughout the years. They wanted to know where you had been, where you were going, and why. If they didn't like your answers, they said so (particularly if you told them the truth).

Not just your relatives minded your business. Everybody in the neighborhood did. Again this had its two sides.

If you walked on the railroad trestle, the phone would ring at your house. Your parents would know what you had done before you got back home. People on the street would tell you to button your jacket, and ask why you weren't in church last Sunday.

But you also had the run of the neighborhood. You were allowed to play in the park. You could go to any store, whether you bought anything or not. They would let you go back behind the store to watch them unpack the cartons and to hope that a carton would break. At the lumber yard, they let you pick up good scraps of wood. At the newspaper office, you could punch linotype and burn your hand on the slugs of hot lead. And at the railroad station (they had railroad stations then), you could press the telegraph key and know that the telegraphers heard your dit-dah-dah all the way to Chicago.

These memories of a gone boyhood have been documented systematically in the research of Professor Herbert Wright and his associates at the University of Kansas. The Midwestern investigators have compared the daily life of children growing up in a small town with the lives of children living in a modern city or suburb. The contrast is sobering. Children in a small town got to know well a substantially greater number of adults in different walks of life and, in contrast to their urban and suburban agemates, are more likely to be active participants in the adult settings that they enter.

As the stable world of the small town has become absorbed into an evershifting suburbia, children are growing up in a different kind of environment. Urbanization has reduced the extended family to a nuclear one with only two adults, and the functioning neighborhood—where it has not decayed into an urban or rural slum—has withered to a small circle of friends, most of them accessible only by motor car or telephone. Whereas the world in which the child lived before consisted of a diversity of people in a diversity of settings, now for millions of American children the neighborhood is nothing but row upon row of buildings inhabited by strangers. One house, or apartment, is much like another, and so are the people. They all have about the same income, and the same way of life.

And the child doesn't even see much of that, for all the adults in the neighborhood do is come home, have a drink, eat dinner, mow the lawn, watch TV, and sleep. Increasingly often, today's housing projects have no stores, no shops, no services, no adults at work or play. This is the sterile world in which many of our children grow, the "urban renewal" we offer to the families we would rescue from the slums.

Neighborhood experiences available to children are extremely limited nowadays. To do anything at all—go to a movie, get an ice-cream cone, go swimming, or play ball—they have to travel by bus or private car. Rarely can a child watch adults working at their trades. Mechanics, tailors, or shopkeepers are either out of sight or unapproachable. A child cannot listen to gossip at the post office as he once did. And there are no abandoned houses, barns, or attics to break into. From a young point of view, it's a dull world.

Hardly any of this really matters, for children aren't home much, anyway. A child leaves the house early in the day, on a schoolbound bus, and it's almost suppertime when he gets back. There may not be anybody home when he gets there. If his mother isn't working, at least part-time (more than a third of all mothers are), she's out a lot—because of social obligations, not just friends—doing things for the community. The child's father leaves home in the morning before the child does. It takes the father an hour and a half to get to work. He's often away weekends, not to mention absences during the week.

If a child is not with his parents or other adults, with whom does he spend his time? With other kids, of course—in school, after school, over weekends, on holidays. In these relationships, he is further restricted to children of his own age and the same socioeconomic background. The pattern was set when the old neighborhood school was abandoned as inefficient. Consolidated schools brought homogeneous grouping by age, and the homogenizing process more recently has been extended to segregate children by levels of ability; consequently, from the preschool years onward the child is dealing principally with replicas of the stamp of his own environment. Whereas social invitations used to be extended to entire families on a neighborhood basis, the cocktail party of nowadays has its segregated equivalent for every age group down to the toddlers.

It doesn't take the children very long to learn the lessons adults teach: Latch onto your peers. But to latch he must contend with a practical problem. He must hitch a ride. Anyone going in the right direction can take him. But if no one is going in that direction just then, the child can't get there.

The child who can't go anywhere else stays home, and does what everybody else does at home. He watches TV. Studies indicate that American youngsters see more TV than children in any other country do. By the late 1950's, the TV-watching figure had risen to two hours a day for the average five-year-old, three hours a day during the watching peak age period of twelve to fourteen years.

In short, whereas American children used to spend much of their time with parents and other grownups, more and more waking hours are now lived in the world of peers and of the television screen.

What do we know about the influence of the peer group, or of television, on the lives of young children? Not much.

The prevailing view in American society (indeed in the West generally) holds that the child's psychological development, to the extent that it is susceptible to environmental influence, is determined almost entirely by the parents and within the first six years of life. Scientific investigators—who are, of course, products of their own culture, imbued with its tacit assumptions about human nature—have acted accordingly. Western studies of influences on personality development in childhood overwhelmingly take the form of research on parent-child relations, with the peer group, or other extraparental influences, scarcely being considered.

In other cultures, this is not always so. A year ago, at the International Congress of Psychology in Moscow, it was my privilege to chair a symposium on "Social Factors in Personality Development." Of a score of papers presented about half were from the West (mostly American) and half from the Socialist countries (mostly Russian). Virtually without exception, the Western reports dealt with parent-child relationships; those from the Soviet Union and other East European countries focused equally exclusively on the influence of the peer group, or, as they call it, the children's collective.

Some relevant studies have been carried out in our own society. For example, I, with others, have done research on a sample of American adolescents from middle-class families. We have found that children who reported their parents away from home for long periods of time rated significantly lower on such characteristics as responsibility and leadership. Perhaps because it was more pronounced, absence of the father was more critical than that of the mother, particularly in its effect on boys. Similar results have been reported in studies of the effects of father absence among soldiers' families during World War II, in homes of Norwegian sailors and whalers, and in Negro households with missing fathers, both in the West Indies and the

United States. In general, father absence contributes to low motivation for achievement, inability to defer immediate for later gratification, low self-esteem, susceptibility to group influence, and juvenile delinquency. All of these effects are much more marked for boys than for girls.

The fact that father-absence increases susceptibility to group influence leads us directly to the question of the impact of the peer group on the child's attitudes and behavior. The first—and as yet the only—comprehensive research on this question was carried out by two University of North Carolina sociologists, Charles Bowerman and John Kinch, in 1959. Working with a sample of several hundred students from the fourth to the tenth grades in the Seattle school system, these investigators studied age trends in the tendency of children to turn to parents versus peers for opinion, advice, or company in various activities. In general, there was a turning point at about the seventh grade. Before that, the majority looked mainly to their parents as models, companions, and guides to behavior; thereafter, the children's peers had equal or greater influence.

Though I can cite no documentation from similar investigations since then, I suspect the shift comes earlier now, and is more pronounced.

In the early 1960's, the power of the peer group was documented even more dramatically by James Coleman in his book *The Adolescent Society*. Coleman investigated the values and behaviors of teen-agers in eight large American high schools. He reported that the aspirations and actions of American adolescents were primarily determined by the "leading crowd" in the school society. For boys in this leading crowd, the hallmark of success was glory in athletics; for girls, it was the popular date.

Intellectual achievement was, at best, a secondary value. The most intellectually able students were not those getting the best grades. The classroom wasn't where the action was. The students who did well were "not really those of highest intelligence, but only the ones who were willing to work hard at a relatively unrewarded activity."

The most comprehensive study relevant to the subject of our concern here was completed only a year ago by the same James Coleman. The data was obtained from more than 600,000 children in grades one to twelve in 4,000 schools carefully selected as representative of public education in the United States. An attempt was made to assess the relative contribution to the child's intellectual development (as measured by standardized intelligence and achievement tests) of the following factors: (1) family background (e.g., parent's education, family size, presence in the home of reading materials, records, etc.); (2) school characteristics (e.g., per pupil expenditure, classroom size, laboratory and library facilities, etc.); (3) teacher characteristics (e.g., background, training, years of experience, verbal skills, etc.); and (4) characteristics of other children in the same school (e.g., their background, academic achievement, career plans, etc.).

Of the many findings of the study, two were particularly impressive: the first was entirely expected, the second somewhat surprising. The expected finding was that home background was the most important element in determining how well the child did at school, more important than any of all aspects of the school which the child attended. This generalization, while especially true for Northern whites, applied to a lesser degree to Southern whites and Northern Negroes, and was actually reversed for Southern Negroes, for whom the characteristics of the school were more important than those of the home. The child apparently drew sustenance from wherever sustenance was most available. Where the home had most to offer, the home was the most determining; but where the school could provide more stimulation than the home, the school was the more influential factor.

The second major conclusion concerned the aspects of the school environment which contributed most to the child's intellectual achievement. Surprisingly enough, such items as per pupil expenditure, number of children per class, laboratory space, number of volumes in the school library, and the presence or absence of ability grouping were of negligible significance. Teacher qualifications accounted for some of the child's achievement. But by far the most important factor was the pattern of characteristics of the other children attending the same school. Specifically, if a lower-class child had schoolmates who came from advantaged homes, he did reasonably well; but if all the other children also came from deprived backgrounds he did poorly.

What about the other side of the story? What happens to a middle-class child in a predominantly lower-class school? Is he pulled down by his classmates? According to Coleman's data, the answer is no; the performance of the advantaged children remains unaffected. It is as though good home background had immunized them against the possibility of contagion.

This is the picture so far as academic achievement is concerned. How about other aspects of psychological development? Specifically, how about social behavior—such qualities as responsibility, consideration for others, or, at the opposite pole, aggressiveness or delinquent behavior? How are these affected by the child's peer group?

The Coleman study obtained no data on this score. Some light has been shed on the problem, however, by an experiment which my Cornell colleagues and I recently carried out with school children in the United States and in the Soviet Union. Working with a sample of more than 150 sixth-graders (from six classrooms) in each country, we placed the children in situations in which we could test their readiness to engage in morally disapproved behavior such as cheating on a test, denying responsibility for property damage, etc. The results indicated that American children were far more ready to take part in such actions.

The effect of the peer group (friends in school) was quite different in the two societies. When told that their friends would know of their actions, American children were even more willing to engage in misconduct. Soviet youngsters showed just the opposite tendency. In their case, the peer group operated to support the values of the adult society, at least at their age level.

We believe these contrasting results are explained in part by the differing role of the peer group in the two societies. In the Soviet Union, vospitanie, or character development, is regarded as an integral part of the process of education, and its principal agent—even more important than the family—is the child's collective in school and out. A major goal of the Soviet educational process, beginning in the nursery, is "to forge a healthy, self-sufficient collective" which, in turn, has the task of developing the child into a responsible, altruistic, and loyal member of a socialist society. In contrast, in the United States, the peer group is often an autonomous agent relatively free from adult control and uncommitted—if not outrightly opposed—to the values and codes of conduct approved by society at large. Witness the new phenomenon of American middle-class vandalism and juvenile delinquency, with crime rates increasing rapidly not only for teen-agers but for younger children as well.

How early in life are children susceptible to the effects of contagion? Professor Albert Bandura and his colleagues at Stanford University have conducted some experiments which suggest that the process is well developed at the preschool level. The basic experimental design involves the following elements. The child finds himself in a familiar playroom. As if by chance, in another corner of the room a person in playing with toys. Sometimes this person is an adult (teacher), sometimes another child. This other person behaves very aggressively. He strikes a large Bobo doll (a bouncing inflated figure), throws objects, and mutilates dolls and animal toys, with appropriate language to match. Later on, the experimental subject (i.e., the child who "accidentally" observed the aggressive behavior) is tested by being allowed to play in a room containing a variety of toys, including some similar to those employed by the aggressive model. With no provocation, perfectly normal, well-adjusted preschoolers engage in aggressive acts, not only repeating what they had observed but elaborating on it. Moreover, the works and gestures accompanying the actions leave no doubt that the child is living through an emotional experience of aggressive expression.

It is inconvenient to use a live model every time. Thus it occurred to Bandura to make a film. In fact, he made two, one with a live model and a second film of a cartoon cat that said and did everything the live model had said and done. The films were presented on a TV set left on in a corner of the room, as if by accident. When the children were tested, the TV film turned out to be just

as effective as real people. The cat aroused as much aggression as the human model.

As soon as Bandura's work was published, the television industry issued a statement calling his conclusions into question on the interesting ground that the children had been studied "in a highly artificial situation," since no parents were present either when the TV was on or when the aggressive behavior was observed. "What a child will do under normal conditions cannot be projected from his behavior when he is carefully isolated from normal conditions and the influences of society," the statement declared. Bandura was also criticized for using a Bobo doll (which, the TV people said, is "made to be struck") and for failing to follow up his subjects after they left the laboratory. Since then Bandura has shown that only a ten-minute exposure to an aggressive model still differentiates children in the experimental group from their controls (children not subjected to the experiment) six months later.

Evidence for the relevance of Bandura's laboratory findings to "real life" comes from a subsequent field study by Dr. Leonard Eron, now at the University of Iowa. In a sample of more than 600 third-graders, Dr. Eron found that the children who were rated most aggressive by their classmates were those who watched TV programs involving a high degree of violence.

At what age do people become immune from contagion to violence on the screen? Professor Richard Walters of Waterloo University of Canada, and his associate, Dr. Llewellyn Thomas, showed two movie films to a group of thirty-four-year-old hospital attendants. Half of these adults were shown a knife fight between two teen-agers from the picture, Rebel Without a Cause; the other half saw a film depicting adolescents engaged in art work. Subsequently, all the attendants were asked to assist in carrying out an experiment on the effects of punishment in learning.

In the experiment, the attendants gave an unseen subject an electric shock every time the subject made an error. The lever for giving shocks had settings from zero to ten. To be sure the assistant understood what the shocks were like, he was given several, not exceeding the level of four, before the experiment. Since nothing was said about the level of shocks to be administered, each assistant was left to make his own choice. The hospital attendants who had seen the knife-fight film gave significantly more severe shocks than those who had seen the art-work film. The same experiment was repeated with a group of twenty-year-old females. This time the sound track was turned off so that only visual cues were present. But neither the silence nor the difference in sex weakened the effect. The young women who had seen the aggressive film administered more painful shocks.

These results led designers of the experiment to wonder what would happen if no film were shown and no other deliberate incitement and were introduced in the immediate setting of the experiment. Would the continuing emotional pressures of the everyday environment of adolescents—who see more movies and more TV and are called on to display virility through aggressive sets in teenage gangs—provoke latent brutality comparable to that exhibited by the older people under direct stimulation of movie of the knife fight?

Fifteen-year-old high school boys were used to test the answer to this question. Without the suggestive power of the aggressive film to step up their feeling, they pulled the shock to its highest intensities (levels eight to ten). A few of the boys made such remarks as "I bet I made that fellow jump."

Finally, utilizing a similar technique in a variant of what has come to be known as the "Eichmann experiment," Professor Stanley Milgram, then at Yale University, set up a situation in which the level of shock to be administered was determined by the lowest level proposed by any one of three "assistants," two of whom were confederates of Milgram and were instructed to call for increasingly higher shocks. Even though the true subjects (all adult males) could have kept the intensity to a minimum simply by stipulating mild shocks, they responded to the confederates' needling and increased the degree of pain they administered.

All of these experiments point to one conclusion. At all age levels, pressure from peers to engage in aggressive behavior is extremely difficult to resist, at least in American society.

Now if the peer group can propel its members into antisocial acts, what about the opposite possibility? Can peers also be a force for inducing constructive behavior?

Evidence on this point is not so plentiful, but some relevant data exist. To begin with, experiments on conformity to group pressure have shown that the presence of a single dissenter—for example, one "assistant" who refuses to give a severe shock—can be enough to break the spell so that the subject no longer follows the majority. But the only research explicitly directed at producing moral conduct by Muzafer Sherif and his colleagues at the University of Oklahoma and known as the "Robber's Cave Experiment." In the words of Elton B. McNeil:

War was declared at Robber's Cave, Oklahoma, in the summer of 1954 (Sherif et al., 1961). Of course, if you have seen one war you have seen them all, but this was an interesting war, as wars go, because only the observers knew what the fighting was about. How, then, did this war differ from any other war? This one was caused, conducted, and concluded by behavioral scientists. After years of religious, political, and economic wars, this was, perhaps, the first scientific war. It wasn't the kind of war that an adventurer could join just for the thrill of it. To be eligible, ideally, you had to be an eleven-year-old, middle-class, American, Protestant, well adjusted boy who was willing to go to an experimental camp.

Sherif and his associates wanted to demonstrate that within the space of a few weeks they could produce two contrasting patterns of behavior in this group of normal children. First, they could bring the group to a state of intense hostility, and then completely reverse the process by inducing a spirit of warm friendship and active cooperation. The success of their efforts can be gauged by the following two excerpts describing the behavior of the boys after each stage had been reached. After the first experiment treatment of the situation was introduced . . .

Good feeling soon evaporated. The members of each group began to call their rivals "stinker," "sneaks," and "cheaters." They refused to have anything more to do with individuals in the opposing group. The boys—turned against buddies whom they had chosen as 'best friends' when they first arrived at camp. A large proportion of the boys in each group gave negative ratings to all the boys in the other. The rival groups made threatening posters and planned raids, collecting secret hoards of green apples for ammunition. To the Robber's Cave came the Eagles, after a defeat in a tournament game, and burned a banner left behind by the Rattlers; the next morning the Rattlers seized the Eagles' flag when they arrived on the athletic field. From that time on name-calling, scuffles, and raids were the rule of the day.

. . . In the dining hall line they shoved each other aside, and the group that lost the contest for the head of the line shouted, "Ladies first!" at the winner. They threw paper, food, and vile names at each other at the tables. An Eagle bumped by a Rattler was admonished by his fellow Eagles to brush "the dirt" off his clothes.

But after the second experiment treatment . . .

. . . The members of the two groups began to feel more friendly to each other. For example, a Rattler whom the Eagles disliked for his sharp tongue and skill in defeating them became a "good egg." The boys stopped shoving in the meal line. They no longer called each other names, and sat together at the table. New friendships developed between individuals in the two groups.

In the end the groups were actively seeking opportunities to mingle, to entertain and "retreat" each other. They decided to hold a joint campfire. They took turns presenting skits and songs. Members of both groups requested that they go home together on the same buses in which they had come. On the way the bus stopped for refreshments. One group still had $5 which they had won as a prize in a contest. They decided to spend this sum on refreshments. On their own initiative they had invited their former rivals to be guests for malted milks.

How were each of these effects achieved? Treatment One has a familiar ring:

. . . To produce friction between the groups of boys, we arranged a tournament of games: baseball, touch football, a tug-of-war, a treasure hunt, and so on. The tournament started in a spirit of good sportsmanship. But as the play progressed good feeling soon evaporated.

How does one turn hatred into harmony? Before undertaking this task, Sherif wanted to demonstrate that, contrary to the views of some students of human conflict, mere interaction—pleasant social contact between antagonists would not reduce hostility.

> ...we brought the hostile Rattlers and Eagles together for social events; going to the movies, eating in the same dining room, and so on. But far from reducing conflict, these situations only served as opportunities for the rival groups to berate and attack each other.

How was conflict finally dispelled? By a series of stratagems, of which the following is an example:

> ...Water came to our camp in pipes from a tank about a mile away. We arranged to interrupt it and then called the boys together to inform them of the crisis. Both groups promptly volunteered to search the water line for trouble. They worked together harmoniously and before the end of the afternoon they had located and corrected the difficulty.

On another occasion, just when everyone was hungry and the camp truck was about to go to town for food, it developed that the engine wouldn't start, and the boys had to pull together to get the vehicle going.

To move from practice to principle, the critical element for achieving harmony in the human relations, according to Sherif, is joint activity in behalf of a superordinate goal. "Hostility gives way when groups pull together to achieve overriding goals which are real and compelling for all concerned."

Here, then, is the solution for the problems posed by autonomous peer groups and rising rates of juvenile delinquency: Confront the youngsters with some superordinate goals, and everything will turn out fine.

What superordinate goals can we suggest? Washing dishes and emptying wastebaskets? Isn't it true that meaningful opportunities for children no longer exist?

This writer disagrees. Challenging activities for children can still be found; but their discovery requires breaking down the prevailing patterns of segregation identified earlier in this essay—segregation not merely by race (although this is part of the story) but to an almost equal degree by age, class, and ability, I am arguing for greater involvement of adults in the lives of children and, conversely, for greater involvement of children in the problems and tasks of the larger society.

We must begin by desegregating age groups, ability groups, social class, and once again engaging children and adults in common activities. Here, as in Negro-White relations, integration is not enough. In line with Sherif's findings, contact between children and adults, or between advantaged and disadvantaged, will evoke mutual affection and respect. What is needed in addition is involvement in a superordinate goal, common participation in a challenging job to be done.

Where is a job to be found that can involve children and adults across the dividing lines of race, ability, and social class?

Here is one possibility. Urbanization and industrialization have not done away with the need to care for the very young. To be sure, "progress" has brought us to the point where we seem to believe that only a person with a master's degree is truly qualified to care for young children. An exception is made for parents, and for babysitters, but these concessions are for practicality; we all know that professionals could do it better.

It is a strange doctrine. For if present-day knowledge of child development tells us anything at all, it tells us that the child develops psychologically as a function of reciprocal interaction with those who love him. This reciprocal interaction need be only of the most ordinary kind—caresses, looks, sounds, talking, singing, playing, reading stories—the things that parents, and everybody else, have done with children for generations and generations.

Contrary to the impression of many, our task in helping disadvantaged children through such programs as Head Start is not to have a "specialist" working with each child but to enable the child's parents, brothers, sisters, and all those around him to provide the kinds of stimulation which families ordinarily give children but which can fail to develop in the chaotic condition of life in poverty. It is for this reason that Project Head Start places such heavy emphasis on the involvement of parents, not only on the interaction with the children themselves, both at the center and (especially) at home. Not only parents but teen-agers and older children are viewed as especially significant in work with the very young, for, in certain respects older siblings can function more effectively than adults.

The latter, no matter how warm and helpful they may be, are in an important sense in a world apart; their abilities, skills, and standards are so clearly superior to those of the child as to appear beyond childish grasp.

Here, then, is a context in which adults and children can pursue together a superordinate goal, for there is nothing so "real and compelling to all concerned" as the need of a young child for the care and attention of his elders. The difficulty is that we have not yet provided the opportunities—the institutional settings—which would make possible the recognition and pursuit of this superordinate goal.

The beginnings of such an opportunity structure, however, already exist in our society. As I have indicated, they are to be found in the poverty program, particularly those aspects of it dealing with children: Head Start, which involves parents, older children, and the whole community in the care of the very young. Follow through, which extends Head Start into the elementary grades, thus breaking down the destructive wall between the school on the one hand and parents in the local community on the other; Parent and Child Centers, which provide a neighborhood center where all generations can meet to engage in common activities in behalf of children, etc.

The need for such programs is not restricted to the nation's poor. So far as alienation of children is concerned, the world of the disadvantaged simply reflects in more severe form a social disease that has infected the entire society. The cure for the society as a whole is the same as that for its sickest segment. Head Start, Follow Through, Parent and Child Centers are needed by the middle class as much as by the economically less favored. Again, contrary to popular impression, the principal purpose of these programs is not remedial education but the giving to both children and their families of a sense of dignity, purpose, and meaningful activity without which children cannot develop capacities in any sphere of activity, including the intellectual.

Service to the very young is not the only superordinate goal potentially available to children in our society. The very old also need to be saved. In segregating them in their own housing projects and indeed, in the whole communities, we have deprived both them and the younger generations of an essential human experience. We need to find ways in which children once again can assist and comfort old people, and, in return gain insight to character development that occurs through such experiences.

Participation in constructive activities on behalf of others will also reduce the growing tendency to aggressive and anti-social behavior in the young, if only by diversion from such actions and from the stimuli that instigate them. But so long as these stimuli continue to dominate the TV screen, those exposed to TV can be expected to react to the influence. Nor, as we have seen, is it likely that the TV industry will be responsive to the findings of research or the arguments of concerned parents and professionals. The only measure that is likely to be effec-tive is pressure where it hurts most. The sponsor must be informed that his prod-uct will be boycotted until programing is changed.

My proposals for child rearing in the future may appear to some as a pipe-dream, but they need not be a dream. For just as autonomy and aggression have their roots in the American tradi-tion, so have neighborliness, civic con-cern, and devotion to the young. By re-exploring these last, we can rediscover our moral identity as a society and as a nation.

Behavior of Man in the Cities of Man

Edward Stainbrook, Ph.D., M.D.

The best things and the worst things in human experience have always happened in cities. Cities provide the conditions and the opportunities for the most creative and the most resourceful as well as for the most primitive and least civilized behavior of men.

More than 80% of us live in cities and, as importantly, the ideas, values and life-styles of the city provide a common culture even for those who continue to live in a nonurban environment.

More people are now trying to live a good and gratifying life in the city at the very time that cities are failing to provide the social organization that is necessary to keep people in effective committed relationship to other people and to the values and directives that maintain the sense of community, common cause and common goals! Administratively and politically cities are becoming more inept and more impotent at the very time when the city must change from a passive, post-crisis adaptation to its tasks to becoming an active, responsive city which anticipates crises and is imaginatively engaged in creating new social functions in existing institutions or in developing even new social institutions as answers to the human needs of the present.

Moreover, all of the causes particularly of the behavioral distress of people in the city are not confined to the city itself. A full employment society as a national economic policy would probably do more to reduce psychological disorder than would a community mental health center on every corner.

The public relations men who manage the impression-making of many politicians have caught from the "eggheads" that the word for the '70's is 'ecology,' a word that originally meant the study of inhabited houses. It is a word, therefore, that is particularly relevant to an emphasis on what man is doing to the city and on what the man-shaped city and the man-created environment is doing to men.

No one needs to argue the advantages of adapting and transforming the natural environs to satisfy better both the basic biological needs and the psychologically experienced and culturally derived motivations of men. Moreover, although the unforeseen or belatedly detected consequences of the adaptations to the natural surround are now what threaten us, the basic meaning of the word, survival, is to live on after a resolution of a life-threatening crisis. We cannot, even if we would, stop

Reprinted with permission from author, Edward Stainbrook, Ph.D., M.D., University of Southern California.

the progressively augmenting alterations of both man himself and his investing nature being made possible by the knowledge and skills of our technetronic society and culture. And many of us, freed from the worry about subsistence success, will respond to the existential anguish evoked by wondering what, then, shall man be for? If, however, we try to save our lives by losing them in the scientific and technological inventions of change, we run the danger of being lost in process and of being completely programed only by our own momentum.

Some of us, therefore, will have to forthrightly raise questions about what it is in the human situation we wish to conserve and potentiate and what new values for man need to be created and accepted as directives for action in our time.

Health concerns rank very high in the man-urban environment dilemma. A few years ago the President's Commission on Chronic Illness defined medicine as merely a branch of the more inclusive science of human ecology. This is a recognition that a population is constantly exchanging substances, energies and information with its environment and is cross organized with it.

Usually, medicine prefers to detect and describe the disease and impairment as purely biological happening. However, an adequate conceptual model of a living person accepts the fact that every self is an uniquely genetically programed body which has become humanized and socialized—that is to say, experience-changed and experience-organized. We do not have a body, as we wrongly so frequently assert. We are bodies. William James had already posed the crucial statement at the turn of the last century. "And our bodies, themselves," he asked, "are they our or are they us?" Our bodies are obviously and indissociably

us. And we are in constant reciprocal transaction with the world around us. Indeed, for some of our body organs what is considered to be inside the body are, like the lungs, really a folded-exterior with the internalized surfaced of the organ in direct contact with the contents of the outside environment.

And just as the complex whole body learns to be human and social, so does each organ system. Depending upon the functions of each system, different organs participate more or less predominantly in different human and social transactions. Organs, therefore, can be differentially involved more frequently, more intensely or more openly and vulnerably, depending upon the character of the situation.

When impairment is monitored only at the biological level, usually after an ostensible structural or functional defect has developed, this information considered, in the case of cancer of the lungs, as feedback information to the self from a noxious atmosphere is already years too late for effective prevention. Hence, many of the really helpful feedback sensors scanning either the internal environment of oneself or the external environment must be ideas in the mind, hypotheses, or conceptual anticipations. It is the function of the mind, the educated brain, to pick up information before the uninformed tissues of the body know and signal what is happening to them.

The many recent demonstrations both in unicellular organisms as well as in complex animals and in man of recurrent genetically programed biological rhythms with 24-hour, 7-day, lunar and seasonal annual cycles point to an early evolved locking-in to biological processes of a correlation between once extant and coexisting sequences of bodily and environmental events. Modern environments with climatic and illumination control, with work organizations and other social institutions structuring wakeful activity around the clock, with a distressingly high and insistent daily input of inadequately integrated information demanding delayed and belated sleep-disturbing attempts at mastery, with the rapid transportation of persons through space and time—all these transformations in and of the environment may now conflict with the innate tempo of the body and with inherent biological scheduling and readiness for anticipated happenings in the world around. Fatigue and inefficiency and perhaps other and more subtle temporary or enduring impairments of adaptation and optimal biological responsiveness may be the price exacted for a mismatch between the preferential ongoingness of the body and the out-of-phase demands of the surround.

The contemporary toxic natural environment is composed not only of the well-discussed air and water pollution but is also formed by objects and events of a more psychological and sociological character. Most of the urban environment is full of noise and of people and of vehicles driven by people. The urban environment is therefore filled with relevant and irrelevant information which must be scanned and filtered out or suitably processed by all of the occupants of the city. As someone has suggested, silence in the city must be defined as unintended or personally irrelevant noise. From birth onward, human beings react with anguish and irritable distress to any excessive stimulation. Hence, noise can insistently evoke a psychosomatic response from the hearer which under suitable subjective circumstances results in increased arousal both of brain physiology as well as an increase in the functions of other body organs, particularly of the heart and blood vessels. In a situation of sustained informa-

tional overload, and perhaps complicated by the subjective state of the person, the increased subjective irritability with which one reacts to the noisy surround may intensify, sustain, and increase the frequency of psychophysiological responses. Over a period of time, this may make a contribution to the actual appearance of a disease. Chronically stressed persons who are busy with "the noises inside" tend to react excessively to the noises outside. For some psychologically susceptible persons, therefore, the noisy external environment can be distress-inducing. Even in more purely physiological terms, prolonged high decibel sound can produce inner-ear changes that may, in the extreme, lead to the complete destruction of sensitive hearing tissue. A metabolic degenerative change ensues as the finally irreversible reaction to the noise.

There is another indirect way in which the noise environment contributes to human stress. The recent study of sleep and dreaming in man has suggested that dreaming may be considered as a delayed processing of inadequately mastered information received during the day. Freed by sleep from the input of insistent external information, the dream experience may represent a time when we can integrate and rationalize the unsettled and unsettling issues directly or indirectly evoked in the waking state into our preferred ongoing conceptions of ourselves, of others, and of our idiosyncratic way of being in the world. When sleep is interrupted by the noisy night, dreamtime may be lessened and the dreamwork interfered with.

Obviously, the density of people in the urban environment has a great deal to do with the constant burden upon our attention which must scan and react suitably to very frequent person encounters. Part of the way this task is handled in the city is by learning not to scan or not to respond to a great number of people. This leads to a learned indifference to others as a protection against the density of the human encounter. It can also by generalization lead to a not-seeing and a not-responding to others even in a context where seeing and responding might be appropriate. And just as city dwellers develop by this perceptual defense of not seeing others a conceptualization of them as faceless and anonymous, so, too, one becomes aware of one's own anonymity and facelessness by getting no response to one's self from the encountered others.

The theologian, Harvey Cox, who sometimes seems to take the position of apologist for the secular city, insists that we cannot approach the city with a village theology. Neither can we approach the problems of the city with a rural conception of nature, nor can we expect in the urban environment rural neighborliness nor a personally shaped reaction to every leisurely encountered passerby. And there are many positive psychological and social advantages to the anonymity and personal freedom and privacy in the city. But one of the basic human difficulties presented to people in the city is that too many of them who are there are almost completely alienated from supporting primary face-to-face relationships and frequently because of their self-isolating and isolated containment find themselves unable to establish a consistent and enduring environment of a very few people who can reflect back to them their continuity and existence as worthy selves. Moreover, many newcomers, particularly into the central city, have migrated to the city primarily because they had lost or moved away from significant supporting persons in their lives.

Perhaps one of the most urgent needs in the large central cities is some new kind of residential places for young people between the ages of 18 and 25 who spend a variable time "in transition" in the central cities until they can establish themselves in gratifying and economically supporting relationships.

It has been suggested that Los Angeles must be a very interesting place from the psychiatric point of view, as indeed it is. One of the reasons for that is that so many people come West seeking the frontier and find only Los Angeles. So many have the problem of coming into the city but are unable to relate effectively to others and find no appropriate social space in which they can effectively reintegrate themselves into social living. Perhaps the basic consideration here is that it is quite possible and perhaps desirable to enjoy the anonymity, the impersonality and the freedom and the privacy of the city. The anonymous environment, however, cannot be managed if one feels completely anonymous one's self. With the support of a few primary face-to-face relationships, however, the anonymity of the city may be transformed from despair into confident and gratifying living. Either implicitly or explicitly we are all asking: "Do you know that I am here?", "Do you value me?", "Am I doing all right?", "What can I confidently expect?"

The congestion of people and their social organization are therefore very relevant to the goals of the natural and social design of the city. There is another derivative to these considerations. We are fond of extrapolating, perhaps too uncritically, studies of the behavior of congested animal populations to the description of congested persons in the cities, forgetting that man is a very resourceful symbol user and has tremendous capacity for organizing himself socially, or for failing to do so. Hence, we have to modify our thinking about the consequences of congestion in the city by considerations of the adequacy or inadequacy of the social organization of the congestion. It is not congestion alone, for example, that creates the hostility, the lack of love, the lack of esteemful supportive mutuality, and the psychological degradation which may exist in the ghetto residence of five or six persons in the same room or 10 or 12 persons in the same small apartment. Large families of 10 or 12 were common occurrences in our own society not too long ago and even larger families and numbers of people in the same small dwelling occur with minimal social pathology in many other cultures. An important pathogenic factor in ghetto congestion is the failure of the social organization of the people crowded into room and apartments. Lack of kinship ties and other socially enforced obligations and responsibilities in many situations keep them a crowd rather than a group. Added to this is their inability to escape from this closed and entrapped situation in which they exist with their unrelatedness to each other, with their lack of reciprocal gratification, and their high anxiety and hostility.

It is worthy of reflection here that one of the great benefits of designing cities for space and openness and for providing walkways by which people may traverse distances is that the possibility is created for persons getting out of the closed space of residential entrapment. Pathways are made out into the social space around and if in that social space around there are also sufficient and accessible social resources in that openness, then you have invited persons to come out of their closed, entrapped pathology into the more resourceful, more self-esteeming and self-confirming environments of the world around.

Closely associated with the spatial and social design of the city is the current recognition that in these times the city can be built anywhere. Moreover, urban-

ity is a culture, a whole way of life, which can obtain wherever the city is in physical space. In the next 30 years we will have to build the equivalent of 150 new cities in this country. These cities need no longer be anchored to the pathways of commerce or to natural energy centers. And there is now no technical reason why a city cannot be built anywhere. Hence, the question must be seriously debated as to how much we shall reconstruct existing urban centers and how much shall we build completely new cities in areas where openness and space need only be used and not obtained by renewal and reuse.

One might apply some of the experience we have had with psychiatric hospitals to our thinking about the interrelationships between the physical and social environment of the city and the behavior of the people who live there. Much of what contributed to the impairment of people who lived for a considerable time in the chronic psychiatric hospital was the environment of the hospital itself. We were impairing people in the very act of trying to help them. We desocialized persons and diminished their self-esteem simply by the way in which we structured their life experience within the hospital social and physical space.

The implications of this for the urban environment are obviously great. They have to do with the self-fulfilling prophecies invested in an external environment of ugliness, delapidation, dirtiness, overbuilt space and the lack of natural surroundings. These characteristics of the surroundings constantly reflect back the low worth, the isolation, and the segregated rejection insistently communicated to the people who live there. In this sense the surroundings add to and confirm the negative self-appraisal which may come also from other ways of being in the contemporary society.

The characteristics of one's self-appraisal have some relationship to how destructive one may be, both toward one's self and toward others. Individuals vary, of course, a great deal in how dependent they are for their own self-esteem and self-appraisal upon the reflections from the physical and social surroundings. However, it is usually those people who are most dependent upon external appraisal and most vulnerable to it, therefore, who live in the greatest numbers in the most unaffirming and demeaning parts of the city, both in terms of the physical surround and the social interrelationships.

The changing relationships of contemporary man and nature, particularly in the city, may also be determined by some of our basic attitudes toward our own bodies as part of nature. In a definite sense, not only has philosophy and religion alienated man from his body but current scientific thinking, even in the behavioral sciences, tends to support the same alienation. The analogy of the body as a machine, first in the Cartesian sense of a "doing machine" and then in the contemporary sense of a "thinking machine" makes a healthy, joyful narcissism about the body a difficult psychological experience. Not since the Greeks have we experienced a healthy narcissistic acceptance of our bodies. Christianity taught that the body was bad, evil and morally as well as physically dirty. Then, before we could recover from that insult, the industrial and electronic society suggested that the body was inefficient, ineffective and much less omniscient and omnipotent than the contemporary machines. The more implicit goal of what may overtly seem to be a resurgence of the hedonistic enjoyment of the body may, indeed, be a nascent attempt to repossess what for so long under cultural directions had to be dispossessed. The acceptance of one's self as a body also implies the acceptance of that body as part of nature. Hence, one can see increasing evidence, particularly among the young, of the return both to the enjoyment of the body and to living in and close to nature.

It is true, of course, that the return to nature can be a "cop out." This might be what the psychiatrist would call a regressive use of nature, trying to restore earlier situations where one could be dependent without guilt or passive without self-castigation and where one could experience, for a time, rather effortless pleasure and unconflicted satiation. Regression, however, can be used as an avoidance of development and responsibility or it can be used in the service of self-enrichment and growth. In our contemporary adolescent world, some do seek the natural environment as a drop-out space but others may use it as a place for creative restoration and for an extended intrapsychic transformation of the self as a preparation for resuming with more awareness and confidence a life career in a highly complicated and difficult world.

Understandably, we give much attention to the behavior of others that makes us anxious or which threatens us. Violent and criminal behavior are concerns of high priority for city-dwellers.

Violence in the protest and quasi-revolutionary sense may be understood generally as a primitive regressive expression of destructive hostility which occurs, certainly more easily in psychologically predisposed individuals, when more constructive alternative action in the service of aggression as a search for personal mastery is not available.

It would seem to be true in human behavior that the more violent your behavior is the less effective is your aggression. The more constructively effective the aggression, the less violence. The task of the urban society and of the body politic generally is how to provide the social resources for the effective constructive expression of dissent. Simple suppression leaves no alternative for the aggressive search for personal effectiveness except violence.

But the most rational methods for shaping and directing the behavior of people in the city have to be executed through the various social organizations and institutions of the city in which people of all ages and characteristics come to do their human business with each other.

The development of inhibitory anxiety about destructive behavior and the learning of a compact of concern about others and about basic values of the society have to occur and be maintained in the socialization process of education and subsequently in human interaction all of one's life.

You cannot really socialize a child in a crowd, that is today, a crowded class-room. And you cannot maintain the reenforcement of concern for self and others which inhibits violence, predation and self-centered, greedy achievement and acquisition if no relationships and communicative interaction even obtain between the body politic and those who have stayed out, never gotten in, or who have dropped out in anger and despair.

At long last all of us need a sense of confident mastery of ourselves and of our situation. We need a constant reenforcement for feeling good about our concern about others. We need a sense of a predictable future. We need a society that binds undue anxiety but at the same time allows its people to worry resourcefully. We need a society that keeps man compassionately related to man. We need an active, self-studying, self-directing society of uncertain but confident self-knowing and self-directing men.

The Temporary Society

Warren G. Bennis

This future is not necessarily a "happy" one. Coping with rapid change, living in temporary work systems, developing meaningful relations and then breaking them—all augur strains and psychological tensions.

Fantasy, imagination and creativity will be legitimate in ways that today seem strange. Social structures will no longer be instruments of psychic repression, but will increasingly promote play and freedom on behalf of curiosity and thought.

The increased level of education and mobility will change the values we place on work. People will be more intellectually committed to their jobs and will probably require more involvement, participation and autonomy.

Professional specialists can hardly be called organization men. They seemingly derive their rewards from inward standards of excellence, from their professional societies, from the intrinsic satisfaction of their standards, and not from their bosses. They are not good company men; they are uncommitted except to the challenging environments where they can "play with problems."

We are now approaching an era when a man's knowledge and approach can become obsolete before he has even begun the career for which he was trained . . . This is, perhaps, responsible for the feelings of futility, alienation, and lack of individual worth which are said to characterize our time.

The ease of transportation, coupled with the needs of a dynamic environment, change drastically the idea of owning a job or having roots. Already twenty percent of our population change their mailing address at least once a year.

The key word will be "temporary." There will be adaptive, readily changing temporary systems. These will be task forces organized around problems to be solved by groups of relative strangers with diverse professional skills.

In a nonmobile society one expects of marriage only a degree of compatibility. Spouses are not asked to be lovers, friends, and mutual therapists. But it is increasingly true of our own society that the marital bond is the closest, deepest, most important, and putatively most enduring relationship of one's life. Therefore, it is increasingly likely to fall short of the demands placed upon it and to be dissolved.

From an organizational point of view we can expect that more time and energy will have to be spent on continual rediscovery of the appropriate mix of people, competencies and tasks within an ambiguous and unstructured existence.

Parents cannot define the parameters of the future for their children—cannot even establish the terms of possible change or a range of alternative outcomes. They are therefore useless and obsolete in a way that rarely befell parents of any previous century.

The tasks of the organization will be more technical, complicated and unprogrammed. They will rely on intellect instead of muscle. And they will be too

Reprinted with permission from Warren G. Bennis, President, University of Cincinnati, Cincinnati, Ohio.

complicated for one person to comprehend, to say nothing of control. Essentially, they will call for the collaboration of specialists in a project or team form of organization.

Our society has opted for more humanistic and democratic values, however unfulfilled they may be in practice. It will "buy" these values, even at loss in efficiency because it feels it can now afford the loss.

Our country, it is important to remember, was founded, built, populated, and sustained by individuals whose characteristic response to social problems was flight, escape, and avoidance. The suburb also springs from this impulse.

It will be almost routine for the experienced physician, engineer, and executive to go back to school for advanced training every two or three years.

"Organizational revitalization" is a complex social process which involves a deliberate and self-conscious examination of organizational behavior and a collaborative relationship between managers and scientists to improve performance . . . The manager has had to make himself and his organization vulnerable and receptive to external sources and to new, unexpected, and even unwanted information.

The difficulty of continually forming new bonds and breaking old ones can be mitigated by developing ways of accelerating the process of acquaintance, an informality, an easy friendliness, a capacity for ready, if superficial, ties.

No matter how imaginative, energetic, and brilliant a man may be time will soon catch up with him to the point where he can profitably be replaced by someone equally imaginative, energetic, and brilliant, but with a more up-to-date viewpoint and fewer obsolete preconceptions.

It will become increasingly necessary to take people as one finds them—to relate, immediately, intensely, and without traditional social props, rituals and distancing mechanisms . . . by the time the individual reaches his "here-is-the-real-me" flourish, he will find himself alone again.

The separation of the individual from those permanent groups that provide him with ready-made values and traits from which he derives his identity will accelerate . . . there will be concomitant feelings—acute and pervasive—of alienation, of anomie, of meaninglessness.

The executive becomes coordinator or "linking pin" between various task forces. He must be a man who speaks the polyglot jargon of research, with skills to relay information and mediate between groups. People will be evaluated not according to rank but according to skill and professional training.

About those phrases on the previous pages: there's no specific sequence.

Mix them around for awhile.

Read them in any order.

That's the way I believe America is moving. Those are some basic ideas and patterns in what I call the *temporary society*.

Although I'm a social psychologist—and most of those introductory phrases describe and probe into social phenomena—my ideas about the Temporary Society develop directly from my work during the past fifteen years with scientists, engineers, and technologists. And also from my belief that of all factors creating changes in our society, the most important and dynamic factor is the increasing pace of technological change.

The Temporary Society has possibilities for creativity, challenge, exciting unpredictability, continuing growth. It also has the potential for increasing alienation, loss of identity, higher divorce rates, executive dropout, and accelerated human obsolescence.

As an optimist, I feel things will go the first route: The Temporary Society already emerging will bring greater human fulfillment than ever before. Either way, the impact on American life will be startling and disruptive. And technological organizations, although they helped spawn the Temporary Society, will not be immune to the dislocations and restructuring it makes necessary.

When I was at MIT on the faculty of the Sloan School of Management from 1959 to 1967, I learned a lot from the scientists and engineers who were my colleagues. Their main contribution to my thinking was the idea of a task force or problem-solving team: Specialists in different fields come together, concentrate on a task, complete their mission, then dissolve as a group. They later regroup with different teams of specialists to tackle new and different problems.

The pattern grew out of the war years when units like the Radiation Lab and Instrumentation Lab were established at MIT. I once asked C. Stark (Doc) Draper, the wise old man who started and still runs the Instrumentation Lab, what his organization looked like. Could he draw a chart for me? Well, no he couldn't. He had about thirty-five task forces, and the best he could do was sketch out a galaxay of these temporary teams.

This task force idea was reinforced in my work with R & D firms and consulting companies such as TRW Systems in California and Arthur D. Little in Cambridge. They realized that the environment in which industry operates is a very active, turbulent place in constant change. Problems no longer come packaged with simple labels of production . . . research . . . or marketing. In order to keep up with changes in the environment, temporary systems are a necessity in an organization.

An extracurricular analogy may provide a helpful perspective. I am now Vice President for Academic Development at the State University of New York at Buffalo, an institution whose students, administration, and some faculty members are trying hard to make strides toward the future. One of our problems is that many traditional-minded academics still think that the universe is conveniently carved up into familiar packages called psychology or economics or biology or classics. But the world doesn't offer up problems with those labels. It has problems called war . . . peace . . . environmental pollution . . . race relations . . . poverty. To tackle these problems, even at a university, requires temporary task forces of specialists drawn from several departments.

But universities have not learned to operate that way yet. And this traditional unwillingness to make courses relevant to the world as it exists is contributing to unrest among students.

In those last sentences substitute corporate organizations for universities, professional specialists for students, and work for courses and you have a preview of new-dimension problems in technological organizations.

The Temporary Society did not spring full-blown upon us in the 1960's. Our ability and desire to keep moving is astounding. It goes deep into the early days of the American nation. Alexis de Toqueville saw in the 1830's. Whenever I read de Toqueville, I get a little discouraged because he almost always articulated my new ideas better than I do, and more than a hundred years sooner. He wrote the following:

"In the United States, a man builds a house to spend his latter years in it, and he sells it before the roof is on; he plants a garden and rents it just as the trees are coming into bearing; he brings a field into tillage and leaves other men to gather the crops; he embraces a profession and gives it up. He settles in a place which he soon leaves to carry his changeable longings elsewhere. If his affairs leave him any leisure, he instantly plunges into the vortex of politics, and if at the end of the year of unrelenting labor, he finds he has a few days vacation, his eager curiosity whirls him over the vast extent of the United States and he will travel 1,500 miles in a few days to shake off his happiness. Death at length overtakes him, but it is before he is weary of his bootless chase of that complete felicity which is forever on the wing."

After waves of immigration before, during and after the conquest of a frontier, our mobility patterns are not much different today.

Recently, a colleague of mine at MIT, Ed Schein, studied the paths of master's degree students after they left the Sloan School of Management. Of the 1962 graduates, 82% had left their first employer; 73% of the 1963 class had left its first employer; in the 1964 class, about half have left. In some cases two or three jobs have ensued. In an even more recent study of executives from 500 corporations, it turns out that the executive mobility rate has increased about five-fold since the Korean War. Almost all of the company presidents have moved at least once as president and 60% in this sample have moved twice.

In contrast, some years ago Daniel Lerner conducted an exhaustive study of life in a Turkish village. Turkey is a country still in a slow transition from a traditional, rural, agricultural society to a modernized, industrial society. One of the questions Lerner asked the villagers was, "What would happen if you had to leave your village?" Most couldn't answer the question, because they just couldn't imagine any possibility of leaving their place of birth. Those who could answer the question usually said, "I'd rather die than leave my village."

Can you imagine a redblooded American middle manager saying to his boss, "Before I leave Poughkeepsie and go out to Chicago to take a better job, I'd rather die!"? Especially these days, when IBM is referred to as "I've been Moved."

There is an obligato underneath all of these human changes—the steady pneumatic beat of advancing technology. The main fuel for the dynamism of Americans—their restless, rootless, itinerate nature—comes from the American gift for being able to apply technology, to take ideas and put them to work as no other people have. It has often brought chaos, but it has provided in many ways an interesting life in this country. For example:

It is still hard for me to believe that the first commercial jet went into operation only eleven years ago.

Consider the changes in the interval between a technical discovery and its commercial application—before World War I there was a lag of about thirty years; between the two World Wars about seventeen years; and since World War II only eight or nine years. Specifically, the transistor was developed in 1948; by 1960 more than half of the electronics industry making delicate devices had switched from vacuum tubes to transistors. The laser was invented in 1960 and the Nobel Prize for its development was received in 1963; by 1970 it could be a $3 billion industry.

The first industrial application of the computer was in . . . 1956.

Look at what the automobile has done to American cities, to mobility, sexual and social patterns, vacations. It also introduces many people to the legal process, because the main felony in America is car theft, and for most citizens the main contact with the law is through the traffic ticket.

The Pill is changing human relationships, sexual patterns, and marriage.

What I'm pointing out here is that changing social patterns are to some extent caused by new technology. Here's a homely but highly graphic example. An outstanding anthropologist, William F. Whyte, studied problems in the restaurant industry about twenty years ago. He operated from the premise that organization hierarchies are based on exchanges of information-leaders, loftier, in the hierarchy, initiate interaction and exchanges of information more often than those below them.

Whyte discovered that in some restaurants there was a great deal of tension between chefs and waitresses, who were much lower in the restaurant hierarchy. As a consultant, Whyte could have recommended a program of human relations counseling in which chefs and waitresses could learn to understand each other's attitudes and problems. But he took a much simpler approach. He put up a spindle on the counter near the chefs. A waitress would write her order down and spike it on the spindle. Then the chef would take the paper off the spindle. No more verbal orders shouted from the waitresses. All tensions resolved.

Other developments in American society, less directly related to technology, are also precursors of an increasingly temporary society which will affect technological organizations.

In our time the inhabitants of organizations have demands and expectations, desires and wishes which are also in a continual state of flux and change. And organizations have to negotiate and transact with their own members in order to remain viable.

Given our increasing mobility and the network of professional friendships a man creates in his lifetime, it's not strange that he can move from organization to organization, or from country to country, in pursuit of new and, to him, more conducive environments.

Very often such people have groups of colleagues at distant places who are more important to them than those in the next office. Even though you have an office next to someone for ten years, you can reserve for him the same vacant stares that people reserve for you in buses and subways. So time and propinquity while terribly important, may not match the kind of congeniality, friendship, or even love, provided by what a friend of mine calls "the invisible colleges." These comprise the people a man writes to and writes for—his imagined audience. He may have more intense relationships with members of his invisible college, whom he may rarely see, than with members of his immediate company.

People of all ages are participating increasingly in retreats of various forms. Retreat—"to step back from." They're interested in stepping back from their daily existence to have a different experience. Brief encounters, for weekends or a few days, often provide a more intense, fulfilling experience in a temporary system than ongoing work situations.

I'm thinking of such retreats as sensitivity training sessions (T-Groups or encounter groups), at such places as Esalen in California, Bethel in Maine, or their many emulators. Even professional seminars and conferences, away from familiar people and surroundings, give some feeling of temporary systems—people live and work intensively for a few days, then suddenly separate and go back where they came from.

Among college students, recent vintage college graduates, or dropouts, there is a growing interest in extended retreats, social-collective experiments in living. Dropping out of the society. Moving into communal life. Within universities there is a parallel growth in courses in utopias, past and future, and as well as present.

Then there is the "demo," as younger

people call the social or political demonstrations—whether it be a march on Washington or a campus protest. Demos take on lives of their own, once again with intense and usually temporary relationships involved.

Temporary systems are also found in psychotherapy—either two-person or group therapy—where intense new relationships are established and later broken, with the participants moving off.

William Butler Yeats once said: "Give a man a mask, and he tells the truth." This strongly suggests the temporary-system quality of carnivals in Europe, in Rio, and in New Orleans. Wearing masks, people can assume new and temporary identities. This also seems to hold true for the temporary systems outlined above: You can become a different person, even for a weekend. Or more accurately, you can allow other parts of your humanity to come forth, aspects of yourself which are not called on or developed in routine organizational work.

Although we are, I believe, moving into the Temporary Society, it will not necessarily be a "happy" one. Moving from temporary system to temporary system will satisfy certain needs and desires, but it will also create personal disorders, alienations, and dislocations. These are suggested in the scattered phrases preceding the article.

The Beatles have provided, unintentionally, a musical theme for the Temporary Society in their song, "Hello, Goodbye." Repeats of the line, "I say hello, you say goodbye . . . I wonder why I say hello, and you say goodbye." There will be a lot of hello, goodbye situations; quick turnovers in personnel; people moving in and out of groups—not quite in phase—so that by the time some are ready to say hello, the group is disbanding and the word of the day is goodbye.

We've all had that experience. Being a new boy in the neighborhood, or a new man in a company or university, or a new member of a club or church brings a mix of interest and anxiety. The main psychosocial consequence of the Temporary Society will stem from the repeated process of being the new boy, over and over. It will affect individuals, their work groups, their families, their goals.

Recent studies show that highly mobile people develop a sense of loneliness, of social disconnectedness, which often leads to imbedding themselves in material possessions. So the mobile executive has more household appliances, more color TV sets, more cars than the person who is relatively static. Security is derived from being able to drop anchor with something solid and durable.

Mobility in the Temporary Society can bring more diffuse, less satisfying, relationships. Commitments can become less focused without the deep gratification of interpersonal contact. While this diffusion of commitment—even a diffusion of libido—is very functional for a mobile society, it causes frustration at the lack of deep relationships.

Marriages will be profoundly affected. Many social scientists consider marriage an increasingly nonpermanent relationship. Some look at the upward curve of divorce statistics and conclude that marriage is a dying institution.

I take a directly contrary view: More people are marrying earlier, and they seem to enjoy it so much, they keep repeating the process. The technical term for this phenomenon is "serial monogamy," a distinctly American pattern which lacks the sophistication of the affair. I think of increases in serial monogamy, not as failure of the marriage institution, but as evidence that people expect far more of marriage today than ever before. They become dissatisfied when marriage doesn't stack up. In the Temporary Society, this dissatisfaction will likely increase as people place more value—and more demand—on an intense relationship with a marriage partner to make up for the absence of other satisfying relationships. Not all couples can handle the pressure.

Other consequences? Of utmost importance will be what I call the new immediacy—the need for immediate gratification, the need to consume something quickly, whether it be a work of art, an idea, or even a person. Artists seem to be showing the path: the emergence of guerilla theatre; self-destructing or self-consuming sculptures; computerized music; the simultaneous bombardment of several senses in multi-media presentations.

This immediacy is the antithesis of things I grew up with: delaying and postponing gratifications to save up for some future ecstasy (that never seems to arrive anyway). You save, you prepare, you delay, you leave the best for last. I still leave the best thing on my dinner plate until last.

But for a new generation, in a world where the past has been so horrible and difficult and so easy to repress, and where the future is so turbulent and uncertain, possibly even apocalyptic, what else is left? The immediate present. What else can one really trust?

Which brings up a new consequence in an old-fashioned word: fidelity. For adolescents, particularly, fidelity is terribly important in their lives; as Eric Erickson has pointed out, without fidelity—commitment to something—maturity and identity are diffused and delayed. While adolescents are torn and ambivalent about many things, in my view they really want things pure, right, and absolute.

But in a Temporary Society, what can be committed to, even beyond adolescence? What does a man love and invest energy in?

A job?

Possibly. However, for reasons already explored, a job or organization will not hold a man unless it answers his needs for more than a home base and income.

Can anyone survive in the Temporary Society?

Over the years, in my work with professionals of all kinds, including literally hundreds of engineers and scientists, I've noticed that people who feel comfortable in such situations have a distinguishable set of characteristics.

They are problem-solving, dilemma-seeking people. They identify with, and thrive on, the process of solving problems. Sometimes they scarcely care what the problem is—atmospheric pollution, a new form of instrumentation, or how do we get the laboratory cleaner faster?

They have a high tolerance for ambiguity. Problems are things with a shifting, elusive quality; the parameters or dimensions are not always clear; sometimes problems develop very quickly or change in unexpected ways. None of these factors contributes to stability or uncertainty in a situation—so tolerance of ambiguity is a strength.

They have a very high identification with their profession and their invisible college, not with their immediate jobs.

They are learning people. Opportunity to learn and the content of a job are more important to them than money or the physical context they work in.

Their work motivation is primarily internal, intrinsic to their interests and the task itself. They respond very negatively to any coercion to work on a task or problem defined and imposed on them by others.

They have a high need for collaboration and involvement in a systemic approach to their work. They recognize that no individual has the knowledge and the perspective to handle new and complex problems alone. (This is much different from the still-typical university pattern where individuals work alone, and make very narrow contributions to their fields.)

On this last point, Donald Pelz's important studies of engineers and scientists have shown how important it is to them to collaborate on making work and goal decisions. They want to avoid the "deadly condition" where the boss or supervisor makes basic decisions for them.

In brief: Pelz categorized scientists and engineers in his study as high, medium, or low performing; the ratings were based on evaluation by their colleagues and bosses and on their work loads. High performing men typically collaborated with the boss before crucial decisions were made; the medium performers made decisions by themselves; and the low performers operated on decisions made by the boss.

Not all people will have an affinity for life in the Temporary Society. But I believe that some established trends plus some methods for quickly attaining intense relationships will allow more people to find a way, *some* way, *their* way, in it.

To begin with, ours will be an increasingly educated society. Twenty years ago there were half a million college and university students; today there are seven million. About half of the college-age population is in college. In fifteen years I suspect that figure will be about two-thirds.

Given the future needs of the society, where programmed production will be done mainly by machines, there will be an increase in professional jobs requiring higher education. By professional, I mean unprogrammed situations that require individuals to exercise discretion.

As part of the advanced education, one learns to rely more on the value of inquiry, on the pattern of thought which considers knowledge as a means to solve social and technological problems. This is still a highly debatable hypothesis—that knowledge can help cure man's social ills—but the assumption that it can, is part of the value system in higher education.

A related factor is that people will require repeated educational experiences in the course of a professional career as their knowledge of a field becomes obsolete. Also, people will simply live longer in the future; this means they can have two or three or more careers in a lifetime, with periodic returns to formal schooling.

Given all these factors, there still remains a crucial human dimension: The need to move in and out of temporary systems quickly, keeping elan high and dislocation low. Since most manifestations of the Temporary Society create pressures toward uncommitted, alienated, highly mobile people, is there any way to help people overcome sociopsychological stresses?

I believe so. It's always seemed strange to me that people understand that individual human development and maturation are slow processes, yet nevertheless expect human groups to develop into cohesive units in quick time. Groups, however, have a maturing process of their own; their slow pace, if left unaltered, could accentuate the stresses of the Temporary Society.

However, I think we know how to make groups come together very rapidly in environments where mutual trust can develop quickly, where open communications can emerge, and where creative and productive work can be stimulated. We don't need to wait for the development of such a group life through chronological time. It can be achieved faster through means represented by such terms as group dynamics, sensitivity training, encounter groups.

The essential ingredient in this kind of group life is mutual trust. Most social systems operate in ways that stifle mutual trust, ways that engender mistrust and a high degree of threat in the environment. Most social systems, particularly those connected with technological work, are highly task orientated. Expression of feelings, emotions, "irrationality" is considered inappropriate, even dangerous. While people in such organizations are very open when confronted with technical matters, they are not open to confronting feeling tones or group atmospheres.

Is it possible to change that situation? To make engineers and technologists become concerned with human and group relations, when many studies indicate their natural preference for *things* rather than *people*? Well, I've had experience with many such people in T-groups, and I see no insurmountable obstacles.

Engineers and scientists tend to use reliable and publicly shared data as a strategy of determining truth. They tend to resist or underemphasize personal experience and feelings as relevant aspects of data and truth. Their strategy of truth emphasizes a validity based on facts obtained outside of the individual.

Understandably, then, scientists and engineers are highly skeptical of group dynamics or, really, *most* social science. However, I have learned that once involved with human relations groups they become highly committed to that framework of experience and strategy of truth. Concentration on personal experiences can also provide publicly shared data. So the spirit of inquiry is carried over from the professional's own sphere to the human behavior all around them. Being empiricists, they see they are learning something about humans and groups which can be generalized.

In order to make it in the Temporary Society, individuals will have to develop the ability to acquire love quickly—and to lose it, let it go. And then acquire it quickly again with new people.

Life in the Temporary Society will not be easy for anyone, least of all for those who take responsibility for attaining the goals of temporary technological groups. Supervisors and managers will have to learn new ways of leadership and evaluation. There are no handy ABC's or how-to-do-it guides.

But trends have been emerging in the construction, drug, aerospace, consulting, and research and development fields. Some specific organizations which have taken conscious steps to set up new organizational modes include TRW Systems, Union Carbide, American Airlines, Polaroid, Federated Department Stores, ALCAN, Harwood-Weldon Mfg. Co., and Hotel Corporation of America.

Most knowledge in one hundred years of research on problems of leadership is pallid and useless; It says that some combination of elements in the led, the leader, and the situation produces either successful or flawed leadership.

In terms of the led and the situations, some direct statements can be made about the changes in our society.

The led—those in the working population—will be younger, smarter, and more mobile than ever before. Data: Half the population is under twenty-five, one-third is under fifteen; already more than half the teenagers from some urban areas go to college; one of five families changes its home address each year.

As for the situations, ours is the only nation to employ more people in service occupations than in production. Manufacturing is no longer the problem being dealt with by new organizations; the focus is on large-scale, sociotechnological systems, and the deployment of high-grade professional talent in growth areas such as education, health, social welfare, and recreation.

Another change in the situation concerns the composition of the American work force. With the introduction of automation and computer technologies to handle programmed production work, I believe that fifteen years from now:

40% of the work force will have positions in problem-solving organizations, most of them technologically based.

40% will be social change agents, that is, individuals working on revitalization of our institutions or with those problems people feel in times of transition, including moral and ethical problems.

20%, to my despair, will do the remaining unprogrammed, low-level jobs of the society—cab drivers, sweepers, kitchen help, janitorial services. I can say something very unfashionable about this category of job: Perhaps, there are enough people with physical or mental handicaps, or people with low aspirations, to do them. It's difficult to think about, because people don't want to confront the problem of unpleasant jobs which society does not value highly. It's clear, however, that these jobs should no longer be filled by people the society has chosen to handicap or defeat in socioeconomic terms.

Now to the leaders.

The prime attribute for leadership in temporary systems is the ability to develop collaborative relationships with subordinates. This does not mean competing in popularity contests. It means negotiating and collaborating with task force members whose interests are directed to problem solving, professional fulfillment, and involvement in work decisions and plans. It also means acknowledging that in new situations, no leader can know everything; subordi-nates will have the complementary information and competencies he needs to direct a successful group and project.

This style requires a moral toughness to take on the most difficult aspect of the job: To transact with, and unflinchingly confront, recalcitrant parts of the system that are afraid to change and grow. This means groups, subgroups, and individuals. To do this effectively, to be actively involved in revitalizing one's organization regularly—to face directly into the choice of growth or decay—means creating an open organization which can develop the data necessary for renewal. Often this means operating with limited information on the nature and direction of changes in the environment, or on unwelcome information.

The main instrument in the art of leadership in temporary systems will be the creative use of the leader's own personality. Thus, it is essential to know the effects of his actions on individuals and the group; once again, this requires an open system with strong feedback capability. It also will require interpersonal skills, including the cultivation of other people's talents while deferring one's own desires and gratifications.

This kind of leadership is more demanding and formidable than any we have ever known, including king and pope. But if successful in enabling people to find commitment and fulfillment in a cycle of temporary systems, then it will contribute to a human aspiration in the Temporary Society contained in a triplet by John Cage which I am fond of quoting:

We carry our homes
within us
which enables us to fly.

Park and Recreation Clientele

WILLIAM NIEPOTH "Users and Non-Users of Recreation and Park Services"
Leisure-Society-Politics: "The Political Environment of Parks and Recreation" *Proceedings 1971,* Park and Recreation Administrators Institute, University of California, Davis, 1972.

DAVID E. GRAY "Crisis in Youth Values"
California Parks and Recreation, California Parks and Recreation Society, Inc., April 1969.

J. S. SHIVERS "Special Recreation Needs of Teenagers"
Parks and Recreation, National Recreation and Park Association, August 1967.

JANET POMEROY "Is He Entitled to Recreation?"
Parks and Recreation, National Recreation and Park Association, June 1961.

LARRY E. DECKER "Recreation in Correctional Institutions"
Parks and Recreation, National Recreation and Park Association, April 1969.

MARGARET MEAD "Aging Differently in the Space Age"
Parks and Recreation, National Recreation and Park Association, May 1964.

ETHEL SHANAS "What's New In Old Age?"
American Behavioral Scientist, Sage Publications, Inc., October 1970.

IRVING ROSOW "Old People: Their Friends and Neighbors"
American Behavioral Scientist, Sage Publications, Inc., September/October 1970.

ADA BARNETT STOUGH "Creative Aging"
Parks and Recreation, National Recreation and Park Association, November 1966.

Park and Recreation Clientele

Evidence clearly indicates that in the first forty years of the twentieth century a far greater number of people participated in recreational activities as compared to those who watched. Statistics now prove that the general public is spending more of its time in recreational and leisure pursuits than ever before.

The spirit of Puritanism still has an important influence on today's recreational life, but conditions have changed so greatly that our whole idea of leisure-time activities has been completely transformed. There is an active encouragement and promotion of every form of healthful amusement. The present-day opportunities for recreation and park clientele are numerous.

". . . By the middle of the Nineteenth century, the problem of the identity of man had begun to receive attention of some of the philosophers of the day who sought to discover what the meaning of man is."

People who go to the park and recreation facilities attend for a reason, probably, for multiple reasons: Some go for the development of a new skill; some go for the excitement of winning or losing a game; still others go for the association of being with and enjoying other people. There is one common denominator and that is these people attend voluntarily and because of their own volition. They want to attend or participate and so they do. The individual's ability to understand his alternatives determines his choice. Furthermore his ability to choose is extended by education and experience coupled with feeling and awareness.

". . . We must always remember that recreation is for all members of the community whatever their condition."

Every man, woman, and child who has received satisfaction through the act of play is and should be considered a future client or recipient of recreation activities.

Whether an individual is confined to a correctional institution, has progressed beyond the age of seventy-five, has a severe physical handicap, or is a teen-ager in the stage in life where values are questioned and identity or conformity is being established, he needs recreation programs and facilities perhaps even more so than those individuals who are considered "normal" in our society.

The above cited individuals have often been neglected and sometimes received mediocre recreation programs. In correctional institutions, for example, the programs are frequently inadequate and deemed unnecessary for some of these individuals who have strayed or broken a law or laws established by our society. But what society has apparently failed to realize is that there may be a possible problem with these persons not being able to cope with a normal social environment, or that the individuals' needs for full, complete, and happy lives have not been adequately satisfied.

"Recreation is often used as a stopgap measure in meeting the major ills of institutional life—the ever-present boredom and overabundance of free time."

Those activities which are scheduled in correctional institutions are generally centered around acquiring vocational skills for the inmates or as aids in determining the psychological problems which caused the individuals to be considered as detrimental to our society.

These confined individuals need the same wholesome recreation programs as those provided individuals who are not confined in an institution. Through recreation they may possibly learn to cope with the problems of socializing with individuals once they leave the institution, and in addition learn to be less afraid of establishing "wholesome" identities when they return to the community.

Individuals who are severely physically handicapped have also been neglected in the process of establishing normal recreation programs that would include them in community-oriented activities. The usual solution has been to place them with persons who are also handicapped. These individuals are considered as being ill, and knowledge regarding their area of sickness is essential before proper recreation programs can be instituted to meet their specific needs. Recreation leaders tend to believe that the desires and interests of these individuals are totally unrelated to nonhandicapped persons. It is generally felt that instead of including these persons in the community recreation program, it

"A recreation leader should understand that the severely handicapped are first and foremost people—who have the same basic needs, desires and interests as the nonhandicapped—that the handicapped are more like others than they are different from them."

would be best to work with them collectively based on their illness and only by people who have special training in the area of their handicap.

The community and recreation leaders who learn to accept the fact that these individuals do have the same needs, desires, and interests of those that are not handicapped will do well. However, complete knowledge regarding the handicap is not absolutely necessary before these people can be included in community activities. Special training may be provided as to how to handle these people physically when they are involved in recreation activities.

Old age is and has to be the most dreaded period in an individual's life. The general attitude has been that this point in life is used primarily for the arrival of death. The senior citizen's life is filled

"Society must work to counteract the pervasive idea that the last of life is only preparation for death."

with a great deal of loneliness and boredom. No longer is he capable of going to the job and carrying out his professional duties because in many cases he was forced to retire. His activities are limited to quiet, passive, and less strenuous games. His demands on his family diminish because the older person no longer feels needed or capable of contributing to the lives of the young. His ideas and values will often conflict with those that are being created by an everchanging society.

The performance of these individuals is based on the assumption that once an individual has progressed beyond a period of years, he is no longer mentally and physically capable of growing. It is felt that he has fulfilled his capacity for production and should be left to rest till the end of his days.

The recreation leader has to construct programs that will show these individuals that they are still capable of growing and expanding their interests. The leader must be creative and experimental and act as an enabler for these aged participants. The fact should also be taken into consideration when planning that he is and will be dealing with two distinct calibre of people—those individuals that are set in their ways and still cling to the Puritan ethic way of life, and those individuals who are products of this everchanging society, those growing old in the space age who have outlived one generation and are dying in another. They are quite capable of communicating and relating significantly to the ever-present young generation.

". . . The world has changed, is changing, and will change, and those who have changed the most are the older people."

New philosophies, creativity, and imagination will have to be used and established in helping to combat the feeling among the aged that they're a problem to society. Recreation programs should be set up so that these people can learn to relate to social problems and would require them to become actively involved with community-oriented programs that include all ages, young and old alike. Activities should be

". . . the man of the present lives on a level of abstraction far beyond the man of the past."

capable of instilling in these individuals the constant desire to grow and be willing to accept challenges beyond those provided by bingo, checkers, and other quiet games commonly offered as programs.

As life progresses and times change a society is constantly confronted with the problems of working effectively with teen-agers. The teen-ager is the future for any society. As a teen-ager, values are questioned and identity is being sought. Their ideas and views are expressed in terms of behavior, adopted philosophies, dress, literature, art, and music to which they expose themselves. Conflicting beliefs in the working of societal institutions and the constant seeking of challenges and change are uppermost in the minds of today's teen-agers. The general feeling among these individuals is to what extent they should consider the moral values of their parents and how conducive are they for the maintenance of a society. The desire to make mistakes and decisions for one's self seems to be the ultimate goal in the minds of today's youth. It seems that there is always the question of "why" in the minds of these individuals who will be the makers of this society.

"Teen-agers constantly seek a place of their own. They need the security of identity in a society which nearly always enforces conformity."

Recreation can be used in helping to satisfy some of the needs and give answers to some of the "why" questions that are plaguing the youth of today. By establishing teen centers and providing adequate recreation programs, a place for identity will be created. Teens would have a place for getting together to discuss social problems. Frustrations can be released and, more important, the establishment of peer relations so that they may learn to trust and benefit from one another.

In establishing adequate teen centers the programs should not be completely sports-oriented as those in the past. If this is the case, only a few will be served and the rest will gradually turn to other forms of escape which are not necessarily healthy or even legitimate.

Today's youth must be able to express themselves in an environment which is free from the constant threat of over-authoritative adults who are afraid that they are conspiring to overthrow the government or that their involvement with peers is resulting in immoral and degrading acts of conduct. Teen-agers must be given the place and a chance in which to think and become involved in helping with the problems that are disrupting the society.

The recreation leader can be the authority figure, but he can also be a friend. He should be capable of intelligently discussing and offering proper guidance in molding and shaping the minds that will create the future American society. The center can be used as a place for satisfying those special recreation needs of teen-agers only if there is trained personnel capable of handling situations as they arise and who know what is going on in this world. The recreation leader might become the consultant, counselor, and leader in helping to restore the faith of teen-agers in their outlook for the societies of the future.

The people of any society are and can be the clientele of any recreation and park program. The problems rest in training recreation personnel so that adequate, meaningful, and beneficial programs may be established which will motivate individuals to participate in the activities and use the facilities that are being offered. If the recreation personnel does not know how to construct a program that is attractive and meets the needs of persons in our society, participation will be minimal. Too, recreation leaders have often geared their programs to those that are traditional. These are old hat to the society. They no longer present a challenge or help the recreation recipient establish an identity through their leisure pursuits.

"We don't allow for the fact that today's babies are being brought up differently, so we're always trying to catch up with ourselves."

The preconceived notion that individuals are afraid of change is one that will have to be erased from the minds of recreation leaders. They must also realize that whatever life style an individual has leaves room for constructive, creative, and imaginative recreation outlets that can be provided for at recreation and park facilities.

"Those who know no culture other than their own," says Ralph Linton in *The Study of Man*, "cannot know their own." The recreation leader should be aware of the clientele he will be working with. He should be able to relate to these individuals. The recreation leader's training should include a broad array of experiences so that he may adequately plan programs that will meet the needs of the aged, the teen-ager, the handicapped, and also those that are confined to institutions as well as the normal person in society. The park and recreation domain is not bound by the conceptual, the factual, the symbolic.

"Deficiencies are readily observable, and in many cases easy to define. The difficulty is in trying to correct the deficiencies and to outline a constructive program for improvement."

It should work in concert with these and include every aspect of human existence that is relevant to our new age.

Users and Non-Users of Recreation and Park Services

William Niepoth

It is abundantly clear that greater percentages of our population are engaging in recreation. However, it is also clear that some people participate on a relatively limited basis and it is apparent that any one supplier of recreation opportunities (public or private) attracts less than 100% of the population it intends to serve. Precise figures are somewhat difficult to establish, but it is probable that fewer than 60% of the residents in any city participate directly in the programs of the public recreation and park department. Hopefully, all benefit from the presence of parks and recreation programs, even if they do not use them directly. However, in terms of direct participation, we attract considerably less than the total potential participant group.

This condition is understandable and not surprising. Depending upon the philosophy and intent of any particular agency, it may be desirable. The great diversity of recreation agencies at all levels of government and in the private sector, provides opportunities to select from among several alternatives.

Two conditions seem to exist, however, which suggest further examination, especially on the part of public agency personnel. *Condition A:* There are people in our communities who are non-users of our services, not by choice, but because of personal or environmental restrictions. *Condition B:* There also are people in our communities who choose not to use our services. In *Condition A*, we have an obligation to expand the user group and reduce the numbers of non-users. Our obligation to citizens in *Condition B* may be less clear; at the least, we may have a selfish interest here. Non-users frequently are non-supporters. That is, they may not be willing to support tax increases and bond elections for recreation and park services. If so, the maintenance, and needed expansions, of our agencies may depend upon changing more non-users to users in this group.

In both cases, it would seem that we would benefit from knowing more about the users and non-users of our services.

CONCEPTUAL VIEWS OF THE USER AND THE NON-USER

What are the characteristics of the user and the non-user? Obviously, there are such great diversities within each category that specific de-

Reprinted with permission from William Niepoth, Chairman, Recreation Department, California State College, Hayward.

scription is not feasible. However, two conceptual schemes seem useful to a general understanding of both the user and the non-user. The first of these schemes is a concept of recreation participation as a segment of behavior. The second is a model of use and non-use factors.

Recreation Behavior

Somewhere in the Sierra, two men move slowly upward toward the notch in the ridge through which the trail passes. At 11,000 feet, their progress is slow and their breathing labored. The packs are heavy, even though each item of food, clothing and equipment was considered and weighed carefully. At the crest, they slip out of their loads and lean back against the rock wall which rises above the trail. The wind cools and dries their sweat-drenched shirts, as they gaze out over the vastness to the south.

Two hundred miles away, a woman bends over a ceramic wheel and digs her thumbs into the mound of clay which spins on the wheel. Carefully, she brings up the cylindrical wall, the clay responding to her search for evenness. Several revolutions of the piece against the sponge, and she straightens to exchange a few words with her neighbor on an adjacent wheel.

At home, the neighbor's 10-year old shakes the dice, and counts out five spaces on the board. As directed by the square he landed on, he draws a "Chance" card. Dismay replaces anticipation, as he reads, "Go directly to jail. Do not pass GO. Do not collect $200."

All three of the above are illustrations of participation in recreation; as such, they also are examples of recreation behavior. All three contain elements which can be defined in most examples of recreation behavior. While these elements interact in a fluid, dynamic fash-

ion in actual behavior, it is possible to isolate them artificially for the purpose of defining a concept of participation as behavior.[1]

1. *The participant's goal, or goals.* It seems safe to assume that all three of the individuals involved are engaged in activity for a reason, or probably, for multiple reasons. We might assume that the packers hike to enjoy the scenery they encounter, or to test themselves against the challenge of the mountains, or for exercise; or for all of these reasons. These are possible reasons among many others. The ceramicist may seek the development of new skills or recognition for a well-thrown pot. Her son might play for the excitement of winning or losing, for a sense of power (unarticulated) in owning property and charging rent, or for the fun of being with friends. All of these can be viewed as possible goals. It seems reasonable to assume that all recreation participation involves goal-seeking of some kind. The goals may be grand in nature, or mundane; they may be sought after intensely or casually; immediately or with an eye to ultimate achievement.

2. *The influences of some of the individual's personal characteristics.* In addition to goals, each individual possesses a great variety of characteristics, some of which influence participation. The health and fitness of the packers influence their ability to engage in the activity they have selected. The participation of the ceramicist is influenced by her skills, and her son's play depends upon his knowledge of the rules. Other influencing factors include financial resources, attitudes, feelings about self, coordination, strength, etc. In some re-

1. The conceptualization presented here is similar to the general model of behavior developed by Cronbach.

spects, these personal characteristics are similar to those possessed by all other members of any given society; for example, we all experience fear to some degree when placed in situations that we perceive as hazardous. In other ways, personal characteristics tend to be highly individualistic; each person's past experiences, and the specific influences of those experiences on such factors as attitudes and feelings about self probably are completely unique. In between the two extremes of near-universal traits and complete individuality, exists a useful concept of "modal" or "typical" characteristics for various sub-groups within the society. For example, we can describe some typical characteristics of teen-agers, with reasonable confidence. They tend to be interested in members of the opposite sex; they tend to be seeking independence from adult authority; etc. Certainly, not all teens exhibit these traits at the same time, and some exhibit them not at all. However, they are typical behaviors for relatively large percentages of adolescents. Most backpackers are conservationists; most mothers feel a responsibility for their children's welfare, and most fifth-grade boys are more interested in playing with boys than with girls. This concept of typical characteristics is useful to an understanding of recreation behavior, when it is coupled with a deep and continuing appreciation for the wide range of possible individual differences, and when the observer guards against the tendency to see what is expected rather than what is actually present.

3. *The socio-physical setting within which the behavior takes place.* The two men could hike in almost any outdoor environment, but the Sierra offer particular values in terms of scenery, challenge, and relative isolation. The influencing elements in the pottery studio include not only the wheels, the clay,

light, heat and other physical factors; the presences of other people also become considerations. The nature of participation may be changed by the individual's interaction with the instructor and with other participants. The emotional climate (i.e., relaxed, friendly, formal, etc.) which prevails also is a potential influencer. The setting within which the Monopoly game is being played includes not only the board, the deeds, and the money, but also the complex web of psychological and emotional relationships that exists between the players.

The actual setting in most recreation behavior is greater than that portion which the participant experiences. There are infinitely more potentially-influencing factors within and beyond the ceramic studio than are perceived by any one of the participants. Perhaps an amateur pottery show is being held in an adjoining community. A knowledge of this might prompt a different kind of effort from the ceramicist in this illustration. Or, perhaps an unexpected visitor is waiting for her at home; a knowledge of this condition might terminate her participation for the day. Both the pottery show and the visitor are part of the total setting within which the ceramicist behaves; both are potential influencers of her behavior. However, if they are not part of her awareness at the given time, their potential influence generally is not felt. She might be influenced by factors which are not perceived accurately. For example, it is possible that the wheel on which she is working is faulty. She may interpret her failure to throw a pot as lack of skill, rather than attributable to the wheel. In this sense, an element in the environment (the faulty wheel) contributes to a modification in her behavior. However, until she is aware of the actual source of her failure to perform, she will behave on the basis of her perceptions. That is, she probably will continue to try to improve her techniques.

The influences of the characteristics of the individual and the nature of the socio-physical setting function in an interacting manner. Assume that one of the backpackers once suffered frostbite from being caught for several days at a high elevation by a late summer storm. This past experience is part of his unique individual characteristics. A cloud build-up may be perceived by this man quite differently than by his companion who has not had a similar experience. In this instance, the influence of the physical setting probably will be different for each of the two men.

4. *The participant's plan for achieving the goal(s).* If one of the goals set by the hikers is to enjoy an environment of relative isolation, they probably formulated a plan by which to achieve this objective. They may have looked over various maps of the Sierra and selected their route based on what appeared to be the least-used trails. They also may have decided to go in mid-September, rather than over the Labor Day weekend. This planning process may be long and involved, or it may be immediate and relatively concentrated. It also is continuous, as ongoing behavior is adjusted to problems and opportunities which are encountered. The ceramicist may plan the shape and size of a particular pot for several days. Then during the throwing, as she attempts to bring the plan into being, she may make several modifications. These, also, are plans, even though they happen in the ongoing behavior. She may find the consistency of the clay inappropriate for what she intends to do, or she may happen upon a new shape accidentally which she wishes to incorporate into the overall design. Planning usually is a continuous process, which is woven into the total behavior sequence. At the early stages, as with the back-

packers going over maps, it can be observed rather directly. As they make adjustments on the trail, planning becomes part of the total experience and, therefore, is more difficult to differentiate.

The selection of a particular plan by any individual may be influenced by all of the previously-mentioned elements (goals, personal characteristics, and perceptions of the setting). An attractive setting (for example, a well equipped ceramics studio) may generate new goals, or intensify existing ones. The setting also may suggest a plan for achieving goals. The example of other people throwing pots, or techniques described and illustrated on a bulletin board may lead a plan of intended behavior. The setting may be experienced directly, or it may be experienced indirectly as in television, printed materials, etc. Similarly, the recollection of past experiences may either contribute to goal development or to plans for achieving goals. Plans may be based on adaptations of earlier successful and satisfying behaviors and experiences. Or, we may imitate the behaviors of others in defining our own plans. Much of our recreation behavior probably is based on the imitation of family and friends. In the context of this description, we follow their plans.

Some of our recreation behaviors may become almost habitual and relatively unplanned. Given certain recurring goals, we may engage in an activity with relatively little planning, or without any reappraisal of an earlier plan on which the response is based. For example, we may frequently seek relaxation after dinner. Watching television has satisfied this goal in the past. Given the circumstances of early evening, in the home, and the goal of relaxation, we may turn on the TV set without really evaluating whether or not that behavior has the greatest potential for satisfying our goal, consistent with available resources, our own energy level, etc.

5. *The behavior, or participation, itself.* It is this element that recreation personnel most frequently encounter directly, and it is this aspect which is most easily observed. For the participant, it is the recreation experience. It is the act of hiking, of throwing the pot, of playing monopoly. It does not exist in isolation from all of the other elements, as has been mentioned previously. The participant's goal(s), his or her characteristics and perceptions of the setting, and the plan which has been conceived all are part of the totality of the experience. However, we typically think of the behavior as it is manifested when we think of participation. The behavior, or activity, may involve quite different expenditures of energy. In this sense, listening to music is an activity, as are square dancing and playing the guitar.

Jensen (2), and others, have introduced a useful expansion of the concept of participation. The total recreation experience includes three phases: an anticipatory and planning phase,[2] the actual participation, and a reminiscence or recollection phase. While these phases may be part of the same recreation experience, they also may be viewed as three different recreational experiences. That is, the planning of the pack trip, and the recollections of it (slide viewings, discussions with friends, etc.) probably contain the elements of goal(s), characteristics, settings, plans, etc. as does the actual trip itself. The distinction is not important however, as long as the observer of recreation behavior is sensitive to the fact that anticipation and recollection of recreation experiences may, in themselves, be recreational.

6. *The participant's perceptions of the consequences of his or her behavior.* The backpackers, the ceramicist, and the Monopoly player all experience the con-

sequences of their behaviors. Usually, these consequences are perceived in terms of varying degrees of satisfaction or dissatisfaction. The packers may enjoy the solitude or the view; or they may meet a large group on the trail and the weather may be unfavorable and they are dissappointed.

Perceptions of satisfaction or dissatisfaction probably occur as a continuing part of the ongoing flow of behavior, and as an overall feeling about the recreation experience at its conclusion. The feeling of satisfaction may be rather intense, or it may be diffused and generalized.

Satisfaction and enjoyment, or the lack of these elements, are, in large measure, a function of the degree to which goals are achieved. We can predict with some confidence which kinds of experiences will be satisfying. However, the perceptions of the behavior are the determining factors in any specific experience. Suppose the ceramicist throws a pot which is admired greatly by her family and other members of the class. Will this condition produce satisfaction and enjoyment? Probably, but we cannot be sure. If she aspired to an invitation to show the pot at the County Fair and the invitation was not forthcoming, she might be quite dissatisfied in spite of the admiration of family and friends. On the other hand, she may aspire to no more than completing a pot, regardless of its beauty. In this case, she might find real satisfaction even in the absence of recognition from others. One backpacker may aspire to hike five miles a day; another may wish to hike a 100-mile section of trail in five days. These varying levels of aspiration influence whether or not satisfaction is experi-

2. Jensen conceives of planning and anticipation as separate phases. Other writers view planning as part of anticipation.

enced. The phenomenon seems to be present in most recreation behavior.

If a participant experiences satisfaction from an activity or a particular behavior, he tends to repeat the behavior, when conditions occur which are similar to the earlier behavior. When the hikers have free time during summer months, there is greater likelihood that they will engage in backpacking rather than in another activity which has not been satisfying. If satisfaction is not achieved, there is a tendency to do one of two things: (1) try a new or modified plan for reaching the same goal, or (2) give up the goal in favor of other goals. If the ceramicist does not receive the admiration she seeks with her first pot, she may try again, using some modification in her technique. Given rather consistent failure to receive admiration (assuming this to be the goal), she may turn her free-time energies from ceramics to jewelry-making or some other potentially rewarding activity.

Schematically the elements discussed above may be represented by the relationships shown below.

The individual *participant* (A) exists within a total environment, which includes an infinite number of potentially-influencing factors. These factors constitute the *"actual setting"* (B). However, the individual will be influenced, largely, only by those factors which are part of his or her awareness—the *"perceived setting"* (C). Within this setting, the individual defines a *goal or goals* (D). The goal may be a result of one or more *"stimulus factors"* (E): needs the individual feels, satisfactions from past experiences, an attractive and stimulating environment, group or peer pressure, etc. The individual mentally formulates a *plan* (F) for achieving the goal. Other possible courses of action may have been *planned*, but not selected (G). The plan leads to a *response* (H). The response may include emotions and appreciations, as well as more readily observable activity. The participant does something. He or she hikes, or goes to the ceramics studio, or moves to "Park Place." As a result of the activity, the participant perceives a *result*. The result may be *satisfying* (I) or *dissatisfying* (J). If the results are satisfying, the tendency to repeat the *response will be strengthened* (K). If not, the individual may try a *modified plan* (L), in an attempt to achieve the same goal. Or, a *new goal* may be selected (M).

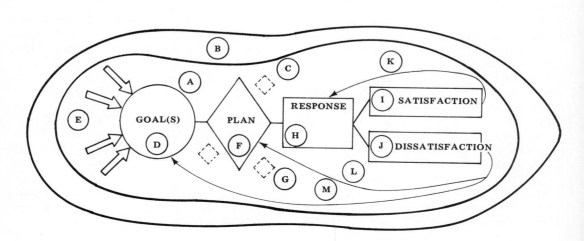

Use and Non-Use Factors

The conceptual model described above suggests several factors which influence whether or not an individual will or will not use a recreation facility or program. For example, the individual may not see the recreation opportunities we offer as being related to his goals. He may not have personal qualifications needed to participate; or, he may not perceive that the opportunity to participate is available. All of these possible factors seem to fit within a second model or scheme.

Edward Sebastian, a 27 year-old accountant, just moved to Sacramento from San Diego. He is in excellent health, and he has a good income. He engages in several low-energy leisure pursuits (reading, movies, etc.), but his physical recreation activity has been limited to surfing. Residing in Sacramento, he has relatively little opportunity to surf.

Shortly after joining the firm, in December, he meets another accountant who skis. They eat lunch together on two or three occasions, and talk about skiing in the Sierra. Sebastian also sees a couple of ski reports on television. One day, on his way to work, he walks by a sports shop. He drops in and picks up some brochures on ski areas in the Sierra, and gets some information on equipment rental.

On Friday, he stops by the shop and rents skis, boots and poles. Saturday morning, early, he heads for the mountains.

At the ski area, four dollars buys a rope-tow ticket. Three hours later, he is wet, tired, bruised, and discouraged. He has spent more time on his back than on the skis, and he is convinced that he is lucky to have escaped from the tow with all limbs intact. After lunch at the lodge, he goes home.

Two weeks later, Sebastian bumps into an old friend who has just moved to Sacramento. The friend works for the Pacific Gas and Electric Company, and has a week-end job teaching skiing at one of the areas at Lake Tahoe. He encourages Sebastian to come up and take lessons.

Over the remainder of the season, Sebastian develops his skill in week-end classes. His interest and his enjoyment continue to increase.

Sebastian's involvement in skiing might be represented by the model described on the following material.

Sebastian was a potential user (i.e., a potential skier). However, there was no likelihood that he would become a participant until he became aware of the activity. This condition simply says that one factor contributing to use or non-use is awareness.

The participant must have at least some awareness of the activity in order for it to be a possible behavior for him or her.

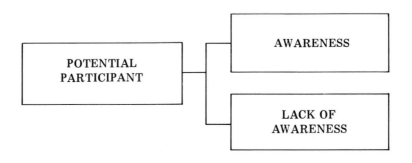

Awareness alone does not lead to participation. The individual must want, to some degree, to engage in the activity. Somewhere along the line, Sebastian developed a desire to try skiing. Interest may have been sparked when he talked to the fellow accountant, or when he saw the television reports, or when he dropped into the sport shop. It may have been strengthened by a deeper desire for physical activity; perhaps, as a replacement for surfing. Whatever the particular combination of events and conditions, he was motivated to try skiing. Without such motivation, he would have been a non-user.

most frequently noted include the wish for achievement, and for affiliation (or companionship or love). In this context, Sebastian may have become a user (i.e., skier) to satisfy a need for achievement, or for affiliation, or both. Improving his skill and developing friendships with other skiers would contribute to the satisfaction of these needs, and to his enjoyment. Why he selects skiing rather than bowling or weaving is a factor of personality and environmental influences.

Hierarchy of Needs. Abraham Maslow[3] has suggested that some needs are more dominant than others; that needs

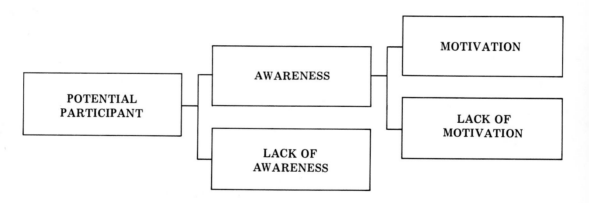

There is little consensus in motivation theory. However, several notions have potential contribution to an understanding of recreation behavior.

Social Motives. Sebastian's participation may have originated in a desire to satisfy one or more wishes or needs, which he might hold in common with most other people in our society. Many theorists support the notion of common wishes or needs. These are sometimes called social motives to differentiate them from physiological needs, such as food, drink, shelter, etc. The social motives or common wishes which are

exist in a fairly predictable hierarchy. At the bottom of the hierarchy are physiological needs, (hunger, thirst, etc.) and security needs. Maslow contends that these must be rather consistently satisfied before other needs become influences on behavior. Next, in order, are social or belonging needs, self-esteem needs, and the need for self-actualization. This concept suggests that Sebastian would not be motivated to engage in

3. That part of Maslow's theory which is discussed here is concisely summarized by Edward J. Murray.

any recreation activity, including skiing, if he had not satisfied basic survival needs.

Moreover, the need for security might cause him to discontinue skiing if he felt a threat to his safety (i.e., fear of heights on chair-lifts, fear of slope steepness, fear of avalanche hazard, etc.). What seems to be crucial at this level is the participant's perception of the risk or hazard. Many activities, including skiing, involve danger elements. For some participants, it is one of the attractions of the activity. Maslow's theory seems to suggest, however, that as long as the participant perceives the risk as surmountable the safety need will be more or less satisfied. If survival and safety needs are reasonably satisfied, Sebastian may ski to satisfy belonging needs (friends, the club, dates, etc.), or, at a higher level, esteem needs (recognition for skill, the possession of good equipment, etc.). At the highest level, self-actualization, he may find in skiing the opportunity to express his fullest capacity in skill, knowledge, and emotion. A downhill run, or a cross-country trek, may afford him the opportunity to manifest his total being in the act of skiing. This level probably is rarely reached in recreation behavior. Suppose, however, that Sebastian was motivated primarily by the esteem need; he skied well and was generally admired for his talent. Assume that, for some reason, skiing became an unpopular activity among his circle of close friends. Maslow's theory suggests that the belonging need might become dominant, as a lower-order and more intense need, and Sebastian might give up skiing.

Conflict. Another concept related to competing needs is the idea of conflict. Psychologists have defined several situational categories where conflicts arise. These may be conflicts between alternative plans for satisfying the same need,

or they may be conflicts between needs. They include (1) approach-approach conflicts, (2) approach-avoidance conflicts, (3) double approach-avoidance conflicts, and (4) avoidance-avoidance conflicts. Since recreation behavior assumes voluntary participation, the fourth category (avoidance-avoidance conflicts) can be dismissed for our purposes.

The approach-approach situation is where we have two alternatives which are equally attractive. If Sebastian was planning a trip to the snow during his vacation in February, and he received a phone call inviting him to spend a week surfing at a friend's beach home during the same time, he might be in an approach-approach conflict. Or, if he was invited to enter the club's downhill race, he might find himself in an approach-avoidance situation. He might be attracted by the recognition afforded racers, but repelled by the possibility of injury in the downhill race. Double approach-avoidance is where both alternatives (e.g., skiing and surfing) have attractive and rejecting elements. Conflicts may result in no behavior; however, we usually select the course of action which seems most likely to satisfy our needs or our goals.

The above paragraphs suggest only three notions related to motivation. There are many others. However, the basic generalization is that we are inclined to engage in those activities that we feel will satisfy our needs or our goals. If we are not motivated to engage in a particular activity, we probably will not become users.

However, motivation alone will not assure use. There must be opportunity.

Sebastian had the opportunity. Skiing was geographically accessible to him; he had adequate health and fitness for the activity, and sufficient time and financial resources to participate. Initially he

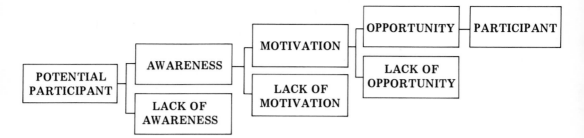

lacked skill, but he overcame this restriction.

These elements—geographic and environmental resources, health and fitness, financial resources, time, and knowledge and skill, seem to define the immediate limits of an individual's opportunities to participate. They are subject to change, but they influence the immediate capacity to use or not to use facilities and programs. Endless examples could be offered. It is difficult to mountain-climb in Iowa.[4] The older adult, with cardiac problems, may not be able to hike into wilderness areas. The poverty mother may not be able to afford the ceramic class. The physician may not have time for continuing his participation in the community orchestra, and the young pianist may not have sufficient skill to do so.

Another factor might be added. The climate for participation must be at least somewhat encouraging or accepting if we are to become users. Some environments are prohibited by law; minors cannot legally frequent bars and the unlicensed driver cannot operate a motor vehicle, even if he has the skill. Restrictions are also imposed, more subtly, in terms of social sanctions and expectations. The beginning tennis player who would like to join the club, may not because he does not have appropriate apparel, or because he does not know the modes of behavior which are expected on and off the courts. The woman who enjoys

billiards may find, in some communities, social expectations strongly against her participation. Restrictions based on expectations and sanctions seem to be lessening. This may be most apparent in terms of what are seen as appropriate activities for women. However, such restrictions continue to exert some influence on the opportunities possessed by any given individual.

Whatever the specifics, each person's unique complex of characteristics interact with the environment to produce what might be called an "opportunity framework." For some, this framework is fairly large. For others, the framework of opportunities is consistently limited. The aged, the poor, and the ill and the handicapped typically fall in this category. It is these people who seem most often to be non-users; not by choice, but because of environmental and personal restrictions.

The use and non-use model presented above attempts to categorize use and non-use factors which are encountered frequently in a recreation agency. The skiing illustration embodies the basic notions. However, the following example may be more germane to the efforts of a public department.

The Broderick Street Recreation Cen-

4. However, technology is creating artificial environments, so that it is now possible to surf in Phoenix, climb a rock face in downtown Tokyo, etc.

ter recently initiated a new morning program for pre-school youngsters. The program was well planned by the Center staff, and there was a high participation potential since many young families live in the area. However, there were very few sign-ups for the program and only two or three mothers have been bringing their children. Analysis by the area supervisor revealed the following contributing factors.

Awareness. The program was publicized in the community's newspaper; two announcements and one article describing the program appeared. The Center Director also asked the Broderick Elementary School Principal if he would ask the three primary-grade teachers to send notes home with children in their classes. Some non-use potential was introduced at this point. Many residents of the neighborhood do not subscribe to the paper, and two of the teachers forgot to send notes home with the children.

Motivation. Broderick Recreation Center has an excellent program staff. They have a good reputation, in the community, for providing effective programs. However, earlier cut-backs in the departmental budget required that the City's maintenance staff be reduced. As a partial result, all of the centers have been less well-maintained. The grass has not been cut as often as it was previously, trash has been collected less frequently, and the general condition of the building has deteriorated somewhat. In addition, older, out-of-school youth have been hanging around the Center grounds, recently, during the morning period. These conditions led to some conflict situations on the part of those parents who were aware of the program. The reputation of the Center staff contributed to a desire to enroll their children. However, the presence of the older youth created some parental fear that younger children might be both-

ered, and the deteriorating appearance of the Center tipped the balance in favor of avoiding the situation (program, in this case).

Opportunity. The Center staff decided to set up the pre-school program on a partially self-supporting basis. A nominal fee was planned to cover the costs of supplies. The program also was organized around the utilization of mothers as aides. Each mother was to volunteer one morning, every other week. These two conditions ruled participation out for most of the parents who knew about the program and who wished to participate. The registration fee, even though nominal, was excessive for young families on very limited budgets. In addition, several mothers also had infants who required care during the times when they would be expected to assist with the program.

IMPLICATIONS

This paper has focused primarily on two concepts: the notion of recreation participation as a behavioral sequence, and a schematic categorization of use factors which influence whether or not an individual will use recreation services. It has not examined different philosophical positions in the provision of services; and, it has not intended to discuss specific implementation techniques. A number of general implications seem apparent, however.

If we want to expand the numbers of citizens who directly use our services, we need to be certain that they are aware of the opportunities that are available to them.

We need to use our resources so as to provide for services which appeal to a broad range of possible motivations, or goals. And, we need to do what we can to help people see how our services can contribute to goals they may have.

If we wish to reduce the numbers of

non-users in our communities, we need to make some inferences about the "opportunity frameworks" within which people live. We need to make some attempt to define restrictions, and to identify those over which we may have influence. In public agencies, these kinds of analyses probably will have to be made on a group basis or in terms of "modal" characteristics—at least initially. However, the more our efforts can be individualized the more effective we will be.

Perhaps most basically, we need to become more sensitive to the socio-psychological and environmental factors which influence the behavior of the people we serve . . . and those we do not serve.

LITERATURE CITED

1. Lee Joseph Cronbach, *Educational Psychology* (New York: Harcourt, Brace and Co., 1954), pp. 45-47, 49-51.
2. Clayne R. Jensen, *Outdoor Recreation in America* (Minneapolis, Minnesota: Burgess Publishing Co., 1970), p. 14.
3. Edward J. Murray, *Motivation and Emotion* (Englewood Cliffs, New Jersey: Prentice-Hall, Inc., 1964), pp. 110-111.

Crisis in Youth Values

David E. Gray

After you lose your membership in it, the younger generation seems pretty bad. Adults view with alarm, the behavior of the young. They see young people rebelling against governmental policy in the United States, Britain, Poland, Spain, Czechoslovakia, Japan, Egypt, Germany, South Korea and Turkey and wonder what possesses the younger generation. Never before today has there been such a widespread discontent among youth. This is not a question of an eccentric minority, the hippies and flower children or the mods. The current movements are sponsored by earnest students concerned with society's future. All of these movements share a common distaste for the preceding generation. The young are revolting, not only against the customs of their elders, but also against the society they inherited from them. The deeply impressive aspect of most of the current wave of unrest is this genuine effort to right wrongs and to stimulate peace and justice. A deep gap exists between the generations in this country. Young people under thirty and older people over fifty live in entirely different Americas; the middle aged try to bridge the gap but their efforts are largely unsuccessful. The generation gap is real, and more severe than is generally recognized. It is caused not only by external things like the length of hair and the mode of dress, but also by different approaches to deep philosophical questions including the nature of reality, the nature of man, and the dimensions of the human condition. There is evidence that, in their need to know themselves, the young are absorbing some of the ideas of existentialism.

The young are deeply influenced by existential thought. Most of our youth have not deliberately and consciously, as a matter of free will, embraced existential philosophy, but the central ideas of existentialism are such a prominent part of the art, the literature, the life style, the education and advertising pressures of contemporary life that these ideas have been absorbed as a consequence of living. When they are absorbed, they begin to condition the responses young people make to the problems of life.

The way man perceives himself influences everything he is or does. The existentialist looks at himself in a fundamentally different way than do those who follow the more traditional philosophies of western man. Existentialism is the climate in which the young draw their breath.

Reprinted with permission from *California Parks and Recreation*, April, 1969, California Parks and Recreation Society, Inc.

Expressions of existential thought are all around us. Modern art expresses the temper of our time. If we could have a finer, truer art in our era we would. The ordinary citizen in contact with modern art reflects confusion and irritation. He finds it obscure and disturbing. He suspects it depicts depravity and spiritual poverty. Modern art depicts not beauty but life, and modern life rests upon values that are not very clear. Even if existential philosophy had not evolved, it would be apparent from contemporary art that a radically different vision of mankind was under development. The world pictured by the modern artist is like the world pictured by the existential philosopher—an irrational world in which the old conceptions of man are no longer relevant.

The literature young people are reading deals with existential themes. The classical format with a beginning, middle and end and logical development of the argument is not the form of much of our contemporary literature. When existential ideas are central the work is apt to be meandering, without climax, almost formless, and dense, opaque, unintelligible. That is the image of the irrational world the modern writer depicts.

In music, we find the young turning toward the Oriental, but the Oriental song confuses the adult westerner. He has always demanded meaning and form in his music—a beginning, middle, and ending combined with a message. Oriental music has no meaning for him. The form of the music preferred by the Oriental reflects his conception of life. He holds that life itself is meaningless and this ought to be reflected in the arts. Since the Greeks, western man has believed that all being is intelligible and that there is a reason for everything. That many of our youth are responsive to Oriental music reflects a profound change in their attitude toward the

world. It suggests the idea that they are no longer sure of the final intelligibility of existence.

Every age projects its own image of man into its art. The tradition of western humanism has faltered and become questionable. We are not so sure any more that we know what man is. The thing that is not clear in modern art is its image of man. In modern art man is a man without identity. He is often depicted as a faceless hero who is everyman and no man, in contact with nothingness. Nothingness has become one of the principal themes of modern art and literature. Modern art and existential philosophy treat similar themes. Both start from a sense of crisis. Both represent a break with western tradition. These are the influences some of our youth are experiencing.

Existentialists hold that rational man has limitations to this rationality. Even in science, we are learning there are limits to our ability to know and predict physical states. Modern science opens up a glimpse of nature that may, at bottom, be irrational and chaotic. What is and what is not rational stands open to doubt. Existentialism opposes rationalism. It suggests that much of the experience of mankind cannot be explained in a coherent rational system.

By the middle of the Nineteenth Century, the problem of the identity of man had begun to receive attention of some of the philosophers of the day who sought to discover what the meaning of man is. Soren Kierkegaard and Freidrich Nietzsche offered explanations which are central themes in existential thought. Kierkegaard recommended rediscovery of the religious center of self in terms of a return to the Christianity of the first disciples of Christ. Nietzsche sought explanations beyond Christianity and science in the early Greeks. Kierkegaard's theme and passion was Christianity. His concern was what it means for an individual to be a Christian. He perceived that his civilization was no longer Christian. Nietzsche said, "In the end one experiences only oneself." The self he experienced was a tormented atheist tearing himself loose from his psychological roots, reporting "God is dead," and demanding that mankind become adult and godless. Thus, almost at birth, existentialism had two mainstreams, one dedicated to the glorification of Christianity and the other the exponent of abject atheism.

Kierkegaard worked out a statement on ethics. He saw an ethical rule as a universal which prescribes behavior of all men under given circumstances. But he recognized the religious personality may be called upon to do something that goes against the universal norm. The individual who accepts the universal but must break with it because in the uniqueness of his own individuality he cannot as a "matter of personal conscience" live with it in a particular instance does so in "fear and trembling." It is precisely this kind of dilemma many of our young men, who are opposed to the Vietnam War, face when they are drafted. Those who choose to violate the laws as a matter of personal conscience, do so with fear and trembling. They are following the principle of existential philosophy which places the individual ahead of the universal and suggests that each man must listen to his own conscience and judge *from within* what is ethical and moral and truthful.

The man of the present lives on a level of abstraction far beyond the man of the past. There is an extraordinary externalization of life, the tempo of living is increased and journalism, both printed and electronic, enables people to deal with life more and more at a distance. These depersonalizing forces are a major theme of existential philosophy which

struggles to awaken in the individual the possibilities of an authentic personal life in spite of the forces for conformity in contemporary mass society.

Existential philosophy does not treat traditional themes and philosophers who work in the tradition of western philosophy find it threatening. Anxiety, death, personal conflicts between the sham and real self, lack of identity, neurotic anxiety, and the experience of the death of God have not been central in our philosophical tradition. But they are central in our lives! We suffer personal conflicts, anxiety, loss of identity and death. These are the problems of modern life—they are also the main concerns of existential thought.

The initial response of America to existentialism was rejection. We found it alien to our patterns of thought. We attributed it to a decadent European society which had lost it's vision and sense of direction. Americans had always believed in the perfectability of man. We are only beginning to perceive his limitations. But gradually, against the will of most of us, the central themes of the philosophy began to flow into the American consciousness.

Existentialism is a complex philosophy. This brief discussion of it has barely sketched some of its central ideas, but perhaps it is comprehensive enough to give us a new perspective of the behavior of youth. Most of our young are not intellectually following existentialism but many who would not know the word are acting out, as part of their day to day living, existential ideas. Although there are many philosophical systems which appear to condition the responses our youth make to the choices of life, one of the main ones seems to be existentialism.

* When a young man refuses to submit to the draft as a matter of conscience;

* When a boy or a girl pickets the Vietnam War on moral grounds;
* When a youth maintains a shining faith in God in the absence of rational proofs that He exists;
* When a young man or woman creases, mutilates or spindles a punch card and refuses to perform by the numbers;
* When a young painter represents man as a faceless non-entity;
* When a young couple have pre-marital sexual relations because they are "really in love" and want to express it;
* When a boy or girl drops out of adult society and refuses to live by the clock, consume goods at a prodigious rate, work at a steady job or do the other things required for success in our materialistic society;
* When a young student challenges his professor to present something that has reference to his life;
* When the young demand that the older generation begin living up to their cherished ideals;
* When a young person confronts himself and tries to understand who he is;
* When a young student denies that science is the final authority on life and living;
* When a young individual makes a moral choice according to the dictates of his conscience without recourse to law or the Ten Commandments;
* When a young person wears non-conforming clothes outside, as a symbol of the non-conforming person inside;
* When a youngster lives his life with passion;
* When a youth does not rule out God but questions organized religion;
* When a young man puts responsibility to himself above responsibility to anyone else;
* When the young say straight out what is in their minds without sham or subterfuge;
* When a man lives in the "here and now" and refuses the frantic rush to make his schedule work;

When the young do any or all of these things, they may be acting out a central theme of existential thought.

The average adult who knows anything about existential thought finds it nihilistic, atheistic, repulsive, threatening, negative, morbid, and sordid. When they respond this way to a youth who finds meaning in it, they have dropped out of his life.

If the generation gap, as this thesis suggests, is real and involved with vital issues of living, how can the adult work with the young? If we would be successful the adult must: (1) leave open every opportunity for an expression of points of view, even hostility, on both sides; (2) the youth and adult together must decide what are responsible and fair limits of behavior; (3) opportunities must be provided for youth to release their potential constructively; (4) the adult must realize that old eternal truths are not here any longer; (5) the adult must remain real; the youth does not want an anonymous adult; he wants someone with feelings and emotions and ideas.

An early reaction to the troubles of this world was to drop out. Now the young have elected to stay and fight. The most articulate of our young are rejecting the kind of world current trends would create in the future. They reject the old notion that politics is "the art of the possible"—they think politics should be the art of the necessary whether it is possible or not. The young are interested in black power, brown power, federal power, student power; they suspect their elders are only interested in electric power.

Religion is much less comforting than it was. One cannot turn things over to God and pray things will come out all right. The young are not afforded the easy comfort of a half-lived Christianity which does not get in the way much here on earth but offers the promise of a life hereafter in heaven. Being young is loving and wanting and waiting. Some things are for some day and some things are for now. The young are more interested in now than some day.

Americans have been busy taming a continent, building the world's greatest economy and developing a society. We have not asked what the ultimate ideas behind our civilization are. We have not looked for human identity beyond the facade of our technology. But the time has come to deal with the problem of human existence. There is evidence that our young people have already begun this task. As they undertake it, they appear to be embracing existential ideas.

Special Recreation Needs of Teenagers

J.S. Shivers, Ph.D.

Young people throughout the country feel uncertain in this age of anxiety, abundance, increased leisure, mobility, and uncertain futures. They must adjust to an environment which admonishes them to stay in school and prepare for a society which is rapidly modifying its demands for vocational skills.

At a time when technical necessities appear to be the single road to youthful salvation, the schools appear bent on graduating those who feel they must enter institutions of higher education to better compete for occupational security and opportunity. In many instances, youngsters no longer trust the schools in respect to future vocational competence and lose interest in the academic program long before graduation.

The teen-age school drop-out has increased the ranks of unskilled and therefore unemployed or unemployable persons having much leisure but little satisfactory utilization of it for their own or society's benefit.

Those who remain in school have certain recreation needs supplied, but with exposure to many avenues for fulfillment and additional leisure skills, they also find it difficult to satisfy newly awakened recreation desires because communities simply have not kept pace with the needs of people.

Too many outmoded, hackneyed programs are offered to individuals with more knowledge and sophistication than their parents. Alienation, disaffection, and outright rebellion can be spawned when this group is denied legitimate recreation opportunities.

Teen-agers constantly seek a place of their own. They need the security of identity in a society which nearly always enforces conformity. The identity thus sought gives them a precious independence and represents, at least to their minds, status or recognition. Many communities can afford to meet this demand for security and independence by organizing a recreation program geared specifically to teen-agers.

A teen program may and should have its inception with the public recreation service department of the community. This is the agency with primary responsibility for the satisfaction of recreation needs for all the people in the community, regardless of age. The public department should attempt, with interested teens, to establish some sort of center which by its very designation indicates its function: The Teen Center. The center may be any structure which can house an organiza-

Reprinted with permission from National Recreation and Park Association. Official publication *Parks and Recreation*, August, 1967.

tion that will effectively contribute toward meeting individual needs of teenagers.

Programs offered through such organizations provide youth the opportunity to discover release from normal tensions and pressures. A well organized teen club will offer participation in a variety of wholesome recreation experiences, comprehensive enough to meet the direct needs of all those who wish to take part. In addition, socially approved outlets for youthful energies can be directed for the mutual benefit of the community and the young person. Recreation activities that afford instruction in a host of living experiences can point the way toward a rewarding series of lifetime skills.

Teen-agers holding membership in the specialized program or club organization may seek needed counseling or guidance from qualified recreationists primarily employed for that purpose. The communicative recreationist is the one professional person to whom the teen-ager may turn to mitigate encountered problems. The permissive atmosphere of the club eliminates overt pressure to attend, maintain grades or perform in ways which may prove uncomfortable. In this environment mutual respect, trust, and understanding on the part of young persons and employed recreationists is more readily developed.

It is unfortunate that many communities do not have such programs. To the extent that there are no public departments of recreation service within the towns, there is a consistent denial of even the most elementary recreation programs. Furthermore, the lack of a public department of recreation service usually means that the community does not offer any recreation opportunities to its citizens—young or old.

In too many cases, recreation activities are generally of an athletic orientation and typically do not satisfy more than five percent of the town's population. Every community, regardless of size, has the resources to establish a public recreation service department. Through this department all segments of the population can be well served. However, the implementation and organization of a teen-age program does not have to wait for the establishment of a town recreation agency.

The financial outlay and initiation of a teen-age program will not necessarily strain the town budget and may be effective if cooperation and coordination exists among all agencies of the community—public, quasi-public, and private.

Teenagers are the future tax payers and potential governors of our social system. They will better be able to fulfill their citizenship responsibilities if the social world in which they circulate meets their needs as they reach young adulthood. The need for a specialized teen-age program within every community should be apparent to all. It provides the environment where peer acceptance, so significant to the young person, social skills, and enjoyable moments may be rendered. To neglect the teen-ager is an invitation to possible social disintegration and economic futility. The principles of effective teen-age group organization to provide recreation activities is mandatory if town governments want to serve their constituents in the best possible way.

Is He Entitled to Recreation?

Janet Pomeroy

People in general, and recreation leaders in particular, need to acquire a new concept concerning severely physically handicapped persons. A person in a wheelchair or on crutches who is severely physically handicapped may not be ill. Yet, people often associate such a handicap with a crippling disease, and either think of the person as ill or as a patient who is recuperating. The word *patient* means, "a sick person, now, commonly, one under treatment or care as by a physician or surgeon or one in a hospital, hence, a client of a physician," according to *Webster's New International Dictionary*. This does not apply to a large number of the handicapped.

The common misconception of the severely physically handicapped—particularly those with multiple handicaps—as ill persons has been a deterrent in the provision of community recreation programs for this group. It brings about a chain reaction that retards or even prevents the inclusion of these persons in regular programs and/or the development of recreation programs for them. Some health and welfare agencies associated with the severely physically handicapped have, no doubt unknowingly, contributed to the general misunderstanding of these persons by creating stereotypes through the use of medical labels. For example, we hear cerebral-palsied persons referred to as "CP's" or "spastics." Recreation activities conducted by some of the welfare groups have been called "spastic activities" or "group activities for CP's." This specialization within an isolated group does little to encourage their acceptance by community groups of any type, including recreation programs. This situation is also found in residential institutions for the severely handicapped.

It is entirely possible that a severely physically handicapped person, even though he may be bedbound, has never spent any time in a hospital, and that his only experience as a *patient* was the time he had the measles or some other illness common to children. His handicap could have been caused by a birth injury that resulted, in cerebral palsy, for example, in a *condition* rather than an *illness*. Even if his handicap was caused by a crippling disease such as polio, he would be considered, following his recovery, merely physically handicapped.

Unfortunately, recreation leaders who are trained in general community recreation tend to believe that they are not qualified to work with

Reprinted with permission from National Recreation and Park Association. Official publication *Parks and Recreation*, June, 1961.

such persons. In reality, however, they may be the most desirable leaders to be so doing. Although working in recreation with persons who are truly *ill* requires specialized training, it does not follow that the community recreation leader needs to be medically oriented to work successfully with physically handicapped persons who are well.

ATTITUDES

A recreation leader should understand that the severely handicapped:

1. Are first and foremost people . . . who have the same basic needs, desires and interests as the nonhandicapped . . . that the handicapped are more like others than they are different from them.
2. Need to participate as regular members of the community through recreation interests . . . not through isolated groups of persons who happen to have the same type of handicap.
3. Have the same right as others to choose and to share in the planning of their own recreation activities, and to participate voluntarily.
4. Can participate in a wide variety of activities in the community, particularly if they have the encouragement and guidance of good leadership.

THE RECREATION APPROACH

The professionally prepared recreation leader's very lack of specific medical orientation may actually be an advantage. As Dr. Ralph W. Menge recently stated in *Recreation* magazine *(October 1960):* "To make therapeutic use of himself, it isn't necessary for the professional recreator to know a great deal about sickness. Nor is it necessary that he be a psychoanalytically oriented psychotherapist." If the recreation leader is not too involved with the medical and technical background of individuals, he will tend to accept and treat these persons as participants in a regular recreation program. If he is not hampered and confused by their presumed "limitations," he does not set up mental blocks in his own mind concerning their abilities and potentialities. Moreover, medical opinion on these so-called limitations is often inconsistent and continually changing.

A severely physically handicapped person needs to be able to express himself naturally, through interest or other normal motivation, without worrying about what muscle he must move or exercise because it is "good for him." In addition, if he knows that the recreation leader is not preoccupied with what is good for him he is more relaxed and at ease as a participant. Therapy is essential and necessary for most severely physically handicapped individuals. However, the recreator is not a therapist, but rather a leader who provides them with incentives and opportunities to exceed their limitations—all of which results indirectly in desirable therapy.

Recreators do, however, need to have special information and skills that will help them in the physical handling of the severely physically handicapped. For example, in preparation for swimming or overnight campouts, leaders must often assist in removing braces. Leaders also need to be acquainted with the handling of wheel chairs, feeding those who are unable to eat by themselves, and in assisting those who require toilet help. When such assistance is required, information is usually requested from parents and is included on application forms together with other pertinent information, including a medical report from the family physician. Advisory committees which include technicians and practitioners in services to severely physically handicapped persons can provide valuable guidance to the recreation staff. Some colleges (for example, San Francisco State College) are now including in the recreation curriculum appropriate pregraduate courses in "Recreation for Special Groups" which include some orientation toward the physically handicapped.

We must always remember that recreation is for all members of the community whatever their condition.

Recreation in Correctional Institutions

Larry E. Decker

Recreation has been recognized as a rehabilitative tool both in mental institutions and hospitals for some time. It is an important instrument in almost any kind of youth work. Strangely enough, not much has been done with recreation programs on a planned, professional basis in correctional institutions.

In the corrections field, recreation's role in the treatment program has been undeveloped; and in a sense, agencies involved in corrections have reflected a general nonacceptance of the role of professionally adapted and applied recreation services. The efforts with the inmates—patients—socially maladjusted—or whatever one wants to call individuals in need of intensive resocialization—seem to be devoted principally to meeting medical, educational, and vocational needs.

RECREATION PROGRAMS ARE INADEQUATE

Recreation programs which do exist in correctional institutions are often inadequate. The findings of a recently completed Recreation Planning Study for the Oregon State Division of Corrections[1] indicate some of the reasons why recreation programs in correctional institutions are frequently inadequate:

- The role and values of recreation are not emphasized.
- There is no professional staff member trained in recreation.
- The emphasis is on custodial care and security.
- Professional guidance and assistance in recreation services are not readily available to the staff.
- Where recreation programs do exist, they often are instituted with little planning and few long-range objectives in mind.
- The administrative climate is not conducive to evaluation and change.
- The professional recreator's efforts have not been directed toward explaining and increasing the role of recreation in the institutional setting.

It is known that an unhappy person, a hostile or conflictive personality, does not lend himself cooperatively to educational programs, clinical treatment, or vocational opportunities. Lack of purpose and objec-

Reprinted with permission from National Recreation and Park Association. Official publication *Parks and Recreation*, April, 1969.

1. *Recreation in Residential Treatment*, Hillcrest Recreation Study, Center of Leisure Study and Community Service, University of Oregon, Eugene, Oregon, July 1968.

tives, too much free time, lack of qualified guidance and direction, all build anxieties and frustrations which must be vented. Recreation is often used as a stopgap measure in meeting the major ills of institutional life—the ever present boredom and overabundance of free time.

Unless recreation programs are professionally adapted and applied, much of their potential to combat and alleviate these institutional ills is lost. Many people in correctional institutions have no knowledge or skills which enable them to make acceptable use of their leisure. In fact, improper use of leisure is often the reason for their presence in the institution. Some lack the ability to engage in any cooperative activity. Many do not have self-control or a sense of fair play.

Professionally adapted and applied recreation can aid in rehabilitation. The inmates can be exposed to programs and activities in which they experience success and socially-acceptable satisfaction—both are too often foreign to their past experiences. In essence, a well-planned recreation program gives institutionalized individuals the opportunity to acquire skills, knowledge and interests. This is necessary if they are not only to return to community life, but also if they are to benefit from other therapeutic efforts during their stay in the correctional institution.

LIFE HISTORIES ARE SIMILAR

The life histories of those in correctional institutions are significantly similar. All have some problem as defined by the social system—family problems, socialization deficiencies, inadequate social functioning, and intellectual deficits or environmental disadvantages. The family experiences of many are characterized by two extremes—excessive over-protec-

tion or the total lack of external and internal family control or guidance. Their experiences and involvement in community institutions, such as schools, churches, camps and recreation centers are extremely limited or negative.

Inmates also share problems relating to daily pressures and conflicts, which may include the following:

1. Immature expectations regarding authority figures
2. Confused self-image in regard to the social implications, their adultness, their self-worth, their vocational goals, and their personal skills, limitations and capacities
3. Parent-child conflicts
4. Confusion regarding life plans and resistance to reviewing them
5. Immature, inadequate and frustrating heterosexual relationships
6. A sense of unreality because of a lack of opportunity to experience group-living situations

RECREATION HAS ROLE TO PLAY

Recreation is not a cure-all. It does not prevent, control, or cure unacceptable behavior. But it does have an important role in the total treatment and rehabilitation process. The use of recreation in rehabilitation allows a varied and coordinated approach with other phases of the treatment process in a more relaxed atmosphere. Recreation is part of normal, everyday life; and as such it can provide institutionalized individuals with an important link with life outside. The knowledge, skills and interests learned in professionally planned and adapted recreation programs have strong carry-over value when the inmates return to society. The hope of any recreation program in a correctional institution is that carry-over will occur and that the results will be shown in a happier, more stable, better adjusted individual.

Recreation is justified in a correctional institution on two basic counts: (1) It satisfies basic human needs by providing outlets for inner urges and drives. For the institutionalized, it provides opportunities for anxieties and frustrations to be vented in a socially-acceptable manner. (2) It can be a useful rehabilitative tool. If a program is well planned and adapted to the participants, they can be guided and assisted in learning self-control and self-discipline, engaging in cooperative enterprises, building more constructive social relationships, and acquiring interests that replace undesirable past interests.

The objectives of an institutional recreation program include:

1. Assisting in the total treatment and rehabilitative process
2. Providing a setting that will aid social adjustment and functioning within the social system
3. Developing living skills that can be carried over into the home, the community, and the work environment
4. Furnishing experiences to help individuals accept themselves and their limitations while encouraging them to utilize their capacities to increase their feelings of self-worth and to focus on the positive aspects of their interest

GUIDES FOR DEVELOPMENT AND EVALUATION

Anyone concerned with influencing the role of recreation in a correctional institution might consider the following as a guide for action and evaluation.

Outside consultation and professional assistance should be sought to cooperate with the staff in evaluation and planning. The history of recreation in the institution should then be reviewed and a study made of the present goals and philosophy of the institution as they relate to recreation's role in the rehabilitative process, together with an account of any needed changes or revisions.

The present staffing patterns for recreation in the institution should be studied. The establishment of an administrative position, if none exists, is most important. The administrator would be responsible for planning, coordinating, training and directing recreation's role in the institution and involving community and state resources in meeting the needs of the institution's recreation program. Staff for direct leadership roles should also be engaged.

Bearing the long-range goals in mind the recreation program should be planned with enough variety and flexibility to meet a wide range of needs and interests. Program areas should include arts and crafts, drama, dance, music, cultural activities, hobbies, outdoor recreation, sports and games, reading, writing, speaking and other creative skills, social recreation, special events, and the opportunity for volunteer services. Individuals within the institution should be able to participate in the planning, initiating and teaching of recreation programs.

Finally, establish a secure financial base to facilitate greater fiscal responsibility and long-range planning and institute continuous research and evaluation of programs, methods and techniques to strengthen recreation's role in the correctional process.

Recreation does have a definite role in the total treatment and rehabilitative process. In most correctional institutions there is room for considerable improvement. Deficiencies are readily observable, and in many cases, easy to define. The difficulty is in trying to correct the deficiencies and to outline a constructive program for improvement. To have the greatest impact, the recreation program must be professionally planned and adapted; an integral part of the total rehabilitative process; and directed toward the ultimate goal of returning a more stable, better adjusted individual to society.

Aging Differently in the Space Age

Margaret Mead

The attitude in the United States that old age is a form of illness, to be lamented but not mentioned earlier than necessary, has been part of our whole cult of youth and our unwillingness to tackle head-on many of the aspects of aging. The picture of aging that people of my day grew up with is no longer valid and the aging that our children will do is totally different from the aging that we have today. One of the complications, of course, is how to handle this moving model of aging—and not pickle or crystalize it in our institutions—whether in Social Security regulations, residence laws, rules for the construction of buildings, rules about driving cars, or any of the thousands of ways in which aging is engaged with the structure of society.

We have to be very careful that we don't do anything with the aging group that we are dealing with now that might limit the possibilities of people who will be this same age twenty years from now. They will be totally different kinds of people. This has been one of our big drawbacks in any kind of social research in this country. We catch a group of adolescents and we make a study about their childhood and we find out what their mothers did that they shouldn't have done and what they didn't do that they should have done. Then, we try to change what's happening to today's babies, so that future adolescents won't be like the adolescents we've got now. We don't allow for the fact that today's babies are being brought up differently anyway, and so we're always trying to catch up with ourselves. We must not let the special characteristics of the people who were born in 1890 determine what we're going to do for people who were born in 1920. We must be ever mindful that in building a moving model of aging, we must build in ways to allow for all these differences.

We've got to stop thinking about a category of grandmothers who all look like what our grandmothers looked like—if we can remember them. Of course, they looked terribly old to us—incredibly old—as older people always look to children. Then, we've had this continuous process of rejuvenation going on in my lifetime. All the women in my age group, and slightly above it, have benefited by the fact that they look younger every year. We need to remember that we don't look younger to the children, but we do look younger to each other and that cheers us up immensely. We need to think in terms of generational, as well as

Reprinted with permission from National Recreation and Park Association. Official publication *Parks and Recreation*, May, 1964.

chronological age—definitely and precisely. We must not lump together and confuse sixty-five to seventy-five years of age, for instance, with being grandparents or great-grandparents.

By stylizing older people as grandparents, we muddle it all up and we don't use the grandparents as we should. We're not recognizing that grandparents are, on the whole, the most vigorous, freest group in the population. Many of the men have gone as far as they are going to get, so they can quit competing. If they are women, they are filled with mild post-menopausal zest. We should be using them in the community. They should never get categorized in any way as out of the picture. We should have grandparents' and teachers' associations, or a grandparents' and school association. Today, we retire people the day their last child leaves public school. They may only be forty, but we put them on the shelf. They turn into disgruntled taxpayers who disapprove of the schools and object to the bond issue. Every community in the country is filled with these people and it's utterly unnecessary.

When we use the words "the golden years of life," roughly speaking, we are thinking of the great-grandparents, and great-great-grandparents. Up to that point, we call them "silver." This "golden" business, of course, I don't think we are going to give up quite yet, though I imagine there are going to be a fairly large number of people who are going to rebel against being "golden" and it might be a good idea if they did.

When I was twenty-six or twenty-seven, all the old people I knew were people one wanted to emulate; they were lively. They tatted without their glasses. They could still read fine print. Their minds were alert. They were a little deaf and they had a lot of rheumatism, but nevertheless they were lively, interesting people. The picture of aging, therefore, combined with "you must live through diphtheria, measles, whooping cough, scarlet fever, pneumonia and, some day, if you're good, you'll be old"—this was a very rewarding picture. The young people who are growing up today are seeing the consequences of this attitude. A new generation will have a different attitude towards human dignity and will be able to set their sights quite differently.

We have to be continually aware of those people who grew up in and outlived one age and are growing old and dying in another, so that they will not set a standard or depress the expectations of younger people, but rather, that they will be able to communicate to younger people other sorts of things.

In building a program for this kind of change, we must keep out of the future the deficiencies of the present, and recognize that what we're doing now is merely palliative. It's making up for the mistakes of the past; it's making up for the changes of the past; it's making up for people who were undernourished in their childhood and whose aging process shows it. At the same time, we are designing for the next twenty, thirty, or forty years a completely different kind of relationship to older people who will be alertly related to the young people and to the community.

We could start, for instance, by eliminating "den mothers." Den mothers are one of the nuisances that have been invented in this world. They are bad for little boys and they are bad for the mothers. They just perpetuate too much female society mixed up with learning how to be a man. There are unlimited potential candidates for "den grandfathers" around and they are at least as able to do the things den mothers do—and a whole lot of other things that den mothers can't do. So, if we could set up grandparents' and teachers' associations, and get the grandparents back in the schools; if we could set up den grandfathers instead of den mothers; if we could do things such as are being planned now by the new Oliver Wendell Holmes Institute, we might make some progress. The Oliver Wendell Holme's Institute is planned for the affluent, but, nevertheless, can have repercussions in models that we can use at every level. The institute will offer courses of high academic excellence to people's parents and parents-in-law while they're on vacation; so that, when the older folks come home after four months in Florida, they'll be very up-to-date.

In fact, they'll be more up-to-date than their children, because they'll have had time to learn something. It will be possible to feed back into the communities remarkably well-informed older people with time to read the newspapers, and time to read Plato, and time to keep alive a knowledge of our tradition. They can teach their grandchildren and their great-grandchildren what they know far better than any young person. This is the nature of change itself.

We have been so impressed in this country with putting grandparents on the shelf because they came from some other country, and they didn't get on with the visiting nurse. The general style of the row between the grandmother and the visiting nurse, plus the row between the two sets of parents-in-law, has become very crystallized in the way we handle things. We have assumed that, on the whole, grandparents and old people are a liability. Old people that only talk about the past are just as tiresome as people who talk only about the present. But old people who can describe vividly and meaningfully to young people the steps from candles to kerosene lamps, to gas lamps, to electricity; who can describe the steps from nothing but the newspaper and the telegraph to the

Morse Code, to radio and TV, and then Telestar—these people have an invaluable contribution to make in building into our young people a notion of flexibility—a recognition that the world twenty years from now is going to be incredibly different from the world of today.

In a relatively static society, too much association with grandparents makes one static, but in a changing and moving society, the only certain way that you can keep a sense of change and movement is to associate with grandfather and let him talk about the past, and fill the listening children's bones with the idea that the world has changed incredibly. The world has changed, is changing, and will change, and those who have changed most are the older people. They are the best living example of change.

All this is going to require a tremendous amount of imagination in the way we structure the relationship of older people to the community. We will have to sort out those who are ready for retirement at an early age because of the vicissitudes of their lives and those who need only protection and cherishing and care. We can't do very much more for them now, because in the past we weren't able to do very much or didn't try to. Yet, we must do this without building a picture of aging in the future that is going to include *any* of these things. Instead, we must develop a picture for the future in which we will have the sort of community, the sort of housing, the sort of educational assistance in which people never finish school, in which we never put husky 65-year-old people into ghettoes, and in which we are able to use almost all the grandparent generation and many of the great-grandparent generation in building a society that is flexible enough to be continually self-renewing—continually able to change.

What's New in Old Age ?

Ethel Shanas

Old people are found in all societies. The age at which a person is considered old varies from country to country and may indeed vary within individual countries. For example, 55 is considered the official beginning of old age in India, just as, for most purposes, age 65 is the official beginning of old age in the United States. Yet, despite official agreement on when old age begins, as codified in federal statutes and in private pension plans, who is considered old, and when old age begins depends on who is making an age judgment. The American young talk about "not trusting anyone over 30," thus relegating to the outer reaches of "too old" about half the American population. At the other end of the life span, at the age of 70, most Americans continue to describe themselves as "middle-aged," thus identifying with what they consider the mainstream of the American population. It is not until after they have reached the age of 75 that more than half of all Americans describe themselves as "old" or "elderly."

In this issue of the *American Behavioral Scientist*, seven Americans, two Europeans, and one Middle-Eastern scholar discuss the elderly in contemporary society. In most of these papers the elderly are considered those over 65; in some papers no age definition is given. The American papers deal with the role of the aged vis-à-vis the young; the family life of old people, widowhood, and friends and neighbors in old age; problems of work and economic support; and the psychological strains of growing old in a society oriented toward change. The two Europeans—one French, the other British—deal with special aspects of aging in their own countries: aging as a political problem in France, and the aged as one of the constituencies with claims on the welfare state in Britain. The third non-American paper, written by an Israeli, focuses on the problems of aging in a new immigrant society, where growing old occurs within a new and often unanticipated social structural framework.

Given the range of the papers, it is somewhat surprising that irrespective of their subject matter, two common themes emerge. For the sake of simplicity, we will call these themes the optimistic and the pessimistic. The optimistic theme deals with the relationships between old people and their families. Earlier social theorists stressed the disappearance

"What's New in Old Age?" by Ethel Shanas is reprinted from *American Behavioral Scientist*, Volume 14, Number 1 (September/October, 1970), pp. 5-11, by permission of the publisher, Sage Publications, Inc., and by permission of author.

of the extended family in industrial societies. The American, British, and Israeli contributors report, however, that studies of the aged in their countries indicate that in old age the relationships between old people and their children and kinsmen increase as old people call upon the family for help in coping with the larger society. Furthermore, children and relatives are the major source of emotional support for old people. As Irving Rosow points out, while the social world of the aged contracts, this does not apply to their association with their children. Indeed, it may be argued that within industrial societies the aged are able to survive only because of the psychological and other supports given them by their families.

The pessimistic theme deals with the relationships between the aged and the larger society in which they live. The situation of the aged vis-à-vis the larger society is expected to worsen in the foreseeable future. There will be greater social distance between the young and the old. The contributors to this issue anticipate that the economic situation of the aged will deteriorate further in comparison with the economic situation of those still at work, particularly should there be sustained economic growth. A downgrading of the aged in terms of their claims on national economies is expected. If societies must choose among various claimants, help will go to the young, not to the old. All of the authors foresee rapid social structural changes in the near future. Such changes will place greater stress on the aged as the latter attempt to accommodate. Many old people, particularly the most work-oriented, the widowed, and the more rigid personalities, will be unable to do so. The aged will be pushed out of the larger society and forced to rely more and more on their families and kin.

As Bernice Neugarten points out,

these are foreseeable short-run effects. It is appropriate that the first paper, that of Professor Neugarten, discusses the roles of the aged both now and in the future. Mrs. Neugarten indicates that increased tension between age groups may be occurring and that overt anger directed toward the aged may also be increasing. In response to such hostility the aged may become a more vocal group, more demanding of what they see as their rights. While hostility between age groups may already confront us, it is possible that, in the long run, the position of the old will improve as they become successively "younger" in body and mind. Age differentiations based on the calendar may diminish in importance throughout the adult life span as other measures of competence are substituted for calendar years.

The next three papers—those by Gordon Streib, Helena Lopata, and Irving Rosow—deal with the family life of old people, and the roles of friends and neighbors in the life of the elderly. Professor Streib begins his paper by pointing out that in our youth-oriented culture, old age is not a captivating topic. Scholars interested in the family are therefore more likely to study the young husband and wife rather than the mature couple despite the fact that maturity may have a longer calendar span than youth. In his paper, Streib outlines the different family structures to be found in later life, and makes some prognoses about which characteristics of older families will persist until the end of the present century. Finally, he considers how the older family would change with the restructuring of various social systems within the United States. As Streib looks into the future, he sees more and more old people living apart from children and relatives, and more and more old people living in age-segregated communities. He points out that, contrary to the teachings of earlier sociologists, there is no evidence that older people find that period of their lives when children leave the parental home particularly painful. Indeed, many middle-aged and older couples view this as a period of freedom. It may be expected then that more and more old people will be seeking family "intimacy at a distance."

As Professor Streib indicates, however, the ability to maintain households separate from the young, although much desired by old people, is related to three problem areas over which the elderly have no control. These areas are widowhood, declining health, and inflation.

The first of these problem areas—widowhood—is the subject of the paper by Professor Helena Lopata. Mrs. Lopata deals with the social involvement of American widows. Widowhood in this country has hardly been studied, but there are more than nine million widows in the United States, their life style must have some impact on the remainder of the population, even apart from its effect on their families and their friends. As one views the family life of the elderly, it is obvious that most older men are married and living in a household with a wife, while most older women are widows. This difference in marital status between the sexes is the result of two factors: men tend to marry women younger than themselves, and women outlive men.

In American society, unlike traditional societies, the role of the widow is not spelled out. On the surface, then, our society appears to offer the widow a choice of social roles and many alternative life styles. In practice, however, widowhood means that a woman's engagement with the social structure is broken. For the older woman, the loss of a husband is more than the loss of a marital partner. In many ways, her ties to the larger community were not as an individual, but as part of a husband-wife dyad. Usually, a woman who is widowed develops no new or replacement roles for the role of the wife. She becomes isolated, and not through her choice. The major reason for her isolation is that American society does not prepare people to reengage themselves once a major social role is removed. Americans lack the competence to cope with changes in the environment that involve changes in their self-conception.

The paper by Professor Rosow deals with the changing environment of the aged. Old people, widowed or not, live in a contracting social world. The dominant theme of old age is loss—the loss of social roles and group memberships. As these losses take place the elderly tend more and more to center their associations on their family and relatives, their friends and their neighbors.

The family remains the core of social relationships in old age. While the social world of old people contracts, this contraction does not apply to their relationships with their children. Friendship patterns, however, tend to be independent of relations with children. The friends of old people, like the friends of the young, resemble them not only in age, but in sex, marital status, and social class. The opportunities for friendship in old age, therefore, are greatest where the neighbors of old people are also their peers. What this means is that the aged in residential concentrations of old people are less isolated than other old people, and more likely to interact with those around them. Housing planners have stressed age-integration, reflecting perhaps their own antipathy to a concentration of old people. The Rosow paper, however, shows that not age-integration, but instead age-segregation where the aged have peers available to them, noticeably increases the social integration of the aged.

The next two papers—those by Juanita Kreps and Harold Sheppard—are closely related. Turning from the old person's family and his friends, these papers deal with the work role of the older person and his overall economic status. In the first of these papers, Professor Juanita Kreps states categorically that, both absolutely and in relation to the income of other segments of the population, the present low incomes of the aged are likely to persist within the foreseeable future. Despite wishful thinking to the contrary, Professor Kreps feels that in an economy distinguished by technological change and an expanding labor force, retirement is necessary. Economic deprivation of the nonworking aged then is generated in the process of technological advance and growth. Further, as real income of the employed increases with economic expansion, the real income of retirees, which is based on earlier work experience, will decrease. It is only through some scheme which will relate retirement benefits to the growth of real income that most retirees can maintain themselves outside of poverty.

Harold Sheppard's paper focuses on the older worker. Like Professor Kreps, Dr. Sheppard stresses that the older worker cannot be considered apart from other workers. In a thoughtful discussion Dr. Sheppard states that while the long-time trend is for men to withdraw from the labor forces at earlier and earlier ages, we still do not know the extent to which the giving up of work is a free choice and the extent to which such withdrawal is a grasping at "straws," with older men choosing to receive Social Security benefits simply because jobs are no longer available to them. Dealing with workers as individuals, Sheppard points out the destructive personal effect of retirement for many men. On the societal level, Sheppard indicates that there may be limits to the extent to which the working-age population will want to pay to maintain the elderly at a decent standard of living. He stresses that greater efforts may have to be made to combat early retirement in order both to lessen the burden of nonproductive persons upon the work force and to make retirement much more of an option or true choice for the individual worker.

The two European papers, by Dr. Jean Huet and Dorothy Wedderburn, deal with special aspects of aging in France and in Britain. It is apparent from these papers that in these industrialized countries, just as in the United States, the aged are now a large enough proportion of the population to present a problem to the body politic. Huet's paper deals with old age as a political problem. Like Dr. Sheppard and Professor Kreps, Dr. Huet is concerned with the costs of the elderly to the society. What proportion of national income should be reserved to the elderly? How much does an old man cost? How much should he cost? Dr. Huet sounds a warning note when he states that a politics of expansion means choices in favor of youth. In effect, this is what one is seeing in the United States at this time. Manpower training, efforts to increase real income, programs to provide health care to the poor—all of these diverse activities are focused on youth.

Mrs. Wedderburn's paper bridges the gap between sociology and economics in a discussion of the economic situation of old people in Britain and of how older people are integrated into British society. Like Dr. Sheppard, Mrs. Wedderburn stresses that work and the income work produces are probably the most important integrators of the individual into a capitalistic society. However, despite the British government's emphasis on keeping older people in the labor force, the proportion of old people in that country taking their pensions at the earliest possible age is rising. In Britain, as in the United States, this creates a group which lives on an income level well below current earnings. Further, the aged in Britain suffer because social services for the aged—no more than for other groups—are not seen as contributing to the overall goal of economic growth. Like Professors Streib and Rosow in their discussion of old people in the United States, Mrs. Wedderburn indicates that the family relationships of the elderly are strong and viable. However, family relationships can integrate old people into only one of the structures of a society.

The paper by Hanna Weihl, "Aging in Israel," deals with the problems of aging in a new multinational state. Israel, as Miss Weihl indicates, has a population of immigrants from all over the world. There are very few elderly Israelis who are native-born. Within the state, however, there is a distinction between veterans and newcomers, the veterans being those who arrived in Israel prior to 1948, the year of Israel's independence. While the veteran aged occupy many positions of power within the society, many of the newcomers are hardly assimilated and, for many among them, only the childrens' services as buffers between them and the larger society make their functioning possible. Israel is an ideal laboratory for the study of a situation in which the old have to adjust not only to their own inevitable bodily changes, but also to a language which they may hardly understand and often do not read, and to structural and normative forms to which they are strangers.

The last paper in the issue is by an American psychiatrist, Dr. Robert Butler. As Dr. Butler views American society, its dominant theme is change, yet the middle-aged and elderly are discouraged from changing. Dr. Butler makes a plea for society to allow greater freedom of life styles for the middle-aged and elderly. The aged, like the young, must be encouraged to change, and must be ready to change. We must cease to be punitive toward those who evolve new life styles in accommodating change. The fact is that much of human behavior is maladaptive. It is only by psychological readiness for what is new that man can continue to cope with the social and technological changes of our era.

Reviewing the papers, one is impressed by their thoughtfulness, and by the way in which all the authors relate the aged to other population groups and consider aging against a backdrop of social structure. No one grows old in a vacuum.

What, then, is new in old age? What's new is the general agreement among scholars that in industrial societies the modified extended family provides a locus for the elderly and assists them in coping with an increasingly complex environment, and, on the other side, the overall agreement that age-ism, or the increasing hostility between the young and the old, will operate to make the situation of the aged more difficult in the foreseeable future.

The aging of populations, however, is inevitable in developed societies. In the long run, people are healthier and they do live longer. One way to control the hostility between the young and the old is for behavioral scientists to focus their thinking and their planning regarding the elderly in the direction of giving the aged more freedom and more options for change and growth. The calendar is a less and less useful index to individual capacities and capabilities. We are coming to accept the emancipation from the calendar for the young; would we deny such emancipation to the old?

Old People: Their Friends and Neighbors

Irving Rosow

The purpose of this paper is to summarize concisely what has been learned about old people's relations to their friends and neighbors and to indicate several significant areas for future research. It is certainly important to be aware of continuities in old age, those relatively stable features of middle age that continue into retirement and the later years. But our present concern is with the specific patterns in old age that typify this stage of life.

SOCIAL WORLD CONTRACTION AMONG THE AGED

The foremost condition of the problem is that the aged live in a contracting social world in which their participation declines, notably sharply after age seventy-five (Rosow, 1962; Smith, 1966). This has two aspects. First, their activity in formal organizations of all kinds is drastically reduced (Wright and Hyman, 1958; Dotson, 1951). At the same time, they apparently also lose friends, and their informal associations with them diminish (Rose, 1965; Rosen and Neugarten, 1960; Blau, 1961). Second, they enter a life stage distinguished by a severe loss of social roles (Rosow, 1962). Of those over sixty-five, almost one-half are widowed, including one-fifth of the men and over half of the women; more than two-thirds of the men are no longer working, mainly because of poor health or compulsory retirement; income declines drastically to less than half of what was earned before retirement and by substantially more than this for widows; and about fifteen percent of the age group is seriously limited in its activity by major health problems (Rosow, 1967: 2-4, 13-20). Accordingly, with their loss of social roles and group memberships, their social participation is diverted from formal to informal arenas and reduced from more to fewer associates. The associations that they do have are centered in informal groups: family and relatives, friends and neighbors. Insofar as their viable sociable world is reduced to these four groups, the groups become alternative possibilities for social intercourse. Consequently, to be set in perspective, an analysis of old people's relations to friends and neighbors should take this into account and be extended to include children and relatives as well. While space precludes a detailed analysis, we will at least review the major outlines of the relations to these various groups.

Reference Group Salience

The relative salience of old people's informal reference groups varies with the context, so that for different purposes they are ordered in different priorities of eligibility and preference. For financial assistance, older persons look only to their adult children (or, in the case of the childless, only to relatives—although much less frequently). However, this orientation is significantly lower (1) in the working class than in the middle class and (2) when there are no children living in town. But under all conditions, friends and neighborhoods are absolutely excluded as possible sources of financial help. People look only to their closest family members, primarily children, for financial aid, and there are no functional substitutes for them among other personal associates.

On the other hand, for care in illness, especially longer illness, people also look first to their children, but neighbors are second in importance—particularly for widows and those living alone. Indeed, neighbors often become primary for persons without local children. Generally, relatives and friends are of minor importance and the aged expect little of them. Thus, there are flexible substitutes for the family in this context, with neighbors the preferred alternative after children.

But for certain problems in old age, children are inappropriate reference figures, and age peers are required. This is most apparent in the selection of possible role models in aging. While few older persons have any particular age mates whom they especially admire, those who have select them mainly from relatives or friends. Neighbors are named often only by those with many old neighbors, but under these conditions, they are extremely important reference figures.

However, each of these contexts is quite specific, and from one to another, family norms or functional appropriateness weight the relative priorities differently. When we consider the prominence of each group in a neutral context without such constraints, a more fundamental picture emerges (although here we lack suitable data on relatives). Basically, as general reference groups, older persons rank these classes in the order of (1) children, (2) neighbors, and (3) friends. This expresses their relative attractiveness and general significance to the aging. Furthermore, their respective strength approximates a mean proportion, so that children are to neighbors as neighbors are to friends. In this fashion, neighbors constitute a viable alternative to children, and friends are an alternative to neighbors. But friends are not a significant challenge to children. (For details on all these reference group patterns, see Rosow, 1967: chs. 5-6.)

The relations to these groups simply reflect that while the social world of the aged contracts, this does not apply to their association with children. There is abundant evidence that the social arenas of the elderly are ordered in priorities. As these shrink, they tend to be shed as successive layers of an onion—formal organizations first, and so on. These priorities form a continuum from formal bureaucratic to intimate personal associations. At the core is the family. Not only are relations with children the last to decline, but indeed they are actually sustained in old age rather than reduced—subject, of course, to limitations of residential distance. In other words, whatever their disengagement or loss of contact with other groups, old people's relations with their children are maintained (Rosow, 1967; Chellam, 1964; Cumming and Henry, 1961; Shanas, 1962; Rosenberg, 1970).

Furthermore, friendship patterns tend to be independent of relations with children, so that these function as separate social arenas. The frequency of contact with children and that with friends and neighbors have no *general* reciprocal effect on each other (Rosow, 1967). But this general pattern is subject to sharp qualification for the most disadvantaged older persons; those who are living alone; those who have no local children, especially daughters; and those who experience high role loss—the retired, the widowed, and the sick. Among these specifically disadvantaged aged, there is an inverse relationship between contact with children and with neighbors and friends. As they see less of their children, they see more of their friends and neighbors (Rosow, 1967; Townsend, 1957). To the extent that old people feel deprived of contact with children, they use friends and especially neighbors as a *compensatory* substitute. This is particularly true for elderly parents with children in town, but less so for those whose children all live elsewhere. For people accept the realities of objective absence more easily than a separation that strikes them as one of insufficient concern or neglect (Rosow, 1967: 225-235).

Specifically compensatory neighboring is strongest among those who are the most emotionally dependent on their adult children in a strictly psychological sense. Yet emotional dependence is literally psychological, probably stable throughout adulthood, and completely impervious to life experience or the specific deficits peculiar to old age. Contrary to what one might expect, widowhood, retirement, poverty, poor health, the absence of children, living alone, social isolation, and growing *objective* dependence have absolutely no effect on

the purely *emotional* dependence on children (Rosow, 1967: 235-240). Yet emotional dependence engenders the pathetic irony that people who are the most insatiably involved with their children and who have no other emotionally meaningful relationships are precisely the ones most likely to interact frequently with their neighbors *if* they do not see enough of their children. But this is essentially a social activity to keep busy rather than an intrinsically satisfying interest; it is not an effective emotional substitute for constant contact with their children.

Against this general background of the relative salience of the four groups, we will now consider several features of old people's particular relationship to neighbors and friends. One concern will be to differentiate the aged in terms of their responsiveness to their immediate social environment. This has several aspects, one set involving differences in the composition of the environment and the second, differences among older actors themselves.

Status Homogeneity

Perhaps the foremost principle about the social composition of the environment is that of status homogeneity: Friendships are formed primarily between persons with similar status characteristics. This covers a broad range of elements, starting with age itself, but also including sex, marital status, race, social class, and their various correlates, such as education, ideology and beliefs (Merton and Lazarsfeld, 1954), stage in the life cycle, and so on. As far as the aged are concerned, the research results are clear. Their friends resemble the elderly not only in age, but also in sex, marital status, and social class (Rosow, 1967). An old person's resemblance to his neighbors in status characteristics is directly related to the number of friends he has and inversely related to his isolation (Rosenberg, 1970). One study shows that friendships of older women are discontinued when their status similarities are disrupted, so that those in a circle who are first widowed are quietly dropped by their friends until they themselves in turn become widowed (Blau, 1961). Consequently, a person's social integration may be governed less by his individual attributes than by how these attributes correspond with the characteristics of people around him.

The functional basis for the affiliation of similar persons seems reasonably clear, especially in the later stages of life when competitive striving for scarce values is declining (Dean, 1960; Cumming and Henry, 1961). Status similarities generally provide a strong basis for solidarity because they join persons of like social position who have the same relation to the larger society and who share a common set of life experiences, problems, perspectives, values, and interests. Accordingly, not only do such friendships confer on them the various benefits of group support, but they also afford a vital continuity during the transition from middle to old age.

Age Peer Concentration

Insofar as status homogeneity is such a fundamental factor, friendship opportunities vary directly with the local concentration of age peers. This relationship increases with older people's proximity to each other and the number of statuses they share. Several studies have definitively established that as the aged live among other old people, their friendships and interaction with neighbors increase drastically (Rosow, 1967; Rosenberg, 1970; Messer, 1966). In contrast with those with few old neighbors, they have more friends, see them more often, and show a higher level of social activity. Indeed, the importance of these

nearby peers is potentially so great that even a single confidant can mean the difference between an older person's stability and demoralization (Lowenthal, 1964a, 1964b). Hence, people are unequivocally integrated into friendship groups to the extent that they have older neighbors who effectively constitute their potential friendship field. Furthermore, the larger this potential field, the less likely are older people to have younger friends. Their social activity and friendships are restricted to age peers by more than the growth of sheer opportunity for such friends (Rosow, 1967). Consequently, their local integration increases disproportionately to the growing concentration of old residents.

This simply underscores the fact that the relationship between the local concentration and social activity of old people is not strictly linear, but increases disproportionately to concentration. There is a threshold effect in which minimally half the dwelling units in a residential setting must have an older person before strong neighboring patterns are stimulated and interaction is significantly intensified (Rosow, 1967).

Mutual Aid

Such socializing is only one reflection of group embeddedness, but other kinds of group support develop as well. Various forms of mutual aid, primarily care in illness, are also correlated with residential concentration (Rosow, 1967). The principal beneficiaries of this care are the most vulnerable older persons, the widowed and others living alone, the childless, those without local children, and those in the poorest health. In areas with high concentration of the aged, neighbors basically provide the care for these most dependent people even in longer, more serious illnesses. Under these conditions, of those who live alone but have comparatively few old neighbors, one-third go completely without any care in contrast to fourteen percent of those with many old neighbors (Rosow, 1967). In other words, more than twice as many of these people are untended at all when they live with few age peers nearby. This simply symbolizes fundamental differences in the character of group life that develops when significant numbers of older people live together, not only in their sociability, but also in meeting various dependency needs and crises. The group provides significant resources for its members and gives them a genuine sense of security about meeting future emergencies (Rosow, 1967). This is reflected in the extent to which elderly neighbors become more significant to the aged than their other friends (Rosow, 1967).

There are also other correlates of high residential concentration. People in these settings are more likely than others to know personally old people whom they greatly admire (Rosow, 1967), and such viable role models can facilitate their own adaptation to old age. Further, residents with more friends among their neighbors are also more likely to be satisfied with where they live and to be less willing to move elsewhere (Langford, 1962; Rosow, 1967). Indeed, in one study, differences in old people's preference for their present residence over their previous one could be accounted for solely in terms of the increase in their friends (Rosow, 1967).

Social Integration

The overall principle is clear: residential concentration of the aged significantly increases their social integration and group supports.

But this general proposition is subject to some qualification. First, older persons are not equally sociable or positively oriented to their neighbors, even age mates. A distinction can be drawn between those whom Merton (1957) in another context called locals and cosmo-

politans. While most persons are quite amenable to neighboring, others positively avoid it, mainly because their significant reference groups are outside or else because they want no friends or involvements at all (Rosow, 1967). However, when these persons are set aside and only those considered who are socially interested, then the original relationship between local concentration and social interaction is strengthened (Rosow, 1967).

Second, aside from their personal sociability, some people are more responsive than others to residential concentration and disproportionately capitalize on its social opportunities. Those over 75, women, and the maritally unattached are more sensitive than others to these opportunities and exploit them; similarly, a high loss of major roles (retirement, widowhood, and poor health) sensitizes middle-class persons to their surroundings and involves them more deeply in them, although not to the general level of those in the working class (Rosow, 1967).

Further, high concentration of the aged reduces by one-half the involuntary isolation of those who are interested in neighboring. However, in terms of these persons, this still leaves one-eighth in the working class and one-fourth in the middle class socially isolated. Their passivity in the face of the active life around them demoralizes them significantly more than those isolates living where there is comparatively little neighboring (Rosow, 1967). This indicates that even under optimal conditions, substantial minorities of socially interested old people cannot take advantage of the social opportunities that are available to them.

Social Class

Finally, the effect of greater residential concentration differs somewhat according to social class. This modifies fundamental class patterns in friendship that are not peculiar to old age. Generally, middle-class persons have significantly more friends than those in the working class. At the same time, working-class people are far more dependent on their place of residence for friendship formation and their social life (Smith et al., 1954; Rosow, 1967; Rosenberg, 1970). Yet despite this local dependence, old middle-class respondents have more friends in their neighborhood or section of town (Rosow, 1967).

This paradox is accounted for by the interaction of two factors that result in different social class patterns: localism selectivity and residential mobility. Basically, working-class people move more often and their social life is locally focused; middle-class persons have a longer residential tenure and are more selective in their formation of friends. Also, length of residence is strongly correlated with number of local friends (Langford, 1962), and this increase with residential tenure is greater in the middle class than the working class (Rosow, 1967). Consequently, because working-class people move more frequently and make friends with successive sets of neighbors, their friends are scattered around town over a larger number of neighborhoods. But, because middle-class persons live where they are for a longer time, despite their selectivity they gradually accumulate a larger number of friends within the neighborhood than the locally dependent working-class people (see Smith et al., 1954; Rosow, 1967: 60-63).

However, this general pattern is modified inasmuch as older people move significantly *less* often than younger persons, particularly the retired working-class aged who tend to be residentially stable. Because of their residential stability and strong local dependence, the working-class old have more friends among their neighbors even though their middle-class counterparts have a larger total number of friends (Rosow, 1967; Kutner et al., 1956; Hunter and Maurice, 1953). This obtains even when residential concentration and interest in neighboring are held constant (Rosow, 1967), for local dependence in the working class tends to be pervasive and overriding. But though the working-class aged have more friends where they live, middle-class persons may respond relatively as strongly to the social opportunities presented by many old neighbors. Despite their different class norms about local friendships, among the socially interested and those who have lost many roles, the proportional increase in neighboring with greater residential concentration is virtually identical in both social classes (Rosow, 1967).

One consequence of manual workers' local dependence is a significant class difference in the sheer definition of friends. Middle-class people distinguish between friends and neighbors while those in the working class do not. Nonmanual respondents differentiate neighbors who are acquaintances, neighbors who are friends, and friends who are *not* neighbors on an implicit basis of social closeness. But among manual workers, the two terms are virtually synonymous. For all practical purposes, their friends simply *are current* neighbors, while former neighbors are in effect previous friends whom they seldom if ever see (Rosow, 1967). In other words, in conceiving their viable social world, their local orientation also subsumes a present time focus.

CONCLUSIONS

This brief review can only summarize a few major features of old people's relations to their friends and neighbors and thereby oversimplifies a complex problem. The aged certainly live in a contracting social world. The relative salience of their reference groups varies with the context and the problem. Basically, they rank their general reference groups in the order of family, neighbors, and other friends. While old people's social worlds contract, their association with children does not. Their friendships are generally independent of relations with children, so that these are separate social arenas. Among the most disadvantaged and vulnerable aged, there is an inverse relationship between contact with children and contact with neighbors and friends. Specifically compensatory neighboring is strongest among persons who are the most emotionally dependent on their children.

Friendships are formed primarily between old persons with similar status characteristics. Their friendship opportunities, group supports, and social integration vary directly with the local concentration of age peers. The relation between this local concentration and the social activity of old people is not strictly linear, but increases disproportionately to concentration. Various forms of mutual aid, primarily care in illness, are also correlated with residential concentration. But elderly persons are not equally sociable or positively oriented to their neighbors. Some avoid local involvements while others are particularly sensitive to residential concen-

tration and disproportionately capitalize on its opportunities. High concentration reduces by one-half the involuntary isolation of those who are socially interested.

The effect of residential concentration differs somewhat according to social class. Because of residential stability and their strong local dependence, the working-class old have more friends among their neighbors even though middle-class persons have a larger total number of friends. But for the socially interested and those who have lost many roles, the *proportional* increase in neighboring with greater residential concentration is virtually identical in both social classes. Middle-class people distinguish between friends and neighbors while these are synonymous to those in the working class.

Many problems remain for future research, but several areas are particularly important: (1) the *qualitative* character of old people's relations to children, relatives, friends, and neighbors; (2) the conditions and limits in which these four groups can be functional substitutes for one another; (3) the continuities and discontinuities in the relations to these groups through different life stages, particularly between middle age and old age; (4) the potential functions of friendship in compensating for the specific losses of status (income, widowhood) and instrumental roles (retirement).

Creative Aging

Ada Barnett Stough

The field of aging is so complex it becomes difficult to discuss in tangible specific terms. It is fallacious to speak of the *older population* as if it were one constant, unchanging homogeneous segment. To speak of the *characteristics* of older people is to tread on equally fallacious ground. The most authentic statement we can make is that older persons are individuals and only in a very general sense can they be said to have certain common characteristics which distinguish them from the young and the middle-aged.

Much of the literature and most of the action programs center around the visible and acute needs of older people, such as inadequate housing, low income, and poor health care. There is discussion and research on the biology and psychology of aging, but much of it centers on the pathology of the aging mechanism. This is inevitable and necessary. The decrements of aging cannot be ignored, and remedies for diseases of either the body or society cannot come without knowledge of sources and causes. This emphasis on pathology, in both the biological and societal aspects of aging, has, however, tended to obscure more positive social-psychological factors. One of these is the failure of society to help the retiring person to meet the debilitating loss of occupational status which follows retirement and to emphasize his potential for growth and development.

Adequate housing, health, and income could be empty achievements if life for the older person has become mere existence without purpose or meaning. A well-rounded approach to the whole area involves many disciplines. The most appropriate role for recreation is to devise and develop ways to encourage the continued development of individual personality through meaningful use of free time.

This task is not easy. The Puritan ethic is strong and many older people want to devote their time to activities that are akin to work and will result in economic reward and social recognition. Activities unrelated to work, pursued for the sheer joy of doing or learning, are presumably less acceptable. I personally do not think that assumption can be validated until many more creative activities have been developed and pursued, and we have a more extensive basis for testing and judgment.

Reprinted with permission from National Recreation and Park Association. Official publication *Parks and Recreation*, November, 1966.

Future technical and social change will bring even more leisure and, along with it, greater social complexity and increasing dislocation and acute problems to persons in later life. Tomorrow's retirees will be more vigorous, with better education and higher incomes. They will be more interested in mental alertness, social involvement, and physical fitness. Society faces the responsibility to encourage them to expand their horizons and build on their unique potential for growth. It must also work to counteract the pervasive idea that the last of life is only preparation for death.

We are discovering that aging is not necessarily associated with disease; that the changes in the aging organism may be triggered by emotional traumatic experiences; a person can learn at middle or later life the same kinds of things he learned in his teens or early twenties; that the art of aging is just another chapter in the art of living; and that old age is a challenge and could, indeed, be the best time of an individual's life. To learn to know one's self, to pursue the avenues of self-development and fulfillment, is what I call *creative aging*.

The challenge of creative aging to leaders in the recreation field might be measured by the answers to four basic questions:

- Does recreation believe it has a responsibility to older adults?
- Does it have a philosophy?
- Does it have or is it preparing for adequate, trained personnel?
- Is it conducting or planning to conduct research on the role of recreation in relation to increased free time?

The critical periods of an individual's life when recreation is most needed, we are told, are when school life is over, around eighteen, and the period around sixty or sixty-five when an individual retires from his life's work. Most of the programs in recreation departments are for young people and recognition of the leisure-time needs for retired persons is slow in coming.

Basic to almost everything else in a discussion of philosophy is whether recreation programs are to be tailored to meet the needs of older people or whether the old are expected to accept and adapt to those activities originally designed for the young. Closely related is the question concerning criteria of success: Is it the number of programs? Number of participants? What they make and what they do? Or is a program judged by what it does for people as individuals?

Important to a discussion of philosophy is the goal of standards against which older adult programs can be measured. Is the activity designed to capture the interest of the older individual and lift him out of his boredom and loneliness—something to challenge his growth potential—or is it a passive program designed to fill time and perhaps afford a measure of socialization? Dr. Max Kaplan (writing for the social gerontologists) has a relevant observation to make on this point. "*Games* are the *least oriented* to people, since they are most rooted in rules and formal behavior. Paradoxically, games are perhaps the *easiest* type of activity for recreation leaders to organize. Thus, wherever games—checkers, chess, cards, bingo, et cetera—are found to be most popular among groups of older persons, we may reasonably inquire whether this is an activity above and beyond a more meaningful program or whether it is the meat of the recreation schedule."

Recreation faces a dual and really very difficult challenge. It needs to offer a wide and varied program because the present aging population is so diverse in background and interest. At the same time it needs to develop a philosophy on which to base its planning for the future.

More and better trained personnel is needed. Right now there is a shortage of qualified persons to staff senior centers. One more indication of the emphasis on the pathology of aging is the current opinion that senior centers must be run by trained social workers. When the potentialities of older people are recognized to be as important as their problems, the services of a recreation expert will be in as much demand as those of a social worker.

Dr. James Charlesworth and other writers on the subject suggest the need for leisure counselors with wide interests, at home in several disciplines. Such a person would see the inner relationship of leisure and recreation to personality, work, family life, and economic security. He would, in a sense, provide help for living not only during the prime of life but also for the later years. Persons with this broad training will be needed not only in schools and parks and playgrounds, but in churches, industries, housing developments, and senior centers.

The last, and probably the greatest, challenge to the field of recreation for older people is a need for research. Recreation is a good area in which to study motivation, because it creates a milieu in which techniques that make for growth can be distinguished from those which merely pacify. Research can result in valuable information on how to change leisure habits and perhaps determine who is most resistant to change—the public, the elderly, or the recreation specialist.

Recreation can devise experimental designs in which all different kinds of people can be immersed in various kinds of leisure experiences to see what happens. Many ways may be found to explore the possibilities for self-fulfillment and continued growth through recreation. Commercial interests will try hard to fill the free time of tomorrow's retired people with empty entertainment and meaningless squandering. These will be bought and used because individual interests are different and all kinds of diversions are needed. It will be sad, however, if persons who can use and enjoy more substance have to settle for mediocrity because nothing else is available. The field of recreation has an opportunity to make a real contribution to creative aging by demonstrating that leisure can be intense, enjoyable, serious, significant, and a source of inner growth. To do so, however, recreation needs to become more creative itself, to become bold in its search for new ideas and determined in experimenting with these ideas to meet new problems.

Serving the Central City

Pasadena Recreation Department, Pasadena, California

BOY SCOUTS OF AMERICA "Urban Poverty and the Dynamics of Inner-City"
Some Characteristics of Poverty, U.S.A., Boy Scouts of America, 1968.

RICHARD KRAUS "Recreation and Civil Disorder"
Parks and Recreation, National Recreation and Park Association, July 1968.

WILLIAM G. McNAMARA "Widening Horizons"
Parks and Recreation, National Recreation and Park Association, October 1969.

DAVID E. GRAY "The Case for Compensatory Recreation"
Parks and Recreation, National Recreation and Park Association, April 1969.

DONALD A. PELEGRINO "Special Demands of the City"
Leisure-Society-Politics: "The Political Environment of Parks and Recreation" Proceedings 1971, Park and Recreation Administrators Institute, University of California, Davis, 1972.

IRA J. HUTCHISON, JR. "Planning Where the Action Is"
Parks and Recreation, National Recreation and Park Association, July 1968.

JUDITH MURPHY AND RONALD GROSS "The Arts and the Poor"
U.S. Government Printing Office, 1968.

Serving the Central City

By the turn of the nineteenth century the trend toward urbanization became a dominant factor in American life. The completion of continental expansion, the development of new technologies, and changes in national economic patterns brought into being the industrial city. Between 1860 and 1900, urban population nearly quintupled while rural population failed even to double. Thus, in 1900 nearly forty per cent of all Americans were living in cities.

"Deprivation in recreation and park services and facilities is a major source of dissatisfaction among ghetto residents."

Immigration from abroad coupled with increasing discouragement of domestic farm life, in part, brought about this change. People saw in the city an opportunity to achieve financial security along with the prospect of a more exciting life.

Cities mushroomed and grew to such proportions that their sites no longer seemed functional. They increased upward and outward in size, often engulfing neighboring communities and becoming giant megalopolis centers. No longer can political boundaries describe the character or size of a city. With increasing growth, most cities lost their unique character and have become sprawling unidentifiable urban complexes.

"Successful activities will be those that are planned with rather than for the citizens of the community."

What, then, were the origins of this urban mess? The answer lies partly in American attitudes of individualism, partly a disrespect for nature, and often a lack of concern for the public environment. These factors in our frontier history are still predominant. These attitudes together with an absence of city planning skills produced an ill-bred urban environment almost from the beginning. Problems became more complex when, during the 1950s, the white middle class, fully mobile and yearning for suburban life, exodused in great masses into a hodgepodge of outlying areas wholly unprepared for them. This produced a need for services, which brought new commercial ugliness along roadsides and in huge concrete centers.

"The recreation profession is at a crossroad. To do and what to do—to act and how to act—in response to the urban crises is being asked by park and recreation people across the nation."

As city and suburban areas grew, population increases were also occurring. Urban problems were created largely by this rapid growth. Municipal governments, therefore, cannot restrict their concern to activities within legal boundaries for they now find that many of their problems also exist beyond city limits. Shared almost universally with areas outside the cities are problems of air pollution, traffic congestion, water and power supply, treatment of sewage, unemployment, and poor educational quality.

The time is a desperate one for urban America. Can the city become a decent place to live, to work, and for recreation? The image of the core city is slum districts, crime, noise and congestion, and of people who are poor, and generally of ethnic minorities. What then of the city in the future? That will depend upon whether this country can find ways and means of making cities more habitable, or whether the problems of the metropolitan regions are beyond rehabilitation.

This task is too enormous for private enterprise or individuals to tackle. It requires federal subsidy and, in fact, the Federal Government has become increasingly involved in tackling these urban problems. In 1965 Congress created the Department of Housing and Urban Development in the President's Cabinet. The Department administers a wide range of activities including: low- and middle-cost housing, programs of urban renewal, planning for urban and metropolitan growth, the use of open space, community facilities, and problems dealing with mass transportation.

"Recreation is an expression of man's need for man."

Another major national undertaking is that of the Model Cities Program which authorizes the Secretary of HUD to provide grants and technical assistance to help communities of all sizes plan and develop model projects. These are local programs for rebuilding or restoring large sections and neighborhoods of slum and blighted areas by the concentrated and coordinated use of local private and governmental resources. The State of the Cities Commission, also under federal sponsorship, has just issued its provocative and exciting report. Its findings are relevent to the complex problems of urban life and city planning, and bear not only study but action.

"Our end then will not be activity; activity will be the means. Our end will be development of human potential in all its richness and variation."

Alongside federal study and tangible aid private enterprize is playing an enormous role in city improvement. Increasingly we are becoming a nation of white-collar administrators, secretaries, professionals, and business people. An overwhelming proportion of new office buildings for banks, insurance companies, and corporations has taken place in the larger cities. With this new infusion of white-collar jobs, there are definite signs of a small but significant move back from suburbia. Many workers are choosing new high-rise luxury apartments as an alternative to suburban home upkeep and the daily freeway traffic struggle into the City. This trend will help the cities, for to remain dominant cultural centers, cities need a core of people to support their theatres, museums, shops, restaurants, and recreational facilities. It is the people who live in the

"The central city has really become the worn out core of the "social city," filled with a myriad of environmental inadequacies and massive contained inner-city areas of urban poverty."

city who make it an attraction for visitors, especially at night, for they help to create its character; without it there is no reason for one to go downtown, or into the Inner City.

On the other hand, big cities are losing blue-collar and retail jobs as industry builds more and more new manufacturing plants and warehouses on cheap land in the suburbs.

"America has a gap between generally accepted goals and the extent to which the low income can realistically expect to attain them."

Thus, for some time now, a somewhat healthy sorting out of functions is taking blue-collar jobs, as well as truck and industrial pollution, away from the core area and substituting white-collar jobs. It is ironic that while this transfer has been

going on, most of those who hold inner-city jobs have been moving out into the suburbs to live, while minorities, in spite of growing job opportunities in industry, have remained concentrated in the cities. Hopefully, people in both groups who must travel to work will move and live closer to their jobs. For this to materialize depends upon whether minorities can gain access to suburban housing, and whether the cities can offer a lifestyle that appeals to the middle class.

A joint solution would be to increase the number of jobs within the city to include minorities living nearby, thus creating a socially and culturally richer middle class.

"It is the arts which can best help man—and, more important, the poor themselves—to understand the dark, complex, baffling realities of the ghetto.

Presently though, most central city or core areas have deteriorated from neglect for they have long been regarded only as a place to work or carry on business. People have more concern for the communities in which they live than in central areas where they work. Residents of the inner city though, for the most part, are not able to afford housing elsewhere and usually settle in isolated "de facto" ghettos with others of similar cultural backgrounds. To provide a better life for city dwellers, special demands must be met. These include improved housing and transportation facilities, better medical care, and open space for recreational activities. As for meeting recreational needs, some local community programs, such as music and

"There is no point in bringing parks to where the people are, if in the process the reasons that the people are there are wiped out and the park substituted for them."

art festivals, drama groups, and athletics, have been established, as have "pocket" parks through municipal government and local group cooperation.

More action must be taken for as long as there are people living in the city, there will be a need for recreation services designed to provide the urbanite a wide variety of opportunities and experiences. The challenge is great for the situation is complex and no single remedy is at hand which could possibly cure the many needs of people in the city. This chapter titled "Serving the Central City" examines closely the predicament of individuals and groups living there, presents a case for increasing action by those in the recreation profession, and presents some ideas as to what type of action is necessary.

"Political boundaries can no longer describe the character or size of a city. Most cities lost their unique character with increased growth and became sprawling unidentifiable urban complexes."

Urban Poverty and the
Dynamics of Inner-City

Boy Scouts of America

Urbanization is one of the greatest crises our nation has ever faced. While space does not permit an analysis of urbanization, a few of its dimensions are important to further understanding the characteristics of poverty in the inner-city.

Since the turn of the century, there has been a mass migration of the American people to the cities. Seventy percent of the population now lives in what the census defines as "urban places." However, almost all of the population is now living under the influence of an urban society even if not living in what the census defines as an "urban place."

The most dramatic aspect of this urban growth has been the mushrooming of vast metropolitan areas. These metropolitan communities are the most interdependent communities the world has ever known. However, in recent decades as the "social and economic city" with all of its interdependent functions has continued to expand almost without restriction, the central "legal city" has stopped expanding with central city boundaries usually limited to those which existed shortly after the turn of the century. Hundreds of overlapping and provincial governmental authorities are now attempting to relate to these metropolitan areas, a condition which has been termed the "hardening of the boundaries."

For the central cities, a vicious cycle has evolved which engages and reinforces the cycle of poverty discussed above: Into those central city neighborhoods which we now call the inner-city pour millions of refugees from a worse poverty in rural areas. People of wealth and marketable talent move out of the central cities. Industry decentralizes and moves out. The flow of resources into the city declines. The tax base shrinks ($3000 taxable land per capita in Newark and Hoboken—$12,000 taxable land per capita in surrounding suburbs). The tax rate of the central cities goes up, and again, more people and industry move out. Throughout the entire cycle, the need for city services, particularly in the inner-city, becomes more and more severe.

The central city has really become the worn out core of the "social city," filled with a myriad of environmental inadequacies and massive contained inner-city areas of urban poverty. Unwittingly or not, the new suburbs have formed a wall around these central cities which did

This article is reprinted by permission from *Some Characteristics of Poverty, U.S.A.* New Brunswick, New Jersey: Research Service, Boy Scouts of America, 1968, pp. 18-25.

not exist previously. ("Suburb" has actually now become a misnomer—they are no longer just "sub" or dependent upon central cities. Rather, central cities are now also dependent upon suburbs.)

It is this growing disparity between inner-city and suburb—the two poles of metropolitan areas—which is most dramatically responsible for the extreme economic and racial segregation expected to produce major conflicts among urban population in interests, needs and values. Although most of our northern cities will have a majority of Negroes in the years just ahead, the split between inner-city and suburb is increasingly one of socioeconomic difference, particularly as middle-income Negroes follow the white flight to the suburbs.

The inner-city is not only segregated by race and economics, but also by education and civic-mindedness.

The inner-city is, therefore, not just an urban community of decrepit buildings; the inner-city is an urban community of the poor who are, to a large extent, socially and economically isolated from the mainstream of American life. It is an environment of pessimism and hopelessness—a personal reality—for its inhabitants. It is an environment for the culture of poverty in which both its victims and its disabling institutions are inexplicably bound.

LOW INCOME LIFE STYLES

For many poor people today, poverty is more than just the lack of money. Economic deprivation accompanies and is linked to a pattern of attitudes, feelings, values, habits and practices which permeate all areas of life for the poor and are in contrast to life styles of the prevailing middle class. These low income life styles are sometimes collectively referred to as the "culture of poverty."

The characteristics which follow do not reflect the position of all low income persons. There is variation. Still, they do point to a constellation of general differences from the way of more favored groups. Differences are usually of degree rather than of type.

A. *Powerlessness*—The poor are often convinced that they cannot influence the workings of society. They may doubt the possibility of being able to influence their own lives. They have a feeling that the institutions of the larger society are not there to serve their interests. They are able to exercise very little bargaining power in the working or political worlds. In places where the poor have recently begun to exercise power, this has been a cause of unrest among the nonpoor.

B. *Fatalism*—The genuine powerlessness experienced by the poor coupled with a belief in religious predestination is a major source of persistent fatalistic beliefs. What will be—will be—and they see little prospect that they can change the course of their own lives. They see life as unpatterned and unpredictable. This is in sharp contrast to middle class people who believe that they do, in fact, have a sizeable measure of control over their own destinies. Even when optimism is expressed by the poor, it is likely to be in terms of a chance that a lucky break will put them on top.

C. *Present Tense Time Orientation*—A characteristic associated with fatalism is the persistent tendency to think in terms of the present rather than the future. To the poor, what can be seen and touched *now* is real. Their orientation may be toward the immediate satisfactions of the moment rather than toward an anticipated future goal. They live from day to day or week to week and long-range planning is both unrealistic to them and largely absent from their background. Experience has taught them that low income life is too unpredictable and unstable and long-range planning does not pay off. A decision is made in the light of its present yield. The poor often do not understand the continuity of past experiences and current ones. This "bird-in-the-hand" outlook seems more logical and natural.

D. *Security Rather Than Status*—Aspirations are of a far more immediate, urgent, and material nature in contrast to the more middle class value of achievement to meet future needs and aspirations. Usually avoiding the worsening of an already unstable situation, the poor are unwilling to take risks, and seek security rather than advancement.

E. *Limited Alternatives*—Throughout life, the poor view and experience a very narrow range of situations and demands. For example, socially, they seldom go beyond the borders of kinship and neighborhood groups—people much like themselves.

F. *Concreteness*—There is a stress of material rather than intellectual things. The verbal style of the poor has less abstractions and fewer concepts. The poor rely more on pragmatic observation than intellectual processes and are more tied to the world of immediate happenings and sensations. Immediate results are important.

G. *Isolation*—Even though people of low income may live in the midst of a large crowded city, they are and react as isolated people. They are isolated in the sense that they read fewer newspapers, join fewer organizations and know less of the current life of either their community or the larger world. They feel alone and detached from the larger society.

H. *Low Self-image*—Low income persons have a relatively low appraisal of their own worth. America has a gap between generally accepted goals and the extent to which the low income can realistically expect to attain them. Television, the world of advertising and other mass media continuously reinforce for the low income their failure and inadequacy. The person living in a defeatist environment may not expect to succeed; or he may come to expect that illegal behavior is necessary to reach such strongly approved goals. This may lead to withdrawal and further isolation. Such persons need a chain of realistically attainable and successful experiences before their self-image can begin to improve.

I. *Spontaneity*—Many poor people react to situations on the basis of emotions and intuitions rather than by design or time schedule. They are often able to share what they have with compassion and enthusiasm rather than hesitate, count the cost and let the opportunity slip by to help a neighbor in distress. They are also less likely to disguise their true feelings except with many outsiders. This can be a real strength.

J. *Authoritarianism*—The authoritarian theme is a strong underlying factor in interpersonal relationships of the poor. Strength is seen as the valid source of authority. There is a reliance on authority, rather than reason, as the proper source of decision. This characteristic is also reflected in child-rearing practices.

Many low income persons are distrustful and antagonistic of the authority figures of the larger society as well as in their own community.

K. *Division of Marital Responsibility*—The division of responsibility between husband and wife is more formal than in middle class homes. For example, child rearing is usually within the domain of the wife with the husband playing a more passive role in the home. There is a tendency to feel that earning the money is the man's responsibility; spending it wisely is the woman's duty. When a large proportion of income must go for routine necessities, there is less need for joint decisions. There is a relative emotional isolation of spouses from each other.

L. *Extended Family*—Among some low income people (particularly among Spanish-speaking people) there appear to be stronger and wider kinship ties than among middle class people. Visiting seldom extends beyond the kinship circle which more readily includes grandparents, cousins, etc. The poor receive more help from relatives than the non-poor.

M. *Matriarchal Families*—In those homes which are mother-centered, children do not experience the much needed influence of a strong, stable, consistent, loving male figure. For the poor child, the supply of available adequate substitutes for a male model is extremely limited. Many boys of low income communities grow up where their only knowledge of manhood comes from their peers on the street.

Poor children may be classified roughly into three categories—one third live in homes headed by men who have regular low paying jobs, one third in the homes of men who do not work, and one third in homes headed by women. This last one third of poor children is compared to only one out of twenty-three nonpoor children who live in a home without a father. Nearly half of all poor nonwhite children live in homes headed by a woman.

N. *Mutual Aid*—Growing out of the extended family and other personalized, primary-group relationships is the low income strength of cooperativeness and mutual aid. Their greater spontaneous giving to and guiltless acceptance of aid from those close to them is in some contrast to the middle class ethic of more formal exchange and individual responsibility.

O. *Informality*—Low income people tend to have a more informal, personal quality of easy comfortable relationship to people. They often have a warm humor. They frequently lack the impersonal and formalized way of doing things so often associated with a middle class life style. Often, if a low income person cannot relate himself to something in personal, informal terms, he will reject it.

P. *Limited Experience with Formal Organizations*—A critically important low income life style characteristic necessary for the understanding and adaptation of community service agencies is the resistance of low income people to formal organizations, particularly highly structured ones. They have had little or no experience with belonging to formal organizations, serving on committees, or playing formal leadership roles. This is in sharp contrast to the highly organized, complexly structured, largely specialized nature of the prevailing middle class culture. (Paradoxically, some of the strong criticism of the poor today leveled by the middle class stems from the extent of success of some institutions—anti-poverty programs, churches, social agencies—to help the poor organize and be effective as groups.)

Q. *Religious Involvement*—Limited evidence suggests that low income people as a group are likely to be more conservative or orthodox in their beliefs than other groups but to be somewhat less attached to the church. A major reason they are less likely to be church members or attend Sunday worship is their more limited experience with all types of formal associations. However, those poor persons who are involved in church life tend to have a more ardent set of beliefs and these beliefs are more emotionally charged than for middle income groups. This large emotional involvement in religion (for some their only overt emotional involvement) is a prominent source of support and encouragement to the poor.

Low income groups are the most likely to engage in salvationist religions. "Denominational families" have been rank ordered according to socioeconomic status of membership. They are ranked from lower to higher in the following order: Jehovah's Witness, Holiness, Pentecostal, Assembly of God, Eastern Orthodox, Mormon, Baptist, Catholic, Lutheran, Disciples of Christ, Methodists, Friends, Jewish, Christian Scientist, Presbyterian, Congregational, Unitarian, Episcopal.

Recreation and Civil Disorder

Richard Kraus

Two recently issued reports which deal with the crucial problems of minority groups in urban slums are of special interest to recreation and park professionals.

The first, the *Report of the National Advisory Commission on Civil Disorders*,[1] was released to the nation in March 1968. Based on a searching analysis of the wave of rioting and looting that has swept through urban ghettos throughout the United States during the past several years, this report has been hailed as a major social document. While some of its conclusions, such as the identification of "white racism" as a major cause of riots, have not been unanimously accepted, there is general agreement that this report is the most detailed and frank examination of the problem yet undertaken.

What does the report have to say to recreation and park administrators?

RECREATION SERVICES FOUND WANTING

First, it confirms the fact that deprivation in recreation and park services and facilities is a major source of dissatisfaction among ghetto residents. The study of cities where serious riots have occurred since 1965 indicates clearly that there is a reservoir of major grievances in Negro neighborhoods which contributed to the readiness of residents to riot. The Commission identified twelve of the most serious of these; recreation was ranked on the second level of intensity.

First Level:
  1. Police Practices
  2. Unemployment and Underemployment
  3. Inadequate Housing

Second Level:
  4. Inadequate Education
  5. Poor Recreation Facilities and Programs
  6. Ineffectiveness of the Political Structure and Grievance Mechanisms

Reprinted with permission from National Recreation and Park Association. Official publication *Parks and Recreation*, July, 1968.

1. *Report of the National Advisory Commission on Civil Disorders* (New York: Bantam Books (paperback, $1.25), 1968), 608 pp.

Third Level:

7. Disrespectful White Attitudes
8. Discriminatory Administration of Justice
9. Inadequacy of Federal Programs
10. Inadequacy of Municipal Services
11. Discriminatory Consumer and Credit Practices
12. Inadequate Welfare Programs

Grievances concerning municipal recreation programs were found in a large majority of 20 cities that were studied intensively; typically, references were made to inadequate facilities (parks, playgrounds, athletic fields, gymnasiums and pools) and the lack of organized programs to serve Negroes. Throughout the study, the Commission gave examples of cities where recreation had been a focus of demands by ghetto residents, or the scene of initial disturbances: Chicago, Tampa, Cincinnati, Atlanta, and a number of cities in northern New Jersey: Newark, Elizabeth, Plainfield and New Brunswick. It documented too that this was a concern of long standing. For example, in a study carried on in Detroit by the University of Michigan (this was before the bloody Detroit riot of 1967), ghetto residents expressed major dissatisfactions which included the following:

> A significant proportion believed municipal services to be inferior; 35 percent were dissatisfied with the schools; 43 percent with the city's contribution to the neighborhood; 77 percent with the recreational facilities; 78 percent with police services . . .

Based on this analysis, one might have expected that the Commission's recommendations would have given serious weight to the need to improve and strengthen recreation and park facilities and services—and to provide funds to do this job. Disappointingly, however, this was not the case.

RECOMMENDATIONS OVERLOOK RECREATION

In two major sections of the report, detailed recommendations were made by the Commission. These included such areas as the development of neighborhood task forces, expanded legal services to the poor, expanded employment opportunities, improved police practices and riot control procedure, and improved political representation. Lengthy recommendations were made with respect to four areas: employment, education, the welfare system, and housing. However, recreation is not dealt with at all in these recommendations—with the exception of a one-word reference to it as a form of community service which might be provided, using school buildings. Typically, in the index of the report, "education" is listed 55 times and "employment" 47 times. "Recreation" is listed once.

What does all this mean?

First, the Commission correctly reported its findings—that the lack of adequate recreation is perceived as a major grievance by black people in urban slums themselves, and that it is frequently the cause of initial disturbances. However, it failed to follow up on this finding by identifying recreation as a significant form of service in improving the status and living conditions of the urban poor. The lack of any recommendation in this area indicates that the Commission failed to assign any real priority to it in its own deliberations and conclusions.

REPORT ON PUBLIC RECREATION AND THE NEGRO

Another dimension to the problem is provided by a study carried out by the author of this article in 1967, under the sponsorship of the Center for Urban Education, a regional research branch of the United States Office of Education. The report of this study, titled *Public Recreation and the Negro: A Study of Participation and Administrative Practices*, was published in April, 1968[2]; it was based on an analysis of program services provided in 24 suburban communities in New York, New Jersey and Connecticut, and in the five boroughs of New York City. Briefly stated, the report reveals the following:

1. In the communities studied, Negroes tended to participate in patterns that varied widely from those of white residents, in terms both of activities and age groupings. In part, this was obviously a matter of social class differences, but other factors seemed to be involved as well.

2. Despite frequent citations in textbooks as to the "democratizing" effects of recreation, it appeared that these public recreation programs were doing little to achieve integrated participation or better relations among ethnic groups in the community. In sports, particularly, there was considerable team segregation, and hostility which appeared to be evoked by inter-district or interracial competition.

3. Directors reported a variety of administrative problems related to the behavior of both whites and blacks in their programs. Suburban recreation directors tended to blame the Negroes for causing their major difficulties; directors in New York City indicated that their most serious problems came from the withdrawal of whites from programs which Negroes had entered.

4. While all programs purport to serve both races equally, and to provide comparable facilities, in most cases Negro neighborhoods possessed the oldest, most limited and run-down recreation facilities in the communities studied.

5. A substantial proportion of Negroes were employed in public recreation and park programs; however, they held few supervisory or administrative positions.

6. In those communities which had developed school desegregation programs, almost no effort had been made to involve Negro youngsters who had been bussed into formerly white schools in after-school recreation programs. Indeed, bussing schedules made this impossible in most cases.

7. Few recreation directors had meaningful contacts with anti-poverty organizations, with groups of neighborhood residents or other agencies that would help them serve minority group members more effectively. There was almost no deliberate effort to achieve co-racial participation, or to provide specially designed services in Negro neighborhoods that might serve hard-to-reach groups.

Fuller details of this study may be found in the report, for which the source is given below.

IMPACT OF REPORTS

What is the impact of these two reports?

The second one reveals many of the details of how Negroes participate or do not participate in public recreation programs, together with the problems surrounding their involvement and the

2. *Public Recreation and the Negro: A Study of Participation and Administrative Practices* (New York: Center for Urban Education, 105 Madison Avenue (paperback, 25c single copies, 21-50 copies 20c), 1968) 100 pp.

administrative policies found in this area—all as reported by recreation directors who are themselves white in every case. It adds up to a picture of inadequate service, despite the concern and in most cases, the determination of recreation directors to do the best job they can in this area.

The first study reveals the effect of such deprivation, in terms of the grievances held by ghetto residents—and the turbulent outcomes that stem from the grievances.

Both studies, finally, lead to the conclusion that, if fully adequate facilities and services are to be provided in disadvantaged neighborhoods, it cannot be done on a stop-gap, seasonal basis—or as a response to immediate crises. For recreation, it is essential that there be a fuller understanding of the role that it must play in enriching and upgrading the quality of community life for all groups, and particularly those who are in the greatest need and least able to serve themselves constructively. This understanding must be accompanied by growing willingness to provide adequate funding for imaginative and well-staffed park and recreation programs and facilities in urban ghettos. If this does not happen, we can confidently look forward to reading a series of later editions of the *Report of the National Advisory Commission on Civil Disorders* in the decades ahead.

Widening Horizons

William G. McNamara

Many sports, recreation and educational leaders labor under the misconception that the supplemental programs so desperately needed by the inner city cannot be initiated until substantial additional funds and personnel are made available. This myth has been exploded by a group of volunteer women in Washington, D.C., who reasoned that there is, in any community, an abundance of educational and cultural resources available to youth which has only to be mobilized and organized into a planned program. "Widening Horizons" was started by a few concerned volunteers and has successfully operated for the past seven years, primarily with voluntary help.

In 1962, Mrs. Arthur Goldberg, wife of the then Supreme Court Justice, organized a meeting of concerned wives of top officials in the federal and District of Columbia government agencies and private business firms. Out of this meeting came a program of "Tours for Teens" called Widening Horizons. Its objective was to acquaint junior and senior high school students with cultural, educational and occupational opportunities in the immediate area.

Staff members of federal and private agencies, industries, cultural institutions, and the District Public Schools joined forces with adult and youth volunteers from the community to build a program designed to encourage potential dropouts to remain in school. The fact that education is vital to success in today's world was constantly stressed.

A LOOK AT THE ADULT WORLD

Originally, the program consisted of free tours, films, lectures, trips to workshops, offices, hospitals and museums. The aim was to give students a close-up view of the adult world of work and to open their eyes to the wide range of occupations available to them.

Supervision of the program was placed under the Urban Service Corps of the District of Columbia Public schools which provided free transportation to and from the various activities. Transportation was originally funded by the Agnes Meyer Foundation and later by Title I, of the Elementary and Secondary Education Act.

From a modest undertaking which served about 150 students during its first year of operation, Widening Horizons grew until the summer of

Reprinted with permission from National Recreation and Park Association. Official publication *Parks and Recreation*, October, 1969.

1965 when nearly 2,500 students participated during July and August. During the winter of 1966 it received additional funding through the United Planning Organization and hired its first full-time staff director, who was charged with development of an experimental in-school program of Tours for Teens. Initially, the three junior high schools with the highest concentration of deprived youth were selected. That year, 100 ninth-grade youngsters from each of the three schools participated in the winter phase of Widening Horizons.

Today, more than 30 agencies are providing tours for Washington youth ranging from the Department of Agriculture to Interior to Treasury. In addition, the Department of Defense runs a large-scale sports program.

VOLUNTEER BOARD OF DIRECTORS

A board of 25 volunteers directs the program. The full-time director, assisted by three coordinators and one secretary, administers it. They work primarily through organized groups—schools, orphanages, Police Boys Clubs and organized neighborhood groups. In each of these groups an adult volunteer functions as the neighborhood coordinator.

Widening Horizons has had its great moments. One of the first came in the summer of 1966 when a small art program, "The Tom Sawyer Project," engaged 30 youngsters, under the direction of the Curator of Education of the Corcoran Art Gallery, in painting 18 panels of a fence around the partially completed Kennedy Center for the Performing Arts. The project attracted national and international attention. Subsequently it was taken over by the Kennedy Center in an effort to involve children from all 50 states and foreign

countries. Today, a new set of panels is unveiled each month.

While the tour program was considered successful, the members of the Board had a vague feeling that something was missing. Various members noted that the attention span of some of the participants was only one to two hours. After that, they became restless. Consequently, the ladies began searching for a productive outlet for the energies of the youngsters.

SPORTS BALANCE PROGRAM

In 1967, Mrs. Cyrus R. Vance, wife of the then Deputy Secretary of Defense, became chairman of Widening Horizons. Shortly thereafter it was suggested that sports might be what was needed to balance the program. And at this stage, the opinion of the author was sought. He pointed out that research conducted by the International Council on Sports and Physical Education revealed that:

1. A youngster's self-image and self-confidence improves as his physical fitness improves.
2. Physically fit youth consistently make higher marks in school than do the less fit.
3. Sports are one of the most effective means for building endurance, self-discipline, will-to-win and teaching teamwork—all vital traits for success in today's adult world.
4. Sports can bridge the socioeconomic differences in society and bring together representatives from all levels for peaceful group experiences.
5. Sports offer youth from the lower socioeconomic levels the quickest and easiest route to national and international recognition.
6. Excellence in sports can be the key to a college education for many poor youngsters.

Consequently, the plan advocated that:

1. Primary emphasis would be placed upon the socalled "minor" sports so that participants might make significant progress in a short period. (Deprived youth *must* win some ribbon, medal or other form of recognition rather quickly. Otherwise, they become discouraged and quit.)
2. Sports would be selected which would require little expense and for which outstanding military coaching might be available, on a voluntary basis.
3. Long- and short-range goals would be established and a challenge issued to the participants in each sport.
4. The program would include only organized youth and neighborhood groups. Each group was to be responsible for the transportation of their youth, discipline and any necessary paperwork. Volunteer coaches would be responsible for nothing but coaching.

The sports, goals and challenges recommended were:

I. SWIMMING:

Goal: Participation in the 1972 Olympics in Munich Germany.

Challenge: The USA has never had a Negro national champion. Be the first.

II. CANOEING:

Goal: To be the first Negro canoeists in Washington, D.C.'s annual Presidential Regatta. And, later, participation in the 1972 Olympic Games.

Challenge: You can win an Olympic medal if you have the determination and the capacity for hard work.

III. SOCCER:

Goal: Participation in the 1972 Olympic Games.

Challenge: America fares poorly in soccer, the national sport in 121 countries. Everyone thinks that Americans can't learn the game. Let's show the world!

IV. BOWLING:

Goal: Introduce youngsters to a lifetime sport and one of the most popular mixed sports.

Challenge: Become a television bowler and win money and fame.

V. PHYSICAL FITNESS:

Goal: Win the coveted Marine Corps Certificate of Physical Fitness and later participate in the National High School Physical Fitness Meet, with a chance at a college scholarship.

Challenge: The Marine Corps builds men. Can you measure up to its standards?

The sports programs were initiated during the summer of 1967. The swimming team selected a name, "Stafford's Sea Devils," registered with the AAU and prepared for competition. Initially, the team took in orphans and wards of the court from the D.C. Junior Village, plus Negro and white youths from different socioeconomic levels. This was the only competitive swimming team east of the Mississippi that would accept Negroes.

Families who could afford to were asked to pay a small monthly fee. From this small treasury, sweat suits were purchased and entry fees into meets were paid for all team members.

Many of the members of the team had to be taught to swim. Nevertheless, they progressed rapidly under the two hour a day, six days a week, training sessions. By the end of the summer, the team had won several meets and they were beginning to "jell" as a team.

PHYSICAL FITNESS INSTRUCTION

At the beginning of the summer, the instructors from the USMC Physical Fitness Academy conducted a day-long course for Police Boys Club instructors on how to train their boys for the USMC High School Physical Fitness Test. At the end of the summer the Marines returned and conducted the tests. The individual championship trophy was won by a boy from Junior Village and the team trophy was won by Police Boys Club #6.

Several days before Labor Day a youth festival was held at Fort Meyer, Virginia. The Honorable Cyrus R. Vance attended and watched his wife present attractive certificates to every boy and girl who had participated in the Widening Horizons program. Members of the school board and a number of other dignitaries also participated. The U.S. Army Band entertained with musical numbers.

When cold weather came, all the teams, except the swimming team, were disbanded. The swimmers continued with their six days a week training grind and a number began to show real promise. In the Thanksgiving AAU meet four placed—against top-flight competition.

Mrs. John S. Foster, Jr., wife of the director of Defense Research and Engineering, succeeded Mrs. Vance as chairman of the program in March 1968. She arranged for the canoeists to train at the Anacostia Naval Air Station and several eight-man war canoes were borrowed from the U.S. Olympic Canoeing Development Committee. The teams went to work.

Students of Shaw Junior High, which has the highest concentration of disadvantaged youth of any school in Washington, participated in the program. The boys worked hard and in September, after 17 months of arduous training, they reached their first goal by becoming the first Negroes to compete in the canoeing event of the Presidential regatta. Competing under the banner of "The Shaw Flippers" they won a bronze medal in their first big race. As a reward, arrangements were made for a charter bus to take them, their coach, and chaperones to New York City the following week to witness the national canoeing championships.

In 1968, Bowl America, Inc. again cooperated with Widening Horizons by making alleys, shoes and a professional instructor available. Five hundred youngsters received 30 days free bowling instructions. The formation of the "Washington Whips"—a professional soccer team generated increased participation in the 1968 Widening Horizons soccer program. This activity will be offered from August 1969 until the onset of cold weather. The Marines again ran their physical fitness program, providing trophies and certificates and a sizable number qualified to receive the coveted USMC physical fitness certificates.

ROWING ADDED TO PROGRAM

In 1968 rowing was added to the program. Two unused sea skiffs were borrowed from the U.S. Navy, and by the end of the summer the crews were rowing beautifully. Unfortunately, there was no competition in which the Widening Horizons crews could be entered that summer. Nevertheless, the participants all had a sense of achievement from mastering the tricky, frail shells and they had learned some valuable lessons in teamwork.

By July 1969, the Widening Horizons swimmers had participated in the Regional Junior Olympics, they had won ribbons in several big AAU meets, and several members had received promises of college scholarships. In addition, all swimmers over 16 who wanted to work during the summer were employed as lifeguards at private and community pools. For many of them, it was the first job they had ever held.

During Summer '69, another 500 youngsters were receiving bowling instructions and the eight-man war canoes were back on the river. The canoeists' sights are set on representing their country in the 1972 Olympic games in Munich, Germany.

Two new programs are expected to be added to the program this year—whale boat racing and orienteering. The Seafarers International Union has promised the long-term loan of two whale boats. When received, that program will get underway, with the Harbor Police and the fireboat crews supervising it. Orienteering, a new sport which is sweeping Europe, combines the arts of using a compass, map reading and cross country running. It is all done against the clock. Simply stated, it is the art of land navigation. The U.S. Marines, the leading U.S. experts in this sport, have agreed to conduct a clinic for adults on how to coach this sport. Later, these neophyte coaches will pass along their new knowledge to Boy Scout troops and youth in the 11 Police Boys Clubs. In the early fall, the Marines will return to Washington to conduct the Widening Horizons Orienteering Championship.

VALUABLE SUPPLEMENT TO SCHOOL CURRICULUM

In the opinion of school officials, the police and community leaders, Widening Horizons has proven to be an extremely valuable supplement to the regular school curriculum. Teenagers have been introduced to sports they might never have experienced; the restless energies of youth have been channeled into healthy outlets; their self-esteem has been raised; they have learned teamwork, and perhaps most important for deprived youth—they have been instilled with the will to win.

Along with their healthier bodies and healthier minds has come a marked improvement in scholastic achievement, an increased interest in the world around them, and some very serious thought about their future careers.

At the same time, the coaches and volunteers discovered some interesting facts about inner-city youth which could prove of value to other people assigned to work with this segment of our society. Some of these facts are:

1. The parents of most disadvantaged youth have never provided them with any goals. But when they are given relatively easily attainable short-range goals and more difficult long-range goals, they react very well.
2. Most deprived youth are woefully lacking in self-esteem. But after gaining even a small degree of public recognition, such as winning a ribbon in a sports event or getting one's name in the newspaper, complete personality changes can be observed.
3. Inner-city youth respond very favorably to strict discipline and heavy physical demands, so long as they believe that the disciplinarian genuinely cares about them and is doing it for their own good.
4. Deprived youngsters are starved for love and for adult attention. Consequently, anyone working with them must have a good feel for human relations and infinite patience. He will soon find that he must serve as: father, mother, advisor, doctor, psychiatrist, hero, and fill in other gaps in their lives.

5. Most inner-city youth see no way of breaking out of their environment. As a result, they have a defeatist attitude and are woefully lacking in motivation. However, once their self-image is improved they can be reached on the importance of education in today's world and persuaded to return to school.

This experimental program in Washington, D.C., has proven conclusively that it does not take a great deal of money to launch a worthwhile program. All that is required is a small budget for transportation, one or two prominent community leaders to serve as focal points, and a group of dedicated volunteers. Such a group can then mobilize the resources of its community and mold them into a program designed to meet the needs of the youth in that community. Washington, D.C., is blessed with unique facilities. But every sizable community has many resources—factories, mines, research companies, service companies, sports coaches, etc. And these resources could be molded into a youth program patterned after the Widening Horizons concept. After all, the whole idea is to open the eyes of deprived youngsters to opportunities in their home community—not to opportunities in another.

The Case for Compensatory Recreation

David E. Gray

The recreation movement was born with a social conscience. It grew up with the settlement house movement, the kindergarten movement and the youth movement that fostered the great youth agencies of the nation. Its earliest practitioners had a human welfare motivation in which the social ends of human development, curbing juvenile delinquency, informal education, cultural enrichment, health improvement, and other objectives were central. Gradually the social welfare mission weakened and a philosophy which sees recreation as an end in itself was adopted; this is the common view in public recreation agencies throughout the country.

In the earliest days of the recreation movement, playgrounds were located in what was then called "under-privileged" neighborhoods. Gradually, as the movement matured and public acceptance increased, the idea grew that any neighborhood which lacked public recreation services was, in a sense, underprivileged, and that centers ought to be provided throughout the city. In some cities where residents of more affluent neighborhoods employed their power to articulate needs and influence political processes, a preponderance of new facilities often went into the developing suburbs and what inequalities existed in distribution of facilities favored the more affluent population.

In the future this will change. Although a basic level of service is likely to be available everywhere, there is growing recognition of the fact that people are unequal in their need for community-supported recreation services. It requires substantially more effort to get results in a "culturally deprived" area of the city than it does elsewhere. It appears that in the future we will take this into account in the construction of facilities and the deployment of recreation personnel. This will result in a disproportionate expenditure of resources and effort in "culturally deprived" neighborhoods.

When we manage our resources this way we will be establishing a program of compensatory recreation, a program of special services, beyond the community norm, designed to help compensate for social and economic handicaps suffered by disadvantaged persons.

NEW PROBLEMS NEED NEW SOLUTIONS

As even the most casual reader of any newspaper can attest, today's world is beset with a host of new and baffling problems—social, economic and technological. In the United States these problems are compounded by massive interdependency and expectations of a material

Reprinted with permission from National Recreation and Park Association. Official publication *Parks and Recreation*, April, 1969.

scale of living far beyond that ever known by mankind. Perhaps the most perplexing aspect of all this is the extent to which all problems are interlinked. Poverty may be due to a lack of jobs; but behind that lack is one of education; and behind that, problems of the family and poverty, and so the vicious circle is completed.

The scale of these social needs has placed them far beyond the reach of the private individual or organization. Increasingly, government's tasks are being seen in a new perspective. There is growing acceptance of the idea that services should be provided from community resources for those who cannot provide them for themselves. Many people can purchase their recreational requirements. There is growing affluence for the majority of our people. But many have been left behind and they cannot pay; if they are to have recreational experience, it must be provided at public expense either through taxes or the donated dollar.

Recreation is an expression of man's need for man. It is not a panacea for all social ills; it is not a substitute for jobs with decent pay, or safe and sanitary housing, or a relevant educational system, or a meaningful role for the elderly in society. But it is an important way to learn democratic human relations, leisure skills and interests, creative expression, and to promote physical, mental, and social growth. In the drabness of the ghetto, as elsewhere, these are not inconsequential benefits.

DEFEAT PRODUCES DEFEAT

Numerous studies show that what matters most in producing a delinquent is not race, religion, or nationality; it is where the child grows up. Official delinquency data are biased in favor of upper- and middle-class youth. It is clear, however, that children in disadvantaged areas of the city are more likely to become delinquent. The environment most apt to produce delinquency is residence in a large city, a broken home, numerous children in the family, poor performance in school, and low economic and social status.

The business of adolescence is to find out who one is, what one can do, and what one believes. Accomplishment of this primary task is much more difficult for a disadvantaged youth than it is for an advantaged youth. Among all the critical dimensions in which the disadvantaged differ from those enjoying advantage, none is more critical than the development of a satisfactory self-image. The disadvantaged youth has difficulty in thinking well of himself. He is not sure who he is or what he can do or what he believes. Often his physical and social environment conspire to convince him he cannot achieve any commendable goals. One learns to be successful by being successful; there is no other way. But for many disadvantaged youth success is a long time coming. Caught in the pressure cooker of poverty and social disorganization, the disadvantaged child grows up to expect defeat and frustration. He is rarely disappointed.

In the development of a stable and satisfactory self-image, adult models are important. The child is encouraged or discouraged in his development by people around him, and the people he associates with during his formative years help determine who he becomes. The child's life space is the home, the school, and the immediate community. If his home and school fail him, his only hope is the community. If the community fails to provide satisfactory models and opportunity for success, he soon learns to expect failure and frustration. He learns he is a nobody, decides he can do nothing, and believes the world is against him. Shortly this becomes a self-fulfilling prophecy.

A skillful and relevant recreation agency can do much for disadvantaged youth. It can provide suitable adult models. It can provide opportunities for him to find out what he can do. It may help him learn what he believes, and if it is particularly relevant and skillful, the agency may help him find out who he is. Disadvantaged youth are often dependent entirely on community sources for this kind of help.

STUDY DEFINES NEEDIEST

There are measurable social characteristics which reflect need for recreation services in an urban setting, the Recreation and Youth Services Planning Council of Los Angeles used four basic factors to measure recreation need: population of youth between the ages of five and nineteen; total population density; median family income, and the rate of juvenile delinquency. The council said that priorities in community-subsidized recreation services should go to those least able to pay; to those experiencing maximum social pressures from high density of population, large numbers of youth, low income, and high social disorganization. To these indices some critics will add the additional criterion of a high population of elderly persons. Retired persons often have the most time and the least money for recreation. They suffer loneliness, ennui, and loss of social role at a time when their need for social experience is high. They are prime clientele for community-supported recreation services.

We have narrowly defined our services in the past. In the future will we be concerned about contributions to the education of our people, the welfare of the elderly, maintenance of domestic tranquility, the quality of American life, beauty and conservation of the urban environment, the design of our cities, improvement of community life, development of the young, and cultural affairs? If we are not, which agencies in local government will be? These are much greater concerns than scheduling and staffing activities and managing recreation and park properties. If adopted, they would represent a major involvement in contemporary affairs. We currently lack expertise in many of these areas, but who is expert in the management of contemporary urban life?

URBAN PROBLEMS ARE HUMAN PROBLEMS

We should be attempting an enlarged contribution to the solution of enlarged urban problems, but many agencies do not exhibit a social conscience or pursue a social mission. Such agencies express their goals as "providing a program of activities for the entire community," or they say "we provide recreation activities for all the people." We cannot divorce ourselves from the great social issues of our time. As we seek ways to make a contribution to the solution of social problems we will rediscover our social consciousness and begin to define our goals in terms of human welfare.

Our end then will not be activity; activity will be the means. Our end will be development of human potential in all its richness and variation. The poor, the potentially delinquent, the elderly, and the disadvantaged are groups with the least resources and the highest need for community-supported recreation services. They will be the recipients of programs of compensatory recreation.

Special Demands of the City

Donald A. Pelegrino

More than three years after the Kerner Commission analyzed the causes of the great urban riots of the 1960's, the racial ghettos of the U.S. are more than ever an environment of decay, distrust, and despair. That is the conclusion of a report, "The State of the Cities" issued by a commission of the National Urban Coalition.

"Housing is still the national scandal it was then," says the report. "Schools are more tedious and turbulent. The rate of crime and unemployment and disease and heroin addiction is higher than ever. Welfare rolls are larger and with few exceptions, the relations between minority communities and the police are just as hostile." If such trends continue, the report concludes bleakly, "most cities by 1980 will be predominantly black and brown and totally bankrupt."

How did our cities get this way? What caused these conditions? What are the origins of this urban mess? To determine the answers to these and other questions, we must historically but briefly reflect on the city and its origins. A city, simply defined by the *Random House Dictionary of the English Language* is "a large or important town—an incorporated municipality, usually governed by a mayor—the inhabitants of a city collectively."

Various factors helped early American cities take shape and grow. The general design of the city was basically derived from its inhabitants' European backgrounds and culture. Natural advantages and terrain and strategic and economic factors played an important part. Sometimes the selection of a place for development as a city or as a capital, to which lesser towns were subordinate, was the deliberate act of a person or group. At any rate, cities had the basic design and components necessary for commerce, culture, habitability, and recreation for its dwellers. It also had diversity and drive as well as the support of its citizens.

By the turn of the nineteenth century the trend toward urbanization became a dominant factor in American life. The completion on continental expansion, the development of new technologies, and changes in national economic patterns brought into being the industrial city. Between 1860 and 1900, urban population nearly quintupled while rural

Leisure-Society-Politics: "The Political Environment of Parks and Recreation" Proceedings 1971, Park and Recreation Administrators Institute, University of California, Davis, 1972. Reprinted with permission from Donald A. Pelegrino, Coordinator of Graduate Studies, Department of Recreation, California State University, Northridge, California.

population failed even to double. Thus, in 1900 nearly forty per cent of all Americans were living in cities.

Immigration from abroad coupled with increasing discouragement of domestic farm life, in part, brought about this change. People saw in the city an opportunity to achieve financial security along with the prospect of a more exciting life.

During this period of city development, the Parks and Recreation movement came into being. It was developed after the broad based philosophy of Jane Addams and had a strong social conscience. Neighborhood parks or park-like open spaces were considered boons conferred on the deprived populations of the cities. In the "then" orthodox city planning neighborhood open spaces were not so venerated as they are now.

Cities mushroomed and grew to such proportions that their sites no longer seemed functional. They increased upward and outward in size, often engulfing neighboring communities and becoming giant megalopolis centers. Political boundaries can no longer describe the character or size of a city. Most cities lost their unique character with increased growth and have become sprawling unidentifiable urban complexes.

The American attitude of individualism coupled with a disrespect for nature and often a lack of concern for the public environment have helped cities arrive at the state in which they presently exist. These factors in our frontier history are still predominant. These attitudes together with an absence of city planning skills produced an ill bred urban environment almost from the beginning. Problems became more complex when, during the 1950's, the white middle class, fully mobile and yearning for suburban life, exodused in great masses into a hodgepodge of outlying areas wholly unprepared for them. This produced a need for services, which brought new commercial ugliness along roadsides and in huge concrete centers.

As city and suburban areas grew, population increases were also occurring. This urban growth has threatened the peace and tranquility of many of the better citizens and groups of our society. This same urban growth brought to the cities overcrowding, pollution, traffic congestion, crime, delinquency, psychological and social ills associated with poverty, unemployment, poor education and poor housing, injustice and frustration.

Insulation and/or protection from these ills is becoming increasingly more difficult. The groups associated by the middle class with these ills, the minorities, the poor, the unemployed and the new foreigners are an increasing proportion of the central city. They are spilling over into the suburbs or threatening to do so. The suburbs, in turn, are taking up more and more open land, building look-a-like houses, saturating the area with children and freeways and along with this all the aggravating annoyances and problems of lower middle-class life. Municipal governments, therefore, cannot restrict their concern to activities within legal boundaries, for they now find that many of their problems also exist beyond the central city and its limits.

The time is a desperate one for urban America. Can the city again become a decent place to live, to work, and for recreation? The image of the city is now bad enough—slum districts, crime, noise, and congestion, and of people who are poor, and generally of ethnic minorities. What then of the city in the future? This will depend upon whether this country can find ways and means of making cities more habitable, or whether the problems of the metropolitan regions are beyond rehabilitation.

Perhaps too much is expected of city parks and recreation places. Far from transforming any essential quality in their surroundings, far from automatically uplifting their neighborhoods, neighborhood parks themselves are directly and drastically affected by the way the neighborhood acts upon them. It must be kept in perspective that cities are thoroughly physical places and it stands to reason that parks and recreation places either permit or discourage ordinary physical interaction with their neighborhoods. Cities have, among other variables, active and different currents of life which function and come to a focus. Neighborhood parks fail to substitute any way for plentiful city diversity. There is no point in bringing parks to where the people are, if in the process the reasons that the people are there are wiped out and the park substituted for them. Parks and recreation places should help to knit together diverse surrounding functions by giving them a pleasant joint facility. It should also be remembered the ability of a neighborhood park or recreation place to stimulate passionate attachment or, conversely, only apathy, seems to have little or nothing to do with the incomes or occupations of a population with a district. In today's society mobility by all ages is a factor to be considered when planning parks and recreation places.

If the object of a generalized park or recreation place is to attract as many different kinds of people, with as many different schedules, interests, and purposes as possible, it is clear that the design of the facility should abet this generalization of patronage rather than work at cross-purposes to it.

Increasingly we are becoming a nation of white-collar administrators, secretaries, professionals, and business people. An overwhelming proportion of new office buildings for banks, insurance companies, and corporations has taken place in the larger cities. With this new infusion of white-collar jobs there are definite signs of a small but significant move back from suburbia. Many workers are choosing new high-rise luxury apartments as an alternative to suburban home upkeep and the daily freeway traffic struggle into the city. This trend will help the cities, for to remain dominant cultural centers, cities need a core of people to support its theatres, museums, shops, restaurants, and recreational facilities. It is the people who live in the city who make it an attraction for visitors, especially at night, for they help to create its character, without it there is no reason for one to go downtown, or into the Inner City.

On the other hand big cities are losing blue-collar and retail jobs as industry builds more and more new manufacturing plants and warehouses on cheap land in the suburbs. Thus, for some time now, a somewhat healthy sorting out of functions is taking blue-collar jobs, as well as truck and industrial pollution, away from the core area and substituting white-collar jobs. It is ironic that while this transfer has been going on, most of those who hold inner-city jobs have been moving out into the suburbs to live, while minorities, in spite of growing job opportunities in industry, have remained concentrated in the cities. Hopefully, people in both groups who must travel to work will move and live closer to their jobs. For this to materialize depends upon whether minorities can gain access to suburban housing, and whether the cities can offer a lifestyle that appeals to the middle class. By the same token, a joint solution would be to increase the number of jobs within the city to include minorities living nearby and thus create a socially and culturally richer middle class.

Presently though, most central city or core areas have deteriorated from neglect for they have long been regarded only as a place to work or carry on business. People have more concern for the communities in which they live than in central areas where they work. Residents of the inner city though, for the most part, are not able to afford housing elsewhere and usually settle in isolated "de facto" ghettos with others of similar cultural backgrounds. To provide a better life for city dwellers, special demands must be met. These include improved housing and transportation facilities, better medical care, and open space for recreational activities. As for meeting recreational needs, some local community programs such as music and art festivals, drama groups, and athletics have been established, as have "pocket" parks through municipal government and local group cooperation.

It is interesting that while "Self-Help" has become a cliche in the literature of economic development, the National Urban Coalition report on cities, which was cited earlier, did find one hopeful sign: a "new tough pride, self-confidence, and determination" of minorities to build their own grass roots institutions of self-help and reach "for levers of power." At the same time, the report warns: The most disturbing point most of those we spoke with made was they had no faith at all in the System—the Government and the private wielders of power—as a protector or a provider.

As a result of this cities report the question arises in the Parks and Recreation profession: How can we deal effectively and responsibly with the citizen community inside the central city? After all, we are part of the system and we must recognize the problem and offer some solutions or at least ways and means for alternates to these solutions. There are countless ways in which our profession can offer solutions. The first of which is not to become anti-urban in our approach to the city. The second is to bring to being all our resources for imaginative exploration of techniques and strong implementing action directed at making our city and its environs of benefit to all of its dwellers. The third is not to resist change. We are not the panacea for the problems but we have to take an aggressive role in social change and bring these efforts down to everyday practice to help ameliorate problems.

What then is involved in these techniques? How do we go about establishing methods of survival and renewal in a city? Why not have the people running the parks and recreation facilities? These could be local governing groups from the neighborhoods who give direction, determine policy, handle discipline, and dole out the budget. The professional staff would be the enablers and the overseers. After all, don't the parks belong to the people?

Why not offer more "demand goods"? If a store in an inner city can be rescued and justified, it will be a dent of heavy concentration on what merchants call "demand goods" instead of reliance on "impulse sales." Demand goods are those which the citizens want not what the maintenance men desire. For example, in one park there is a big swimming pool, which sometimes contains more people than water. Another park has a band shell which is used six times a year when thousands of people pour into the park to hear a concert series. Another park has a tot-lot center where hundreds of mothers and children come only in the mornings. And yet another park has a building used exclusively for teen-agers on the weekends. Here are illustrated demand goods operating although too limited in quantity and too desultory in time. It is clear, however, that people do come to these facilities for special demand goods, although they simply do not come for generalized or impulse park use. Effective diversity of use, drawing deliberately a sequence of diversified users, must be deliberately reintroduced into the facility itself.

Magnificent views and handsome landscaping do not make a park anymore. They fail to operate as demand goods. They can work as adjuncts only. On the other hand, swimming operates as a demand good, so does boating and fishing, carnivals and music, and drama and ethnic festivals, and the like. Why not provide free transportation from park to park for recreation programs. If the people can't go to the park, bring the park to the people and provide the Park and Recreation Department with free publicity in doing so. Why not bring smaller facilities to the streets and into the apartment buildings or backyards or churches or even empty warehouses. Use what they—the citizens—have. We might just learn something about our neighborhood and its residents.

This suggests more cooperation between the people and the parks. This further suggests more democracy in decision-making as well as more diversity of use and scheduling. It may mean giving up the old arbor festivals and halloween parades and giving in to a black arts day or a Purim carnival or a street festival. It may even mean fighting those who think the middle class think the poor are their enemy, thereby letting the wealthier classes get away with more. Perhaps the central thesis here indicates that we should take strong stands and not worry about being loved by everybody.

City Parks and Recreation facilities are not abstractions or automatic repositories of virtue or uplift any more than

sidewalks are abstractions. They mean nothing divorced from their practical tangible uses.

This task of uplifting all city parks and recreation facilities is too enormous for private enterprise, municipal governments, and individuals to tackle. It requires federal subsidy and, in fact, the Federal Government has become increasingly involved in tackling these urban problems. In 1965 Congress passed the Housing and Urban Development Act establishing it (HUD) as a Department in the President's cabinet. The Department administers a wide range of activities including: low- and middle-cost housing, programs of urban renewal, planning for urban and metropolitan growth, the use of open space, community facilities and problems dealing with mass transportation. Parks and Recreation are not specifically mentioned, but nevertheless, they are included in the activities and funding.

Another major national undertaking is that of the Model Cities Program which authorizes the Secretary of HUD to provide grants and technical assistance to help communities of all sizes plan and develop model projects. These are local programs for rebuilding or restoring large sections and neighborhoods of slum and blighted areas by the concentrated and coordinated use of local, private, and governmental resources.

Alongside federal study and tangible aid, private enterprise is playing an enormous role in city improvement. Finally, as long as there are people living in the city, there will always be a need for recreation services designed to provide the urbanite a wide variety of opportunities and experiences. It seems clear that the traditional services are no longer the answer and that self-help is only one answer. The challenge is great for the situation is complex and no single remedy is at hand which could possibly cure the many needs of people in a city. In reaching for new approaches and solutions to these problems new enemies may be made and hostility encountered, for there are those in our own ranks who do not want the city improved. However, in this rejection by some, new allies may be discovered. With these allies and their approaches coupled with the self-determination of citizens, the special demands of the cities will be met.

NOTES USED IN PREPARATION OF THIS PAPER

1. Arbital, Samuel L., *Cities and Metropolitan Areas In Today's World* (Mankato, Minnesota: Creative Educational Society, Inc., 1968).
2. Chapin, Stuart F. Jr., *Urban Land Use Planning*, 2d ed. (Urbana: University of Illinois Press, 1965).
3. Dickinson, William B. Jr., ed. *Editorial Research Reports On the Urban Environment* (Washington, D.C.: Congressional Quarterly, Inc., 1969).
4. The Editors of Fortune, *The Exploding Metropolis* (New York: Doubleday & Company, Inc., 1958).
5. Gordon, Mitchell, *Sick Cities: Psychology and Pathology of American Life.*
6. Jacobs, Jane, *The Death and Life of Great American Cities* (New York: Random House, Inc., 1961).
7. Isenberg, Irwin, ed. *The City in Crisis* (New York: The H.W. Wilson Company, 1968. The Reference Shelf Volume 40, Number 1).
8. National Recreation and Park Association: *Parks and Recreation* Vol. VI, No. 7, 1971.
9. *Time Magazine*, Vol. 98, No. 15, 1971.
10. The Twentieth Century Fund, *CDCS: New Hope for the Inner City* (New York: The Twentieth Century Fund, Inc., 1971).

Planning Where the Action Is

Ira J. Hutchison, Jr.

The recreation profession is at a crossroad. To do and what to do—to act and how to act—in response to the urban crisis is being asked by park and recreation people across the nation.

The social and economic problems that are plaguing our society have swiftly become ones that are demanding our immediate attention; we have our choice of two roads:

- Dynamic innovations and readjustments within the structure of our recreation programs and services is the one road—.
- Apathy, negativism, and insensitivity to the needs of the disadvantaged and the problems of the inner city is the other road.

Recreation practitioners have the choice of taking a more active and responsible role in the national effort to solve some of the problems associated with economic and social deprivation or retreating to the comparative safety of proven services and predictable participants.

Challenges are not new to the profession. We live in a world that is constantly revising its value system and assuming new concerns for its citizens. The positive growth and development of the park and recreation movement has been characterized by its ability to react successfully to these revisions or reassessments of societal priorities. Beginning with the pioneer recreators who first encouraged a stubborn society to realize the true meaning and value of recreation and leisure programs, our professional progress has been steady and meaningful.

Once it gained a respectable role and function in the area of public programs and services, recreation quickly became a tool or resource that society often asked to aid in its efforts to meet the physical, social, and psychological concerns of its people. Present day recreation services for the ill and disabled, the aging, and mentally retarded persons are examples of that kind of societal involvement.

CROSSROADS HAVE BEEN MET BEFORE

So in effect, crossroads have been encountered before. Fortunately, the road leading to innovation and readjustment to the existing crisis or need has most often been chosen and navigated successfully. Is this to be true again?—The purpose of this article is to share some observations

Reprinted with permission from National Recreation and Park Association. Official publication *Parks and Recreation*, July, 1968.

and opinions that might speed up the problem solving and decision making that will enable us to answer this question.

In the past, no crisis has been so complex or unique that our profession has not been able to rise to the situation. That is—until community programmers and planners turned their attention to the recreational needs of the urban inner city and its disadvantaged and deprived residents.

Puzzled and discouraged recreators are finding it difficult to understand why there is often such a limited response by the inner city resident to the programs and services that are planned and offered for his use. Some administrators and practitioners have assumed the blame for these failures. Others have attributed the lack of response and involvement to factors peculiar to the inner city residents themselves. Perhaps there are elements of truth in both reactions but more than likely situations such as this are due to factors far more serious in nature and content.

INAPPROPRIATE GUIDELINES USED

It is suggested here that the root of the problem is the use of inappropriate or inappropriately interpreted principles and guidelines in the development and presentation of recreational programs and services for the inner city residents.

There might be reason to believe that the concepts and guidelines we have developed and use have become oriented to serve the middle and upper socio--economic population. It is further suggested that the profession, lulled into a state of complacency by past successes, might be supporting a syndrome of professional practice that cannot be successfully implemented in any but a

middle or upper socio-economic setting. If this is true, then what next?

Action—meaningful, appropriate and immediate action must be the guide post for the future. Concepts and guidelines that govern existing recreation programming must be re-evaluated for their capacity to meet this new challenge.

The key to success can be the willingness of the practitioner to create recreation programs and services that are compatible with the cultural, social, and economic characteristics of the inner city.

New concepts and guidelines must be developed that will spawn recreation programs that can meet basic health needs of the inner city resident as well as those needs arising from the comparatively unique aspects of the inner city environment.

At this point some factors are offered for the consumption of recreation professionals who are faced with the challenge and responsibility of organizing recreation programs in deprived or disadvantaged communities.

FAMILIARITY WITH ENVIRONMENT NEEDED

As has been stated before, there are social, cultural, and economic aspects of the disadvantaged community environment that are most often unfamiliar to the recreation practitioner. He should not attempt to practice his profession until a solid familiarity has been established with the essence of these differences and their relevancy to the concepts of community recreation programming.

How do current concepts of leisure or recreation for the individual match the life style of the inner city resident? Does he in truth have "leisure" time or does he exist in an almost continuous and undefined flow of time without meaning or purpose? Many now believe that the latter situation prevails and recreation services designed from the "leisure time" conceptual standpoint are alien to the social and cultural atmosphere of the inner city and thus are consistently rejected. The customs, standards, and preferences of the community govern the actions and performance of its members and are the cornerstones upon which successful recreation programs should be constructed. It then becomes possible to provide services that meet basic health needs as well as introduce new or desirable activities that can reduce the isolation and alienation of the inner city resident from the societal mainstream of cultural and social opportunity.

How does the practitioner gain the necessary knowledge and familiarity with the urban inner city environment? Certainly no one needs to do more than remind today's recreator of the necessity to inventory and evaluate the existing facilities and services in any recreational setting that becomes his responsibility. This is no less true in the depressed community. He will want to know how, when and who uses these facilities both by sex and age group. He will want to know the days and the hours the maximum number of persons can be attracted to his programs. The following example indicates how important this factor can be:

The recreation director of an agency for a ghetto area in a metropolitan city reported that a camping program scheduled on the usual Friday evening or Saturday morning was a failure. Upon switching the program to Mondays and Tuesdays, camping became one of the most popular and well attended activities. Fortunately, this director came to recognize that the social life of this ghetto community reached its peak on

Friday and Saturday. This meant that the attractiveness of camping was at its lowest level during the weekend.

It is equally important that the recreator take the time to identify the appropriate leadership in the inner city community. These people can provide reliable advice and assistance in the formulation and implementation of recreation services. Successful activities will be those that are planned with rather than for the citizens of the community. Indigenous leadership is a known quality in programming and should be utilized at all levels; planning, directing and supervising inner city programs.

USE AVAILABLE FACILITIES

A common tendency among recreation practitioners is to limit their planning and presentation of recreational activity to the public and private community facilities and resources for recreation activity. Community centers, public parks, and other municipally owned facilities are in this category. In the inner city community, the bowling alley, the pool hall, the motion picture theatre and other establishments such as churches, barber shops, taxi stands, restaurants, and the neighborhood grocery store might be more popular than the most elaborate public recreation facility. The recreation planner should enlist the support of the proprietors and directors of these establishments for they often have excellent relationships with the teenage or young adult inner city residents. Pool or bowling tournaments in the local pool hall or bowling alley might be a beginning step that will aid in creating positive interaction between the inner city residents and the public recreation department.

In summary, recreation services in the depressed urban community should be organized within a context that avoids insult to existing socio-cultural patterns or customs. To offer recreation programs in the inner city that are limited in long range value to the participants and unrealistic or inappropriate in relation to the resources and the life-style of the community's residents will be hollow exercises in recreation leadership.

This then is the present challenge to a profession that has already successfully met others. The question is not really which road we shall choose to travel. We are strong enough and most often, wise enough, to preclude our taking the wrong one. The real concern is whether or not we can harness our strength— whether or not we can temper our wisdom with the kind of meaning and objectivity that will enable us to synthesize our concerns and efforts into meaningful programs and services—programs and services that respond adequately and appropriately to the needs, the desires and the birthright of the citizens of our urban inner-cities.

The Arts and the Poor

Judith Murphy and Ronald Gross

CAN THE ARTS HELP THE POOR?

Many artists, educators, and sociologists believe and would like to prove that the arts, by meeting disadvantaged children where they are, can lead them on to a number of highly desirable goals beyond the substantial pleasures and values of art per se. These goals include a novel sense of their own worth as individuals, an appreciation of their own heritage—whether African, Sioux, or Sicilian—and an openness to the learning process in its broader dimensions. Taken by itself, the maxim "Through art to arithmetic" may sound blasphemous to the aesthetic purist; but as one facet of the arts' constructive potential, it obviously has its points. Through intensive experiences in the arts, children from impoverished environments may, by finding themselves, find ways to change themselves and their environment to something nearer their own deepest needs and the needs of a healthy society.

These children, deprived of the simple delights of childhood and often denied much of their mother's attention, are dazed by the abstractions of arithmetic and letters. By ordinary school standards they are "nonverbal," meaning that they boggle at the language they must learn to speak, read, and write, although there is plentiful evidence that these very children can be magnificently verbal when freed from the constraints of approved English usage.

Even as they are intimidated by abstraction, poor children in particular warm to whatever they can touch, see, hear, and manipulate: the concrete, in short. Seeing a movie about a train, visiting a railroad yard, building a train out of blocks, acting out the parts of the locomotive and cars themselves, joining in a railroad song—such activities relax their bewilderment over T-R-A-I-N in a book, on a flashcard, or intoned by the teacher.

ART EDUCATION FOR THE POOR

That the arts could play a primary role in meeting the challenge of poverty seems at first glance a frivolous notion—a strained attempt to relate an essentially peripheral, ornamental pastime to individual misery and a deeply disturbing social problem. Yet there is remarkable evidence that makes it foolhardy to dismiss the proposition.

Reprinted with permission from the United States Government Printing Office.

In Job Corps centers around the country, for example, psychologically damaged teenagers are turning their hands to painting, pottery, dance, music, and creative writing. A large exhibit of Job Corps art is now on national tour. Even more important than the intrinsic merit of the painting or sculpture itself is its effect on the boys and girls who produced it, only a few of whom plan to earn a living in the arts.

Barbara Dean, for instance, had been making her perilous way alone in the adult world since she was 12 years old. In her own words she was "generally falling apart" when she joined the Job Corps at 17. With only 7 years of schooling she soon displayed an unusual ability to express her ideas and feelings both in words and in paint. Now, after winning a Job Corps writing contest and a place in the touring exhibit, Barbara has a scholarship to a California high school and hopes to go to college, perhaps to study sociology.

Other examples abound:

- In Los Angeles, the Watts Towers Art Center has for over 5 years been running free classes for the young people of the community. They come to paint, carve, build, and act.
- On a dingy street in the same sprawling ghetto, for more than 2 years a dozen or so teenagers and adults have been meeting regularly with a famous novelist in a writing workshop. School dropouts and poorly educated adults turn out work of sometimes astonishing quality. One man whose job is sweeping out a local bar has had a piece published in *West*, the Sunday magazine of the *Los Angeles Times;* another has had a television play produced on a national network; and a 55-year-old woman, who did not finish the eighth grade, has nearly completed a novel based on her childhood in the South—a novel whose drive and emotive power astonish her tutor and deeply move her classmates.

- In Harlem, a world-famous soprano, retired from the concert stage, now gives full time to the school she organized in her husband's parish. Hundreds of impoverished children come after school and on weekends to sing, dance, and learn to play instruments.
- At the other end of Manhattan, on the Lower East Side, the Arts-for-Living Program at the Henry Street Settlement embraces a music school, a playhouse for drama and dance, and a pottery and art school—all designed to reach young people not yet motivated toward the arts or toward any kind of disciplined study. Experienced artists team up with trained social workers to help children find new ways to express themselves, gain self-confidence, and taste the joys of creation and collaboration.
- In Santa Fe, New Mexico, a special boarding school supported by the U.S. government enrolls every year several hundred young people from the nation's "forgotten" minority, the American Indian. They usually arrive silent, repressed, uneasy, and—by accepted academic measures—retarded. Immersed in a curriculum rich in art work of all kinds and keyed but not limited to their Indian heritage, the students blossom into individuals, develop self-esteem and pride, and gradually transfer their new-found confidence to mastering the routines of arithmetic and English and the other standard school subjects.
- In Delano, California, the striking fieldworkers who pick grapes have formed a traveling theater. Performing on the tailgate of a ton-and-a-half truck, going out where the farmworkers are with the message of "Huelga" (the strike), El Teatro

Campesino uses strikers as actors. Improvising their parts, these performers help an impoverished community to understand and define itself.

Many other examples, some described in the pages which follow, could be adduced—perhaps hundreds, if one were to include all the unconventional but effective learning of this kind that goes largely unheralded in schools and less formal settings all over America.

Although the "implausible notion" that the arts can "turn on" deprived youngsters and adults may have neither tradition nor everyday logic to recommend it, it does have one thing worth considering—it actually seems to work. Many times, in many places, with many youngsters who desperately need to be reached, it has worked. The challenge to teachers, educational researchers, and administrators is to understand better how this happens so that it may be made to happen more often, with greater assurance of success, for the millions of children to whom it could mean so much.

WHO KNOWS THE WAY?

"Compatibility between the artistic and the administrative personality," said artist-administrator Melvin Roman on the first day of the conference, "is simply not in the nature of things." Thus, a nagging and embarrassing problem landed on the conference table.

HIP VERSUS SQUARE

Can the tension between artists and administrators be resolved, alleviated, or end-run in some way that will permit artists to contribute their unique gifts to educational programs under conditions which they can accept? Can administrators in and out of schools, who after all carry the responsibility for the success of their programs, be assured that their worst forebodings will not come true?

But the dichotomy is a little too easy. Many artists like Roy Lichtenstein (the pop painter specializing in blown-up cartoon panels) run their studios and their professional lives with the precision and orderliness of an insurance office. And the conference included at least one administrator, William Birenbaum of Long Island University, who obviously prides himself on his genuinely impulsive, irreverent style of administration. There are, in short, square artists and hip administrators.

Yet the essential truth remains valid: the artist and the administrator more often than not do clash in temperament, outlook, and style. There is nothing invidious in the contrast, just that, through self-selection, the process of professional training, and day-to-day conditions of work, the two groups tend to develop divergent viewpoints.

The artist is typically engaged in exploring and expressing his own personality and sensibility. He cultivates what is most personal and intimate in the hope of making it, through mastery of his craft, a widely appreciated perception of reality. He is deeply engaged with the concrete materials of his art, the observation of reality in its most specific manifestations, and the feel and tone of things rather than their everyday utility.

On the other hand, the administrator is characteristically devoted to the control and manipulation of resources to achieve a desired end. He is not, or should not be, concerned primarily with expressing his own personality or thrusting his own interpretation of experience upon other people. Rather, he applies his efforts to achieving goals that are publicly conceived, objectively measurable, and socially useful.

Caricatured at their extreme, the artist

and the administrator are irreconcilable antipodes: the long-haired artnik glowers from behind his shades at the stodgy, hypocritical, repressed bureaucrat swathed in red tape. Fortunately though, such caricatures are rare among artists and administrators, who should be able to work well together given common goals and a congenial atmosphere.

In formal education, such an atmosphere has yet to be established. Artists and performers feel that many teachers of the arts in our schools today are not fully committed to the arts as a way of life and lack true insight into them. Most teaching, therefore, they consider pedantic, inhibiting, authoritarian, and unenterprising. On the other hand, art educators suspect artists of lacking a basic commitment to children, as well as the pedagogical skills and understanding of the learning process required of anyone who takes responsibility for children's growth and development.

In practice, artists are usually prevented from contributing their talents to the school program by certification requirements which exclude unaccredited persons from regular classroom work, while art educators are frequently barred from continuing intercourse with professional artists by the snobbishness of the artistic community. In short, the artists, who are "in" artistically can't get their hands on the kids; the art educators, who are in control of the arts in the schools, are snubbed if they try to make contact with the "real world" of art.

There are other problems. The arts in the schools suffer from the cold hand of academicism. The conventional school schedule, whatever its advantages for the formal academic subjects, sharply interferes with the freedom the arts need—freedom from time restrictions, from constraints on spontaneous behavior, and from taboos on what can and cannot be expressed.

What is the solution, given the perennial conflict between the artist and the bureaucrat or art educator, and given the constraints, indifference, and occasional outright hostility the arts face throughout the school system? What could break through this negative grid of powerful forces to put at the service of the poor—particularly in the schools but throughout the ghettos, too—whatever significant values the arts can uniquely or most abundantly supply?

CULTURAL IMPERIALISM

More than personal and professional styles are involved in bringing the arts and the poor together. A recurrent question at the conference might be summed up as: "Just who do we think we are?" Accepting the hypothesis that the arts in their many uses have special importance for improving the lot and the lives of the poor, do artists and teachers know what they are trying to accomplish? And if they do, are they presumptuous to seek to impose these values on the poor? What's so great about "our" values, artistic and social, whether these are the prevailing middle-class values of America or the radically different values of those who would transform America? Maybe the poor would just as soon "not be done good by." Maybe dwellers in the ghetto have something going for them that outsiders either fail to see or else misunderstand.

This complex question involves social and political issues that go far beyond the potential benefits of the arts to the education and life of the poor. And it has been getting increased attention in recent years.

Francis Ianni stated the issue forthrightly when he attacked the presumptions of so-called "do-gooders" that they can bring light into the ghetto. Predictably, as an anthropologist, he put cultural imperialists in their place with an unsettling analogy from Melanesia, citing "the destructive results on the unifying ethos of Melanesian culture and society when the British imposed their own cultural norms and prohibited head hunting . . . the organizing principle, the passion, and the fountain of social and individual ambition in Melanesian society." In Ianni's view, the net effect of the enlightened British suggests "that social betterment, even planned social change and reform, can be disastrous unless we comprehend and appreciate how it is perceived by those undergoing change and how the change relates to what went before." He went on to say that art's role in social betterment was neither here nor there: that what counted was the give-away of our own pretensions and false values in the very use of the term "culturally disadvantaged." Said Dr. Ianni, "We admit by the term itself that this age of American culture has nothing better to offer them as a cultural milieu than what they already have," and he added, "I have seen very few programs in the arts which do not attempt to take the best of what 'we' have to offer in order to help 'them' fit better into our world."

This accusation of "missionaryism" through the arts haunted the conference deliberations. On the one hand there is no gainsaying the value of simply bringing the arts to the poor, or vice versa. The conference heard about a number of such projects. For example, Nina Perera Collier described Youth Concerts of New Mexico, which brings professional musicians to the isolated and deprived schools of the state. The work entails strenuous dedication of the part of the performers and of those who run the program. The rewards can be measured only in human terms of bringing beauty, warmth, and excellence to children who

might otherwise never experience these through the arts.

Among other examples are New York's Theater in the Streets, vividly described by Patricia Reynolds; the federally supported Educational Laboratory Theatre projects in New Orleans, Providence, and Los Angeles; and efforts in New York City and elsewhere to expose high school youngsters to the theater, museums, and the opera.

As Commissioner Howe pointed out, the Office of Education, under provisions of the Elementary and Secondary Education Act of 1965, can support such enriching activities and experiences, and many school systems across the country are already embarked on new programs under ESEA's titles I and III.

Clearly, such direct exposure to the arts—not only through books, records, and films, but also through live theater, ballet, opera, instrumental performances, and museum visits—can have a powerful positive effect, particularly if the "hit and run" pattern is avoided. Students should be prepared beforehand for each experience; they should be involved to the greatest possible degree while going through it—by meeting musicians, performers, and artists, for example; and they should have the opportunity to distill something of lasting value for themselves out of the experience after it is over.

Despite this recognition that the arts are to be appreciated as well as produced, however, the conferees seemed disposed to consider such programs of exposure as worthy but insufficient. There seemed to be a general feeling of the need to go beyond artistic missionaryism. "We've had it with bringing the Pittsburgh Symphony into the ghetto," proclaimed a veteran poverty worker quoted approvingly by one conferee. "The arts must be nurtured from within the community of the poor. Otherwise the effects are ephemeral, or worse." The reason, explained another participant, is that art brought in from outside may be good art but it's bad social action.

The conferees felt that actual participation is essential if people are really to benefit from the arts. At the easel, in the writing workshop or music studio, on stage—wherever art is being made, the poor can, should, and must join in the making. That this is possible and desirable was evident by the exhibit of Job Corps paintings and sculpture that surrounded the conferees, by the moving account of Budd Schulberg's writing workshop in Watts where students who had flunked out of high school English are creating stirring and beautiful poems and stories, by the arts center in Watts that Lucille Krasne reported so vividly to the conference, and by Dorothy Maynor's music and dance classes in Harlem.

Perhaps the best example is the Free Southern Theatre, a touring company based in New Orleans that brings plays to Negro communities of the South, free of charge. The theater is composed of Negroes and concentrates on plays written by, about and for Negroes. Its primary function is to communicate with its audience, and to plant its seeds so well that members of that audience will, in time, *become* the Free Southern Theatre.

Such direct involvement of the poor should, it was widely felt, also extend to planning and administration. Melvin Roman early put forward a formula for achieving such participation: "Democratize decision-making; search for indigenous leadership; relax the boundaries of authority; recognize that change involves the entire environment; make the organization fit the people, not the other way around." Concluded one work group:

"The ends pre-exist in the means. In all programs this value should be asserted from the beginning: the poor should be included in the planning and operation."

Beyond the negative effects of imposing the arts from outside, there is also a positive value in the lives of the poor which could be endangered. Francis Ianni went further than anyone else at the conference in evoking and extolling the "rich culture of poverty." He pointed, for example, to anthropologist Oscar Lewis' demonstration that "what causes the disjunctures and the disharmonies is our attempt to tell [the Puerto Ricans] that they don't know what they are missing." Some conferees were willing to go at least part way along this road, but more of them supported Ianni's related point that the artist "must work with and within the society and the culture he hopes to change." Julian Euell, Lloyd New Kiva, Dorothy Maynor, and others stressed the critical importance of imbuing the culturally disadvantaged—especially the Negro, Puerto Rican, Indian, and Mexican minorities—with a vivid sense of the aesthetic contributions, past and present, of their people. This concurrence led, in turn, to debate between those who want to preserve the distinctive values of ethnic, racial, and religious groups as essential to America's vaunted pluralism, and those who, granting these values, would subordinate them to the greater good of removing barriers between men. The old melting-pot idea took a beating at the conference, but it survived.

These troublesome issues produced some odd currents and cross-currents. Under questioning even Dr. Ianni granted that "middle-class" culture could provide two important desiderata—openness and access. It could bring new experiences to children in the ghettos and open *them* up for the experiences. Dr. Ianni's diagnosis of

Negro entertainment as a put-on for the white audience (Stepin Fetchit, the Clay-Liston fight, inter alia) drew mixed fire from both Negroes and whites in his audience. Ann Flagg cut through the argument and, if only to judge by the applause her moving plea evoked, got close to the heart of the matter. She said, in part:

> Not only must we be concerned with the building of a satisfactory and strengthening self-concept for the disadvantaged child—and now I'm talking about the Negro child, though this is not the only problem—but we must also look through the window from the other side, and have the larger society recognize that Negro culture is a part of the American whole. And until we can look at it in that way, and deal with it in that way, I don't know that anything very much is going to happen with the children.
>
> I don't think there's a Negro in this room who doesn't know that there was a time when the Negro spiritual was a thing to reject in getting to be a part of this larger society. Why do some Negroes still reject it? Because we do not understand, deeply understand, that this is an art form that came out of experience; and it touches everybody. Jazz says something to everybody too; and it's all a part of the mainstream. I am saying let's do something with the teachers, too, who have this open access to knowledge, to truth. We're in the same soup.
>
> Let us use the arts for truth. When I have worked with Negro children, using Negro history, I have not worked with it entirely from the point of view of the black power motif that is being talked about. I've been talking about this kind of understanding— "When you say 'Land where my fathers died,' you are talking about your very own fathers, honey. Your fathers had as much to do with this way of life, this culture we're talking about, as anybody else." And if the middle-class things are arbitrary or artificial but represent the good way of life, then no American should be denied access to that. He helped to make it. Why is it not a part of him? What is wrong with wanting the good life? Let's not have our children start out

with the same misconceptions and misunderstanding of each other that we have started out with. Let's strip away the masks and understand why the Stepin Fetchits came about. Let's give the children a chance to understand what we ourselves don't even begin to understand.

CAN THE ARTIST
SHOW THE WAY?

Much of what is most characteristic and exhilarating about the American art scene today centers on a new relationship between the arts and society. The formalistic boundaries between the arts have been swamped under a tidal wave of "mixed means"—poetry moves off the printed page and into the bars and coffee houses; painting leaps from easels to sidewalks and hospital walls; theater moves from Broadway to off-Broadway and to off-off-Broadway, onto the streets and into the parks and playgrounds. The Happening—a mixed form (or formless mix) including poetry, painting, film, theater, and music—involves the audience and the entire environment. Artists seem to be reaching for a new relevance, a new role to play in creating the conditions of modern life. The artist seems to be seeking to regain his political voice with such anti-Establishment or protest plays as "Viet Rock," "Dynamite Tonite," "MacBird" and "America Hurrah." New social uses of the arts are emerging; the conference was reminded of how New York City's Central Park, which had become a symbol of nighttime terror, was being transformed through events staged to involve every visitor as an actor. Through such events and other improvements the crime rate has dropped, the park is becoming a place of joy; and Thomas P.F. Hoving, former Parks Commissioner, was hailed as "King of Fun City."

The example is neither frivolous nor

unique. At the other end of the country, leaders of the Watts community achieved something of the same effect when they sought to counteract sensational stories in a national weekly magazine on the first anniversary of the 1965 riots. "Watts still seething . . . the ghetto today is close to flashpoint," announced its cover story. Infuriated by what they considered an irresponsible misinterpretation of the state of their community, Watts residents launched an arts weekend to enlist residents in a creative and constructive display. Sargent Shriver led a gala parade, the "flashpoint" never came, and the arts won justifiable praise for the achievement. A similar festival of the arts took place in Watts again in the summer of 1967 and may become an annual event.

The broad question of how the arts might promote desirable change in society received sporadic but intense consideration by the conferees. Melvin Roman's paper on "The Arts as Agents of Social Change" posed it the first morning. Quoting Ralph Ellison, Roman said that his thesis was that art, through its "organized significance . . . alone enables man to conquer chaos and master his destiny." It is the arts, then, which can best help men—and, more important, the poor themselves—to understand the dark, complex, baffling realities of the ghetto.

How can the arts do this? There are several ways. Roman finds the best model in the so-called "therapeutic community" developed in certain progressive mental hospitals, which puts "a great deal of emphasis on self-help and community responsibility." Such a pattern, he believes, can "harness the power of the artist to help the community articulate its feelings and to catalyze whatever action may be necessary to improve its social and physical environment."

A somewhat different perspective on the role of the arts in improving the relationships of poor people to their society was offered by Julian Euell, formerly director for the arts program of HARYOU ACT (a community action program for Harlem youths). His experience has convinced him that people in the ghettos have a craving for the arts that is often ignored and sometimes actually stifled by the job-oriented grants criteria of OEO, for example. Adding that the sheer ugliness of the slums is a prime cause of alienation and isolation, he quoted Kenneth Clark:

> The most concrete fact of the ghetto is its physical ugliness, the dirt, the filth, the neglect. The parks are seedy with lack of care. The streets are crowded with people and refuse. In all of Harlem there is no museum, no art gallery, no art school, no sustained little theatre group . . .

The description would apply, Euell sadly noted, to almost every impoverished area in the United States.

To break down ethnic and racial barriers, then, Euell suggests the arts as a connecting tissue with the outside society—motivating personal growth and development, and at the same time generating sympathy among divergent groups and groups and individuals. This effect is commonplace in popular culture: pop music, folk songs, sports, and nightclub entertainment, as well as activities not usually included in the arts, such as Chinese cooking—all have helped from time immemorial to create good will across national class or racial lines.

Do-gooders, however, once they begin trying to engage the poor in "art" programs, all too often tend to introduce things like basket weaving and handicrafts. Dance and drama are conceived as recreation rather than as deeply joyful, highly important experiences. But, Euell says:

The HARYOU program firmly established in my mind that we can take the disenchanted youngster and, through the arts, show him a way to ready himself to join the mainstream of society.

He believes, in fact, that this course may be more than another option; it may be essential to an effective antipoverty program. The efficacy of job-focused programs may have been relevant 20 years ago, but today, according to Euell:

> . . . the degree of deterioration and alienation in low-income areas is at a point where much more is needed. Programs that reach deeper must be introduced. Many young men and women from poverty areas do not carry enough confidence with them into a job-training situation. We cannot build up that confidence and a positive self-image overnight or just because we want it that way . . . [Besides] people who live in poverty are not just interested in jobs, housing, social welfare, etc. They are hungry for programs that allow for more individual achievement and expression. Most important is that the flow comes within themselves and their community.

For those who share Roman's and Euell's views, the ghetto can and must be transformed by the creative powers of the poor themselves. The way is hard and contrasts sharply with the usual services-from-without formula of conventional social work. But perhaps the artist knows the way and can help others find it. His way of life draws nourishment from within to come to terms with an environment that is usually indifferent and often hostile.

The Physical Environment:
Parks and Places

JERE STUART FRENCH "The Decline and Deterioration of the American City Park"
Parks and Recreation, National Recreation and Park Association, August 1970.

MAYER SPIVACK "The Political Collapse of a Playground"
Landscape Architecture, July 1969.

DAVID E. GRAY "The Un-Hostile Park"
Parks and Recreation, National Recreation and Park Association, February 1970.

R. BURTON LITTON, JR. "Ode to the Vacant Lot"
Landscape Architecture, July 1969.

MAYER SPIVACK "Listen, Hide, Build, Sing, and Dig"
Landscape Architecture, July 1969.

IRA COHEN "City Streets as Play Areas"
Parks and Recreation, National Recreation and Park Association, September 1968.

V. MICHAEL WEINMAYR "Vandalism by Design A Critique"
Landscape Architecture.

ROBERT SOMMER AND FRANKLIN D. BECKER "The Old Men in Plaza Park"
Landscape Architecture, January 1969.

CONRAD L. WIRTH "A Measure of Success"
Parks and Recreation, National Recreation and Park Association, November 1961.

ARCHIE D. McDONALD AND ROBERT J. NEWCOMER "Differences in Perception of a City Park as a Supportive or Threatening Environment"

JAMES ALEXANDER, JR. "Urban Esthetics *Can* Be Functional"
The American City, December 1969.

JOSEPH E. CURTIS "Pragmaesthetics"
Parks and Recreation, National Recreation and Park Association, July 1970.

J.E. CURTIS "How Parks Will Shape Urban Development"
The American City, October 1969.

The Physical Environment:
Parks and Places

Parks are for the people. They provide the public with a place where they may go to socialize and interact with other individuals. The park has served as a place for family gatherings; as a place to meet to plan a "revolution"; or as a place to refresh and renew oneself in the middle of an urban megalopolis. Parks have also served as a social arena for the individuals who use them. Although parks function differently in the inner city and the suburbs, they provide a place and often the services to meet the needs and interests of the urban resident.

In recent years, however, the use of parks in the inner city has declined rapidly. As a result of urban growth, individual social preferences, mobility, increasing crime rates, and deterioration of neighborhoods, parks no longer satisfy all the needs of all the people. The physical environment of the park no longer supports the activities being sought by some people in the society. Planning of park areas has often tended to reflect ideas of individuals whose only concerns are for the physical appearance of the park and not how well the park will meet the demands brought on by changing developments in our society.

"Many of the old parks and green areas still remain but their use is changing so rapidly that one has difficulty recognizing their original character."

Parks are viewed differently by all individuals. Children see it as a place where they can go to utilize the swings and other play apparatus that have been provided. Interacting with the equipment available, the ever-present curiosity and inventiveness of the child develop a variety of play patterns. The opportunities to develop, create, and be imaginative in his play habits are a constant challenge to the child, but parks and playgrounds may sometimes stifle children in trying to attain this self-realization. It is as though adults at times forget how curious children are and how imaginative they can be when left to follow their own nature. When standardized swings and jungle gyms are supplied, adults expect children to be quite content and happy while playing. This equipment at times does provide children with the challenge to think and create their own play devices, but some parks and playgrounds do not provide play experiences that create adventure and excitement. Faced with a sterile park environment, children seek the excitement and adventure which can often be found in the city streets.

". . . curiosity takes things apart."

In the adult world the park can be viewed as a place for social interaction, a "commons" where adults may assemble without a host-guest relationship, a place where they may go and be free from some of the pressures of contemporary life.

Some people in urban areas do not see the value of parks as other individuals do. They feel that the funds used to construct parks could be used for more important purposes like providing adequate housing or improving the overall community. Some feel their time is fully spent in trying to survive in this society—leaving them little time to enjoy and benefit from park experience. Others believe that their own backyard which offers more privacy or visiting neighbors will satisfy their need for social interaction.

"Parks are for the people, whether located on the suburban fringe or deep within the urban core."

By providing parks for these individuals, additional problems are created. Poor maintenance and vandalism are often evident. Few care about what happens to the park or how it looks. The general feeling of some of the people is that they did not want the park so why worry about what happens to it. Vandalism and destruction only confirm their attitudes about the significance of parks.

Another factor contributing to the decline in park use is the move from urban areas. Industrial and commercial expansion has forced many people to live lives that are concentrated in two distinct environments—the suburbs in which they live and the urban areas where they work. The city centers, alive with activities during the day, are largely deserted at night with relatively few remaining in the urban core. This severely inhibits day-long use of parks.

"America's city parks are dying. Their rejuvenation will depend largely on a rebirth of the city itself, for the public parks, like no other aspect of the urban scene, reflect the status of life and vitality of the city and its people."

The suburban dweller has a different kind of park experience. In development of tracts, little open space has been left to provide adequate parks. The facility often provided is the private club house, complete with golf course, cocktail lounges, and green spaces. These facilities are geared for the adult population. Lacking even rudimentary facilities the youth are seeking adventure that can be found in the streets of their neighborhoods. Lack of challenge, and the opportunity to express creativity, and imagination creates a hunger that is not being completely satisfied in these new neighborhoods.

Individuals who are served in city parks are often senior citizens—primarily older men and some women. They like the park. They have few places to go and little to do so they usually go to the park where they form relationships with individuals who have the same basic life styles as they have. The daily congregation of a group of elderly men sometimes discourages others from attending. If there is a substantial number and they appear shabby to the passerby, oftentimes they are looked upon with distrust by other people who use the park. It is felt, by some, that they make the park look like a place for vagabonds and useless old men. This physical resemblance appears to make the park unsafe for women and children, and over a period of time it may restrict the park to an all-male clientele.

The environment of the park clearly plays a vital part in attracting participants. The park must be capable of providing an environment which is attractive, safe, and one which offers facilities that will interest people sufficiently so they will want to take part in the services being provided. The park, like any other recreation facility, must create an environment where people will be comfortable and relaxed. Some parks have a welcoming profile, others are foreboding. This image is reflected in the uses made of them.

There are other factors which influence the use of parks. Although inhabitants of many low-income neighborhoods want facilities that are on a par with facilities in other parts of the city, their parks are sometimes old and poorly maintained. In these instances the facilities available are not adequate to their needs. In other sections of the city ridden with high crime rates the anti-social behavior in and around parks may inhibit their use, particularly at night. These problems are being addressed in many communities where, with the aid of self-help programs, redevelopment and model city funds, new facilities are being developed. Residents are volunteering in some cities and making a personal investment in neighborhood redevelopment by taking personal pride in their local parks.

"Destruction is the expression of a need."

The middle- and upper-income park areas are often equipped with facilities that are better developed and which add to the cultural enrichment of their participants. Because of their higher income, these people have other alternatives. To these individuals the type of facilities and physical environment of the parks are extremely important if they are to become active participants in park activities. Factors which inhibit use of parks in other areas of the city are not as strong in these areas.

The park, in this country, is no longer considered the ideal place for social interaction by an ever-increasing proportion of our society. Its future is uncertain. The public must learn to make these areas an asset to the communities in which they exist. It must be made more understandable that parks are not the sole responsibility of local government but that all people must continue to work to ensure that parks are desirable entities in the community.

People in urban areas must be encouraged to help establish the parks in their communities and to have a voice in their design. Only with their interest and support will parks remain an asset. They must realize that a gracious city requires parks and that the residents are entitled to the benefits and pleasures that parks offer.

In the future parks will have to be designed so that they provide adventure, the opportunity to think and to be creative. They must be attractive to draw attention, and to let the public know they are there to be used in helping to fulfill some of their social needs.

"A park that is to draw a diversity of users must offer a diversity of settings."

The articles in the following section represent a kaliediscope of thinking about parks—past, present and future.

The Decline and Deterioration
of the American City Park

Jere Stuart French

Today, more than any other time in our history, American cities are faced with calamitous problems that threaten to turn them into gray jungles of misery and chaos. The salvation of the cities, where more than 80 percent of the population lives, can be, in effect, the salvation of the nation. What has gone wrong? What can be done to return beauty, peace, and goodwill to the great urban centers?

The structure of the typical American city is over 40 percent commercial and 10 to 20 percent industrial. Streets and parking facilities claim about one-third of the city's area. Less than 10 percent of downtown centers is usually residential. The American city pictured as a center for industry and trade dates from the pioneer days of our machine age when the young nation was flexing its muscles. In trying to compete successfully with Europe's growing industrial strength the charm and dignity of the colonial town centers were sacrificed, perhaps unwittingly.

The rapid and even chaotic expansion during the industrial revolution was damaging to urban life in countless ways. For European cities, which had had centuries to develop a base in humanistic values and logical order, the changes wrought were distressing. For the new, delicately structured American cities, they were disastrous.

For one thing, European cities had parks. Most of these were once the private estates of titled and wealthy European families. Nondemocratic at their inception, they nevertheless eventually formed the basis of public park systems for Europe's older cities.

Moreover, these cities, with their medieval, renaissance, and classical histories, possess street patterns and civic organization which are more organic and humanistic. Streets were originally planned for pedestrians and slow-paced carts which allowed an intimacy that still persists today. The topography of the land was incorporated into the design of the cities rather than being demolished by bulldozers in order to effect the stability of a gridiron system. Thus, at the peak of development a typical European city possessed great open spaces, centrally located, and a tight, organic nucleus which could lend itself to continued development of pedestrain scale and linkage.

Amsterdam's traditional canals, which radiate from the city's center

Reprinted with permission from National Recreation and Park Association. Official publication *Parks and Recreation*, August, 1970.

like ripples in a pool, offer both a means of civic separation of the radial axis and continuity in concentric movement. Amsterdam's modern plan calls for linear development in three directions from the city's heart—like a three-fingered hand—thumb, index, and little finger. Replacing the ring and forefinger are narrow green spaces of agricultural and recreational development. This interlacing of rural and urban fingers gives structure to the city's growth patterns and maintains contact with nature as well. The super park, Amsterdamse Bos, represents one such green finger and offers 2,500 acres of carefully planned watery wilderness to the nearby citizenry—easily within cycling distance. The middle finger, extending out from the city, is represented by the new town of Amstelveen. This model city from nearly every standpoint has been carefully planned to include a system of linking greenways and canals, while at the same time to provide boundaries which are fixed permanently by adjacent parks and polders.* Although the corridor park was invented by the American, Frederick Law Olmsted, it is probably seeing its greatest development in the cities of Northern Europe.

Paris' two super parks, the Bois de Boulogne and Vincennes, in conjunction with Vie de Triomphe and the Seine, create the framework for a highly stylized urban system. Based on existing urbanography, a far-reaching plan by Baron Haussmann and a penchant for both density and *elan*, Paris emerged in the 19th century as the most exciting and urbane city of Europe. Her two green lungs help to separate the city proper from her inner suburbs, and are themselves connected across the heart of the city by the river and the Vie de Triomphe (Champs Elysees and Acoutrements). In this manner Paris remains distinct from her surroundings in a way

which was never accomplished in London. Inner-city green space is provided by medium sized parks, such as Luxembourg, Buttes-Chaumont, Jardin des Plantes, Montouris, and the Tuilleries.

CITY BUDGETS STRETCHED TO LIMIT

Some American cities have benefited from inherited estates, world's fairs, and so on. But more often the creation and expansion of public city parks in this country has been a long uphill battle requiring outright purchase. Since private capital determines the value of land, city budgets have been stretched to the limit in competing with private finance to obtain park sites where needed. Most American cities, especially in the West and Midwest, reflect this characteristic—gridirons of traffic interspersed with a few disconnected rectangles of green.

By European standards, American cities are park poor—and getting worse. The growth in park acreage is nowhere near proportional to the growth in area of our cities, particularly the faster growing cities like Houston, Phoenix, Dallas, and Los Angeles.

Los Angeles can boast of only two well-located parks of respectable size, for a city of three million people (eight million in the metropolitan area). One of these, Griffith Park, is largely undeveloped while the other, Elysian Park, is in a serious state of decline due to inadequate maintenance. Griffith Park, an extraordinary gift of some 4,000 acres, after some 50 years still waits for major development. Except for its observatory and zoo (a major controversy itself), park improvements include only the creation of three golf courses. (Two large dam basins to the west and northwest of

*land reclaimed from the sea.

the city's center have been appropriated and will eventually serve as city parks.)

The gridiron sprawl and accompanying lack of developed parks in Phoenix is even worse. Save for memorial parks, Houston is every bit as park poor—and getting worse daily! For a city which prides itself on the accomplishment of private enterprise and the absence of governmental regulatory organization, the results are indeed depressing.

EMOTIONAL AND POLITICAL FACTORS INVOLVED

In addition to an urban growth rate which is outstripping park growth and the decline of existing parks through lack of sufficient maintenance funds, there remain emotional and political factors which further damage the imbalance between city and park. Some of these are:

1. *Social and political unrest has led directly to the reduction of park funding, programming, and use.* Denied access to public parks in several southern cities in the early '50s, Negroes rebelled against this injustice and forcibly integrated such parks and bathing facilities. This resulted in angry retaliation, property damage, and eventually the closing of parks and pools. Since that time, city parks across the country have become scenes for continuous demonstration and rebellion against political and social inequities and injustices. The various counterreactions of civic and military authority, as well as general citizenry, have made some of our parks virtually synonymous with battlegrounds. Lincoln Park in Chicago, and more recently the "People's Park" of Berkeley, have become internationally known as such. The parks are not to blame, and curtailment of limitations on use of public parks for peaceful gatherings is tantamount to denial of free assembly—a constitutionally guaranteed American right.

2. *Decline of Public Transportation.* Studies taken from percentage of use at established city parks seem to bear out the affinity between public park use and public transportation. Where transportation declines or is terminated, park use falls off accordingly. The deterioration of public transit systems is largely the result of an increasing dependence on the automobile and the resultant strain on public transit systems trying to function on shrinking profits. There is, however, an additional psychological factor which is infecting public facilities—parks as well as transportation—and that is a growing mistrust, fear, or even disdain for public institutions. Urban, and more so suburban dwellers, continue to express a greater desire for private, enclosed yards and autos even when proven to be more expensive and inconvenient than *public* parks and transportation. Indications of this nature suggest a continuing erosion of public trust—a basic tenet of urban life.

3. *The erosion of urban residential areas by expanding commercial and industrial facilities continues to threaten urban balance.* Beginning in the late 1940s, the exodus from the cities, to establish new homes while keeping old jobs, has led to a schizophrenic way of life for many Americans who must wrestle between two environments and two lives neither of which is able to gain dominance over the other. And the city centers, alive with activity during the day, are abandoned at dusk to another society—a variety of "night people" and bizarre if not unsavory activities. Only the ghetto continues to maintain the tradition of live-and-work stability. Perhaps, with careful planning and sufficient insight, these older residential communities could point the way towards a

healthy rehabilitation of what is presently considered uninhabitable. Philadelphia has already taken the lead in experimenting with new ways of restructuring and revitalizing urban residential patterns of living. In the meantime, the great city parks continue to suffer from abandonment. Parks are for people, whether located on the suburban fringe or deep within the urban core. When the "frame of residential constancy" is impaired, the park will fall victim to night, even day uses, wholly unsympathetic to neighborhood integrity and social well-being.

4. *Stratified suburban communities, so common since the great "exurbanite" housing boom of the '50s, have also failed to promote the growth of public parks.* The typical suburban tract has been unable to meet the needs or desires for public open space, and to see kids playing in the streets is perhaps as common a sight in such middle-income tracts as in the ghettos. Again, for other than financial reasons, stratified communities appear to offer less challenge, excitement, or interaction than do neighborhoods of less homogeneous composition.

5. *Decentralization, including suburbia, and low density areas tends to impair the development of public parks for another reason—substitution*—the backyard can and does offer many of the essentials of the public park, with a measure of privacy as well. Without backyards, Los Angeles would be uninhabitable with a ratio of developed public park acreage to total urban area within the city limits of only one-fifth that of Philadelphia. Los Angeles' park-city ratio becomes absurd when compared with Stockholm, where an intense emphasis on public park facilities exists. In terms of public recreation, Stockholm's giant park system offers a great variety of organized programs for all ages

including amateur and professional outdoor theater—all free and readily available to the public. Los Angeles' park system offers golf for a fee and a few limited recreation activities.

URBAN PARK REFLECTS VITALITY OF THE CITY

America's city parks are dying. Their rejuvenation will depend largely on a rebirth of the city itself, for the public park, like no other aspect of the urban scene, reflects the status of life and vitality of the city and its people. But even then the character of city parks and park systems must be made to reflect the hoped for renaissance in terms of basic demographic, climatic, and topographic characteristics of their respective cities as well as trends in growth patterns and advanced technology, which can be made predictable for summation. Certain laws of thumb seem to apply:

1. **The greater the population density, the higher the percentage of acreage in parks and other public open space—**

Statistics for Los Angeles, St. Louis, and Philadelphia can be compared. Sprawling Los Angeles, which covers over 460 square miles, continues to outstrip its presently inadequate park capabilities. Considering only those living within the city limits, Los Angeles maintains a ratio of less than two acres of developed park for 1,000 residents compared with 4.5 acres per 1,000 in St. Louis and Philadelphia. Moreover, comparing total urban area to developed park area, we see that Los Angeles maintains a ratio of 50 to 1 whereas St. Louis, with a compact and better established urban base, has a ratio of 15 to 1 and Philadelphia, one of our oldest and greenest cities, approximates 1 park acre out of 10.

Los Angeles controls several thousand acres of undeveloped land in Griffith

Park and two dam basins which offer great potential to the city as does the great swath of the Santa Monica mountains containing over 150 square miles of well-located, undeveloped land representing perhaps the city's greatest hope for new space development. For sprawling, low-density cities, however, more small parks, interlocked through pedestrian systems, are needed—especially in low income neighborhoods where ample private yards are not available or readily maintained.

2. **The greater the emphasis on private ownership of land, the less acreage devoted to public parks—**

The outstanding examples for park comparison in the western world might be Phoenix and Stockholm. In Stockholm, where virtually all land within the city limits is city-owned, the ratio of city to open green space is about 6 to 1 whereas Phoenix, a city devoted to a great extent to independent development, is largely devoid of public parks and public transportation. Such conditions create virtual prisons for the poor and the old who can't afford private recreation facilities such as golf, tennis, and swim clubs. A sense of public trust must be awakened if public institutions are to be maintained and enlarged in keeping with normal population growth, earlier retirement, and ever-shortening working hours. The spending of public funds is at an all time high—most of it, however, for national defense. Boston's Mayor White declares, "Every American city is on the verge of bankruptcy," while at the same time the federal government spends between 350 and 400 million dollars every day of the week for military purposes alone!

3. **The greater the economic stratification of neighborhoods, the lesser the emphasis on public park use and development—**

Some improvements in this situation have been attempted by developers through variation of lot rise and housing styles. Much more study is needed, especially in older, more organic neighborhoods, to find the formulae for neighborhood economic balance.

4. **The greater the degree of commuter living, the lesser the emphasis on park development in either suburbia or center city—**

Urban schizophrenia creates a sense of confusion in values, purposes, and life style. Schools and other public institutions as well as parks suffer the fate of public neglect, whether in bedroom communities or the nocturnally abandoned center city. A return of "live-where-you-work," as Philadelphia has attempted to create, sounds fine, but only if the city center can provide the life style and public facilities required.

5. **The greater the public trust, the greater the use and development of public parks and recreation—**

Our city parks are declining in America because the public is losing its faith in public institutions—and apparently in itself as well. A city which lacks the soul of urbanity ceases to be a city in the finer sense of the word, as expressed by Aristotle, Sixtus V, Georges Haussmann, Daniel Burnham, and the other visionaries throughout the ages who have always considered the city to be man's greatest accomplishment on earth.

Public trust would seem to have two implications here. One calls for a reconfirmation of our faith in cities as civilization's greatest experiment in human endeavor. The other meaning suggests a need for greater public trust in itself. The future of our city parks depends on it.

The Political Collapse of a Playground

Mayer Spivack

A few years ago while working as a city planner I became involved in the design and construction of a neighborhood playground located in a very dense old urban area near Boston. I had for some time been interested in the problem of designing physical settings for children which could provide a spectrum of play satisfactions.

My new play facility was to be constructed on the site of an older one whose originally uninteresting and meager equipment had been further incapacitated by vandalism. The city under whose auspices I was working agreed to supply tools and earth-moving equipment and specialized labor where it was required, as in the installation of water supplies and drainage pipes, and drivers for the heavy equipment.

The city also made available a small amount of money (under $2,000) from a special fund. It was our intention to build an inexpensive, appropriately designed play world with the aid of children as designers and constructors. My services were available as a kind of technical consultant to both the city and the children.

For two or three weeks prior to the beginning of construction, and while involved in measuring the site and drawing up tentative proposals for its use, I was able to observe the play and intensity of use on the old playground and to become friendly with the children.

School had let out for the summer and yet in none of my visits to the site were there ever more than three or four children on the playground. Characteristically, they would sit disconsolately in a corner against the chain link fence in the shade—for it was already quite hot on that black desert—or they would ride bicycles in lazy figure 8's, obviously bored. The space was huge in relation to the scale of a child, and totally flat. Broken pavement showed where old, damaged swings and slides had been torn out and the holes had been left unpatched. One could have turned it into a parking lot without altering a thing.

There were children of all ages, from tots through advanced teens everywhere on the streets, sitting in doorways, and leaning on lamp posts. When I talked about the idea of rebuilding the tot lot for the small children, the teenagers left no doubt in my mind that they had felt unfairly treated when, in the presence of an official from the Recreation Commission, they had been ejected from the old space. They soon told me that, reacting to this kind of treatment, they had found it

Reprinted with permission of publisher of *Landscape Architecture*, July, 1969.

satisfying to tear out the jungle gym, to break the slides and to steal the swings used by the younger ones. In response to this the Recreation Commission had given up trying to maintain the area.

The neighborhood was populated in the main by working-class Italians. Many of the children had no access to the interiors of their own houses during the day while their mothers were away working. Children were put in the charge of other families, left to themselves or in the care of some other, older, child. The only play space, possessable space, or homeplace that they could hope for was that which the city would give them. They looked for space in someone else's backyard or alley, or in the street. These children had no place to keep anything of their own, in which to hide their toys, or to use them.

As often happens in such close old neighborhoods, children were noisily and actively discouraged from using vacant lots next to houses, side alleys and back yards by the abutting property owners who feared the litter of broken glass, vandalism, and the noise.

Between us, the children and I devised a plan for the playground whose layout was based upon safety requirements and on the necessity to separate more violent active play areas from those needing some peace and security. The equipment was designed to be built by and for children with materials they could, with a little help, manipulate and control. Our goals were very limited and simple. Given the budget, we were restricted to using industrial surplus materials, and to scavenging what we could. The city would provide us with fencing material, with paving, water pipes and conduit, and with fill.

Within a few weeks we had accumulated on the playground stocks of railroad ties, telephone poles, cable drumheads and many truckloads full of wood

chips. These were to be our raw materials; they would also to some extent dictate esthetic.

In addition, the playground was a kind of compromise or halfway point between the athletic field amusement park and the intimate play space required at various times.

The plan represented that compromise by providing the older children with such facilities as a basketball court in return for their guarantee of protection and maintenance of the playground for the younger children. It was hinted by the older children that if this were not the case they would not protect the facilities that they were not interested in. I learned quickly and gave them their due. In return, they more than kept to their bargain, throwing themselves into the work of building the whole playground with an intensity reserved only for play. There were no further problems with vandalism, and the playground began to have a life of its own.

Arrival of the first construction equipment carrying the hulk of a strong tree-trunk galvanized the whole community. The tree-trunk was placed on its side in temporary storage and within seconds after it was maneuvered into position it became the property of the playground population which had risen to about 25 or 30 children. The new high level of use and involvement was maintained throughout the summer. Many of the children had court records, some of them by the age of 9. I had been warned by city officials that it was impossible to do anything with or for these children for they were hardened delinquents and would destroy anything that we gave them.

Perhaps we were all fortunate that our plan made it necessary for the children to match, by giving their effort and involvement, whatever the city and I gave on our side. In the course of the summer there never occurred an incident of theft or of willful damage to materials on the playground. The children were on the job every morning long before I arrived. Nearly every day I would find the children had torn down and completely rebuilt their little city. The first of these structures, ambitious quasi-shelters constructed of railroad ties, appeared in a shaded corner of the lot and, as I approached, one of the littler kids came running out, pleading, "Mr. Spivack, Mr. Spivack, you're not going to tear it down, are you?" That was their image of "adult authority" and of "city hall," each of which I represented to them.

As the summer progressed this same structure, modified time after time into new forms, would reappear. I was amazed at the ease with which these kids could move the railroad ties, some of which were 17′ long and weighed over 300 pounds. I suspected adult collusion for I never saw them building this way in the daytime: apparently construction was a nocturnal act.

Building the playground became play. The only fights I observed were over the privilege of using a shovel or a pick, or some other tool, for there were not enough of these to go around. As the children built the space it became clear that they were building themselves as well. Pride in accomplishment, in competence, and just plain pleasure were almost always visible on the faces and in the movements of the children while they worked. Having invested themselves so obviously and so thoroughly in a community sponsored, valued project, they also developed a sense of identification with, and responsibility for the publicly owned property. The work and the playground were theirs.

They became visible members of a child community which had a certain amount of effect on, and esteem from, the adult community. They learned to get along with older people because they worked and played with them. They had the chance in a short span of time to participate with adults in the conception, planning, and implementation of a complex piece of work which had obvious and tangible consequences in their world. They widened their repertoire of social roles and contexts within which they could experiment and search for new notions of self-identity. They became, in a very real sense, political actors whose opinions were valued, whose responsibilities were clear; citizens of a small, organized, functioning community—leaders and followers at once. They experienced a sense of community.

Since much of the work and its planning was the responsibility of the children, problems encountered during construction and planning were often unanticipated, and the children, when challenged, time and time again had problems of organization and process which required considerable resourcefulness individually and as cooperating groups in their solution. Perhaps more important, they generated the problems which they encountered in the course of their work on their own initiative. They were not told what to do unless they asked for advice.

Average children discovered in themselves abilities to lead and found that they had attitudes and aspirations towards leadership that might otherwise have been undeveloped. They were glorious in the eyes of younger children and therefore became natural nominees for leadership roles, although such roles were never formalized. Hero worship patterns, however, could easily be observed.

The work-play fusion was complete. Work was played and play was worked. Builders must play on a job like this or it won't be done well. This is an easy, natural way to a good working habit or at least a good attitude towards work, where work comes to be viewed as an experiment with oneself and an exploration of one's stocks of resourcefulness and one's limitations. Children who, for one reason or another, participated less in the building process, came to the playground every day anyway, and in the course of the summer saw their playmates scheme and plan and convert an ugly pile of raw materials into wonderful structures. They watched and they learned vicariously and they enjoyed it immensely.

By late August the land had been molded and distinct activity areas or zones had taken shape. We were within a few weeks of completion. Raw material stockpiled for so long was now being used in construction. It became apparent that we intended to use these materials in their final form without refinishing them. The children were perfectly happy with the materials and may even have thought them beautiful. Their parents and neighbors, however, considered telephone poles and railroad ties as industrial surplus, or as one of them put it, "a bunch of junk."

This esthetic conflict became the issue which was destined to destroy the project. I remained naively unaware that the neighbors were beginning to resent the fact that other areas of the city received shiny new playground equipment while their area was given used, ugly, wooden cast-offs. My original attempts to arouse substantial adult community involvement and support for the project had never been very successful. The neighborhood obviously preferred to have things done for them as was the case elsewhere. (Community action programs were at that time relatively new.) Their preconception also appeared to involve some notion of gaining, or at least not losing, status, by having the services of

the city performed for them by "servants" as was the case in middle class and upper income areas.

Thus without the support and involvement of the neighborhood, and without feedback, we were completely taken by surprise when one Monday morning in early September the children and I appeared at the site to find the project demolished and replaced by a perfectly flat, black, hot, top paving. We now had the equivalent of a parking lot. Later, in a conversation with a city councilor, I learned that an irritated property owner had persuaded him to "eliminate the mess" (sic) and that he had done so, even though previously he had been enthusiastic about the work and had gone so far as to propose to me other sites in his area which might be similarly transformed by neighborhood children.

Now, in the wisdom of retrospection, I understand how differences in esthetics are closely tied to concerns about community status and to the relatively different value structures held by the adults of the community, their children, and myself, the "expert consultant" or technician. Had I identified these differences as conflicts early enough and effectively dealt with them the project might not have failed so drastically.

Perhaps the lessons of failure are the more profoundly learned. If so, then the children have learned as well. For them, a positive image of City Hall and government formed through the optimistic period of their work and participation was inexplicably and insidiously shattered. A truly democratic experience was negated by the powerful gestures of one or two people who remained unidentified.

Most of the children were acutely disappointed and were either unwilling or unable to understand the underlying reasons for the collapse of their efforts. They became uncommunicative and resentful.

Soon the city installed some shiny new fencing and playground equipment. Within days unmistakable signs of vandalism were visible. Fence posts were bent to the ground and the new paving covered with broken bottles. A new kind of junkpile had been created.

Even though the project failed, many ideas we explored concerning the spatial requirements of play behavior and the nature of play behavior itself have been an impetus to my continued thinking and research.

The Un-Hostile Park

David E. Gray

A downtown park may be viewed as a physical environment, an institution, a society, an ecology, or as a system with subsystems and interfaces with the surrounding city. From one point of view, a downtown park is an island in the paved urban world; it is conditioned by the physical environment and the social system of the surrounding territory. The park society is a subsociety of the neighborhood and the neighborhood is a subsociety of the community and so on. There is a dynamic relationship between a park and its neighborhood. The relationship may be friendly, with people moving easily from social roles in the park society to social roles in the neighborhood or it may be hostile with mutual deep suspicion of the park people and the neighborhood dwellers and little exchange of social interaction. Lincoln is an unhostile park! The neighborhood dwellers and the park people are one and the same for the most part.

Lincoln Park attracts several thousand visitors each week. Considering the large number of people who frequent the park and its downtown location, the number of offenses serious enough to attract the attention of the police is relatively small. During the 1967 calendar year, 262 persons were arrested in Lincoln Park, of these 232 arrests were for intoxication, and 11 for drinking in public.

If one eliminates the activities of the drinking class, only 19 people caused trouble in the park serious enough to be arrested. The fact that so many individuals were involved in the problems of drink is significant. It is one measure of the necessity for the park and the services it renders.

PARK EXPERIENCE AIDED BY ENVIRONMENT

A prime characteristic of mankind is the requirement for human interaction. There are human urges and potentials which can only be expressed in a culturally defined social environment. The park also provides a physical environment, of course, and this supplies many things from which people who attend the park can construct their experience. Obviously, one cannot watch the movement of trees against the sky if there are no trees, or feed birds unless there are birds, or doze

Reprinted with permission from National Recreation and Park Association. Official publication *Parks and Recreation*, February, 1970.

in the sun without sun, or sit on a bench where there is no bench. Thus, it is from the physical environment that much of the park experience stems.

At any one time there is apt to be present in a downtown park a number of people who are "regulars" and a number of casual visitors who come to the park infrequently. This is another way of saying that the park environment and the park society are a central concern for some people which prompts frequent, perhaps even daily attendance. But for others, the park is of so little concern that it merits infrequent visits. For the majority of the people, of course, the park does not have enough interest to draw any attention.

For those who attend regularly, since attendance is voluntary, the park environment or the park society, or both, appear to satisfy psycho-biological needs. For the regulars, who spend long hours in the park almost daily, the psychological income derived is adequate to forego alternative uses of the time and energy expended.

ATTENDANCE
SAMPLED REGULARLY

The Long Beach Recreation Department samples attendance during four weeks each year. In the November 1968 sample week there were 790 units of attendance in chess and checkers, 1,292 in cards, 1,618 in shuffleboard, and 547 in roque. These "participants" in organized programs were far outnumbered by those who used the park for their own purposes and were not included in the attendance figures.

Participation in the park is something we know little about. The shuffleboard player is a "participant" according to any definition of the term, but the person who eats a sack lunch, reads a book, feeds the birds or converses with

friends is not. This arbitary distinction between participants and spectators has little meaning. Who among us can say that the psychological income of the shuffleboard player is greater than that of the reader? Each in his own way is a participant in the park society.

There is a well-developed social system in Lincoln Park. The society there is not monolithic, but, like societies nearly everywhere, it is criss-crossed with cliques and groups of various kinds. The card players, the roque players and the shuffleboard players have organized clubs, but there are also more subtle groupings.

There is a class system. The lower class, made up largely of indigent men— the homeless, "winos" and the like— occupy the older section of the park. They are more argumentative and more radical in their politics. Their conversations may erupt into oratory. They have a well-defined territory which is seldom visited by any of the other regulars. Here some pass the time of day, look for a handout and sleep in the bushes at night. For a few, the park is "home" between visits to jail. They look to the park for satisfaction of their biological as well as their social needs.

The upper class—composed for the most part of elderly retired middle-class men and women—belong to the recreation clubs and occupy the redeveloped section of the park. They play cards, shuffleboard and roque, sit on the benches in the sun and carry on endless discussions. They avoid contact with the lower-class individuals whenever possible. Generally people of their class are clean, well dressed and orderly. They look to the park primarily as a source of satisfaction for their social needs.

Within the societies there are groups based on shared recreational interests and within the groups there are cliques based on skill in the activity, shared socioeconomic background and compatibility of personality.

As an illustration, consider the card players. This group has 500 to 600 members, all white, about half men and half women, and living within walking distance of the park—usually within five blocks. The members have a variety of economic resources; some are wealthy, many are on pensions, nearly all live alone in an apartment or single room in the neighborhood. They vary in educational background also; most have grade school or high school educational attainment but there are several retired professionals including teachers, dentists and lawyers. On an average day 150-200 members come to play contract bridge or pinochle. A typical day for a male member would be: get up about 8:00 a.m., eat breakfast, do some light chores around the apartment, arrive at the club about 10:00 a.m., talk with other early arrivals until 11:00 a.m., play cards with a sack lunch at the table until 2:30 p.m. or 3:30 p.m., go out to dinner in a local restaurant or coffee shop, and then return to the apartment to watch TV until bedtime. For the women the day is similar except that they devote an additional hour to chores around the apartment and personal grooming, prior to departure for the club.

PARK KEEPS PEOPLE ALIVE

Asked to articulate the benefits of the club one of its members said, "It keeps us alive, keeps our minds alert (you have to think to play cards), maintains social contact, encourages interest in current events and politics, provides exercise walking back and forth and prevents us from giving in to our feelings and becoming neurotic." These are not inconsequential benefits.

In their recreational interests elderly people tend to be specialists. The card players never play shuffleboard, although occasionally a shuffleboard player may play cards. In cards and shuffleboard men and women are about equally divided; in checkers, chess and roque players are usually men.

On a typical day in Lincoln Park the night people are up and away before dawn seeking a bit of warmth and a handout. If it is a market day the merchants are setting up their booths and beginning to display their wares while it is still dark. At first light, the earliest park visitors appear. One old gentleman makes his rounds picking up trash from the flower beds and walks and deposits it in the nearest trash can. Shortly after, another man, equipped with a shopping bag, investigates the most promising cans to see what treasures have been left there. Soon pedestrians begin to traverse the park, hurrying to get to work. By seven the first roque players arrive. One makes coffee; the others begin the intricate task of preparing the courts for the day's play. By seven-thirty the first housewives arrive to shop in the outdoor market. By eight-thirty the card players have begun to assemble. They are soon followed by those who play shuffleboard. By nine, those who are on the bum have begun to return. Soon the park is occupied and another day has begun. Single men sit on the sunny benches. The walks which had been paths for workers now carry shoppers who, at a more leisurely pace, cut through the park en route to the downtown shopping area. By mid-morning women visitors appear, to sit on the benches and play cards and shuffleboard. At noon the street market closes and the stalls are dismantled. Occasionally a mother brings a child to explore the park. Off-duty sailors stroll through. Library users come and go. This continues until the chill and the fading light force departure. Gradually the benches empty and the players disappear. First the shoppers and then the workers return through the park. Shortly, except for the library users, the park is returned to the night people.

Observations of Lincoln Park—extending back over a four-year period—suggest:

1. To be successful a downtown park must be attractive—literally attractive—that is, it must attract the physical presence of a large number of people.

2. The single most important clientele in Lincoln Park is the elderly retired. It is they who have the leisure and diversity of schedule which gives the place dawn to dusk vitality. For them the park becomes a great outdoor living room in which a daily open house takes place. There people are visited, games are played, issues are debated, and the time-of-day is passed.

3. Lincoln Park is a successful park by any standard. It is successful because it has tremendous vitality. It is used every hour of every day and except when it is in the care of the night people it is usually crowded. Its vitality stems from diversity of opportunity and its location.

4. A downtown park is a creature of its surroundings. There is evidence to suggest that the really successful downtown park is possible only in a diverse neighborhood with a wide variety of development because it is only in such a neighborhood that people's schedules are different enough to populate the park all day, every day.

5. The thing that makes a downtown park successful is use. There is no substitute for occupancy. No size, no feature, no nicety of design, no superiority of maintenance can compensate for lack of public use, but the design can limit use.

6. It appears that the downtown parks must have enough separation from the city to give them identity but not so much separation that it severs park users from the streets about them.

7. Some Americans have a veneration for "open space" that is almost mystical in its reverence. Open space is not of itself a universal good. It is the uses that are made of the space that establish its character. Open space for what? For muggings? As a vacuum between buildings? Unused city parks become places for crime and vandalism, but if the use is heavy they provide their own surveillance.

8. To be successful a downtown park must have a design that fosters social groupings. It should offer a variety of focal points and clearly defined limits.

9. A park that is designed only as a physical environment without regard to the needs and wishes of the potential park society is not apt to attract heavy use.

10. A downtown park that does not encourage the sale of goods—particularly food and drink—forfeits an important service and source of interest.

11. A park that is to draw a diversity of users must offer a diversity of settings. Such a park must have sun and shade, openness and seclusion, sites for activity and contemplation, places to walk and to sit, grass and pavement.

Even these preliminary findings raise some questions about the ways downtown parks are traditionally designed, about the uses that are thought appropriate, and particularly about the way these parks are located. What is a park? Do we really know?

Ode to the Vacant Lot

R. Burton Litton, Jr.

I've got a thing about vacant lots. No park department in its right mind would set out to have vacant lots as a part of its system. But nothing is more useful to kids than to have a fallow lot close at hand, say, a half-block away. It is true that there is a big push on now for vest-pocket parks, something akin to open lots so far as area is concerned, but philosophically no relative. For one thing, the park superintendent couldn't take visiting colleagues around to see how many vacant lots were part of the system, but vest-pocket parks would qualify nicely and think how, if proliferated, they would swell the number of jurisdictional parcels as they appeared in the annual report!

A vacant lot is an adult euphemism for something that should be filled, presumably with a house. This may be all right for a real-estate bias but my impression is that no youngster sees a vacant lot as empty. Let's take the matter of grass (not *Cannabis sativa*). It's a crop that never fails; adults consider it an invention of the devil, and firemen can't rest easy until the torch has been applied. In the meantime, it proves highly useful to the neighborhood's younger set. For the individual there are two kinds of grass whistles, the reed type and the raspberry type, the latter available in three octaves. Wild oats make the best snares for post lizards; you strip off the immature seeds and throw them at someone handy, then the terminal tip can be fashioned into a slip-knot snare. I never saw a lizard hurt that way, surprised, no doubt, but nothing more. For group action, grass fights are the thing. Technically, the projectile is root mass with dirt attached; the stems are the handle, a humane weapon with high trajectory and low speed. Attacks are best mounted from grass tunnels or similar camouflaged positions. Spring is the season for being wary, although adults are normally quite apt to be spared. For those who are concerned, the signs of action can be read from the spent grass clumps in the street. Should any grass survive the pressures of springtime use, and particularly the fireman's later zeal, it will be handy for autumn sliding if the lot is blessed with an excessively steep slope.

Should the empty lot have a grove of trees on it, so much the better. We've had several near us and they've borne their share of tree houses. At a certain age there is a powerful urge to build such assemblies that can be broadly categorized as tree houses. It strikes most boys and even

Reprinted with permission of the publisher of *Landscape Architecture*, July, 1969.

afflicts some tomboys. An important factor is a tolerant landlord, or better yet, an absentee land owner. Where the materials come from is somewhat mysterious, but my shop has been known to supply hammer and nails.

This kind of carpentry-building action has been institutionalized in junk playgrounds in Sweden and England, but in this country it hasn't been given much formal encouragement. The official attitude here is probably more influenced by possible liability claims than by recognition of what kids enjoy doing. I'd like to believe that some day we might think in terms of vest-pocket parks that are dynamic enough to accept action like tree-house building, tearing down, and starting all over again. Some trees are tough enough to take it and still provide an air of local respectability. The ordinary landscape is what you start with.

Listen, Hide, Build, Sing, and Dig

Mayer Spivack

It is perhaps the fault of the Protestant ethic that we so habitually, as adults, separate the activities of children into play and work. For the child, however, things are not quite so clear; given proper conditions, children, in the name of play, will become thoroughly invested in enterprises that would make many a strong man a work shirker. However, on a visit to nearly any public playground in mid-summer we are likely to encounter a meager population sitting discouragedly on swings or near the edges of the playground, leaning against a fence, or perhaps aimlessly riding a bicycle around in circles. The often expensive and "esthetically pleasing" equipment purchased by adults for children with the best intentions stands either unused or unusable because of vandalism.

Lately there has been much attention given to the subject of public playgrounds in urban areas. In Boston the Metropolitan District Commission has for several years, been constructing its version of improved playgrounds for children. Manufacturers have sprung up nationally to add their notions of proper and beautiful play equipment for children. Annually architects, sculptors and designers are invited to enter one of several competitions for the design of better playground "sculpture."

Well-intentioned, as such efforts certainly are, the greater part of them miss the point. Playgrounds, if they are useful at all, must serve many purposes, only one of which is the satisfaction of a child's needs to play in the conventional sense.

Children are rarely conscious of the fact of their playing which may consist of intense learning and the satisfaction of curiosity about the natural world and the human one. It may involve testing of social roles, development of physical coordination and strength and competition with age mates in contests of skill of various sorts. Fantasy-based play may or may not be accompanied by the physical manipulation of objects in the environment—the "working out" or "playing out" of conflicts, fears, and other troublesome emotion-related material. In childrens' play we may see a wide range of behaviors.

Against this rather sketchy background of what children may do while playing, consider the range of settings available to an urban child in a "modern" playground. Most often playgrounds are designed to be miniature athletic fields or do-it-yourself amusement parks, in which

Reprinted with permission of publisher, *Landscape Architecture*, July, 1969.

the child is challenged only in the physical modes of his play behavior. There are bars to climb and hang on, slides to slide on and swings on which to swing. But for a child who wants to build or dig, hide, sing or tell stories and listen to them, there is no proper setting. It is true that children are capable of modifying almost any setting to their needs, but on a playground where other children are flying and kicking there is often little quiet space in which to sit tranquilly and play with a tiny toy or immerse oneself in dreams or fantasies.

Most playgrounds being built today resemble huge squirrel cages. They challenge and exhaust the child with a variety of intriguing and enjoyable muscle testing experiences. This is satisfactory if it does not have to fill the play space needs of the same child or children day after day throughout the year. Unfortunately, this is the kind of playground so widely photographed and discussed in Sunday supplements and most often used as a model by cities and towns. A playground at a school or in a community mental health center, or in an urban or suburban neighborhood must be capable of serving many requirements especially if the group of children using it remain fairly constant. For the child in a dense urban area, ability of the space to provide a variety of play settings may be of superlative importance to his well-being. When a child makes something, or attempts to change his environment, he becomes invested in the object and his work on it. The act often symbolizes his power to change himself. To deprive a child of this opportunity may work unnecessary hardships on his efforts at self-realization and self-definition.

The esthetics of the adult, and the basis for these esthetics, appear to rest on criteria very different from the esthetics of the child. And so adult-designed playgrounds tend to be neat, clean, flat surfaces with sculpture-like objects firmly attached to concrete or tar paving. But children like to play in the rather loosely organized vacant lots that adults seem to dislike. Neighborhood play areas probably require the greatest setting adaptability of any designed environment anywhere. And manipulability of the environment appears to be their essential property for play behavior that is fluid, changing and unpredictable.

City Streets as Play Areas

Ira Cohen

Playing in city streets carries inherent dangers that attract youngsters.

Driving a car through New York offers easy evidence of the street's popularity as a playground. Most city driving is done with one hand on the wheel, the other on the horn. Frequently the horn and verbal admonitions produce more headway than the accelerator.

Also attractive to urban youngsters is the parked car which can, and most often will, be stepped on, climbed on, sat upon as well as crawled over, under and around. Parked cars can double as tag bases in the summer or snow ball fighting forts in the winter.

Ironically enough, there is usually a playground or park within walking distance of everyone's home in New York. After all, most schools have play spaces. Why then do children prefer streets to parks and playgrounds?

What is so motivating about the street? The answer is simple: the street is dangerous. The child is naturally adventurous and the inherent danger of the street motivates him to seek out this adventure. For instance, dodging cars and playing "chicken" seems to provide unending fun.

STREETS CHALLENGE CHILD'S IMAGINATION

The street's curb even has certain play properties. It can become a balance beam, a boundary line or a convenient ledge off which to throw a ball. Sewers may mark the distance for a homerun, be a base, or become a perfect fishing hole for pennies and an assortment of junk. Parked cars become mountains, tunnels, obstacles or lookout stations. In fact a car might become anything the child wants it to become.

The streets also provide stoops to jump off, slide down, and sit upon. Car windows may also be used in many ways. They may be looked in, looked out of, and, of course, broken.

The street does indeed provide a creative experience for the child. Its play devices do not, however, provide continuity and safety.

Reprinted with permission from National Park and Recreation Association. Official publication *Parks and Recreation*, September, 1968.

CONVENTIONAL PLAYGROUND IS BORING

Compare the street setting with a typical city playground on a sunny Saturday afternoon. The playground is adjacent to a city housing unit offering homes to many people. In the playground are four women watching ten children ranging in age from about seven to ten. The playground contains slides, see-saws, monkey bars, and a number of swings, strictly conventional equipment. One boy approached the slide and proceeded to play on it. He slid down the slide five times. At first he slid down normally, then head first, then partially standing, and finally backwards in staggering motions. Having exhausted his repertoire, he then proceeded to the swings. He twisted the swing around and then rode it until it unwound. Following this he looked around and left. The reason for this abrupt departure is best explained by the failure of the play area to provide a creative experience for the child. The other children did not use any of the equipment. Perhaps they had already used it. A parent reported that the children had been in the playground 20 minutes without using any of the equipment. Most of the children ran around, played tag or kicked a piece of broken glass until the pieces were so small that the glass would no longer break.

In contrast, a park adjacent to a school has some equipment that is continuously used. A popular piece is a hollow cylindrical tube standing in a vertical position. The children pile one after another into this tube and seem to have great fun. It is described by children as everything from a rocket ship to a fort. The traditional equipment (slides, see-saws) is used less and less. When traditional equipment is used, however, it is seldom used in the traditional way.

As a result, it becomes unsafe for use. For some reason, which seems to go deeper than just a pure lack of motivation, children appear to lose interest quickly in conventional equipment.

The street, however, seems to provide children with more meaningful experiences. Unfortunately, the playground becomes "old hat" too quickly. The street setting challenges the child to think, then create his own play devices and provides more of an educational experience.

PLANNING PLAY AREAS IS NECESSARY

The problem of developing motivating play spaces for children is relatively simple if funds are provided and a little imagination in planning is used. We need new and stimulating ideas to motivate the child to think and be creative. We must provide the child with a new experience every time he enters the playground. Items of irregular and unconventional shapes should definitely be used. Old discarded automobiles, small aircraft and old subway cars can be made immobile and safe for use. Children love to imagine that they could fly an airplane or drive a car. These items could provide an immeasurable experience for an uncountable number of children, any number of times.

Let us not completely forget the traditional equipment. We must resolve that we are not going to use this equipment in the conventional way. It must be used as a complex rather than the neatly spaced regimented way. A tower combining a spiral slide, staircase ladder, sandbox and lookout post allows children to play more than one-at-a-time with many different perceptions in their minds. This type of arrangement multiplies the number of different activities by the creative ability of the group as a whole.

COMPLEX PROVIDES CONTINUOUS EXPERIENCE

A complex of equipment also provides a continuous experience for the child; whereas the traditional arrangement forces the child to completely leave a piece of equipment in order to get to another. Traditional equipment should not only exhibit continuity, but it should also be colorful and provide gaiety in the setting.

Too often, in the name of time or economy, we lose sight of the real needs and interests of our children. Architects design and contractors build playgrounds with little real knowledge or insight into the interests of children. A sadder note is sounded when these playgrounds are constructed and then found to be unsafe. Before play areas are built, professionals in the field of recreation and child development should be consulted. With expert information, safe, durable, motivating, and creative playgrounds can be built. Let us not waste valuable tax dollars on playgrounds that force our children to play in the streets.

Vandalism By Design A Critique

V. Michael Weinmayr

The real vandals in our society are the designers, specifiers, and installers who provide the opportunity for so-called "vandalism" to occur.

The term, vandalism, is a marvelous catch-all for public apathy, ignorance, lack of concern, and/or intellectual laziness. Ninety per cent of what is labeled vandalism can be prevented through design; the remaining 10 per cent is malicious and unaccountable. Vandalism is an attitude, and controllable. Its prevention should be a concern in the design and construction of playgrounds, and of objects, open places, or events in the urban environment that invite vandalism. Vandalism happens because a hypocritical generation presents opportunity for misuse, then shifts the blame for deterioration to "vandalous youth." Clucking at the ravages solves nothing. Destruction is the expression of a need. An interpretative look at the motivations behind these kinds of playground vandalism may open the door to innovative solutions:

1. *The Vandalism of Over-Use* may be the most frequent form of destruction. You can swing only so many times until the chain wears out, and the merry-go-round has only so many turns. How many kids can sit on a bench? How many balls can go through the hoop?

2. *Conflict Vandalism* is the reaction to a tot lot built in the middle of the baseball field, a concrete climber built on a basketball court, a fence where a gate should be, and grass where kids want to walk. It is an expression of kids doing what is most logical, most natural and/or most appropriate to them, regardless of the designer's intent. Conflict vandalism may be the tree branch too low to walk under, too long to walk around and just the right height to swing on. Or the tree may be planted where kids want to play ball, or it may be in the perfect place to use as second base, and to swing around on the way to third. The tree breaks; vandals get the blame.

3. *Curiosity Vandalism* is the answer to what is behind the locked door and what is under the manhole cover. Curiosity is jamming a stick in the drinking fountain to see how high the water will squirt; plugging a drain to see how high the water will rise; pulling up a tree to see what the roots look like; taking apart the jungle gym to check the

Reprinted with permission of publisher of *Landscape Architecture*.

construction. Curiosity takes things apart. It needs avenues to information provided by the designer.

4. *Leverage Vandalism*, usually prevailing during baseball or hockey season, is finding a hole or slot just the right size to pry with a baseball bat. First the bat is stuck in a hole and a board in pried loose from the bench. The loose board is carried to the jungle gym where it is propped in the bars to form a cantilever. Now the board is a ship's plank, it is a spring board, or a tree branch. Finally the jungle gym bends, the board breaks, and the kid has learned something about the strength of materials.

5. *Deleterious Vandalism* is the concrete trash can which couldn't possibly be stolen. Of course it also can't be emptied because it weighs too much, especially after the removable steel liner has been carried away. If it doesn't work as a trash can, maybe it can be used as a battering ram. The can is dumped on its side and rolled into the bench, then into the lamp post, then into the fence, leaving destruction in its wake.

6. *Irresistible Temptation Vandalism* is writing on a shiny painted surface with a magic marker and riding a bicycle through the big mud puddle in the new lawn where the drainage is improper. It is climbing out on a tree branch to see how far it will bend, and throwing a bottle against a concrete wall. Irresistible temptation is picking flowers or unscrewing the beautiful little brass thing on top of the fountain because its fits so nicely in the palm of one's hand.

7. *The-No-Other-Way-To-Do-It Vandalism* is why the bicycle is leaned up against the tree when there is no bicycle rack. It is throwing papers and bottles on the ground when there is

no trash can and using the sand box when there is no restroom. It is sitting of the fence and hanging your jacket in a tree.

The designer, administrator, and maintenance engineer, faced with finding solutions to vandalism, express their reaction in two classic attitudes:

A. *The Bastille Approach* is building something so strong, so massive, and so simple that the kids couldn't possibly tear it down. And just to make sure, a high fence is erected around the playgrounds so the kids can play only when the administrator lets them, and if equipment still gets broken the gates are locked.

B. *The Zero Approach* provides nothing, therefore there is nothing to break. Put up a fence with no gates. Pave the area but don't plant trees or grass.

8. Neither approach really works because both stimulate *Ugliness Vandalism*. Kids are inherently responsive to an ugly environment. So the Bastille gets cracked, the gateless fence is bent, the seatless swing is uprooted, and the paving is strewn with glass.

The only solution is a creative approach. It is to understand a boy in search of diversion after school; to anticipate the alternatives and opportunities open for over-use, conflicting use, or misuse of playground environments. These approaches must respond to nonconforming uses.

Creative solutions for the above eight varieties of vandalism include (listed in same order as the types of vandalism):

1. Provide sufficient equipment to discourage overuse.

2. Build the path where the kids walk; provide a gate near the hole in the fence. Don't build a tot lot in the baseball diamond and don't plant a

tree on second base. Plant more trees, plant larger trees, and provide a way to run through the planting bed so kids and plants can grow together.

3. Unlock the gate so it won't be torn down. Prevent the gate from becoming a swing. Lock the manhole cover to protect the plumbing. Design a fountain which is easily repaired.

4. Remove loose boards and stray cobbles used as levers and hammers.

5. Mount trash cans on poles; replace when damaged, and empty when full.

6. Use timbers, difficult to write on, but can accommodate graffiti, and they mellow with age.

7. Bicycles should have racks and people should have benches.

8. Iron rail fences control cross circulation, stop kids from running into the street, but don't catch wind-blown debris. Dirt is a legitimate play surface.

There is no such thing as a maintenance-free park. Maintainable, yes, but not maintenance-free. Parks need care every day, improvements every year, and major rehabilitation about every five years.

Kids do not destroy what they want, like, and use. The burden of solution lies with the designer. What have you vandalized lately?

The Old Men in Plaza Park

Robert Sommer and Franklin D. Becker

Social distance between the design professions and the poor is a major obstacle to effective urban planning. Frequently architects and the poor don't speak the same language and their goals differ.

This became very clear in a case study we made of an older park in Sacramento frequented on a regular basis by a large group of older men. Many American cities have parks like this located close to the city center and serving a run-down rooming house district.

To the casual bystander the occupants of the park seem a faceless agglomeration of older men. However it is quite easy to differentiate two distinct groups—the old-timers and the alcoholics. The old-timers are retired men who dress cleanly, are well-shaven, play cards, stay predominantly on the north side of the park, and are not drunk. The alcoholics are generally unshaven, walk unevenly, dress sloppily, and stay on the south side of the park. They often sit or lie in the inner ring of grass in groups sharing a bottle of wine.

Plaza Park comprises one square city block not far from the Sacramento River and is only a short distance from slums and boarding houses now in the process of being torn down by the redevelopment agency. The park was originally given to the city by John Sutter along with several other blocks to be used for public benefit. At the center of the park is a fountain surrounded by a circular flower bed. Around the flower bed is a cement pathway with arteries leading to each of the four corners of the adjacent blocks.

The park was redesigned three years ago. According to the former chairman of the City Planning Commission, the redesign's objectives were: (1) to make the park more attractive, (2) to correct the failing water system, and (3) to open the park up for use other than by elderly persons and transients. Objectives (1) and (3) are related in that a major source of concern to the planners was the "ominous crowd look" that resulted from the older men clustered around the park. Passers-by often complained about the unkempt men and maintained that they would rather walk around the park than pass by the benches full of old men. The planning commission decided that the unsightly congestion should be relieved by permanently dispersing the benches and tables around the park.

Reprinted with permission from publisher of *Landscape Architecture*, January, 1969.

Specifically, the following changes were made—(1) 16 large elmwoods which provided an abundance of shade were cut down. (2) Heavy, tough moveable, wooden benches were replaced by permanent benches to prevent the men from dragging them together to talk or to follow the shade. (3) All benches were removed from the diagonal paths and were relocated out of the way of people walking through the park from one corner to another, to relieve the complaints.

It should be clear that these changes were not intended to make the park more attractive and functional for the regular users, but to benefit passers-by. Even from this standpoint the new design did not succeed. Cutting down many of the old trees, and placing the benches around the park did not succeed in dispersing the occupants. On the contrary it produced a greater congestion under the remaining shade trees. During the hot summer afternoons the tree shaded benches and lawn are virtually deserted; the men follow the shade rather than sitting where the benches are. Typical comments from the men were, "There was more shade in the park before they cut down 16 of the big shade trees. Now all of the benches are in the sun." And, "The benches now are a waste of money. They are out in the sun, all vacant." Most men interviewed mentioned that the park had been better before it was redesigned.

Another problem now is the checkerboards which are permanently fixed to the permanent card tables. There is only one checkerboard per table, which seats four persons. It means that while four men sit at the table, only two can play at one time, leaving the other two as observers. There is room on the tables for two checkerboards. The men also mentioned the need for benches and tables beneath trees and for light moveable tables that could be moved for elderly persons to the shade.

Our interviews also made it clear that the old-timers regard themselves as distinct from the alcoholics. Police vans periodically come around to the park to pick up stray drunks. Most of the old-timers approve of this, saying "It would make the park look a lot better if they took away the winos." Most passers-by, however, do not distinguish between the two groups of users. The major goal of redesign had been to remove or at least disperse the present occupants and open the park up for use by white collar workers. In the planning stages, installment of a putting green was even discussed. It was the hope of the Planning Commission that more downtown workers would then use the park. This plan failed because there was simply no other place for the old men to go.

When asked about special facilities for the older men, one planning official stated that what the men would like was a covered card room. Architect Louis Gelwicks has studied the use of such a card shelter in a small park in Los Angeles. That shelter is a three-sided building with a roof, containing four long tables with benches and a toilet in the rear. The shelter is filled seven days a week from 11:00 a.m. to 4:00 p.m. by a regular group of old-timers. It is not a club, and the activity is spontaneous. No card shelter had been included in Plaza Park, according to the former chairman of the City Planning Commission, for fear that gambling would occur. He conceded that gambling occurs even without a card shelter.

In evaluating this situation, it is first of all clear that there is no lack of information about the needs of these men. The old men would like a nice shady park where they can play cards and talk; the alcoholics want a place where they can drink. These goals were not acceptable to many of the individuals involved in the planning process. The result is a compromise design satisfactory to no one. While failing to discourage the old-timers and the alcoholics from using the park, it did not encourage the downtown workers to use the park. Instead of relieving the "ominous crowd look" through dispersion, it added to it by crowding the men together under the remaining shade trees. The shaded area has brought the alcoholics and the old men into an unwelcome physical proximity. Periodic visits of the police to pick up alcoholics do provide some interest for the old-timers but most would prefer to have a quiet area to themselves.

This sort of situation is all too common in the urban landscape. Not only are the poor and their needs ignored, but they are deliberately frustrated. Certainly the needs of passers-by and pedestrians must be taken into account. In the present instance, the priority given to these needs appears to be excessive. It also appears that there was a "blindness" to the presence of the old men. While everyone admitted that the old men had no other place to go, one objective of the redesign was to rid the park of them. This attitude has characterized many of the redevelopment projects around the nation. Slums are torn down without adequate thought as to what will happen to the present occupants. Most often they are simply pushed into another area. One senses a fervent hope among some planners and city officials that the poor, the old men, and the alcoholics will vanish or at least keep out of sight. Yet the most reasonable and challenging solution is to develop parks and facilities that meet the needs of local residents and are attractive as well. The opposite course of action—making the areas unattractive in order to drive away the poor—is a sure prescription for failure.

A Measure of Success

Conrad L. Wirth

As a boy, there was not an acre of woodland that I didn't personally claim for my own, and I stood ready to defend it against all Indians, outlaws, wild animals, or other interlopers. There is no disputing the eminent domain of a small boy; he needs no general warranty deed; his estate is carved out of the universe in fee simple.

Strangely enough, many years later, I still have the same feeling—that every acre of open space is mine, and I am either pleased when the occupant of the land has taken prideful care in preserving it, or I am righteously indignant when he has allowed his land to become gullied and eroded or sacrifices it to unplanned urban expansion. It is not that I am covetous when I claim this personal ownership. In essence, it is an attitude that I feel every American should have. The farm I do not own is still mine to enjoy visually because it is part of the American landscape, and I feel a deep personal loss when I see a beautiful natural setting leveled for development.

Unlike Don Quixote, I do not intend to challenge the bulldozer to mortal combat. I recognize that landowners cannot be blamed entirely for responding to the dynamics of a changing economy. I am concerned, however, about the vanishing recreation opportunities in America and about the steps we must take to reverse this trend.

The ceaseless motion and transformation of our society calls for a dynamic and forward moving program to meet new demands brought on by changing developments. I am especially concerned with the paradox of rising population and vanishing open space, further complicated by the increasing demand for this self-same space in response to increased leisure time and money to be spent in recreational pursuits.

Cities respond to population pressures by expanding upward as well as outward. How convenient it would be if we could just expand our *natural parks* vertically as well as horizontally. As a matter of logic, however, there is no substitute for extensive open space, and once it has been developed the price of reclaiming it becomes prohibitive—even assuming that we could restore the original natural value. Thus, we have the dual problem of acquiring additional recreation lands now while they are still available and of protecting the parks we already have against encroachment.

Reprinted with permission from National Recreation and Park Association. Official publication *Parks and Recreation*, November, 1961.

We cannot say that all urban expansion to date has been undisciplined and without plan. On the contrary, there have been hundred of plans behind our urban renewal projects, our growing suburbs, and our expanding system of highways. The obvious weakness has been a lack of coordination. The need now is to draw all of these plans together, insofar as they are related, into a cooperative national plan in which all levels of government, individual citizens and civic groups will participate. It is my sincere belief that adequate parks and recreation areas go hand in hand with good public policy and sound government.

I see the job of park-minded people as being more than just the administration of parks—our job is to see that provision is made for outdoor recreation opportunities adequate for *all* the people. And it is not a job solely for the national government, or for the state government, or for the local government, or for individual citizens and civic groups alone. It is a cooperative effort in which we must join unselfishly—but the individual rewards will be great.

Our objectives, of course, depend on our individual concept of recreation. My own philosophy has always followed the democratic principle of the greatest good for the greatest number, but this does not mean that each area must meet the needs of everyone. I favor a recreation plan that will be truly balanced in quality and one that will respond adequately to the needs of our high urban population densities. At the same time, the ultimate success of such a plan must be measured in terms of individual satisfaction.

How do we achieve individual satisfaction when there are so many to satisfy? We need a *variety* of public parks and recreation areas, ranging in kind and location from remote wilderness to highly developed playgrounds near densely populated areas. I would like to see the National Park System rounded out in sufficient *breadth* to portray the major exhibits of our natural and cultural heritage—the best scientific and biological exhibits, characteristic and spectacular views, historic monuments, and natural museums. These would include, among others, natural seashores, free-flowing streams, prairies, swamplands, mountains, deserts, canyons, and wilderness areas. These would be the irreplaceable exhibits and treasures that are of national interest and which we want to pass on to future generations unimpaired.

Then, I would like to see throughout the nation a system of parks and recreation areas in sufficient *depth* to provide all segments of our present and future population with adequate nonurban areas near their homes for frequent day and weekend use, as well as remote areas for vacation use. At the same time I am particularly concerned about the fact that the numbers of campgrounds for our youngsters are inadequate for the demand. No matter how our population increases, the amount of land remains the same. Moreover, the capacity of the land is limited and with the numbers of young campers certain to increase, more and more sites are needed. This is an area where private enterprise is rendering exceptional public service, supplemented by organization and government programs. It is only through family camping and organized group camping that many of our youngsters today obtain their most lasting impressions of nature and outdoor living. In planning for our future needs, let us, therefore, assure the perpetuation of our conservation ideals through our children by providing them with adequate camping opportunities to develop an appreciation of the great outdoors.

Let us also consider the dynamics of

our motorized population. We must continue to give increasing attention to highways and roads of the nation. As Secretary Udall recently stated: "We can do a better job of wedding roads and recreation. It has seemed to us there has been too much tendency in the past to keep them in separate compartments. Our country badly needs a modern highway system; but, above all, it deserves a system that works with nature and makes our highways places of beauty and recreation as well as avenues of commerce."

I would like to see included in all future highway rights-of-way hundreds of acres, here and there along the route, selected for scenic advantages and providing areas for future campsites, picnic areas, or historical and scenic turnouts. These would provide pleasant variety and opportunity to enjoy motor travel on the ride-a-while, stop-a-while basis. Additional campgrounds and other attractions of scenc and historical nature en route mean that vacation motorists will be able to enjoy the entire trip instead of driving hard and fast each day in order to reach a destination—a park for instance—where thousands of others have congregated. The important thing is to acquire the necessary open space at the same time the right-of-way is acquired; development can follow at a more leisurely pace.

We cannot expect future generations—fifty to a hundred years from now—to do retroactively what we fail to do now. The next ten years are crucial. Within the next forty years the population of our country will probably double. In setting aside these areas—and the present area of the present National Park System is less than one percent of the land of the United States—it is not a question of holding lands idle; it is a question of devoting exceptionally attractive and significant sites to the kinds of use that will

make the adjoining lands more valuable, stimulate commerce and its related employment, and, at the same time make it possible for ourselves and our descendants to enjoy these choice places as we have enjoyed them in the past.

We are not actually demanding very much. The principal question seems to be whether the community, the state and the nation can find suitable means to set aside these relatively small areas to keep as historic sites, parks, recreation areas, and other attractive open space for the people of our country to enjoy for all time. The National Park Service is presently cooperating at all levels of government—local, state, and federal—in studying park and recreation area needs of all the states, looking toward a nationwide program that will provide adequate outdoor recreation opportunities for everyone.

While the primary responsibility of providing close-to-home recreation areas is largely that of local and state governments, there is evident need for a concerted and cooperative program involving all levels of government—particularly in planning and land acquisition. It is my personal feeling that the need for immediate acquisition of lands for city, county, metropolitan, state and national parks, including open spaces and shorelines, is such that only a nationwide cooperative program of land acquisition will suffice. Under present parkland acquisition programs park needs cannot be met. Moreover, with present financing, it does not appear possible to undertake an extensive land acquisition program without the necessity for some kind of federal grants-in-aid program. I am hopeful that some means can be devised by which federal aid can be provided for the acquisition of park and recreation lands by state, regional, and local governments on a matching-fund basis. We must remember that although such land acquisition will be for the states and for local use, the problem remains a national one, and aid now is actually an investment in the future welfare of the entire nation.

Perhaps our success will best be measured one hundred years from now when some small boy stand on an open stretch of seashore or on a mountain top rising out of natural wilderness—monarch of all he surveys and wonderfully appreciative, but little realizing the struggle that went into its preservation.

Differences in Perception of a City Park as a Supportive or Threatening Environment

Archie D. McDonald and Robert J. Newcomer

This paper reports on a pilot study which was intended to find out how and in what ways a city park is important, i.e., supportive to its elderly users and to determine why other elderly persons who live in proximity to the park do not use it. Our survey instrument was designed to measure activity patterns, social networks, social involvement, social and physical dependency on resources. More specifically, attention was given to the influences of the present social and physical milieu, lifestyles, and social status on the perception and the use of the park. For example, attempts were made to determine the degree to which living accommodations affected a respondent's use of the park as the availability of social contacts within a residence might reduce the desire for seeking social interaction elsewhere. Perceived differences were also investigated for their possible influences on park use. Among other possible influences considered were such physical barriers as landscaping, heavy street traffic and the presence of panhandlers, winos, and prostitutes.

The study, area for this investigation consisted of two sites: MacArthur Park, located in the Westlake district of Los Angeles, California, and a senior citizens' residential hotel located adjacent to the park.

The Westlake area offers a variety of potential environmental supports for the elderly including low rents, a high concentration of elderly persons and such facilities as the park, senior citizen clubs, convenient location to shopping areas and low-budget restaurants and cafeterias.

The hotel selected for this study features rooms with two meals a day (six days a week) for $90 to $140 a month, depending on room size and bathroom facilities. In addition, the hotel has a large lobby with color TV, card table and sitting area. There is also a small library, porch swings and a garden area for hotel residents.

The overall attractiveness of the Westlake area, however, from the aged person's point of view, has begun to decline in recent years due to an influx of a skid row population following an urban renewal project in downtown Los Angeles. Occurring during this same time period has been the establishment of half-way houses for alcoholics and ex-convicts within the area, and more recently, an increasing immigration of a younger Black and American Indian population. These factors are believed to be responsible for an increasing incidence of violence and potential violence in the area. Other factors preceived as a danger to old people, though these have existed for a number of years, are several bars along one of the streets adjacent to the park, a homosexual population, and prostitutes. Police protective services to the area appear to be limited to one patrolling squad car and maintenance personnel during park operating hours.

SAMPLE DESCRIPTION

The sample used for this study consists of two purposefully drawn subsamples. One (N-23) includes about 25 percent of the total hotel population. This sample contains both park users (N-13) and non-park users (N-10). These park users represent about 90 percent of the hotel's park-using population. The other subsample was drawn in the park (N-14) and includes park habituees selected from such specific park activity settings as the card-playing and shuffleboard areas.

Generally, the sample can be characterized as being Caucasian, in the age bracket of middle to late seventies, and former blue-collar workers. There are no appreciable differences in samples regarding health status, educational attainment, former occupation or present source of income. (The sample used for this inquiry was limited to individuals physically capable of visiting the park without the assistance of other individuals.)

With the typical demographic indicators of age and socio-economic status thus providing no apparent explanation for park use, the remainder of this analysis will focus on personal and environmental factors. In doing so, attention will first be given to general activity patterns before looking specifically at park activities.

FOCUS OF SOCIAL ACTIVITIES

The analysis of social activities was conducted on three dimensions; a recording of activities by type, place of occurrence, and person or persons with whom the activity was conducted. By this process, it was hoped that indicators of social engagement and life space would be derived and that some aspects of an individual's supportive environment could be determined. One's room, the park and acquaintances all emerge for the sample as being the most widely utilized supports or resources. It was further discovered that almost one-half of the sample believed that they functioned mainly alone. Most of the remainder were involved with role specific friends or acquaintances. Only two individuals placed themselves in activities with a peer group or relatives.

These data suggest a number of possibilities. First, involvement in social activity is most easily done on a role specific basis such as card playing and dining. This type of involvement could also account for the greater reliance upon acquaintances than friends. A second possibility apparent in this data is that there is greater reliance upon the self than upon peer or family contacts in establishing appropriate behavior.

The average length of residence for all respondents was four and one-half years and only ten individuals had lived at their current address for less than one year. This information on the one hand implies a higher degree of residential mobility than is commonly attributed to the elderly, but it also indicates that sufficient time has elapsed for significant social contact to have been established by most individuals if they were making an attempt. That such contacts have not been made, we believe, is largely resultant from individual choice rather than exclusionary efforts of others. This supposition is supported in that only one half of the sample presently claims any church affiliation, and only one-fifth indicated any past or present fraternal or civic organization affiliation. In addition to the lack of these membership propensities, few persons expressed a desire to alter their present activity patterns. The reliability of these suppositions is further supported by two additional measures; the high expressed indication of sufficient social contact (78.4%), and the fact that two-thirds of the respondents described themselves as either very happy or contented.

An additional support for the validity and satisfaction with existing activity patterns is evident in the way individuals respond to their problems of loneliness and stress. The reported means of overcoming or avoiding these conditions finds one half of the respondents relying upon themselves or their religion to counteract loneliness or conditions of stress. In short, the conditions of loneliness and stress do not generally appear to stimulate social interaction as a resource for personal assistance.

In brief then, it would appear that the typical individual in this sample has tended to isolate himself somewhat from social interaction but remains capable of choosing selected avenues into groups. The focal point of this entre tends to be in such role specific relationships as card playing, chess or checkers, and visiting. These actions generally are confined to the home, club, church, or park setting. The room appears to be a private domain. The nature of social interaction being role specific, and the high incidence of self-reliance during times of loneliness and stress, both indicate a lack of intimate friendship and an unwillingness to foster such relationships.

Given these social activity characteristics, it next becomes important to determine the influence of one's residence on both activity patterns and their place of occurrence. This influence is one of two basic types: the supportive qualities that could attract a self-selected dependent population, and an environment which provides so little support that individuals must seek these resources elsewhere. This dichotomy does in fact appear to exist for the hotel sample in the former case, and the park sample in the other. Three-fourths of the hotel sample reported that many of their activities were home centered while only one-fifth of the park sample so indicated.

These two samples also differed regarding their dependency needs as expressed by a desire to escape household burdens and obligations and the desire for such activities as meals and maid service. Two-thirds of the hotel respondents indicated their desire for these supports while only one of the park respondents had similar requirements. With 80% of the total sample expressing current satisfaction with their respective accomodations, it would appear that in both samples residential needs are being reasonably well met.

PARK USE CHARACTERISTICS

Because of the differences in residential environments, and residential needs, a difference in park activity patterns can be clearly anticipated. Park activity patterns were investigated from the following perspectives: frequency of use, length of use, rationale for use, activities engaged in and social network involvement.

Length of park use appears to be associated with length of residence in the park area, and years since retirement. As the park sample has tended to reside in the park area longer, there is a difference between samples on this factor. Sample size prevents further meaningful testing of the association between this variable and park use characteristics. This is also true for frequency of park use, but it should be noted that non-hotel residents in the sample are twice as likely to use the park daily as are hotel residents. The non-hotel residents generally visit the park five to seven times a week. Patterns such as these suggest a possible effect on park activities and park friendship associations as well as differences in utilization of the park as a supportive resource. These possibilities are again suggested in the differences in expressed rationale for park use. The hotel sample uses the park almost exclusively as a place to be outdoors, and a place to watch people, to watch birds and to stroll. For the park sample, the attraction to the park is principally as a place to watch and interact with people. Its importance as a natural setting is much less evident. Also for the park sample, the park is more clearly used as an escape from one's residence and as a "place to put in time."

These differences in park use are clearly seen in park activity patterns. The hotel sample engaged in activities such as bird watching, strolling and people watching, which did not involve participation in the social networks of the park. In contrast, the park sample found most respondents engaged in visiting and such other socially involved pursuits as card playing. The natural-setting-oriented activities received scant attention by these individuals. These findings are further substantiated in that practically all of the hotel residents reported that they spend most of their time alone while in the park. Three-fourths of the park sample were meanwhile involved with role specific friends or acquaintances.

From the residentially controlled patterns of park use rationale and activities presented here, it would appear that the park for the hotel residents functions principally as an outdoor resource and ampitheater to view activity, while for the non-hotel residents the park is an important attraction and focus of social activity.

In this latter regard, it might be useful to examine the quality of the social involvement for non-hotel residents. For these individuals, most park friends and acquaintances are described in role specific contexts, but, in spite of the frequency of contact, these associates do not appear to be considered "intimates." This is clearly evident in that park associations do not generally extend beyond the park setting. Once an individual leaves the park in the evening he eats and goes home alone to him room. Thus we find that in the park as well as the hotel, true friendships are not obtained, and the indications suggest that such relationships are not sought.

In general then, it appears that the differences in residential setting contributes to understanding the supportive character of a park. The importance of the park as a center for social contacts diminishes as these contacts are available within the residence. In those cases where social contact needs are fulfilled, the park becomes increasingly important for its "natural" setting qualities.

The desire for "intimacy" in one's social contacts is not readily evident in any of the subsamples and consequently, does not appear to be an important park use attractor.

PARK VIEWED AS A THREATENING ENVIRONMENT

Having established probable park use attractors or supports, it might now be useful to explore the perceived negative aspects of the park. Recalling that the Westlake area is by police accounts a high crime area, it becomes our task to determine the nature of threatening perceptions by area residents, and to discover what other, if any, variables might be influencing this perception. To accomplish these tasks, respondents were questioned regarding the types of people they prefer to be with, their attitude toward park users, their rationale for non-park use and their opinions regarding both possible positive and negative events in the park.

Both samples—park and non-park users, had similar opinions of the types of people using the park. The park is seen as primarily serving former blue collar workers like themselves. Similarly there were no apparent differences among these samples regarding the types of people they prefer to be with. In this case, optimistic, considerate, tolerant people and those with common experiences seem to be most desired.

The similarity between samples as noted earlier in current income, education and former occupation appears to account for these congruencies.

Regarding reactions to possible incidents in the park, both samples agreed on such positive indicators as the park being a place to engage in a variety of activities. An important difference occurred in the perception of such negative events as the possibility of being attacked, molested or robbed. Non-park users were more likely to agree with this possibility. These apprehensions are further clearly evidenced in expressed reasons for non-park use. Here the presence of panhandlers and bums was cited almost unanimously as contributing to non-use. Health reasons, and fear of violence and moral offensiveness, though also mentioned, were of much less importance.

In short, having examined impediments to park use which ranged over social status differences to perceived physical danger it appears that the presence of panhandlers, bums and winos is

the single most important factor contributing to non-park use by our sample population.

A final factor examined for influence upon park use was satisfaction or interest in existing park activities. In the absence of expressed desires for additional facilities other than cleaner and nicer toilets and better park maintenance, it would appear that present activities are satisfactory, and that this factor is not an important deterrent to park use.

POLICY IMPLICATIONS

The two important findings of this study, that residential supports influence both park use and activities, and that the presence of panhandlers, bums and winos is the primary reason for non-park use, raise a number of important design and policy questions.

First, is the broad ecological question of how city policy such as urban renewal and half-way house location carried out in one part of the city (as occurred in this case) can have an important impact on other areas of the city as the relocated population moves into other areas of the city.

Secondly, should, and if so, how can highly supportive environments for the elderly such as the Westlake area with its low rent, convenient location and other facilities be safeguarded against the onslaught of possible threatening or non-supportive intruders who would also be attracted to such areas.

A third issue raised regards the design of parks as a facilitator of social interaction and as an outdoor space resource. Parks designed for high social activity appear to be most potentially successful and needed in those areas where elderly people reside in facilities which do not foster or permit social interaction within the residence. For such individuals, these parks should provide a range of activities, particularly those promoting role specific interactions. Park or outdoor space near residences that themselves promote social interaction can perhaps be most usefully designed to serve outdoor space or "natural" enjoyment needs. Thus here attention would focus on natural features of the park rather than the activities provided.

Finally, a research question concerning the impact of dependency on park use needs to be explored. The hotel population in this study was markedly more "dependent" in terms of its desires for specific hotel services. But it is not clear from our data how this fact influenced park use. With less than 20 percent of the hotel population using the park, it would seem that an important issue still needs to be resolved, which goes beyond the scope of this paper.

Urban Esthetics *Can* Be Functional

James Alexander, Jr.

Improved esthetics need not be the only benefit of a beautification program. Definite functional advantages also can result. Trenton, N.J., has been conducting a comprehensive beautification and improvement program purposefully designed to promote both.

Two grants from the United States Department of Housing and Urban Development, totaling over $300,000 have made the work possible. Any municipality of course can have such a program without federal aid, but the 50% assistance greatly enhances its scope.

The Federal Urban Beautification and Improvement program, as authorized by Congress, provides 50% reimbursement for such activities as the following, provided that the activities are above the normal level of activity:

- Upgrading and rehabilitation of parks and playgrounds.
- Design, construction of improvement of public places such as malls, plazas, waterfront areas and neighborhood commons.
- Comprehensive improvement of the appearance of streets and public rights of way.
- Improvements to beautify public building sites or historical sites.

REHABILITATION

Improving our parks and playgrounds came first in our planning. Of necessity, most money-short municipalities rate these somewhat lower on the priority scale than police and fire protection and other critical services. This often produces a long-term deterioration and lack of many necessary improvements.

However, current urban tensions and the pressures of life in densely populated neighborhoods tend to raise priorities on open spaces such as parks and playgrounds that fulfill a real need for recreation, relaxation and relief from crowding, traffic and noise. Funds allocated for them are a constructive investment in healthy urban life.

Trenton was able to rehabilitate and improve 25 existing parks and playgrounds, with new sidewalks, trees and shrubs, modern playground equipment, benches, water fountains, etc. at a cost of just over

$250,000. Some of these sites still need further improvements, but the results were most noticeable.

MINI-PARKS

Many cities find themselves owning more and more parcels of land as a result of tax foreclosures. Ugly and unproductive, they become mudholes and attract litter and abandoned cars, exerting a serious blighting effect on neighborhoods. Since many of these lots in our city are in congested areas far from major parks, we have been able to build 23 mini parks on them. Intended primarily for adults, they are attractively designed with walks, sitting areas and shrubs.

As a result of Dutch Elm and other diseases, storms, and old age, Trenton had hundreds of dead and dying trees on the streets. Through the beautification program we removed 685 dead trees. To replace them, and to provide shade at other locations required 1,380 new trees.

Street trees are not just a matter of esthetics, just as new parks are not. They provide valuable shade, enhance property values, and provide ecological benefits through their oxygen-producing capabilities. Barren streets take on a new appearance with tree planting. Residents in some of the poorest sections literally adopted the trees as a symbol of the city's interest in investing in, rather than abandoning, their neighborhoods.

Another portion of the program involved blacktopping four back alleys. Previously dirt covered, they posed a constant maintenance problem, having to be graded and treated for dust control several times a year.

An unforeseen benefit developed beyond the anticipated lower maintenance costs. Because traffic is minimal on them, many people found them to be convenient play areas for growing youngsters, just as today's adults often played on residential streets before the advent of heavy automobile traffic.

Another benefit, and the reason that alley paving was eligible under this program, was that it encourages homeowners to park their cars in the alleys, out of sight, thereby enhancing the front street's appearance and facilitating the flow of traffic.

We also undertook improvements that serve the entire community, rather than various sections. For instance, at Trenton's City Hall, elaborate bronze doors and ornamentation had deteriorated over the years. We were able to have them professionally cleaned and refinished.

In addition, a barren concrete plaza in front of the building has been enhanced with a carefully designed set of planting areas that include eight trees, water fountains, ornamental lighting, and flowering shrubbery. Now, civic groups hold concerts and art shows there, which helps bring people downtown.

A particularly striking visual improvement occurred on a large open lot behind City Hall. Originally acquired for future construction, the lot initially had been roughly graded, a snow fence strung around it, and was used for employee parking. Using city funds, we blacktopped it, and demolished an old building on one corner. Then it was laid out properly as a parking lot.

This still presented the rather bleak picture of asphalt. Using beautification funds, we created a green strip five feet wide around the two exposed sides of the lot, planted trees, and installed decorative coach-type lamps on posts. We also erected a planter box at the corner.

The result: an extremely attractive and functional facility that is used during the day for employee parking, and at nights for shoppers' parking.

PROBLEMS

Like any program, problems developed. Public acceptance was one. Some contended that what funds we do have should be spent on "more important" needs than parks, trees and plazas. Fortunately, others supported the work, argued that this is just what the old cities need—that not only are esthetics important in an urban environment, but that vital functional needs can be served as well by the same programs if properly conceived.

A related comment is that if federal funds were not available on a 50-50 matching basis, few cities would assign a very high priority to beautification, and that even the 50% local share cannot really be afforded.

The new mini parks had their advocates and opponents. Some residents eagerly sought them, while others feared that they would bring loiterers, kids and noise into their neighborhoods.

Street trees also weren't always welcome. Many clamored for new trees. Some didn't want anything to do with them, fearing they would just cause leaves and that their roots would damage sidewalks.

At certain points in the program, the availability of such large numbers of trees posed a burden; sites had to be checked for location of water, sewer and gas lines, availability of growing room, and neighbors' reactions. When a majority on a street wanted trees, but several did not, the resulting planting pattern lacked symmetry.

In such cases, we found that forcing a tree on a resident, even though it was in the public right of way, caused no end of complaints to elected officials, and in the end those trees received no water from the homeowner and tended to do poorly anyway.

Design of proposed projects, writing of specifications and actual execution of projects proved to be more than existing personnel could handle. Architects and consultants had to be employed, and in the end, the designs and the plans proved to be very refreshing.

What is commonly called red tape, federal requirements such as equal opportunity, prevailing wages, and an endless sea of forms in quadruplicate, on top of existing city and state requirements, tend to inundate the program at first. But once understood, they are quite manageable if a competent person handles them. The most difficult part is getting some contractors to submit required payrolls, certifications, and other information on time.

A related problem is that the necessity of securing federal reviews and approvals of the various steps in the program is rather time-consuming. For a one-year contract with the government, work should be initiated as soon as possible to allow sufficient lead-time to get all contracts awarded within the period covered by the grant. As this is written, the government has curtailed the number of reviews of proposed contracts, and this hopefully should expedite such programs.

The nature of the federal funding places a temporary financial drain on the municipality. Essentially, the municipality must first finance the program, with the federal funds coming in as reimbursement only after federal requirements have been met. Regional HUD offices have recently been given greater flexibility in making payments, and they are most cooperative in expediting payments, but the municipality must expect to see its money tied up for a number of months.

A well-planned financial strategy will permit the reimbursement from the first year to be used to finance portions of the second year, and so forth.

Perhaps the biggest headache is the maintenance of the new parks, playgrounds, trees and facilities. Chances are that if maintenance forces had been at the desired strength in the first place, there would have been less need to have a special beautification program. An increase in the maintenance budget is a logical consequence of such a program. Of course, those existing sites that are merely rehabilitated do not require much additional attention, but new facilities will.

Even here, the resourceful municipality may be able to take advantage of some of the state and federally aided training programs, providing proper supervision can be arranged.

Vandalism is an increasing problem at all public facilities. We found, however, that even in the most difficult neighborhoods, vandalism was least serious where the facility met a real need, where the residents were made aware of the intended benefits, and where their comments were listened to. The worst vandalism, for instance, occurred in mini parks where the people either didn't want them, or a playground was needed more.

Notwithstanding such problems, a comprehensive urban beautification and development program can be most worthwhile.

Perhaps the basic problem is the program's name itself. To the hard-pressed urban community, "beautification" tends to sound like a frill that can be done without in deference to more serious needs. One must show that such a program, when properly conceived and presented, is a tool that can be used to meet real needs in improving urban life.

Pragmaesthetics

Joseph E. Curtis

The customary description of a junket abroad, even an educational trip by a professional, can make dreary reading. Bromides that include "the lovely beaches," "the warmth of our host—the governor," "they are such a happy, friendly people," and "spring is a riot of color there," leave me cold. Such saccharine descriptions depict every country outside America a veritable paradise, a shangri-la of beauty and idyllic living. The world simply isn't that simple. A research trip abroad can be a challenging and exciting experience for the park, recreation, or urban planning professional if he prepares himself in advance with motives, areas of concentration, and a kit of search techniques that will dig beneath the surface of the society he is observing. Only then will the real essentials, the fascinating idiosyncrasies and oddities of alien philosophies come to light. Only then will he bring home something fresh, intriguing, and productive from those far-off lands.

In May of 1969, I joined a group of 32 zealous travelers heading for a 17-day tour of major cities in Holland, Germany, Finland, Sweden, and Denmark. Labeled the "Urban Design Odyssey," the group included architects, city planners, urban renewal specialists, businessmen, elected officials, and interested homemakers. It was my privilege to serve as tour director, though many of the group knew Europe far better than I. We met months in advance of the trip and discussed in detail what we would search for. It was an intense and dedicated assembly, and a finely detailed planning and observation schedule was forged.

An absolute minimum of wandering and conventional sight-seeing was included, and a maximum of significant stops, visits, and educational side-trips plotted. Advance arrangements were completed with chief gardeners, planners, consuls, park directors, museum officials, conservationists, and expert guides in each of the major cities to be visited. Each member of our group contacted friends who had already visited the target cities and inquired for details and tips which would help us in our quest.

The painstaking efforts paid off. An enormous amount of productive visiting, interviewing, questioning, and sampling occurred. Large quantities of demonstration materials, and thousands of photographs were collected. During the trip, frequent buzz sessions and "brainstorming"

Reprinted with permission from National Recreation and Park Association. Official publication *Parks and Recreation*, July, 1970.

periods were held to digest what had already been acquired and to sharpen our senses for the targets ahead. Ideas were cross-pollenated en route, and revised editions of these ideas were restudied every few days. Keen self-analysis and constructive criticism characterized these sessions.

The result was a rich crop of ideas, impressions, concepts, and philosophic gems which our group brought back to our home cities. These ideas have been under further study since then and several will soon be implemented.

Aside from the broad, clearly defined urban patterns of each city, we discerned second magnitude, less defined characteristics, syndromes, and impressions. These, acquired subconsciously through our sharpened sensitivities, saturated our thinking upon returning home, and will color our permanent images, perhaps more than the earlier, heavier, more obvious impressions.

The following are a few of these concepts:

The word, PRAGMAESTHETICS, an amalgam of the pragmatic and the aesthetic, aptly describes a delightful characteristic of European urban planning, particularly in the smaller details of decor.

In the magnificent City Theater of Helsinki, Finland, we viewed a stunning piece of bronze wall sculpture which extended 30 feet in length, suspended from the low ceiling, parallel to one long wall of the lobby. It appeared to be a great wavy bronze snake with hooked barbs coming out of its body. Only as we looked, did it dawn on us that it was a magnificent coat rack, and each of the hooks would accommodate several garments. We oh'd and ah'd, but it was only the beginning of countless illustrations of this quaint European eccentricity.

In a tiny men's toilet room in Solvang, Germany, I entered through a beaded doorway curtain, suggestive of Somerset Maugham's *Rain*, and approached a commode over which hung a beautiful small crystal chandelier. Pragmaesthetics!

In Amsterdam and Copenhagen the variety of street bicycle racks was endless. They appeared as circular drums, metal fountains, as cuts in the sidewalk, in the form of tree-shaped racks supporting bicycles from above. Nowhere did I see the conventional American straight-pipe bicycle rack.

Stockholm marks its parking slots in small city parking areas with outlines of raised Belgian block, contrasted against the flat surface of the red brick paving. No ragged painted white lines are used. Amsterdam's gaily painted houseboats form inner linings along the retaining walls of many of its centrally located canals. These charmingly adorned vessels are houseboats of the old-fashioned barge style and have little in common with out new fiberglass Florida types. They add a medieval touch to already charming waterways.

In Hannover, Germany, I observed my first *deikvagenlarums*, five foot-high grass-covered dirt walls which, if sliced through the middle, would present triangular cross sections about five feet wide at the bottom and tapering to the top. These lined both sides of roads that pierce the mid-city forests in this German industrial center. They insulate the nearby picnic groves and campsites from noise, headlights, and noxious fumes to a surprising degree. In addition, they heighten the feeling of remoteness and primitiveness for the camper, though he is only a few feet from a main road.

In the lobby of a Stockholm restaurant, we observed a tapestry-like item, about three feet wide and nine feet long, hanging on a wall. It was made entirely of scrap pieces of heavy metallic embroidered and brocaded materials, cut in square, overlapping swatches. The pattern was casual but repetitious, and it contained fluted effects, overlaps, and a variety of tones. We nicknamed it "scrapestry" and it epitomized the European imaginative treatment of commonplace things to produce an aesthetic effect.

On the floor of the City Council Chamber of Hannover, Germany, is a vast map-like depiction of this city of 500,000 and its land-use masterplan. Made of terrazzo, inserted stone blocks, and long thin strips of bronze, this living map enables councillors and city officials literally to walk across and through various discussion items which happen to be on the city's business agenda. At intervals of three to five years, craftsmen are brought in and any significant revisions are made to bring the design up to date. The result is the striking image in miniature of a growing city for visitors to view, and a practical, working device for city officials to study in their municipal ruminations.

Banners, banners everywhere is a message we brought home from northern Europe. Gay, colorful banners, long slender streamers, and huge city flags are lavishly displayed throughout the downtown areas. Wherever a small plaza or open plot is available, cities and private businesses install towering poles and hang from them a variety of colorful and interesting banners. Depicted are Boy Scout Week, National Wine Week, national holidays, birthdays of celebrities and, in many cases, no special event at all. As one strolls the main streets and sees the sensuous, undulating banners in all their colors, it is mindful of the streets of an international World's Fair.

The City of Stockholm, suffering from the writings and scribblings on its walls and buildings that all cities endure, erected a huge, public graffiti wall, measuring eight feet in elevation and 100 feet in length, in the heart of its busiest public plaza. Painted white, this surface is available for all writers, markers, defacers, or protestors to inscribe their messages in paint, ink, lipstick, or other medium. One warning is printed at the top of the graffiti wall: "Write anything you like, but remember that you are responsible for what you write." During my visits to that wall, I was impressed by the antipodal points of view, by the cute cartoons, the clever humor. Relatively little smut appeared. At the end of each week, Park Department employees arrive and paint the entire length of the wall in flat white paint, providing a vast new tablet for the writings of the next week. It was one of the most interesting things—pragmaesthetics—that I brought back from Europe.

During the trip, we were impressed by the apparent disinclination of Europeans to pound home their public relations points, as we might have expected. Rather than tell us, "This is the way you Americans should do it," they would simply, casually, lead us to rare sights and subject us to experiences without the Madison Avenue commentary. Frequently, at the end of a busy day, my Odyssey companions and I would be discussing aspects of the day's tour over a leisurely drink. Only then would certain subtle movements and exposures of the day surface for us, and we would be all the more stunned by their delayed impact. Illustrations of this would include the "allotment gardens" so prevalent in The Netherlands and Germany. These small squares of open-space land at the edge of major cities lay side by side over hundreds of acres. Each square measured about 30 feet by 30 feet and was carefully tilled by a fee-paying urban weekend farmer or gardener. Some squares produced corn and vegetables, while its immediate neighbor might be clothed in a splash of chrysanthemums. The next two squares might have carefully cultivated ginkgo trees, with the following spaces returning to vegetable production. These thousands of patch quilt mini-gardens are relatively unheralded throughout the world, and regardless of which city we were in at the time, our guide would pay them only the slightest attention.

Invariably, our party members would ask, "What about vandalism?" and just as invariably our guide would shrug the question off as hardly worthy of reply. Our readers should consider carefully the significance of this urban confidence in today's American culture!

The existence of flower carts, pushcarts, fresh fruit wagons on countless corners, the strategic location of downtown "forests" in the very heart of built-up urban cities—these and other pleasant surprises were treated with the utmost candor by our guides and hosts. The cumulative effect of these sights, and of this low-key unmerchandising we summed up in the term, "Osmoculture," (osmosis and culture).

NO SUBSTITUTES

As I admired a particularly stunning fabric-covered living room set in the Scandinavian Trade Center of Copenhagen, Denmark, I asked the director of the Center if the material was a plastic. "Plastic?" he said. "We use no plastics in our furniture. In fact, we use no substitutes at all. That furniture is covered with genuine Danish Red cowhide!" If this were an isolated case, it would hardly deserve mention, but time after time I found that Europeans, wherever the economy permitted, demanded the real thing and decried substitutes. In a small restaurant in Solvang, Germany, I again innocently questioned whether a series of paintings on the wall were "prints." The restaurant manager, with mild indignation, pointed out that he would have no prints in his restaurant, and that these particular originals had been done by an elderly gentleman who lived upstairs above the restaurant. Wood carvings, ivory, inlaid work, even pencil drawings adorning walls were invariably originals rather than copies or substitutes. This has deep significance in our American culture when one considers our enormous productive machinery that creates and distributes substitutes and synthetics in all types of handicraft, and in many cases, mass-produces things that purport to be custom-made.

Northern Europe can boast of its share of tall buildings, great bridges, large industrial plants, and many of the frustrating rushes, jams, confusions, and congestions indigenous to all major cities of the world. Nevertheless, these same Germans, Dutch, and Scandinavians have retained and cultivated a delightfully cozy, scaled-down-to-human-size quality in much of their urban design, planning, and street appointment.

The City of Stockholm maintains over 400 human-scale sophisticatedly comic sculptured pieces on its streets and in its parks. A pregnant young lady, a workman arising from a manhole, two overweight professional boxers squaring off in a ring—these and other quaint, earthy and human-sized figures are strategically located throughout the park system and on the busy downtown streets of Stockholm. Each figure is mounted on a three-foot square granite block.

Small squares and parklets dominate the urban scene in Europe. The very smallness and the neatness of these parklets lends a quaint, lilliputian charm to many ancient neighborhoods. Attention to the finest detail is an obsession. The pupils of eyes are carefully drawn in on figures placed in parks and open spaces. The ornamental scrollwork of garden furniture is carefully etched. Intricate details in such things as bicycle racks, drinking fountains, and park benches make them appear as the furniture on the lawn of a wealthy man, rather than apparatus installed in public parks.

The presence of large numbers of bicyclists, in close contact with heavy downtown traffic, reduces the scale of urban transportation to one more tolerable by people. There is something very intimate and social about a bicycle passing by, pedalled vigorously by a gray-haired grandmother, two bags of groceries jiggling in her rear basket.

The human scale, repeated in an infinite number and variety of ways on the downtown scene of Europe, provides much of the intimacy and quaintness that Americans hungrily absorb, and for which they seek despairingly in their own home cities.

A trip abroad for the professional person can be simply a *Baedeker*, a travel talk, a sojourn, a vacation. I find no fault with these. On the other hand, a professional on an educational trip abroad should seek those subsurface signals, connotations, movements, and vibrations which no book, film, lecture, or record album can transmit. It was the discovery of these precious subtleties that made the 1969 Urban Design Odyssey so significant to me.

How Parks Will Shape Urban Development

J.E. Curtis

Crystal-balling the future of our nation's parks and recreation facilities is as risky as guessing the exact shape of interplanetary travel. Discarding the crystal ball, I would prefer to utilize a technique called "synectic perspection."*

Traditionally, America has shaped its parks and recreation facilities after Europe's great parks and its small urban green spaces. From the Civil War until the early 1900's, our parks presented great, formal, beautiful green sights in large cities and towns, kept in neat order, and treated like the front lawns of a tycoon's home. The magnificence of New York's Central Park, Chicago's Lake Shore Drive, the Boston Gardens, and, in Sacramento, Calif., the park-like setting of its State Capitol, all suggest this Victorian period. The nation added to its inventory of parks and recreation facilities during the dark depression days of the 1930's when armies of jobless men and women employed on WPA-financed projects, built baseball diamonds, tracks, small parks and large play facilities in municipal areas throughout America. At the time, many thought them expensive luxuries. Today they would cost ten to fifteen times the price paid in the early 1930's.

Throughout this 100-year cycle, the tone of the park was generally formal, graceful, lovely and ornate. Fences, railings, banisters, walking surfaces, decorative lights, all showed the distinctive mark of the artist, even if the item eventually was mass produced. Curlicues, gimcracks and gingerbread showed everywhere, and delighted the eye of the park buff. Play facilities themselves were relatively simple and unadorned, consisting usually of open, grassy meadows, with an occasional baseball diamond.

CHANGING TIMES

World War II, spiralling costs, labor-saving machinery and the crush of the post-war baby boom have changed these park policies as well as almost everything else. Record-breaking use of city and national parks have brought a host of new service problems. The upward climb of

Reprinted from *The American City*, October, 1969. Copyright Buttenheim Publishing Corporation, 1969, permission of publisher.
*Synectic perspection is the assembly of related established corroborated factors to produce a logical vanishing-point extension into the future, a form of induction, rather than speculation.

labor costs and, ergo, the temptation to replace human labor at every turn with new, efficient machinery, have revised markedly the appearance and operation of our parks and recreation areas. Many of the old formal parks and green areas still remain but their use is changing so rapidly that one has difficulty recognizing their original character. Open lawns have been converted to asphalt parking areas. Dainty, filigreed bandstands are inadequate for today's frenetic musical units, and are being replaced by mobile showwagons and acoustically designed music shells. New buildings in large parks accommodate modern food services, souvenir sales, artificial ice rinks and mechanically operated swimming pools, model boat and plane facilities, marinas and a host of facilities which consume park space, and which compel major facelifting in the Victorian park of the past.

Simultaneous with these changes, a massive convulsion is coursing the world. Powerful forces are in conflict in all major centers of the world and, frequently, public parks and recreation areas provide convenient arenas for the joust. The mall in Washington, Lincoln Park in Chicago, Griffith Park in Los Angeles, Central Park in New York City, the Boston Common and the lovely greenswards of Atlanta, Memphis, Dallas, San Francisco, and Omaha have borne the foot pressure of revolutionary meetings, protest marches and encampments, confrontations with police and National Guard forces, and the social explosions felt around the world.

Dr. Richard Kraus, Columbia University, sees this development as a "direct and priceless opportunity to involve the disenfranchised fully in park policy making and in major decision making where parks and recreation are concerned."*

BATTLE AGAINST LITTERING

The Visigoths of litter, filth, trash and waste are also bugling to the attack. Overflowing waste baskets, acres of broken glass, ruined shrubs and flower beds, mutilated benches, defaced statues and building walls have turned some parks into pigstys. Conscientious citizen resentment against these onslaughts and against the loss of parklands is on the rise, and conservation and urban beauty movements are gathering considerable strength. The first skirmishes have been held but final winners are nowhere in sight. Battles against auto junk yards, the erosion of green hills, the pollution of swimming waters and beaches, and the rapacious stripping of trees and top soil—these evils are being fought more bitterly every day by modern day Joan of Arc and Horatios.

Two opposite-coast classics in this are the Santa Barbara, Calif., offshore oil operations and their impact on neighboring bathing beaches, and, in the east, Consolidated Edison's five-year tussle with nature and park enthusiasts over the proposed power plant on the Hudson River. Both promise decades of struggle.

Alfred North Whitehead, famous architect-philosopher, said: "the major advances in civilization are processes that all but wreck the societies in which they occur."* We see the wisdom of his words in our present urban spasms.

DESIGN

The design and construction of playground equipment is evolutionary. As recently as 1950, playground designers

*Youth Service News, N.Y. State Division for Youth, Spring 1969, Vol. 20. No. 2.

settled for what was termed, "A plumbers nightmare," pipe-constructed units added one after another in a splash of color, on the assumption that this was exactly what the child was seeking in his playgrounds. Today, this riot of color has been modified by the introduction of timber, fiberglass, concrete, rubber and natural materials which soften and make more lifelike the all-pipe, all-color pattern. The brilliant designs of J. Paul Friedberg playgrounds in New York City's newest housing projects demonstrate the enriching effect of rock, paving stone, timber, sand and subdued materials, as compared to garish pipe and color patterns.

FINANCE

Changes in the philosophy and rationale of parks and recreation have brought corresponding changes in public attitude toward costs. Segments of the American population which, until recently, would regard a park or recreation facility as a "frill," are demanding larger units and more advanced planning in their parks. Expensive swimming pools, ice rinks, artificial bathing beaches, marinas, golf courses, tennis areas and picnic groves are being constructed at a record rate, and the costs involved are astronomical. Annual gross costs for public recreation and park operations are inching up into the low billions, according to the latest Yearbook of the National Recreation and Park Association. This is still modest when considered in the light of America's $75 billion spent annually on all forms of leisure and divertisement, but it is a marked rise from the several hundred million figure of the late 1950's.

From this eruption in new life patterns, in new finance, in new public action, we have a base pattern from which our parks and recreation facilities may be projected into the next ten to 15 years.

The need for more manpower is obvious, despite the many advantages of new machinery and automation. A recent national study indicated that from 200,000 to 400,000 potential jobs exist in our nation's park and recreation areas if we restore the human parking attendant, the food concessionnaire, the patrolling security man who maintains order in remote parkways and remote footpaths, the matron in the rest room, etc. There is a protesting clamor from the general public over broken vending machines, filthy rest rooms, a lack of information centers and a dearth of courteous personnel throughout our entire recreation and parks system. This has offended the public and created fears about safety for women and young children in these public areas.

The use of power mowers, for example, should not preclude the presence of a trained and concientious worker system strategically located. Nothing is more frustrating than facing an emergency in a park and being thwarted by locked doors, mal-functioning machinery, vandalized telephone booths, and the total absence of policemen or other uniformed personnel.

The design of the park and recreation facility of tomorrow will, very likely, be less formal than our turn-of-the-century English or French garden. The tone of American life becomes increasingly less formal and in many ways, closer to nature. Massive central entrances in large parks, will give way to scattered small, attractive, convenient entrances. Softer

*"The American Aesthetic" by Alfred North Whitehead.

lighting, illuminated information signs, great publicity on coming events, these are part of the new parks.

SCHEDULING

Scheduling of activities year-round will replace the former warm-weather monopoly in urban park use. This will be assisted by air conditioned all-weather buildings, and the use of temporary shelters such as bubble structures or air inflated structures. The conventional 9:00 to 5:00 p.m. scheduling, and the five-day per week heavy staffing to the exclusion of other periods must be replaced. A leisure calendar and a leisure clock will be devised which will have little in common with the standard clock and calendar of the day. Personnel will be employed, trained and utilized to relate to the new public living patterns rather than the customary clock. Long afternoon and evening programs, many going far into the early hours of the morning, massive scheduling for the weekends, and total programming for year-round operation is already under consideration by most progressive recreation and park agencies. This wider variety of activity will justify a much wider collecting of revenues and fees and charges. The public will pay more willingly for activities which are obviously geared to their convenience and timing, than they have been in the paying of fees for conventionally planned activities. The traditional ten-cent entrance fee to a children's zoo in a public park is no more realistic than a five-cent bus ride.

PROFESSION OF RECREATION

The profession of recreation, park and leisure administration will receive substantial aid from universities and from all levels of government. The quality, quan-tity and stature of the leisure time administrator will rise proportionately, and larger numbers of our bright young people will select this field for careers. Moreover, due to the changing nature of our work, increasing numbers of highly skilled retired people and semi-retired people will turn to this enjoyable field of endeavor and spend more years in it than their original retirement plans suggested. The great advantage of these two developments is that we should have a happy mixture of youthful new careerists together with matured and well-experienced retired and semi-retired professionals.

High mobility, and expanded international travel facilities herald a strong element in tomorrow's recreation. Movements of great numbers of people, in some cases entire small communities of 2,000 to 5,000, will be carefully engineered, and relatively commonplace.

PLANNING EFFECT

One of the most intriguing concepts for the future is one that was hatched in the city of White Plains, N.Y., that is, "The City in the Park" concept. Though White Plains is still far from obtaining this dream of a city laid out on the framework of one all-encompassing park, other cities have moved in this direction. Tapiola, Finland, nicknamed the "Garden City," is perhaps the nearest thing at the moment to this accomplishment. The concept of a city being literally and totally a park with all fixtures, living needs, activities and accommodations placed within it, is becoming increasingly feasible. Rather than a city *with* parks, rather than a city *having* beautiful parks, this concept suggests the total acreage of the city identified as a living park. Hospitals, gasoline stations, schools, streets, fire stations, stores, shops and other essential urban appointments would be placed within the park structure so that all elements were complementary. To do this with an old existing city is not easy, but we try. On the other hand, to do this in a relatively new virgin city like Tapiola, Finland, or Reston, Md., is exciting and far more attainable.

The foregoing cannot be realized without the commitment of massive financial resources. I believe that the amount being invested in parks, recreation and leisure services of all kinds will more than quadruple in the next ten years.

We must expect changes in public policy that will encourage this investment. This observation emerged from a recent park forum:

"Private investors should be given tax incentives for land dedicated for recreational purposes. Individuals or groups should be encouraged to purchase land for recreation as a holding bank until governmental agencies purchases are able to prevent land speculation. Tax benefits should also be applied to this effort. Furthermore, private enterprise should be encouraged to invest in recreation in urban inner-city areas through favorable zoning regulations, building code modifications, and the availability of insurance and liability protection."*

Enormous business empires to service leisure needs and the development of a great complex of power structures to deal in this precious commodity, "good living," will rise in the next ten years. The financial base for this massive expansion and refinement of our parks and recreation structure throughout the world already exists, and simply needs the galvanizing force of new thinking and new triggers for investment.

Parks and recreation of the 70's and the 80's represent, indeed, a most dynamic, exciting, and almost unlimited area for new design and development of this fast-changing urban civilization.

*From minutes of National Forum on Parks and Recreation in the Urban Crisis, convened by the National Recreation and Park Association, Washington, D.C. March 19-21, 1969.

Problems of Policy and Management

Pasadena Recreation Department, Pasadena, California

ALBERT M. FARINA "Legal Aspects of Recreation"
Parks and Recreation, National Recreation and Park Association, March 1967.

DAVID E. GRAY "The Tyranny of the Chain-Link Fence"
California Parks and Recreation, California Parks and Recreation Society, Inc., August 1968.

RICHARD I. McCOSH "Recreation Site Selection"
Parks and Recreation, National Recreation and Park Association, December 1971.

THOMAS L. GOODALE "The Fallacy of our Programs"
Parks and Recreation, National Recreation and Park Association, November 1967.

DAN W. DODSON "Community Relations"
Twentieth Century Recreation: Re-engagement of School and Community, AAHPER, 1963.

JAMES R. MARTIN "Renewing Management Skills"
Forum, Journal of the Association of Professional Directors of the YMCA, January 1969.

DIANA R. DUNN "Motorized Recreation Vehicles"
Parks and Recreation, National Recreation and Park Association, July 1970.

MAYNARD HUFSCHMIDT "A Summary of Environmental Planning"
American Behavioral Scientist, Sage Publications, Inc., September 1966.

ROBERT B. DITTON "Wreckreation in our National Forests"
Parks and Recreation, National Recreation and Park Association, June 1971.

Problems of Policy and Management

Never have park and recreation agencies been more difficult to administer. Never have the problems of public policy been more intense. Never has public support been greater. The concern for people which has been and is now a primary theme in the philosophical foundations of the recreation movement has become the major thrust of contemporary life in this country. This change is apparent in the humanistic movement that is sweeping the nation and the world. It is evident in humanistic psychology, attacks on the abuses of technology, the peace movement, empathy for the poor, the drive for improved medical care, the move to reject possessions as the symbol of identity, the effort to improve education, in women's lib, in race relations, and in a thousand other ways. These ideas are being acted out in programs and demonstrations and individual efforts all around us.

The fundamental themes of the park movement are also major national concerns. Conservation and ecology are the watchwords of the age. The realization that man is not independent of nature but a part of it has seeped into the national consciousness. The few that have been concerned about survival of the California Condor are now joined by thousands who are deeply concerned about the survival of man in the cities of man.

"Governments should be held accountable for their negligent acts as are the people under their jurisdiction."

The park and recreation movement and the agencies that administer programs exist in a political and social environment that is increasingly complex. The state and most communities are politicized to a degree we have not experienced before. Concurrent and interwoven into this increase in the tempo and intensity of political activity are technical and social developments that are changing the social environment dramatically.

It is in this rapidly changing social environment that the recreation and park movement must operate. The magnitude of social change is so great it defies description; it may defy comprehension until it is seen in the framework of history. But some trends can already be seen as highly influential. Among them the changing of family relationships, deterioration of the sense of neighborhood, the development of an urban man, altered conditions of work,

"The key concepts in the community role are engagement and participation—engagement in the great problems and issues of our time and participation in the lives of our communities."

the changing role of women in society, race relations, sorting of society on the basis of age, and revolutionary changes in our system of values appear to be highly significant.

There are risks in the contemporary social environment. Alienation, in which the individual lacks a relationship to something external to him when such a relationship is considered to be both natural and desirable, has been amply documented in the written and visual literature of our time. The theme of this thesis is alienation of man and God, of man and man, of man and woman, of man and the earth, and of man and his institutions. As population increases, the psychological distance between people seems to increase also. The most sensitive individuals among us complain of the lack of meaningful relationships with others, particularly with people whose life experiences have been different. The rate of technological and social change is so rapid that two generations do not have enough congruence in their life experience to understand each other readily. The government and other institutions seem impersonal and remote. Our affairs are so complex, the media play such an important part, and decisions are made so rapidly, and events occur so quickly, the problems seem too big to be managed by human beings. Disillusionment is greater when people feel they have no means of influencing events.

"In our era, when people have better health, more leisure, more material possessions, when more are married, more have children, and more live longer, it is strange that there should be at the same time more of a sense of alienation than ever before."

There is a broad and growing humanistic ethic permeating America. It sees the great needs of our nation in human terms. It would not rank improved technology or an improved economy as central needs in our national life. It would see the primary social needs as human development, improved processes of human interaction, and protection and restoration of our environment, as central. It is precisely in these fields that the recreation and park movement must operate. It is in these fields that the movement finds its mission and identity.

"Some of man's basic conflicts are involved in the MRV (motorized recreation vehicle) issue—controversies such as the rights of the individual versus the state, individual property rights versus common public rights and economic growth versus the quality of life."

There is considerable criticism of city management these days. If the criticism is merited where did management go bad?

The answer is it didn't; it failed to keep pace with increased demand made on the cities of America. Urbanity is a cultural style and a way of life. True urbanity has been lost in most of our cities. The best of things and the worst of things happen to cities. The central question is what men do to the city and what the city does to men. Redesigning the city will not of itself create a satisfactory social environment. One must develop in the city a circle of responsive others. City living cannot be mastered if one feels anonymous. If there

"Bad planning is nothing more than an extremely complex or complicated procedure that will enable you to choose the wrong course of action with an extremely high degree of assurance."

is no response, no satisfactory life is possible. Recreation agencies must help make the social environment of the city human. The problem of keeping social institutions current in a period of rapid change is a difficult one. There are not many social organizations older than a year or two that are really current. Educational institutions, churches, youth organizations, and recreation agencies, fraternities, women's clubs, and many other institutions are substantially out of phase with the wishes and perceived needs of their intended clientele. Organizational obsolescence is

"Since the dawn of civilization it has been a mad and sometimes ineffective race for man and all living creatures and living and vital organizations to keep up with the changes in their environment. The dinosaur didn't make it."

widespread and growing. Social and technological change is overwhelming most institutions because the processes of change are more rapid than the processes of adaptation. What is needed is a continuous process of organizational renewal that updates the agency's values, programs, and procedures at a pace equal to the processes of social and technological change.

One of the great needs of the park and recreation movement is improved management of our agencies. Our literature does not reflect current thinking on management problems. One of the interests of social scientists has been individual and group behavior in organizations. Their research in these fields has greatly revised our understanding of management and organizational behavior. The beginning of this influence is usually dated from the "Hawthorne studies" undertaken at the Western Electric plant in the thirties but some of the ideas which have been substantiated by social science investigations can be found in the literature earlier. The Hawthorne studies, however, were landmark investigations that affected the way we think about organizations and the way we manage most of them. Since those studies were published, a vast literature has grown up that has altered our ideas about the character and influence of authority, motivation of employees, interaction of people in work groups, and most of the central concepts in modern management.

With the advent of humanistic psychology, these interests have been reenforced and expanded. The results are reported in an extensive literature on the "human relations" movement and many other aspects of organizational theory. The recreation and park movement has been largely insensitive to this ferment and unaware of the findings of social science research as it affects management of park and recreation agencies. Some of the articles in this section have been selected to add a dimension of social concern to our management processes; others were chosen to represent some of the social issues that involve park and recreation agencies.

Legal Aspects of Recreation

Albert M. Farina, Ed.D.

In every state, county and municipality in the nation, questions are being asked concerning the legal aspects of recreation.

For example: can my city use tax funds to build and conduct a community center, a park or a camp? Can it provide art exhibits, music programs, or festivals? How is the program to be administered? What is our taxing power? Can we, under the present law legally hire personnel to take charge of our program?

Recreation in every state is administered basically by the local agency. Recently a few states authorized state recreation agencies by statute. Although recreation is increasingly becoming a state function through the authorization of state recreation authorities, it is highly doubtful that it will ever dominate the "grass-root" services provided by the local unit. Therefore, many special problems must be met by the local government in administering the general enabling act.

In administering the recreation program two types of legislation are necessary. These are enabling legislation by the state making it legally possible for the local unit to act, and ordinances passed by the local unit to put the enabling legislation into effect. If the administration of recreation in local governments is to rest on a sound legal base, clear, concise and comprehensive legislation must be provided for the local unit.

Because recreation legislation is usually drafted by professionals in this field or by legislators themselves, clearly established principles are necessary to serve as a guide in establishing effective recreation legislation.

After careful consideration of state constitutions, certain principles and criteria tend to evolve as guides for developing future recreation legislation.

EXPERTISE AND CONSISTENCY

When writing legislation, it is advisable that experts from the recreation profession as well as legal advisors who have had some training in drafting such legislation be selected. New laws must be consistent with other forms of legislation, and careful consideration must be given to

Reprinted with permission from National Recreation and Park Association. Official publication *Parks and Recreation*, March, 1967.

objectives and basic principles. Recreation practices which are enacted into law should always be: (1) consistent with the spirit of the law, (2) consistent with other legal principles, (3) comprehensive or inclusive, (4) peaceably agreed to, and (5) neither obscured in meaning nor merely implied.

NEED FOR FLEXIBILITY

American society is dynamic and constantly changing. Effective legislation must be consistent with the interests of that society. A mandatory law in recreation could create a hazardous lag by forcing a changing society into steadfast law. Under some circumstances it is desirable that grants of power be made by state constitutional enactments to assure permanence, but such changes are difficult because a state constitution can be changed only by a direct vote of the people. Therefore, the use of more flexible and more easily obtained legislation is urged.

Recreation, like many other functions of government in America, has been a local concern. Therefore, recreation should be looked upon as a function of the local unit. As in other issues concerning human welfare, many of the communities of our nation decide local issues by referendum vote. State legislatures must pass permissive legislation in the form of enabling laws which allows communities to decide specific issues in a democratic manner, while adhering to the state enabling act.

STATE RECREATION AGENCIES

It is evident that local communities need state assistance in planning, securing supplementary resources, advising on operational procedures and setting physical layouts and personnel standards. A state department is needed also for the clearance and interchange of recreation information and for the stimulation and strengthening of the local organization. A state recreation authority should follow similar procedure of health, education and welfare services in the various agencies.

SPECIFICALLY STATED POWERS

Legislation which confers broad powers on all governmental units, both urban and rural, has the advantage of meeting the immediate problems of municipalities. And it provides for flexibility in the event of future reorganization. Recreation legislation cannot be broad and inclusive when the authority for its establishment and conduct is not specifically given. The Federal Constitution's welfare clause, police powers, and charter authority are the base for implied powers. Implied authority for recreation is not an adequate basis for recreation because it fails to give direct or express powers for the establishment and conduct of recreation programs.

Communities are sometimes without badly needed recreation services due to slow action of reluctant local officials. And this inactivity is blamed on vague powers within implied authority encountered during previous experiences. If recreation is to serve the needs of the public, direct legislation empowering administration to act must be passed.

CONSTITUTIONAL CHARTER AUTHORITY

A broad municipal charter is almost as important to public recreation as broad state legislation. Together they provide the best form of recreation legislation. It is advocated that a charter which extends those powers invested in cities by constitutional provisions, especially provisions that extend to cities the authority of adopting their own charters of self-government (as in home-rule), is the best form of authority. Constitutional power-granting authority of self-government allows the community maximum freedom desired in administering state recreation legislation. State enabling laws express only the authority to act, not the manner of acting. Thus, local charters, as described above, must be effectively used in administering the state act.

JURISTS AND PUBLIC RECREATION

By educating the jurist many decisions would be more favorable to the community program. For example, a claims board versed in municipal organization for recreation could place the cases in a form familiar with recreational patterns. Thus, a large percentage of claims would be settled by a claims board. Those claims not finally disposed of would pass on to claim courts in large population areas and to the courts having jurisdiction is sparsely populated areas.

IMMUNITY DOCTRINE

Most legal authorities believe that the government and its instrumentalities should be liable in tort. There is in common law the principle of following precedent. The principle of sovereignty has grown and persisted due to the refusal of the courts to break with this precedent. Legal experts and courts believe that the doctrine, "the King can do no wrong," is a misinterpretation of an ancient legal manuscript. The rule becomes more and more unpopular as our social culture changes. Much opposition to this rule has been in some courts. But other courts contend a helplessness to change the rule and say that such changes in established law must be effected by the legislature.

In the future, legislators and jurists must broaden the scope of the immunity doctrine to include due respect for the individual rights of the private citizen. Governments should be held accountable for their negligent acts as are the people under their jurisdiction. Recreation programs suffer when government assumes the attitude of immunity in torts since citizen's rights are undemocratically infringed upon.

FINANCIAL SUPPLEMENTS

Recreation in most instances is financed through tax appropriations and other lesser means, but community resources are either taxed to the limit or statutory power is lacking. Often political authority interferes with recreation funds as a result of curtailments in other budgets. Thus, many states have by law enacted legislation setting up a "separate fund" for recreation. This will assure a definite sum upon which to budget needs.

Certain states have aided their local units by authorizing grants of money through state youth commissions, inter-agencies and other state organizations. State recreation departments do not provide direct financial aid but they are contributing valuable services. In addition, organizations (private, public and voluntary) have contributed to public recreation. If and when aid to recreation is made by states, monies should be appropriated according to an established need. Municipalities should gain such aid directly and be permitted to distribute it through their recreation departments.

IMPLICATIONS OF COURT ACTION

Public recreation officials can do much in protecting the municipality, recreation personnel and themselves from law suits. This could be accomplished in two ways: (1) by briefly orienting personnel in the legal aspects of recreation, and (2) by supplying each employee with a pamphlet or a brief form of literature containing essential material covered during the orientation period. Such instruction would include the state recreation law and municipal ordinance, if any; and personal legal responsibilities in connection with each individual's position. In addition, this literature should cite a few court cases involving the various phases of the recreation program. Finally, the implications for personnel and their responsibilities under these conditions should be revealed. This approach, involving little time or money, may save the municipality or employee an expensive and embarrassing law suit.

PUBLIC UNDERSTANDING

One of the greatest problems in recreation is the education of the public to the need for a philosophy of play. Without public understanding, recreation will not receive support. Inadequate recreation personnel, programs and appropriations in many cities reflect inadequate public support. Many leaders who use publicity techniques encourage the public to participate through a better understanding of the values of recreation. Mass media help carry the recreation programs to the people. Favorable opinion should be systematically cultivated so that a whole citizenry can appreciate how an expanded recreation service can prove valuable to a community.

IMPLEMENTING RECREATION LEGISLATION

Implementation of recommended legislation comprises the most woeful lack in the field of public recreation today. Because legislation usually originates with the people through their leaders, new or improved statutes must wait to be initiated by the people. While various state and local bodies have been a great help in securing needed legislation, much is left to be desired. Knowledge of acceptable methods applied by other professions and organizations in obtaining needed legislation is of immediate importance.

A method that has proven effective is that of "pressure group dynamics." A thorough knowledge of this technique by the recreation profession would be of great value in obtaining needed legislation.

For example, if a group of interested citizens, including the director of recreation, desired the passage of specific legislation to conduct the local program: First, the local committee should formulate the objectives or goals of the desired legislation. Second, a preliminary survey must be made by the committee to ascertain what changes or suggestions are needed in the recreation laws of the state. Third, once all the data relevant to the needed revisions are compiled, and the laws and practices of other states are considered, a plan of procedure must be worked out by the appointed board or committee. The plan of procedure would then include the following:

1. The committee should familiarize itself with the existing laws section by section, making note of conflicts where they exist and of criticisms already expressed.
2. The committee should call together all groups of persons in the state who

are interested or have direct concern with the community recreation program. Other groups that have an interest in the recreation laws of the state also should be asked to cooperate.

3. The committee must receive suggestions from these groups with relation to the difficulties involved in changing the present law or in adopting a new one.

4. The committee must assemble the information to present a picture of operation of the existing law both in terms of its strengths and weaknesses.

5. The committee must formulate, in consultation with the various groups, suggestions for changes.

6. The committee must then present the proposed changes to legislative leaders, for the purpose of gauging the legislative reaction.

7. The committee, with the aid of an attorney, must then draft a bill for introduction to the legislature.

8. The committee must select key legislators, both to introduce the bill in the senate and assembly and to interest the members of each house, who are willing and able to defend the bill later in the session.

9. The committee should distribute copies of the bill, with suitable explanatory material, to organizations and individuals throughout the state who might be persuaded to support it.

10. The committee should prepare suitable newspaper and published material for the purpose of building popular support.

11. Finally, the committee should explain the bill to members of the legislature, answer questions concerning it, see that the bill is effectively presented at public hearings and stand by the bill until it is passed.

Publicity channels should be employed before direct contact with the legislature begins, and the use of these channels should be intensified during the legislature drive. Most groups pressing for the passage of legislation realize that it is difficult to succeed by simply putting pressure on the legislators. Therefore, the various media for publicity should be drawn upon to influence a wide variety of supporters.

It is believed that public recreation interests in America are as vast as those of any other organization in existence. It has always been the custom for the legislature to carry out the public will, determined and manipulated through mass media and reinforced by the old and tried methods of lobbying. If recreation is to meet the people's needs leadership must be fervently undertaken by national, state and local agencies who are interested in the recreation problem.

Tyranny of the Chain-Link Fence

David E. Gray

Recreation Centers can have friendly or forbidding profiles. They can welcome or frighten. They can invite or repell.

On many municipal recreation centers, the most conspicuous design element of the physical plant is a chain-link fence. It is never quite clear whether its purpose is to keep the staff in or citizens out. Proponents of the fence argue that it separates the public property from adjacent private property, establishes boundaries for the center, limits access and improves control of the center, keeps balls in and stray dogs out, provides a foundation for perimeter planting, helps control vandalism, and enhances the security of the center. It may do all of these things.

The fence also separates the center visually, physically and psychologically from the community. The kind of thinking that put it there conditions the goals of the recreation department, helps determine the number, capabilities and deployment of the program staff, influences who is served and how, and expresses an attitude and philosophy about the work. An accounting of the chain-link philosophy suggests that its liabilities far outweigh its assets. The program staff of many municipal centers is as indentured to the land as any serf. They often are charged not with the development of people but with the management of a center, not with service to the community but with the supervision of grounds. The chain-link fence which surrounds their professional world limits their service to the confines of the center, supports a come-to-us philosophy, limits their professional role, restricts the horizon and the concepts of service of the recreation movement.

The most deleterious effect of the chain-link philosophy is on the deployment of staff. Such a philosophy holds that the primary concern of the staff is to operate the center. It identifies the primary tasks as surveillance of grounds to assure compliance with rules, safety, proper use of facilities and control of equipment; development of a schedule for use of the facility; planning and execution of a program of activities with the staff in face-to-face leadership roles; coordination of maintenance activities to insure the readiness and sanitary condition of the premises. Such a philosophy rewards facility managers and holds that what happens on the center is what counts.

In contrast to this view, there is a concept of role for professional recreation personnel which perceives them as *community* figures. This

Reprinted with permission from California Parks and Recreation Society, Inc., *California Parks and Recreation*, August, 1968.

concept identifies as central, development of people, community interaction, improvement of the community, preservation of the virtues of urban life, and concern for the social problems of our time.

A really good recreator working within this concept can operate in a community without *any* facility and earn his salary. He can become a person of stature in his community for the contributions he can make to community living and the growth of people, without ever throwing a light switch, handling a ball, taking in a flag, or locking a gate. His job would be to generate events that would look for a place to happen, not to fill up a facility that he was hired to manage. This vision of the recreator as a community organizer raises serious questions about the way we recruit, educate and deploy staff and about the nature of professional work. There is no doubt that most "professional" recreators do much work that is sub-professional. Such tasks are easily identified. The challenging undertaking is to identify and describe the character of professional service.

The really difficult professional task in these times is the role of community catalyst. In this role, the job of the recreator assumes proportions as organizer, moderator, mediator, stimulator, interpreter, advisor and teacher. Using recreation content and method, such a figure seeks to improve the social climate of his community. There is no precise model for this kind of professional. The task may be accomplished in one community by an outstanding minister; in

another by a particularly able school principal or an effective YMCA secretary, but most communities lack such a person; they are the poorer for it.

Under the direction of an individual performing well in this community role, our recreation centers could become true community centers. This would require abandonment of the chain-line fence philosophy, broadening of the concept of what constitutes recreation involvement in community affairs, re-education and redeployment of the staff, and a new interpretation of the mission of the center.

The key concepts in the community role are engagement and participation—engagement in the great problems and issues of our time and participation in the lives of our communities. The community center cannot be a withdrawn, uninvolved island and perform its potential community role. The center cannot continue to serve a small, clean orderly segment of the community while there is violence in the streets and expect the populace to continue to support it. The vital community center is a "commons" where diverse elements of the community can interact. For many recreators the chain-link fence which surrounds the center is the new frontier of expanded, more meaningful service. It is there that a new world begins; it is there that the center interfaces with the community; it is there that movement begins and abrasion begins and interaction begins and support begins and service begins. Our recreation departments must become participants in the action. The goal is not less than the survival of our cities.

Recreation Site Selection

Richard I. McCosh

Most recreation work calls for a good deal of pre-planning. This is particularly true in site selection. You must know before you start what the needs and objectives of your organization are; you must have a list of requirements on where, how many, and what type sites are needed. With such a program you can make constructive selections of the best sites available.

Begin the examination of a site with a good map and aerial photos if possible. These are becoming more and more available through the work of counties and other government agencies. The new editions of topographic maps being made by the federal government are excellent for orienting yourself to the natural features of the site. These are inexpensive and available from the U.S. Geological Society, Washington 25, D.C. In recent years many counties and the U.S. Forest Service have taken aerial photos which show features in detail and are very good for planning use. Most counties also have maps available from the county engineer showing roads and other features and from the assessor's office showing ownerships of land.

Inspect the site in the field during the time of the year when the area will be most heavily used for recreation. This gives you a better opportunity to get the feel of the climate conditions, the exposure to the sun and wind, the water interests, etcetera, which vary greatly with the seasons. It is usually helpful to make a sketch map in the field, showing the size and location of the features of interest and to take photographs at the site. These are a great aid for planning use back at the office.

For site planning work, it is best to have a qualified and experienced park planner to carry through the study. However, there is also much to be gained by making use of the abilities of the local people who are available and interested in recreation. County judges, commissioners, engineers, assessors, and others who have lived in the area for a long time may have valuable knowledge regarding the site or opinions to offer from their varied professional experiences. A visit to the site by a group of several persons can usually bring out new ideas or verify opinions most helpful to the planning study of any recreation area.

How much study is required? This, of course, depends on the character of the site itself, the previous experience of the investigator, and the

Reprinted with permission from National Recreation and Park Association. Official publication *Parks and Recreation*, December, 1971.

number of factors needed to arrive at a good decision. It is too easy for the inexperienced person to make a quick judgment of a few values of the area and base a decision on these alone. Usually there are more factors to good site planning than first impressions. A site may be a rundown slum or a desolate piece of desert in appearance today but have excellent potentials for the future with a little development or water. The same is true of areas which at first look good because of a few existing recreation features but may actually be poor areas to develop for general public use.

In looking for the best sites available that meet the requirements, you need information to compare the site with others. You need answers to four important questions.

- What are the existing recreation features?
- How well can the site be developed?
- How useful will it be to the public?
- Is this site available?

Check the quantity and quality of all of the recreation interests already existing at the site. Naturally, a park site with scenic views, a good lake, trees, and sand dunes, will attract more people than a nearby area with only trees and dunes. Quality is vitally important. Frontage on a body of clear, clean water will be vastly different from the same amount of frontage on polluted water. Some recreation features, such as scenic values and water interest, also have greater overall value than other interests.

One of the most desirable features for a park are beautiful views or scenery. It may be distant views of a valley or the mountains or natural features such as a small lake, colorful rock formations, or unusual trees. A site which overlooks a harbor or river may offer interest in the activities of boating traffic. An area on the coast may have relaxing views of the surf rolling in on a beach. A site may also be attractive just through the beauty of its trees and shrubs. Note extent of these interests and how available they will be for the public to enjoy.

Water interest is one of the most valuable factors you can find for a recreation site. Most park planners look to water frontage for basic park areas. This follows naturally since frontage on an ocean, strem, or lake provides scenic values and opportunities for the very popular recreation activities of bathing, fishing, boating, and other water sports. A body of water is usually the center of interest at parks which attract the greatest picnic and camping use. It also cools the air in summer and nourishes the trees and wild life.

The amount of water frontage, the quantity and quality of the water, and the recreation afforded by it are important. A restricted frontage may be too crowded an area for public use. The quantity of water flow may be critical; a stream or pond which is attractive in the springtime may become stagnant or dry in late summer. If the site is on a reservoir, the level of the water at various seasons as it affects recreation should be studied. Check the quality of the water. A stream which has all of its watershed within a national forest or other lands under good conservation practices is less likely to be affected by pollution than one passing through unrestricted logging or past an industrial area. Other factors, such as water temperature, depth of water, the fish life it supports, wave action, flooding, etcetera, will affect its recreation value.

Other natural features which can be of high interest are the forests, canyons, mountains, deserts, seacoast, beaches, sand dunes, waterfalls, springs, etcetera with which the area is blessed. Just as the national and state parks place emphasis on features which are of national or state significance, counties should seek out these features which are distinctive of their area. Although the site may not contain the features themselves, there are often opportunities to include them as additional interest to the site. The route to the park may lead people past them or display views of them. A group of native trees or plants which are outstanding in a particular county can be featured at the site.

The fish, animals, and birds which may be found at the site are another interest. Fishing interest calls for a check of the species found, quantity and size, the season they are available, and the stocking program of the fish commission. Animals may be present at the site or provide hunting in nearby areas. The site may be on one of the major flyways of migratory birds or have its own resident bird life. Clams, crabs, and other marine life may add interest at coastal areas.

Each area has its own historical interests with which much can be done. Park visitors are always eager to learn more about the area they are in. The historical sign tells its story, but nothing gets interest across as well as some of the original historical items or places themselves which still have the character of the period covered. Notice should be taken of unusual rock formations, deposits or shapes of the earth's crust in your region. Those which tell a story of the earth's formation in each area can add geological interest to the recreation sites. An old shipwreck, a high dam, an old covered bridge, a place to find agates or other semi-precious stones or a place to pan gold, etcetera may be of interest. Some areas may provide archeological values such as ancient Indian village sites or hunting areas, caves, artifacts, etcetera.

How well can the site be developed? Look at the physical features of the land to determine how desirable it is for use,

what can be done to correct the faults, and what it will cost to make the area meet your needs in comparison to other sites. Many things need to be checked:

Size and Shape—The size of the area alone can be a determining factor. An area may be too small for the needs of the project. Areas should be large enough to include the attractions, have ample space for the use of facilities needed, and have room around the edges to protect the values of the area from encroachment by private developments. Acreage in excess of the minimum is good practice as recreation areas are never too large for the future and it is often more economical to operate one large area than several small ones.

Shape of the area is also related to the use attractions and needs of the development. A large picnic area or camping development is most efficient in shape as a square or rectangle several hundred feet in width in preference to a long narrow area less than one hundred feet wide. This is true because of savings in utility lines and the fact that your buildings have a useful radius equal in all directions. However, a narrow strip may be very practical for small developments, or to provide additional stream frontage for a fisherman's trail, or include scenic strips within the park unit.

Adjoining Areas—The values of the site may be affected by the appearance of the adjoining lands, ownership and use of the land, and the utilities available there. For instance, a site adjoining other publicly owned lands, such as a national forest or a public road, may be desirable, whereas a site next to an industrial plant might not. The utilities available nearby may provide a savings in the cost of extending electricity or water to the site.

Topography—Topography is very important. Check the elevation of the ground, degree and direction of slopes, drainage, rock outcrops, topsoil types and quality, as well as subsoil. Nearly level areas are required for parking areas, beaches, camp areas, ballfields, etcetera. Determine how much the topography limits useful area or what the costs of earth moving or grading might be.

Water—In addition to its recreation interests, water is needed for drinking, sanitation, and irrigation. The quantity and quality of water sources is often a big factor in site selection. The area may provide good springs or opportunities for a well or be near to municipal water lines. Figure the cost of providing water to the use areas.

Plants—The existing plant growth calls for thorough checking. Look at the trees as to size and interest, the amount of shade they provide, how healthy they are, the problems of maintenance, fire hazards, wind throw, etcetera.

An area may have been partially logged and requires removal of stumps or clean up. Some shrubs may be of good landscaping value, other areas of brush may need to be cleared. The extent and location of open areas is noted.

Exposure—How much will wind, rain, sun, and temperature affect the use? An area sheltered from strong winds may be highly desirable for recreation use. The direction, velocity, and season of these winds should be noted as to just how they will affect the recreation use and your maintenance and operation of the area. Lack of rainfall and extreme temperatures may call for the development of shade and irrigation of a site to make it useable. Sometimes, you have a choice of exposure for sites where the topography or trees of the area will provide afternoon shade, morning sun, or whatever may be most desirable for the use intended.

Improvements—Some areas may already have been improved and contain buildings, roads, utilities, cleared land, etcetera which may raise the cost of the site. If they can be used in the recreation development or resold, this amount can be discounted from the costs. If not, their removal adds to the costs.

Access—Examine access both as regards the routes to the site and the various recreation interests within the area. The type and condition of roads leading to the area will greatly influence the usefulness of the sites. Safe and convenient access points are needed to handle public traffic. Some recreation interests within the site may be almost inaccessible due to steep ground or other barriers such as a roadway or river which divides the property.

Undesirable Features—Few sites are without undesirable features—it is difficult to list all of the possibilities. Make note of some of the following:

Physical barriers: cliffs, flooding, swamps, bodies of water, ditches, dunes, blow sand, slide areas, etcetera.

Hazards: traffic, fire, falling tree branches, water currents or wave action, deep holes, insects, snakes, ticks, poisonous plants, animals, cliffs, hunting, water pollution, high voltage lines, etcetera.

Annoyances: noise (trains, airplanes, automobiles, trucks), dust, water algae, turbidity, pollen, aquatic weeds, smoke, fumes, etcetera.

Others: objectionable views, existing structures not adaptable to park use, stumps and logging debris, driftwood, nearby liquor-dispensing establishments, lack of usable area, small size (no expansion space, shade lacking or limited), exposure protection lacking, erosion, reservoir water-level fluctuations, lack of water and utilities, poor access, objectionable easements or land use, cattle grazing encroachment, items required for maintenance but not necessary to increase enjoyment of area, highway relocation, lack of traffic controls, etcetera.

Many of these will not seriously limit use and can be corrected or controlled. A sand dune can be stabilized, a swamp drained, mosquitoes sprayed, pollution reduced, etcetera. The added cost of correcting these features may be in the public interest other than just for the park use itself.

Potential Developments—The planner will need to determine how well the site is adapted to the kind of recreation use we seek to provide. What portions of the site are suited to parking area, picnic use, camping use, active games, natural area, roads, trails, etcetera. Note the additional features of interest which can be enjoyed by the public over and above the basic needs. For cost estimate comparison of sites, prepare an overall plan of the circulation of roads, basic facilities, and development work needed.

Maintenance and Operation—A part of the figuring of the development will be how the site is to be maintained and operated. Will additional personnel, housing, and new service equipment be required or is the area located so existing nearby crews can be utilized?

A preliminary estimate of the costs of providing equal facilities at one area in comparison with another site is required to bring out how much the various site conditions affect the overall cost. This cost comparison will need to include the acquisition of land, development of the site, and its maintenance and operation.

How useful and important will the site be to the public? In order to estimate attendance and other benefits, check the population, the economy, how good the access is, tourist travel, the degree of interest in the recreation attractions provided, how badly the site is needed, and the benefits the development might create.

Location of the site with relation to population centers will determine how many people are served by the area. There is a definite relationship between the number of people close to the area and the attendance, but it is only one factor. Figures on the rate of growth of population will also give a clue on future needs within a given area. Recreation interests of the people, how much time and money they have, and what parts of the state they like to visit will also affect the use.

Convenience of access to the recreation site greatly affects the use. Good access from main travelled routes increases the opportunity for heavy use. Sites which are difficult to reach are apt to have a very limited use. The amount of existing traffic on roads can serve as a guide to the potential attendance. The state highway departments have traffic flow charts of the main highway routes helpful in comparing road traffic and routes of heavy tourist travel.

Although some sites may be remote today, they may be opened up by new routes in the future. Improved access routes and transportation are continually extending the distance which people will travel to find recreation.

Another factor in figuring potential attendance is the nature of the recreation attractions. What is the quantity and quality of recreation features at the area? How do the facilities compare with other areas? Will the public have such a pleasing experience at the area that they will want to revisit it again or to tell others about it? A site with a variety of features for people of all ages and providing popular activities has a distinct use advantage over an area of limited interest.

What is the need for recreation in this area? How badly and how soon is it needed? Perhaps another public agency has plans to develop a site nearby. In such a case, your development may be unnecessary or can be combined in such a manner that one helps the other.

Sometimes we do not recognize the full value of a recreation development. A good park can stimulate the economy of an area by raising the adjoining land values, attracting tourists, and holding them in an area long enough that they spend more money in the region, and increases the money spent on recreation equipment, supplies, etcetera. Improvements made to an area in the form of improving and maintaining roads or scenic values, protecting watersheds, stabilizing sand dunes, draining swamps that breed mosquitoes, etcetera can have value to the surrounding area as well.

Some areas which would make good recreation sites are not available or would be too expensive in cost for the benefits offered. Certain publicly owned properties, such as military reservations, game reserves, etcetera may not be available to other agencies. A number of private properties are too highly developed to purchase at a cost reasonable for recreation. Sometimes, however, these sites may later become available as they are declared surplus to government needs, or improvements decrease in value. Ownership and availability must be checked and sometimes an appraisal must be made of the current market value of the property. Ownerships should be examined for easements, right of way, reservations of mineral rights, etcetera, to make sure that nothing would impair the usefulness of the area for a park.

Even though your funds may be limited, there are always other opportunities which make it possible to reach recreation objectives. Lands may be leased for a long term rather than purchased, easements for recreation use obtained, or land exchanges worked out. Sometimes a site may be purchased as a rock source for highway construction without losing its usefulness for recreation use later. A scenic viewpoint turnout might be made as part of new highway construction as little or no cost by using removed rock or fill material in the road construction. Agencies such as the U.S. Corps of Engineers, Bureau of Reclamation, etcetera may have sites available to an agency which will maintain them. Donation of land, funds, or labor are often available or can be promoted for recreation and the public good.

Your parks reflect the amount of study and good judgment used in selecting the sites. Poor ones will become inefficient areas with problems that can't be solved. Good areas will grow in interest for the future. If you choose the better sites you can develop a balanced, flexible program which will best serve the public's needs.

The Fallacy of Our Programs

Thomas L. Goodale

Recreation programs provide treatment for symptoms, but not the problem. They may, in fact, compound the problem.

The problem, of course, is the constructive, beneficial, creative use of leisure. Programs are intended to solve this problem. Whether or not they do is subject to discussion. While they may not be constructive, at least they are not destructive. If programs are not particularly creative and beneficial, at least they provide acceptable ways of using time according to the standards of the community. Still, such programs have undoubtedly been the salvation of many. Perhaps, too, they have been the downfall of many.

We have been expounding the positive aspects of programs (develop new interests, acquire skills, social adjustment, etc.) for over 60 years. They also consume time, keep kids off the streets, provide relief for mothers, lend structure to otherwise unstructured lives, and serve as the only link with community for many, especially the young and old. Through programs, the recreation function forfeited by the family is absorbed. Churches, schools, private agencies, industries, commercial enterprises, and governments at all levels are providing recreation programs, sometimes tripping over themselves and each other in the process.

For two-thirds of a century we have used programs to stuff a vacuum of time and individual resourcelessness created by an increasingly complex mass society. The vacuum, however, remains. For two-thirds of a century we have used programs as the vehicle to catch up to a demand which continues to outstrip us. It is increasingly evident that we are not, and perhaps cannot, catch up in this way. But we have been so busy trying that we have made inadequate advances on other fronts with other vehicles.

Besides being a stop-gap device that got out of hand, the preoccupation with programs has other causes. First, most programs are successful since the demand usually far surpasses our resources. Since we measure success by counting heads, our conclusion is automatic. We have long challenged attendance as an index of success, but the use of other indices is extremely rare. Counting dollars and cents is not the best substitute either.

Reprinted with permission from National Recreation and Park Association. Official publication *Parks and Recreation*, November, 1967.

In addition to being successful (even if by default), programs provide tangible, visible evidence of a profession at work. The very existence of the profession hinges upon its visibility. Such proof is of great significance for a profession that has been almost continually on the defensive. Of course, visibility may not really prove anything. It is quite possible to see programs, count heads and dollars, read newspaper accounts and annual reports, without having witnessed one shred of recreation.

Because of a need to be visible, we frequently admonish ourselves to do something, even if it's wrong, or perhaps even if its value as a recreation opportunity is questionable. How else can we explain beauty contests for three-year olds, Easter egg hunts for masses of children, or arts and crafts projects which may be neither artistic nor craftsmanlike?

Is there not a covert feeling that a poor program, or one of questionable merit, is better than no program at all? Or is a program on any terms better than no program at all? Should the winner of a contest be awarded trading stamps if the event is co-sponsored by a grocery chain? Should ten-year old ball players serve as walking advertisements for anyone sponsoring their uniforms?

Unfortunately, we have developed only our capacity to provide programs. Much of our literature is devoted to the choice and conduct of programs. This is the easy part. We have more difficulty determining the value of what we are doing, not in terms of visibility, numbers, or public relations, but in terms of recreation value for the participant. We go around telling ourselves that what we need to know is "What does the ball do to Billy?" This has become trite. After two-thirds of a century no wonder.

Our program emphasis, then, presents us with many problems; determining their recreation value is but one of them. Our commitment of time and resources may be another if, and apparently this is the case, we have little left to approach the problem in other ways. Further, the proliferation of programs may, in some cases, have a negative effect on recreation, the free element of free time, and leisure.

We know, for example, that many high school and even junior high school students carry pocket calendars to keep track of schedules of activities, meetings, and other commitments which equal and surpass our own hectic schedules. We know of students who have what is described as "a tired businessman's complex." We know, too, that there are many whose lives are even more markedly characterized by total lack of activity and involvement. Thus, we find patterns among our teen-agers that are duplicated and reduplicated later in life. We find a compulsive busy-ness about many people, young and old, and we are hard pressed to call such busy-ness recreation, or even the use of free time, as the free element is often conspicuously absent. Others are in a torpor.

We find among both young and old, that those best prepared to use leisure have the least leisure available, while those least prepared have the most leisure available. The case may be, as a result, that we are providing services for the wrong people. We may, in fact, be providing a disservice for many.

Warnings of such a happenstance have appeared in literature for a long time. A "best time" for example, has been described by George A. Lundborg as one which "nobody planned for me." A classified advertisement in *The New Republic* promoting a small summer resort area indicated that there were "no hectic programed activities" to follow.

Coincident with the problem of the distribution of leisure in relation to the ability to handle it is the attitude of anti-planning. Those most capable resist efforts of others to plan their time for them. Those least capable are also those least inclined to plan for themselves.

Again, the question arises—whom are we serving, and how much service is being provided? Our middle class values, interests, and trappings result in middle class plans. But it's those in the lower class that are reluctant to plan for themselves, and lack the resources as well, according to David Riesman and Robert Weiss.

Of course, planning is absolutely essential to the recreation profession. Without it we could not even begin to cope with the burgeoning demand in so many areas. But the planning element introduces problems of its own. It is a daily occurrence for many of us to have to decline invitations or forego opportunities which did not arise in time to be fit into a schedule. "I'd like to but I can't because . . ." is frequently a good excuse for declining, but frequently it's used in truth and is thus a poor excuse for failing to avail one's self of the best opportunities; another sacrifice to planning. It has become virtually impossible to do something on the spur of the moment. Everyone else (and everything else) has been booked for weeks. The impulsive element, out of which may arise the most pleasurable moments, has been undermined by the compulsive element of planning and scheduling from here to oblivion.

We have, then, become enslaved to our own plans. Might a similar result evolve for some of those for whom we do the planning? Do recreation programs create a dependency on the part of some of those who participate? Are recreation programs part of someone's busy schedule, and only that? Need mothers be resourceful when they can rely on elaborate playground programs? In providing a myriad of activities, might we destroy opportunities for recreation and leisure?

Programs, by their nature, can only be partly successful. Recreation, on an hour-to-hour basis, is hardly recreation. Interest in music, dramatics, literature or whatever does not necessarily occur from three to four p.m., M-W-F. A thirst for knowledge may not be quenched at the precise moment the library closes. Nor is everyone hungry precisely at noon.

What of those lost in the shuffle, the millions who do not participate in our programs, or any programs? What about the millions lacking not only the inclination to plan for their leisure but the resources as well? What of those whose alternatives are so limited that each choice is to pick the lesser of two evils?

Thorstein Veblen would not recognize today's leisure class. It includes the aged, the handicapped, and the unemployed. Great effort has been put forth by recreation professionals to provide opportunities for at least two of these groups, the aged and the handicapped. These efforts have included our most rewarding, and most frustrating experiences. The programs we provide for them are desperately needed, but at best they alleviate symptoms. Here are groups with a great deal of time, and very limited opportunities. So we conduct senior citizens' programs and programs for the handicapped. In so doing, might we be creating more dependency? Do we create an artificial environment they will not find elsewhere? Are we furthering their isolation from the mainstream of life?

Schools, camps, and programs for the handicapped provide vital services. They are often beautifully conceived and operated. But why should they be separate, segregated facilities and programs? Why should not every school and camp, program and facility be so designed and operated as to provide equally for everyone? Yet every day, hundreds of facilities and programs are conceived and constructed without even lip service being paid to the handicapped. To do so would be very impractical and costly. But does cost and practicality justify segregation? Should the wealthiest people in the world enslave themselves to feasibility at the expense of humanity?

There are other difficulties, of course. Lack of leadership is perhaps chief among them, but it seems not insurmountable if more effort were directed to it. Human ignorance and indifference looms as a larger, more tenacious enemy. We can never admit to defeat at its hands, but must we accept peaceful co-existence? Certainly not, and therefore, should we not redouble our efforts in this area?

Senior citizens, I am told, are very happy living in their own communities. Mild climates, vast and varied recreation programs; what could be better? And so we commend ourselves. Sure they are happy. They have escaped from a society where they are unneeded and largely unwanted; where they are excess baggage on a trip to the moon. Such segregated communities provide a far superior way of life to the alternatives available. But are there no better alternatives? Can they not be integrated, contributing, accepted members of every community? Should they, in the richest nation of the world, be plagued with the problems of housing, income and the like? While we are making some progress toward solving the economic problems, can we solve the problems of isolation and rejection?

Programs for such groups as the aged and the handicapped are very worthwhile and beneficial. They are, by far, the best alternatives available to these people. But the best alternatives are not available. No one can be complacent until they are. "Next to evil, the good is

the enemy of the best," declared Jay B. Nash in his *Philosophy of Recreation and Leisure.*

The unemployed remain largely unreached by our profession. Perhaps our largest short-coming, as they have two strikes against them at the outset. First, they are marginal to their society and community, lacking the skills to participate in the work force. Thus they are not only without the financial resources available to those who work, but are also shorn of that essential link with society which jobs provide. Even the millions who are educationally or emotionally underemployed at least have that important point of contact with the world around them.

Secondly, the Protestant ethic dies hard, and while it shows signs of weakening, little consolation is provided for those out of work. The stigma attached to unemployment is only slightly allayed by the fact that one is looking for work. Free time, by definition, is for those who work. Recreation is impossible under such conditions; even diversion is suspect and to enjoy one's self borders on sin. Pleasure neurosis, in fact, is an affliction of even our hardest working men and women. The unemployed are doubly damned.

Additional programs will not likely contribute enough toward solving some of these problems to justify the emphasis currently placed on them. They help in a stop-gap way, but much more is needed.

Needed, for example, is a massive campaign against the nation's value system; the sacredness of work, the sacredness of consumer goods, and the sacredness of busy schedules must be challenged and changed. We need to place humanity before expediency. We need to provide opportunities for dignity in addition to mere activity.

For those whose alternatives are not happy, or even humane, we must provide better alternatives. We must go to war against human indifference and ignorance, not program by program, but generation by generation. We must devote much more of our energy and resources to *Education for Leisure Centered Living* (the title of Charles K. Brightbill's book). We must conduct basic research. We must quit compromising our programs, and we must stop depending on them to solve the problems of the leisure age. In short we must attack the problem instead of treating, for better or for worse, its manifestations.

The problems are not exclusive to our profession. They are more than problems of recreation and leisure. They are human problems. But by our own claims and proclamations, we must be the self-appointed vanguard unit in the assault. Besides, we were humans before we were recreators.

Community Relations

Dan W. Dodson

In our era, when people have better health, more leisure, more material possessions, when more are married, more have children, and more live longer, it is strange that there should be at the same time more of a sense of alienation than ever before. In our great accomplishments in outer space, automation, togetherness, expanded church rolls, group emphasis and program, we have still not achieved community. The job is becoming more automated and less fulfilling; hence, if the needs of man's innermost soul are to be met, it must be through aspects of his nonwork time, that is, in leisure and what is done with it.

Your job is not merely to teach people to be healthy, as important as that is; it is not to help them to be physically developed, as important as that is; it is not to keep them re-created, especially if this means keeping them amused. A dictator can deal with these problems far faster and more efficiently than can we of a democracy. Our job fundamentally is to develop a citizenry imbued with those attitudes toward life which will cause them to value and prize health, physical well-being, and leisure. The seeking of these values will contribute to worthy involvement in a complex society.

This brings us squarely to the issues of community relations and what is implied in them. My points are stated in ten questions involving the problems of community relations.

The *first* is: can we cope with the problems of population movements in America and, specifically, in our school programs? Americans are people on the move in many ways. There is circular mobility as we move from one place to another, a movement across sectional lines of the country. It is not uncommon that some schools must enroll 107 children each year to keep the register constant for every 100 youngsters. On Manhattan Island, 50 percent of the children move each year during the course of the school year. This situation has its counterpart in every inner city of America, but many of you who work in other places know that mobility is a problem in almost all communities. The corporation gypsy is with us, as is the upwardly mobile young fellow in the business establishment who moves frequently from this town to the other. Many communities tend to specialize in serving this kind of person, who stays three or four years and then moves on.

Reprinted with permission from the American Association of Health, Physical Education, and Recreation.

Population movement involves peoples with attitudes and values which differ from the majority of those in their section of the country. In the past decade, about a million and a half people who are Negro in background have moved from the Southern states to the East and the West and across the United States. When we realize that other groups are equally mobile we get some notion of the great challenge before us—that of developing skills in dealing with population movements.

In our section of the country, we are increasingly concerned with the emigration of Puerto Ricans or people of Spanish culture. In the Southwest and the Far West, the problem involves the Spanish speaking peoples of Mexican background. In the Ohio Valley, we are concerned with the movement of peoples up the Ohio Valley from the Kentucky mountain section of the Appalachian Mountains and with what is involved in serving these mountain people as they come into our communities.

A *second* question concerns a type of mobility, not unlike the first and closely related to it—movement in the community and across the community. This is the great out-migration of the middle income, heavily white population from the inner cities to the suburban communities and the taking of their place by low income, marginal populations in the inner city.

For the New York metropolitan area, between 1950 and 1960, there was a loss of over a million in the middle income, heavily white population, but others took their place. Between 1950 and 1957, New York City lost to the suburbs a middle income white population the size of Washington, D.C., and gained a lower income, heavily marginal, ethnically identifiable Negro and Puerto Rican population about the size of Pittsburgh, Pennsylvania. Chicago has a

Negro population of about 800,000 in the inner city, along with the Puerto Rican, and the same kind of movement to the suburbs.

Philadelphia has a comparable kind of mobility problem. The mayor of Philadelphia referred to his problem as a tight noose around his neck, referring to the white ring of out-migrated suburban type population.

This means that we must deal with populations of larger and larger concentrations who tend to be caught in the throes of reshuffling the metropolis and its suburban branches. It means attrition in the smaller centers of populations, as people migrate increasingly to the larger centers.

Population movement has been toward the urban places of America. At the present time it is conservatively estimated that there are a million more people living in the slums of the cities of America than there are living on all the farms, and there are still a million more, or a million and a half more, who are marginal on the farms and should be moved to some other location.

This gives you some notion of the problem with which we are faced as we try to come to grips with the challenges of recreation and the responsibilities of the schools and other agencies that must deal with it.

The *third* question is: can we deal effectively with trends toward segregation, both enforced and imposed, that are produced by these kinds of movements? For instance, whatever new communities are being established, the tendency is for them to be homogeneous in nature and to attract people who are as much alike as the planners can make them. The whole trend is to lump us into these file-cards-kind of community situations. This problem, I believe, is going to be one of the real challenges to us in the years ahead. One of our most vital tasks is to help develop among these people a community consciousness, a sense of mutual involvement in common activities aimed at the common good.

Somebody has said that if an anthropologist ever scratched around in the ruins of our civilization a thousand or so years from now and ran across a modern church that had been destroyed, finding the cooking facilities, he would say what strange gods these people worshiped that they had to have such equipment to make their burnt offerings. But it is suggestive of the fact that the major thing we are teaching our children today, in too many places, is how to hide from each other respectably, whether it is a segregated neighborhood in the suburbs, a housing development in the inner city, or an all-inclusive social, recreation, and religious program in the church. I suggest that if we are to ask for ourselves the privileges that this brings, it imposes upon us an attendant obligation to find ways through which meaningful encounters and confrontations of peoples across lines of differences can be provided to the end that we develop the skills of leadership commensurate with the space age of which we are a part. Failure to do so results in a kind of mentality that is the reverse of the type required for today. Withdrawal from reality and withdrawal to homogeneity is the opposite of the very demand that takes out into wider encounters.

A *fourth* problem relates to the effects of automation in our society. Instead of the machine serving man, man is almost becoming a slave to the machine. The job description of a designer for a computer carries with it the notion of what is involved here, in that the computer is the main thing and man serves it by developing the program for it. But it is suggestive of some of the kinds of problems we will undoubtedly face in years ahead, if we are to involve all of our people in making a living meaningfully. The work hours probably will be reduced to 20 a week. Work that formerly was a means to an end will become an end in itself.

Since we live in a work-oriented society in which one's status is determined in large measure by one's work, how is a forcibly retired individual to feel useful, important and wanted? Here we face, I think, one of our greatest challenges.

The *fifth* problem is the problem of social class. The study being done by the Community Council of Greater New York has impressed me with the differences in the recreation programs offered in neighborhoods with major social class differences. In the higher socio-economic neighborhoods, there are cultural activities and involvements of all sorts. In the low income neighborhood, it is pretty much mass recreation and, I fear, not too high quality, either. Is it possible for us to be professional enough, and to prepare youngsters who are going into this field to be professional enough, that we do not become simply handmaidens to the middle class? Are we capable of achieving involvement of people across the lines of social class? Can recreation and recreation leaders become a means of breaking down the barriers which divide people and of establishing a sense of community so vital to the welfare of the individual and of a democratic society?

The *sixth* question concerns our ability to understand the function of power and the role of power in intergroup and human relations. I've been impressed as I have worked in New York City and other places with the fact that it is probably impossible for a youngster who is a member of a group that is powerless in a community to grow to maturity without some trauma to the perception of himself. The way we have tended to serve such powerless groups is to get the

bright ones involved, get them to participate, make them ashamed of their heritage and background of which they are a
part, and siphon their sentiments and
sympathies away from the group of
which they are a part. Group self-hate
has been a phenomenon of every minority group, or powerless group, that has
wrestled with the problem of trying to
come into mainstream participation. We
transmute the bright ones into so-called
ideal Americans, which means that they
take over in superficial ways the values
of the other group. This has ultimately
worked, but the erosion of human resources in the second generation is an
indication of the extent to which these
youngsters have been hurt. They have
paid a tragic price in human personality.
We have never really solved the problem
of the slum or of the powerless group.
We left the group itself to stew in its
problems and only siphoned off its
bright ones.

Adler's conception that people over-
compensate for their feelings of impotence, or inferiority, is only half correct;
people also withdraw in apathy. All of us
realize this when we understand that we
ourselves tend to be apathetic about
things we feel powerless about. For
instance, what are we going to do about
the atomic warheads that are pointed at
us every night as we go to sleep? We
realize that they are all set with our
name and address on them, and yet we
seem tremendously apathetic about
them. The apathy of the slums of American cities is testimony to the sense of
impotence and withdrawal that is
plaguing us in our efforts to bring
creativeness and leadership into the lives
of these people. You cannot give power
to a group; it has to take it. You can't
give people power; they have to take it.

Dr. Gabrielsen and I have been involved recently in a community in one
of our suburbs where 40 percent of the
children in public schools are of a
minority group that constitutes 22 percent of the population of the community. This group is completely shut out
of the decision-making councils in the
community. The alternative has to be, it
seems to me, that these people take
power and come as peers in the decision-
making process in the community. And
yet most of us, as people in leadership
positions in agencies, would not see this
as goodness, we would not understand it
as goodness. We'd see it only as a break
in the processes of our leadership responsibilities, and we'd not see it as a
necessary step to the achievement of a
sense of community in which all people
had a sense of belonging and a capacity
to have their wishes heard in our decision-making processes.

A *seventh* question involves the degree
to which we understand the role of
conflict in community involvement. It is
impossible for most of us to lead programs in a permissive, creative fashion in
a community that is in tension. When
the community is in tension, we tend to
become insecure, to take no chances,
and to do simply that which we can
defend—which means that we are not
going to stick our necks out in anything
creative.

I was working in a community on the
West Side several years ago when a
principal, who had a great reputation
and had done his thesis with us on
democratic school administration,
moved into a new junior high school
building. Before this building was finished, it had 200 more children than it
was designed to serve. They were Puerto
Rican children, half of them illiterate in
their own backgrounds. I said I would
like to use the wonderful auditorium in
this building at least twice a month with
anybody I could get into it from the
neighborhood on any topic that would
attract them—that I would be trying to

interpret the new school as a resource and community facility. Instead, the principal became insecure and started administering by directive, rather than getting the teachers together and saying "Gang, how do we do this kind of thing?" He transmitted his insecurity to his staff, who likewise started only what they could defend. What had been a permissive school in the old building, a few blocks removed, shortly became a very traditional, stifling, regimented type of school situation.

In the Bronx, the Negro parents descended on the teachers and said: "You're teaching white kids how to read. How come you can't teach ours?" And this is a good question. Instead of relying on reading readiness and all the things that they knew they should do, the teachers fell back on that which they felt they could best defend, which was rote learning. The amount of time they spend drilling scuttled all the dimensions of creativity in the program.

Most of us carry in the backs of our heads a vision of the time when swords will be beat into plowshares and spears into pruning hooks, when man will lay down his arms and war no more. And while we'd better find a substitute short of war for settling disputes, you and I know that we cannot have freedom in a society and not have difference; we cannot have difference and not have differences polarized. Group polarization of differences always results in some conflict. In fact, a case could be made that some conflict is the hallmark of a free society.

If this is so, and I believe that it is, then one of the biggest jobs that we have is to work creatively in tension and conflict situations. The conflict points are the points at which the new answers or the new designs are being forged, at which the creative things are emerging. There's no conflict about that on which

the community is in consensus. One of our major challenges is how to work in conflict situations, how to deal with conflict creatively, how to keep from withdrawing from it, and how to see it as a good rather than a bad thing. How to keep it from becoming stultifying and destructive so that it may play a creative role is, I think, one of the highest arts of leadership that we will be dealing with in the years ahead. This, I believe, is absolutely essential in the kind of mobile, fluid, changing society that we're talking about.

The *eighth* question I would ask is: to what end do we provide the services that we perform? A case could be made to interpret service as a middle-class people's way of trying to keep the community sufficiently tranquilized so that people will not get impatient and launch out to seek the promised land. To stay content is easier than to hunt the promised land.

I am also convinced that service by itself will not solve the problem. If you believe that you can solve your teen-age problem by simply serving, look at the places where they've taken group self-direction for themselves in some little hole-in-the-wall place while the services you're offering lie idle a block away.

If you believe that services will do the job that is necessary in dealing with low income population, I suggest that you take a look at some of our cities. In my community, we have build public housing to the point that every thirteenth residential address in our city is now city owned. We have built a new seat in the school system for every third child since the war. You cannot say that we have not made every effort to serve in accordance with the needs as we have seen them. But has this service been effective in releasing the creative energies of these people or has its main function been to serve as a tranquilizer, a kind of psychological deep freeze, especially for the youth of the community?

The *ninth* question I ask is: can we beat the growing pattern of bureaucracy in which we work? Not the least of the problems with which we're dealing is that, as we work with increasingly larger aggregations of people, jobs become increasingly specialized, responsibilities increasingly defined in the small print of manuals. Promotions and increments are made not on merit but on the basis of tenure. Increasingly we become people who serve not the total person but some narrow segment of the individual or of life, such as youth recreation. Bureaucracy has its strengths, and we need to learn how to use these strengths. Bureaucracy also can be stultifying to the human spirit. We must do everything in our power to keep from developing into a group of petty bureaucrats who provide a kind of service largely mechanical in nature, lacking the human touch, and devoid of any efforts to involve all the people with whom we work in a common effort to achieve common goals. It has been said that one of the greatest tragedies of modern man, especially the urban man, is his lack of involvement in community affairs. Let us set ourselves to the task of working *with* people rather than *for* people.

The *last* question is: what is the relationship of what we are doing to national purpose? I am concerned that we now must be physically fit to meet the national purpose. I believe America was built on the faith that if every individual were helped to develop his own unique talents to the fullest, the national purpose would be best served thereby. It may be necessary for us to produce youngsters who will be Russian beaters in some things, and we'll have to crack the academic stratosphere in doing this. But I think it is a great danger to assume that we must build bodies strictly to make the nation strong; if we build on this basis we're certain to be disappointed and fail.

To be truly meaningful and significant, purpose must originate from within the individual rather than be imposed from without. It must arise out of the needs, interests, and desires of people, and its pursuit and attainment must result in a deep sense of inner satisfaction and fulfillment. I do not believe that national goals and individual goals are mutually exclusive, but I do believe that we should not put the cart before the horse. Let us not sacrifice the basic values and principles of our democratic faith in order to match the power of Russia, else we may find that we have nothing left worth defending. Power alone in this international crisis will not save us. The strength of our nation lies not alone in our missiles and other armaments but in the moral and spiritual dimensions that characterize a free democratic society.

Renewing Management Skills

James R. Martin

Since the dawn of civilization it has been a mad and sometimes ineffective race for man and all living creatures and living and vital organizations to keep up with the changes in their environment. The dinosaur didn't make it. So far, you and I and the YMCA have. The editor of Steel Magazine recently pointed out that during the past 25 years there has been more technological changes in his industry than in all the history before then and he also pointed out that in the next succeeding 8 years, there would be more changes than the past 25 years.

It is hard for us to realize that as recently as in 1950 there was not a single effective electronic computer, there were no national TV networks and not one piece of hardware put up by any country floating around in space. Yes, as each of your speakers must have pointed out, changes have been most significant and the most significant change of all is that the rate of change is going to be accelerating in the future! What we are here for is to talk about how we can best cope with this.

You know there is one style of management that has made this country great and has built great enterprises that many of you may still be using today. And I should add, if you are in a YMCA that is very small in size, it's called management by intuition! And if your enterprise is small enough so you may act personally as its administrative head, know all about its market, know each of its customers personally, know all about your own employees, know about the problems in your community and know all about your products, then management by intuition is probably the best thing to do. But its greatest danger is that you will slowly become so large that you won't recognize the time, that you won't recognize the fact that you don't know all of what is going on. But you will continue to use this style of management. If you do you will be in trouble. Another one which most of us still believe in and that I would like to look at just a little bit. This is called management by experience.

You know there is all kinds of experience, each of you, to your regret used it in your organizations or had a good "Old Joe" with 30 years experience. One year, repeated identically for 30 times. It's experience like that which gets all of us in trouble. But there is a more

Reprinted with permission from *Forum*, Journal of the Association of Professional Directors of the YMCA, January, 1969.

modern type, a little more insidious that we are also beginning to encounter. It's typified though not duplicated in the administrative world by let's move ourselves back a few years and let's suppose we are now 28 and we have just finished training for Ajax Airlines as a jet pilot. We have had all the modern training and all the experience we need and we are just about to take off on our first commercial flight as the co-pilot. We slip into the seat on the right side and we are just a little nervous because we haven't met the senior flying officer yet. But here he comes through the door. "Capt. Edwards is my name, Son. I'm the Senior Pilot for Ajax Airlines. I have 27 years of experience. I'm one of the first men they hired, you know." He expects me, a new pilot to be greatly impressed by this.

But the fact is, I am terror stricken, I recognize that 27 years consists in the main of flying an airplane that had fans on the wings. I worry about the reactions he may have when we come into the landing pattern some day when, as a result of his experience, he may reach for the knob which will adjust the pitch on the propellers which we just don't have anymore. The counterpart to those actions exists in every corporation, in every YMCA, in every institution which we have in America today. They are dangerous.

Do any of you remember the Pierce Oil Company, Baldwin Locomotive, or American Woolen? Or United Mercantile & Marine? Each of these and 22 others are now completely out of business in 50 short years. The commercial giants of the American business world, 24 of them went completely bankrupt and out of business. And another 28 on that same list are no longer on the list at all, though they are still in business. More than one half of the 100 largest companies in America failed to recognize that their day was changing and through management by experience have either run themselves out of business or are no longer ranked among the top.

The same thing can happen to any of us! There are no magic answers, there is no single answer that is the right one, but one to which I would like to direct your attention for the balance of my time with you is long-range planning. Now I can see visually most of you are relaxed now because you are saying to yourselves, "I know all about that!" And perhaps you do. Unfortunately the comments of Mark Twain about the weather also apply to long-range planning. The weather you know is something everybody is talking about but nobody is doing much about it! Everybody is talking about long-range planning, but from my observation and my searching I don't find many people doing much about it!

Maybe, you have had some disappointments there? Perhaps it is something you have tried and found out it didn't work! Well, if you have let me assure you that you are in exceedingly good company. I don't know a single corporation president who is satisfied today with the quality of the long-range planning job which is being done within his organization. The result, all too often instead of just good long-range planning is even worse than no long-range planning, is bad planning. Bad planning is nothing more than extremely complex or complicated procedure that will enable you to choose the wrong course of action with an extremely high degree of assurance. There are a lot of misconceptions about this new management technique that is really just emerging as far as being able to be perfected in our organizations. I would like to touch on some of them now.

Some of the things, first, that which long-range planning is not! First and foremost it is not aimed at deciding what you are going to do five or ten years from now. But rather it is aimed at helping you to decide what to do now and for the course of the next year in order to shape the things which would otherwise come about five or ten years from now. It's not an activity to be carried upon by your staff or by some form of professionals but rather it is something that requires active participation, day-by-day, by every key member of your staff. Long-range planning is not forecasting, drawing pretty lines on a chart which shows where we are going to be if you keep on going to be right there with Baldwin Locomotive and American Woolen. Right smack out of business!

Finally, it is not a one shot proposition! Effective long-range planning is something which we must be doing day in and day out. It is not a question of whether it is Tuesday and we are going to be involved in long-range planning today, but rather only which phase of the planning cycle we will be devoting our attention to? If done right it is a system of management! It is a way of influencing your actions and the actions of each of your associates.

One of the most fascinating books that I have read this year is called "The American Challenge" by the French author, Servan-Schreiber. His main theme is this: that within the next ten years, the three great economic powers will be the United States, Russia, and the investment of American business in Europe! Now he is quite aware of the fact that today only about 10% of the invested capital in Europe is American owned. But the thing that he stresses is that it is the "Key 10%." Forty percent of all the petroleum distribution in France is American owned. Farm machinery manufacturing and distribution, electronics, telephone communications, the key industries are in the hands of Americans.

You would expect his next step, or at least I did, to be how can we figure out how to throw the rascals out of here. But, instead, says he, if the Americans would desert us now, whether they would take out their 10% of capital or not, if they would leave physically, our economy would collapse. The answer that he has not described as long-range planning but rather he describes it as American know-how which is interpreted in its component-steps which he delineates as the very things I am talking about now.

Technology, inventions, those he said we have already demonstrated the ability to copy or perhaps to beat you Americans at, but the thing we have not yet learned how to do is to organize and to effectively predict and to anticipate and cope with the future in the way that you have. It's a great book. I think you would enjoy reading it. Long-range planning is again a means of coordinating the efforts of all the departments. That's a great statement. Who doesn't like to have his departments coordinated. But who, in fact, does?

You know one of the curses of all large organizations today is what I would call "Energized Stupidity." This is the eager beaver in your organization who has just successfully completed an outstanding project which had no business being started in the first place! Simply because you do not have effective long-range planning with the necessary checks and controls, he is able to start off on something which sounds absolutely beautiful but just doesn't belong in your YMCA. The fault is yours not his, because you have not spelled out exactly what your purposes are and have not made him a part of it. He is exactly like the so-called eager beaver who having lost sight of his directions, sort of corrects that by redoubling his efforts. He's like the airplane pilot, Captain

Edwards, who announced to his passengers while flying over the midwest, "Ladies and gentlemen, this is your captain speaking. I have some news for you. Part of the news I have for you is good and part of it is bad! First let me tell you the bad news. We are at 30,000 feet and we are hopelessly lost. I have no idea whether we are over Indiana, Iowa or Ohio! But now let me tell you the good news. We are making marvelous speed."

Too many of our staff members are making great speed, are making great records, are making newspaper headlines, are doing things which really don't fit in with what we are trying to achieve in the organization. One of the things that long-range planning is—is to avoid this.

Finally long-range planning, if you use it effectively, is a system of measurement! It will establish standards of performance which will let you and all your associates know just how well they are doing! You know every psychologist will tell you very quickly that people, deep down inside, really don't like to get measured! Each of us is measured every day in every way. Within the framework of your YMCA, you are measured annually when your salary is being considered, or your transfer or promotion! And you have just two choices. Either that measurement can take place by your board or by others who are influencial on you. In terms of what or how much of a growl his wife may have given him when he left for the office that morning. Or instead, by the use of long-range planning, you can jointly, with your subordinates, establish standards of measurements which they participated in bringing about and remove the curse of all second line management today and that is the very indefiniteness and the inability for a man to really know if he has really done the kind of job you have wanted him to or not! This planning process must divide itself into two distinct parts. And best you know what you are doing at any particular time! In long-range planning, in every sense, you are like the playing baseball manager. Do you baseball fans remember Lou Boudreau? He was manager of the Cleveland Indians and also effectively played shortstop at the same time. Well, he got away with that but he got away with it only because he made it crystal clear which job he was performing at a given time! When he was on the field playing shortstop he played like a shortstop but didn't manage the team from that vantage point. When he was on the bench with someone else playing that position he didn't try to manage that either. Whether it is strategic or operational planning you are engaged in at a given moment, they are quite different things.

Strategic planning is the process whereby we evaluate and reach decisions on the fundamental important issues that are affecting the long term success of your organization as an integrated whole! Out of strategic planning comes the strategy to make your YMCA to achieve its mission! To improve the spiritual, intellectual, physical and social condition of those people whom you have elected to serve! Strategic planning is in a sense the grand design and it involves major policy decisions. It is not a detailed operating program. It is not concerned with upgrading efficiencies within the organization itself, it does, however, provide the indispensable framework within which operational planning can be developed.

Now operating planning in contrast to this can translate these strategic plans in integrated sets of quantitative and qualitative plans for each of your departments. These are the detailed operating programs which will tell you what, when, who and how action is to be taken to fulfill the strategy which you had agreed upon in a separate process altogether. It's operational planning which will set goals and measures of performance which I stress again, can help to relieve and remove the frustration of second line management who wonder whether or not they have really done a good job. It need not be as complicated. I had some time to kill in Chicago enroute here. In the 2 hours available to me in the evening I spent it at the beautiful Art Museum in Chicago. I would not want to pose to you as being either an authority or a real enthusiast on this. But one thing I learned inside from the guide that conducted me around! Do you know how they measure the effectiveness of the art displays? It's how quickly the tiles wear out on the floor in front of them. If they must replace the tiles once a month, man they know they have a winner! But if the tiles don't begin to wear thin at the end of 6 months they take it out and put something else in its place! One of the curses of the long-range planning that I have seen in most instances is that when it comes to standards of performance, they try to measure everything! From the way the man is tying his shoes until the way he gets his job done! The simpler they are, the better they are in this area.

I would like to touch on four of the environmental changes that are taking place today that I think are having a profound impact on your strategic long-range planning!

I would describe the first one as the edge of affluence. This is not an original term of mine. We worry and think about what we can do about inflation, but every statistician on earth can show you how much we have in net spendable income and in terms of dollars or by any term you want to set, can increase the money that we want to spend, and so do the people you are trying to serve. This has produced a whole new set of problems for us and one which you must cope with in planning your YMCA of the future. Actually, the basic fundamental economic problems of the American people are now within our group to solve. Yes, we can continue to have some pockets of poverty, I'm sure. But the level of affluence of all the people who are accustomed to using the YMCA has risen so far that the things they seek from us as recently as 5-10 years ago are much different. Now, their economic choices now were not made available to them before. As you do your long-range planning you had better know the impact on your market that these will have. You had also better understand the impact it will have on your financial position. What was the financial mix of your YMCA last year? For you know, 5-10% from endowments; another 25% from United Fund or Community Chest; with the balance to come to you from fees and dues for services rendered? I don't know what that was. I don't know what your financial mix will be in 1973 or 1978, but I assure you without a shadow of a doubt that whatever it will be 5 years from now it will be distinctly different than it was last year. Unless you know what your income needs will be and how you are going to cope with them—you will have no chance of succeeding at that time.

One of the most obvious and, in some ways, most difficult changes that I have had an opportunity to observe is the changing environment in our own local United Fund. It isn't localized however, because it is true of each of the United Funds in the State of Massachusetts and also nearby Hartford had little different experience in 1968. For the first time in several years they failed to reach their goal. This in spite of this age of affluence we are living in. As our budgets are curtailed it must have an impact on us.

Something else which is happening

within the United Fund, one of our sources of income. It is the United Fund results of long-range planning. As they turn their attention more and more to the problems of the disadvantaged and become more and more reluctant to spend this same proportionate share of their fund raising dollar with us, I don't have the answer to this one, but I would urge you to place it at the very top of your list as one of the long-range planning problems you had better be prepared to solve. Yes—I know how difficult it is to predict the future. But as long as you have a frame of reference to start with and make some effort in that direction you will be better off than if you had no planning at all!

A second environmental change which I think could best be called individualism. Here again, this has an impact on our market. The courts have helped to foster this because this certainly is known as the age of the freedom of the individual, individual rights and that, of course, is a good thing. But it manifests itself in many different and distinct ways. One of these is best described within our teenagers today. Now I'm not talking about the Hippies, the Yippies, the Yappies, and the Sappies, I'm talking about your kids and my own. You know we have different ways of dealing with problems than our parents did. This problem of discipline is difficult. There must be times when, at least in the back of your mind that bullwhip you saw last Sunday night, sounded like it wouldn't be a bad idea. We don't dare try that. First of all, the kids are getting so big that they just might take that whip away from us and show us the wrong end. But the problem of disciplining youngsters is quite different today and we must recognize it! It's different because they don't have the same dependence on us that they once did.

Each of us is entitled to some prejudices. I am prejudiced against motor cycles. I don't like them in show windows. When I returned from a trip not long ago I found a note on my desk from my son that he had withdrawn his savings, bought a motorcycle and headed for California.

But you know, he got back alright. It was a great adventure. I was dead wrong, and one of the problems was that I failed to keep up with the changes in my environment and my attempts to raise a son. There are a lot of sons in the YMCA and I hope you are more understanding than I was as far as they are concerned.

At the other end of the spectrum in this age of individualism there are some different things happening too! First of all, people didn't use to retire. They would just work as long as they could. Well, being able to retire now is a way of life and not unusual. But they don't do it the way they once did.

People retire now by going to a kind of "elephant's grave-yards" for human beings. Have any of you been to a place like "Sun City" or something like that? Where everybody is over 65, everything is planned, sterile. Everything is organized!

Maybe it isn't up to you. Maybe it isn't up to me to do anything about this. But if that's the way of life that is going to be led and if those are going to be in the environment of our YMCA's, we had better understand that environmental change because this is part of our market. We had better be able to do some things for them because they can become problems. I say that they can become problems, because remember, I'm in the life insurance business. One of the things we are discovering to our financial pain is that these old people just go on and on and on and on! Our annuity tables just don't work anymore. This is another one of our marketing changes that we need to be equipped to deal with.

A third concern is the Urban Crisis! The cities are where the YMCA's are. We talk of problems from housing to racial conflicts, transportation jams, pollution of everything. From language to thought, to water, to air, to nose, from the recreational problems involved. This is an area that you in YMCA, better than anyone else, can help us to solve. One quick illustration. Our company was very anxious early this summer to do something about unemployed. We made a flat conclusion we were going to employ 20 people who did not meet any of our standards of employment, but who were worthy cases? Do you know we had a hard time finding them. In Springfield Mass., not a large city, there are more than 76 organizations who hold themselves out to public as being representatives of this group and can help you to find people to be employed—up until you ask them to do something! After our employment manager had made that 72nd call I had him all worked up about this and he thought this was the worst idea I had had all week!

So—I set out to solve this on my own! I never ran into such a can of worms in my life! We are not the people who can do it. First, we are a large corporation, we don't have the respect that we would like to have with the people we are trying to serve in this respect, **But you do!** Somebody had better organize these people. Somebody had better act, either themselves or in concert with others, as a focal point around which these problems can be solved. Then, when a corporation is ready to get up off its seat and request some money to help solve this problem, you can at least find the people with whom they can get in touch.

I think the theme presented to you last night "If Not You, WHO?" is exactly the one I would like to restate for you. We need you badly for this and for other problems of the cities. Without

you, I'm afraid they are going to go unsolved.

The fourth and final environment change really concerns the businesses in your community, and they have a direct impact on you.

I refer to what might best be known as a maturation of corporate responsibility. A more responsible philosophy of corporate life. Two things are happening to business now! Each of which can have a big effect on you.

First, a reluctant recognition of both business and government that they need each other, that they are not gladiators competing in the pits of the Roman Coliseum, but neither one by itself is capable of solving the economic and social problems which face this nation. But in concert they can achieve a seemingly impossible task. The businessman who says today, "he is not interested in politics and government" is like the drowning man who says he's not interested in water. If you don't think the city and state government is in the environment of your YMCA, have much to do in the way you conduct your business, then you just don't know where the action is. I urge you to get to know your governmental officials. Doing this can have great impact on what you are doing and recognizing that these corporations in your community can do the same.

The other one is a little more complex. The emergence of a sense of social responsibility by large businesses and corporations. The model which Mr. Patrick and Detroit are setting should be repeated all around the country. We think we have been doing our best but it is peanuts compared to theirs.

Will you think for a few minutes, of 4 or 5 of the best business men you know in your community, those whose standards of success are the highest. Men whom you personally like, whose character you admire! Have you ever wondered why they are doing it? I would say that these business men are administering to the people just exactly as you are. They are guiding a very complex and a very difficult segment of our society. They are doing it; first, so it will be successful; but, second, so that it will be a healthy, vital and constructive part of the society in which they are trying to work. These men are constantly balancing their obligations to a variety of groups of people with whom they must deal. Of course, they seek a profit, and that's not a dirty word. You must recognize that unless their corporation makes a profit, it won't be there, nor will the businessman be there. They do have a prime obligation to safeguard and build the investment placed in their hands by their stockholders. But, getting a profit today, no matter how large it might be, is not enough to fulfill a corporation's real responsibility. This is being recognized by more and more businesses today. The heads of these businesses must recognize that they must deal justly with their employees. They must merit their confidence and their respect. They must fulfill the needs of their customers with skill and efficiency. They must deal within the spirit as well as within the letter of the law. But this, plus a profit, is only a halfway start. If they are really going to be successful, they must be a good citizen in the community in which they operate. They must make a contribution to the welfare of that community and to all the nation.

What is the impact of all this on you? The answer is not for you to go to them for a larger contribution. But, if you would instead, tell them you are concerned about the efficiency of your long-range planning. I know you will have common subject of discussion just by saying that. Would he be willing to help you by having his professional staff within his company look over your long-range planning and suggest areas for improving it?

You will find two things. First, here is where a lot of the bright young men in any organization are today. This is where the action is. This is where the up-and-coming people are. You should be getting to know them. Secondly, you will find that you do need a professional in long-range planning. You can't do it on your own. These men can be helpful to you. They will be a soft touch in helping you get the job done.

Here is how. If you come to me with a right sort of build up and suggest to me that I lend to you for a period of 6 months to a year one of the best 20-30 thousand dollar a year young executives I have, on a full time basis, not an after-hours kind of a deal, so he can be assigned to work just for you. You know I would be a soft touch for that.

Because this young man would be a better executive for Massachusetts Mutual after he has worked for you for a year and it comes at a time of his life when he can get this and will never have such an opportunity again.

Right now we have the number two man in our comptroller's department working with an organization called Unity Associates which has all sorts of financial organizational problems. This is going to be our next chief Comptroller and I bet he will be one of the best we have ever had, as a result of this experience.

I don't care what field of endeavor that you have where you have a problem, if you want a bright young man to give you a lift and you let me know. I and my counterparts around the country are eager for opportunities like these.

Come to me with a specific program. Tell me exactly what he is going to be doing so we can jointly sell him on doing the job.

You know, Dr. Livingston, when in darkest Africa, was alleged to have said, "You don't need to worry so much about the Lions and the Tigers but look out for those darn gnats, because they will eat you alive." The details of long-range planning, if you don't work it right will consume you. You must be careful of that.

May I quote from Mr. Gardner, former Secretary of Health, Education and Welfare who said, "The mechanic who is faced with a defective carburator can put it back in working order and stop there, or, if he is a gifted and imaginative mechanic, he may sit down and design an improved unit that will break down less frequently. But, if he is a still more imaginative man, he may think of a whole new means of mixing air and fuel in proper proportions to get combustion."

At this critical point in our history we can less and less afford to limit ourselves to the emergency repair of breakdowns in our institutions and businesses. More and more we must undertake a complete redesign.

We see clearly that many of our institutions are ill-fitted to cope with the tasks which the modern world has pressing upon them. Yet, we find too many of these are incapable of change even in the face of savage attacks by those who would not hesitate to destroy them.

Motorized Recreation Vehicles

Diana R. Dunn

On Christmas Eve 1968 pictures transmitted from Apollo 8 slammed home to millions of earthlings the fact that our planet is a very finite, very fragile, and very unique spaceship—"a grand oasis in the big vastness of space."

Readers of PARKS & RECREATION include the managers of some 500,000,000 acres of our nation's public outdoor recreation land,* approximately one fourth of the land mass of the continental United States. The Apollo 8 photos made it clear that these managers—federal, state, and local—have an awesome responsibility. So does this magazine. The fact that this burden is often complicated by conflicting responsibilities is the crux of this article.

Some of man's basic conflicts are involved in the MRV issue—controversies such as the rights of the individual versus the state, individual property rights versus common public rights, and economic growth versus the quality of life (Interior Secretary Hickel's Net National Environment versus the Gross National Product).

Critical factors in the MRV issue are the land, the vehicles, and man.

THE LAND

All land is biologically and geologically fragile. Enormous variances complicate measurement of fragility, and we have only recently begun to show proper concern with the science which addresses the task—ecology. We are also just beginning, on a broad citizen scale, to understand and to believe that our planet is an exhaustible and irreplaceable resource.

The United States contains less than 6 percent of the earth's population, yet it is well documented that Americans contribute more per capita to irreparable ecological damage to our planet than do the people of any other nation. We have conquered frontier after frontier; each more expensive in terms of long term ecological cost than its predecessor. Our aggressive pioneer spirit *must* be redirected from its traditional focus: Nature.

Reprinted with permission from National Recreation and Park Association. Official publication *Parks and Recreation*, July, 1970.
*The role of the contemporary administrator is that of managing man's relationship with and impact on the land. The pioneer approach of controlling, dominating, and defeating the land is not tenable in 1970.

THE VEHICLES

The vehicles are too new to be a well-understood factor. Even if we discount the typically unquantified warnings of authorities who claim we should not waste frivolously the nonrenewable resources of man and earth necessary for the creation, use, and maintenance of these vehicles, knowledge gaps still exist. For example, research commitment to such attendant problems as pollution control, ecological damage, and user injury prevention have been on the same priority level as they were throughout the early days (roughly 70 years!) of the automobile. We have no "index" against which to measure these sins, or their successful (or unsuccessful) amelioration subsequent to remedial action (an exception is the sound level meter used to assess noise).

We do not know the exact numbers of each type of MRV now in use, but production projection graphs show nearly vertical annual output estimates to 1980. We do know that recreation vehicles are increasing at a faster rate than cars did during their first decade even when population variances are considered. We also know that there are now over one million snowmobiles in use, valued at over one billion dollars!

Positive and negative aspects of MRVs were liberally sprinkled through the letters and literature received. One outstanding recreation value of the vehicles was proclaimed: they are FUN. Utilitarian values reported included their convenience to land managers, utility company personnel, physicians, researchers, ranchers, and rescuers.

Negative charges were leveled at both the users and the vehicles. The vehicles themselves were accused of tearing up trails and turf, creating fire hazards, frightening birds and animals, destroying wildlife habitat and plant life, causing the erosion of lands and the siltation of streams and lakes, creating air, water, and noise pollution, and ruining the dignity, beauty, and serenity of wilderness areas.

MAN

Man is by far the most crucial factor in the MRV issue, for he is responsible and can be held accountable for actions affecting the vehicles and the land. Man is manufacturer and user of the vehicles; he is manager and steward of the land.

Man, the manufacturer, has been given one supreme challenge in the economic picture of the United States: to make money (indeed, until quite recently, this has been a noble goal for all Americans). His social conscience was long separated from his product. Although signs point to some concern by industry in the social and environmental problems besetting us all, this concern frequently requires careful nurturing (tax incentives, good publicity, etc.). The Ford Motor Company is already planning an orderly transition from Ford's traditional and current products to ones which will better serve man's post-auto society. "Now that public expectations are exploding in all directions, we can no longer regard profit and service to society as separate and competing goals, even in the short run," says Ford. "Business should look upon the rising public standards as opportunities for profit." Coincidently, MRV sales emphasis on "family fun," safety, and regulation encouragement is significant, although their admittedly pecuniary motives may distress conservation purists.

Man, the vehicle user, has received few good report cards; as with any group, the "bad guys" attract the publicity. MRV users have been accused of littering, poaching (alligators, waterfowl, frogs, deer, moose, wolves, eagles, and polar bears were among the reported victims), endangering highway motorists and pedestrians, harassing stock and wildlife, and ignoring safety regulations. The "good press" of vehicle users is less abundant, and one must turn to sports organization newsletters and other publications for copious documentation of virtues. Organized users, for obvious reasons, are the first line of defense for manufacturers. They serve as voluntary buffers between and among the abrasive groups which seem to gravitate toward conflict wherever MRVs proliferate. Their sword is service in behalf of the goodwill required to keep them in the driver's seat. They organize safety programs, raise money for charities, organize clean-up campaigns, work on trails, and perform similar service functions.

Man, the recreator, clearly requires more of the land both quantitatively and qualitatively when he is aboard an MRV than when he is on foot or otherwise using his own power. The use of horses and burros is harder on the land than man on foot, as documented by stock grazing restrictions in our wilderness areas. One can envision a recreation area where annual carrying capacity might be:

1,000,000 man days on foot
250,000 man days with stock
100,000 man days with MRV

With the population increasing geometrically, and with a national commitment to serving more Americans on modestly arithmetically increasing public recreation land, man on foot or under his own power becomes progressively more desirable. This is simply because user saturation levels are higher.

Another important dimension of carrying capacity is that of user and use diversity. MRVs tend to restrict large public areas to single use; areas which could be expected to service larger numbers of people, a wider age range of people, and a broader socioeconomic range of people. Further, these areas could be expected to provide opportunity for a fuller spectrum of recreation activities. Public land managers cannot ignore the social implications of these factors.

Man, the steward of the land, has always had a very difficult task, whether protecting royalty's forests from poachers, or the local, state, or national park from freeways. Perhaps nowhere is the conflict inherent in the task better exemplified than in the charges assigned the United States Secretary of the Interior—developer and steward! At the local level, the conflict is as old as "keep off the grass" signs. Man, the enabler of recreation on public lands, has had a complex assignment too. Generally, it has been to provide safe and legal recreation programs, services, and opportunities for all citizens. It is submitted that the permitting of MRVs on public recreation land, particularly at the local level, is not compatible with the intent of this trust, especially when viewed as an extension of the land stewardship function.

WHERE WE ARE

Many commonalities emerged from the information sent from across the country, and they eventually formed a pattern. The message: by permitting interim use of land (marginal, extra, or otherwise), managers are actually creating a market in which investors, manufacturers, and users will flourish, creating a land demand which probably cannot be met now, and which will be even more difficult to satisfy as pressure mounts for other land uses in the future. To explicate the pattern, The Dismal Cycle has been outlined.

THE DISMAL CYCLE

1. MRV sales produce a small, identifiable group of owners of a particular vehicle displaying one common problem: no land of their own.
2. They begin to use public or private land, with or without permission.
3. The group grows, damage occurs, and initial conflict develops.
4. Either (A) Users are prohibited completely and no alternative site is offered (return to #2), or (B) some informal agreement is reached, usually with public land managers.
5. The existence of approved site is publicized by the users (to friends) and by vehicle dealers (to potential customers): more sales, more users.
6. "Bad apples" emerge to jeopardize the initial agreement; conservationists, neighbors, other user types form a coalition which forces a "shot-gun wedding" between recreation vehicle users and the manager. More sales, more users, and more outsiders begin to come.
7. "Self-organization and policing" as well as explicit management controls are initiated. Subtle co-optation of public agency has occurred, and the manager feels compelled to make the "marriage" work.
8. Publicity about favorable features is distributed; *Equilibrium* is attained; more sales, more users.
9. Too many "bad apples," too much damage, too few "police," and the *Saturation Point* is reached. The anticoalition reactivates. A "final straw" event occurs.
10. The manager declares total elimination of MRVs from the area. If alternate site is offered, go to #4B; if not, go to #2 and repeat cycle.

Earlier, the claim was made that the premise that MRVs are here to stay would be challenged. The materials received from across the country give evidence that they have come and gone in many areas already. It would be foolish to suggest, however, that the demise of all MRVs is imminent, or even that it will occur within the decade. In many areas they are still increasing exponentially! Ultimately, however, they will go, for they will become increasingly philosophically untenable and physically nonsupportable. The secondary cause of their extinction will be related very much to that of endangered wild species—not enough land, and too many people. The primary cause of their end will be bitter irony to MRV buffs— success caused by too many vehicles.

As with threatened wildlife species, there will probably be a few types of recreation vehicles which will survive all onslaughts, much as the wild burro and the starling. Perhaps they have not yet been invented, but man's ingenuity is at work. Watch for the second and third generation MRVs which will include "amphicats" (capable of swamp, lake, and beach travel), and "hovercraft" (45 mph on water, 60 mph on land, 75 mph on ice). Of the current crop, a likely candidate for longevity seems to be the snowmobile (typical speeds of 30 to 50 mph, with at least one claim of 170 mph on a straight run).

PARK AND RECREATION MANAGER STRATEGY

Park and recreation professionals have been far too ambivalent about their environmental commitment. Many have been co-opted by the very threats they were hired to regulate, becoming promoters as well as protectors of the presumed regulated group. Nearly all MRV-related "ecocatastrophies" result from successive nondecisions and nonactions. Being a nonmanager is no longer tolerable. Managers can no longer *not* look forward and *not* make decisions and *not* take stands. Isolated and hoc holding actions and maneuvers against specific vehicular threats to the environment are not working. Particularly impotant are defenses where there has been inadequate consideration of potential alternate land uses. Managers must exercise appropriate interventions regarding potential disfunctions over which they have responsibility at the strategically expedient moment.

The choice is: will public land managers satisfy the demands of MRV users now, or will they severely limit present opportunity so that the land will not be monopolized and degraded, but will be available for broader use both today and for generations?

TEN MANAGER STRATEGIES

The following strategies are offered as tentative; they are suggestive of some of the tactics which might be used by managers tired of *re*acting to new MRV challenges.

1. Support efforts to identify alternative, less destructive recreation forms. Surely if this country can reach the moon, other ways of having FUN can be found. The human race got along without MRVs for over a million years!

2. Support efforts to identify less objectionable MRVs and encourage their use over that of more destructive and dangerous types.

3. Become informed—be sure your agency has the informational capability to make intelligent decisions about the long-range social and environmental consequences of its actions. Look back to see if the ecological effects anticipated from past actions were accurate. If not, are you

still using the same information source?

4. Inform the public and encourage them to inform themselves. If you have information and are basing decisions upon it which affect the lives of your constituents and their children, give them all the information they will absorb. You can't expect people to accept "no" for an answer without good reasons.

5. Don't confuse feasibility and advisability. If you're planning actions which will affect ecosystems and social systems, list the good reasons why NOT as well as the positive rationale.

6. Discourage proliferation of MRV sales by prohibiting use rather than entering into short-term compromise agreements which mislead buyers into a false sense of land supply security. Avoid the marginal or interim land-use trap. This is a very relative condition, and implies an obligation for further land provision when the interim or marginal condition has passed. (The proposed Everglades jetport site was less than marginal just a few months ago!)

7. Encourage private enterprise to meet the need for land. Private campground growth is helping to fill the gap near crowded national parks, and such supplemental effort will be needed even more in the future. Develop incentives to influence positive involvement from the private sector.

8. Pressure MRV manufacturers and dealers to increase vehicular safety and diminish those undesirable damaging capabilities through design modification.

9. Encourage special taxes and licenses for MRV manufacturers, dealers, users, and vehicles to pay for costs of

added legislation, police patrols, damage, insurance, and ultimate product disposal.

10. If ensnared in The Dismal Cycle, try to reach *Equilibrium* quickly and maintain this condition as long as possible.

It may be argued that these strategies are Utopian, but as President Nixon said, "We have had too many visions and too little vision." And, as Pogo eloquently observed, "We have met the enemy, and he is us."

This article, and the selected comments which follow, offer insight into the current status of motorized recreation vehicles and bring into sharp focus the responsibility of the park and recreation administrator. When viewed collectively, they substantiate the thesis of this article: motorized recreation vehicles are operating "on borrowed time."

SELECTED COMMENTS

The following observations and information were abstracted from materials received from individuals representing conservation groups, MRV associations, and federal, state, and local park and recreation agencies.

1969 Congress for Recreation & Parks, Chicago, Illinois: With more than one million snowmobiles in operation by the end of this winter, it is imperative that public park and recreation lands be adapted to the controlled use of snowmobiles, the National Recreation and Parks Congress was told by a top executive of the world's pioneer and largest manufacturer of the winter fun machines. "All of you in the recreational field must take a serious look at whether you are fully serving members of your community if your program does not include snowmobiling."

Canadian Parks & Recreation Association: Will snowmobile regulations be enacted before ruination of the sport? Some users are carrying chain saws to cut down any fencing that gets in their way. The answer may be to urge snowmobilers to organize themselves into many more closely knit, self-policing clubs, much like ski patrols.

Michigan State University: The Recreation Research and Planning Unit has started a pilot study of snowmobile use. Questionnaires concerning socio-economic characteristics, use patterns, attitudes, preferences, and related activities are being mailed to a sample of users.

CONSERVATION GROUPS

National Audubon Society: Perhaps most important of all, on public lands, laws and regulations must establish zones of use and access which will assure that off-road vehicles do not interfere with the enjoyment by non-motorized users of a substantial part of our wild areas, do not destroy wilderness, and do not jeopardize the existence of other fragile ecosystems.

Potomac-Appalachian Trail Club, Virginia: Construction of the "Big Blue" trail to the west of the Appalachian Trail is underway. Some fallen logs are being removed from the trail, and others are being left as barriers to trail bikes.

Save the Dunes Council: Dune buggy use along the beach foredunes, and inland are becoming an increasing hazard and threat to the dunes region. The vehicles "tear up the beach grasses, wild flowers, and other vegetation, creating blowouts and erosion. They level dunes, disturbing the natural contours of the region. They are noisy, destructive, and dangerous." The Council is recommending that all beach communities pass ordinances prohibiting their use.

National Parks Association: Motorized vehicles are "a substantial threat to virtually all national parks, as they damage the ecology of the area they travel through or over." NPA supports the premise that parks are for people, not vehicles, and recommends that park traffic be restricted to official, emergency, and service vehicles which would bring visitors into and through the parks. Tourist accommodations should be provided outside the parks by the private sector.

National Wildlife Federation: NWF recommends "that federal, state, and local land-managing agencies adopt and strictly enforce regulations which zone governmental areas in manners so that uses of multiterrain vehicles will be restricted to suitable locations or trails which will result in the least possible impact on the environment or impairment to other legitimate uses of public properties."

The Conservation Foundation: The Foundation has prepared a publication, "Off-Road Vehicles and Environmental Quality." The document offers vehicle profiles, recreation, trail, and noise effects, effects on fish and wildlife, and discussions of trespass, vandalism, and thefts, safety, law enforcement, policy recommendations, and model state laws.

The Salt Water Sportsman: "We are witnessing the passing of the beach buggy in many areas due to stringent laws imposed primarily by local seashore communities. Self-policing had a beneficial effect for many years, but there are now too many vehicles, and too many other people on the beaches." The Massachusetts Beach Buggy Association was the first in the United States, and at one time its membership was over 2,000. This has declined as beach buggy operations have been restricted.

MRV ASSOCIATIONS

International Snowmobile Association: "Our member clubs perform valuable services and cooperate with all government agencies and industry for the benefit of the user in safe and sane snowmobiling."

National All Terrain Vehicle Association: "ATVs have come a long way since John Gower's 'Jiger' was introduced back in the early '60s. Production in 1969 was a mere 15,000, but the estimated output for 1975 is 225,000! The world is the market—we are not hindered by seasonal restrictions."

International Snowmobile Congress, Duluth, Minnesota: Delegates attending the January 1970 Congress were urged to help states regulate the design and use of the vehicles before their numbers and indiscriminate operation became a public nuisance.

International Snowmobile Industry Association, Minneapolis, Minnesota: Report of the Committee on Environmental Quality, Major Recommendation One: "The land managing agencies should take the lead in designing, developing, and maintaining areas and trails where snowmobilers can enjoy quality recreation experiences in harmony with other special interest groups."

FEDERAL GOVERNMENT

Bureau of Indian Affairs: America's Indians are determined to protect their environment. Some tribes have closed parts of their land to one or more specific vehicles; whereas others have closed areas to all motorized vehicles.

Tennessee Valley Authority: At TVA's Land Between the Lakes area, use of mini-bikes by large groups of unlicensed minors has prompted regulations banning their use. Regular motorbikes, motorcycles, and 4-wheel drive vehicles are restricted to developed roads. Future intent is to accommodate MRVs where practical.

National Park Service: "Operating a vehicle outside of established public roads, parking areas, or routes designated by the Superintendent is prohibited."

Forest Service: The anticipated increase in all-terrain vehicles could cause saturation and the beginning of extensive restrictions of the use of such vehicles on public lands. The Wilderness Act already bans all MRVs from these areas.

Bureau of Land Management: In addition to a 16-million acre garbage dump already in the Southern California desert, BLM is worried that motorcycles, dune buggies, 4-wheel drive vehicles, and other off-road vehicles traversing the desert may wipe out plant life, archaeological sites, and centuries-old Indian trails. A 15-member BLM off-road vehicle advisory council wants to mandate strict laws and regulations to protect these public lands. It is asking for a desert ranger force to patrol a beat from the Sierra Nevadas and Death Valley to Mexico, and from the Colorado River to the Pacific.

CITIES, COUNTIES, AND STATES

Bryan, Ohio: The Parks and Recreation Board passed a resolution to prohibit the use of recreational vehicles on parkland, but enforcement is difficult. "The vehicles have their place, but not in multiple-use local public parks."

Hermosa Beach, California: "The best idea is to have a very close study of the situation today and how it will shape up in the future. Then we can decide on some sane rules and regulations to be applied to all vehicles before greater destruction is realized."

Kansas City, Missouri: "Hundreds of cyclists weekly thrill to the jumps and banked curves in a marginal area between the Missouri River and river levee. We should set aside and develop such lands for motorcycle use to keep cyclists off other parklands and make issuing citations justifiable."

Midland, Michigan: A campaign is under way for larger license plates on recreation vehicles, especially motorcycles.

Anchorage, Alaska: "The problem is becoming acute—there are probably as many or more snowmobiles per capita and per square mile as in any other location in the country." The city manager has a committee working on the problem.

Ardmore, Pennsylvania: Motorizes vehicles have been prohibited except at locations specifically designated for such purposes.

Concord, New Hampshire: Snowmobiles and the noise they make are the concern of a special committee working on new statewide regulations. Private development of facilities should be encouraged to reduce pressures on public lands which have more value for other use, according to the Governor's office.

Winston-Salem, North Carolina: The city is building a 91.5-acre "hobby park" to accommodate recreation "nuisances" including archery, rifle and pistol ranges, model plane, rocket, sky diving, go-cart, and motorcycle areas.

Appleton, Maine: The town was invaded by snowmobiles, causing extensive damage to blueberry bushes and forest seedlings. An improvement committee made 50 miles of trails, provided maps, and a warming hut, and proclaimed, "Don't fight 'em, join 'em!"

Southern California: Some cities are investigating the possibility of sponsoring cycle parks. A "mechanical park" is being considered by the Orange County Parks Department, and a study has been completed for a 24-acre cycle park along the Santa Ana River in Anaheim, possibly to be leased to a concessionnaire. Costa Mesa has a motorcycle and mini-bike club for boys 16 and under, "designed to keep the kids off the streets, playground, and parks with their bikes."

North Dakota State Outdoor Recreation Agency: "The step by government to tighten up rules has been a direct result of foolhardy snowmobilers who cannot tell what time of night it is, or the difference between public and private property, or have any common sense for the safety of passengers, pedestrians, and the like. A cut fence, trampled crops, dead livestock, and assorted abuses have ruined the hunter-farmer relationship. Snowmobiling is approaching this unreconcilable plateau."

New York State: Steps are necessary to cut down the growing number of snowmobile-auto accidents, and to provide identification for the estimated 100,000 snowmobiles now in use. Mufflers to cut noise to 73 decibels by June 1974 is in pending legislation.

A Summary of Environmental Planning

Maynard Hufschmidt

Public health historically has been the first concern of environmental planning and management. This took the form of protection against the major hazards of the burgeoning urban growth. The very success of environmental health controls on water and food supply, general sanitation of public and private spaces, and insect control has provided opportunities for environmental management for other purposes unrelated to public health.

TRADITIONAL AND NEW CONCEPTS

Traditional environmental planning for public health had two important characteristics. First, although based upon using existing and developing natural science theory and technique, it was basically man-oriented. The public health of humans was the overriding purpose, and any modification of natural ecological processes necessary for these public health goals was usually accepted without question. In this manner the drainage of marshes or the application of pesticides for mosquito control were planned and carried out with little concern for the possible adverse effects on the natural environment. Second, the control techniques used were arbitrary and usually took the form of inflexible standards, this too stemming in large part from the overriding concern with human life. Thus a single standard of drinking water quality was adopted by the public health administrators in this country and applied universally regardless of the circumstances.

This simplistic approach of the traditional environmental health planners, although adequate and indeed necessary for the intended purpose, has become increasingly inapplicable to the complex environmental problems of today. Today standards are less meaningful when applied in this traditional manner due to the fact that cause and effect relationships of new environmental hazards are difficult to establish. Further, it can be said that the very purpose of environmental management has moved beyond the obvious concern for public health to the more general concern for human welfare, including dimensions only indirectly related to health, such as enhancement of esthetic pleasures.

Natural resource policies are undergoing a parallel metamorphosis.

Reprinted with permission of Sage Publications, Inc., *American Behavioral Scientist*, Vol. 10, No. 1, September, 1966, and with permission of author.

Until rather recently, concern for our resource position was largely in terms of quantity. This point of view is clearly traced to the Malthusian population doctrine. Although the question has been posed in more sophisticated terms as a result of development in resource economics (e.g., "Are real costs of natural resources likely to rise significantly over the next few decades?"), it remained fundamentally a question of quantity.

More recently there has been a startling shift in emphasis in the United States from concern with resource quantity to a pervasive interest in resource and environmental quality. Two factors are the primary causes of this shift. First, rapid technological progress in industries like agriculture, synthetic chemistry and others, has demonstrated that rising per capita incomes (in constant dollars) can feasibly be provided for in a rapidly growing population with little strain on the natural resource base. Secondly, the very rise in population and living standards, accompanied by a major shift of population from rural to urban-metropolitan areas, has intensified problems of resource and environmental quality which were formerly present only in moderate degrees. Air pollution from automobiles became a serious problem when a combination of large urban concentrations of population and high rate of automobile use became common. Water pollution became critical in many areas with high concentrations of industrial facilities and urban-metropolitan populations, operating on a fixed natural-resource base of land and water-drainage networks. Also, it must be recognized that with increasing affluence and mobility the population understand the problems better, and believes it can afford an environment of higher quality than it now has. In this regard, national attention to the problem of quality has played no small role.

To a considerable degree, *natural resource* planning and policy are now being reinterpreted and cast in a framework of *environmental* planning and policy. Examples of this trend include:

(1) concern for outdoor recreation and open spaces which led to a national study commission and the establishment of the Bureau of Outdoor Recreation;
(2) the shift in emphasis in water pollution control from public health to broader esthetic values, and the transfer of Federal responsibility from the Public Health Service to the Department of the Interior;
(3) increasing importance being attached to environmental aspects of our primary industries, reflected in research and regulation in the handling of pesticides, herbicides and solid wastes;
(4) redirection of natural resource research efforts in universities and research institutes.

If the strands of public health and natural-resource planning are to be woven into a sound fabric of comprehensive environmental planning, there must be a suitable conceptual framework which ties together human behavior and the natural processes relating to the environment. In practice no such framework exists. However, the rational decision-making approach of economics may offer some insight into the form of such a scheme if it ever does become generally operational.

FORMAL FRAMEWORK OF THE RATIONAL DECISION-MAKING APPROACH

In many if not most situations the variables and functions required for field use of this approach may be unavailable, either because they are undefined empirically or too expensive to obtain. Still, the framework is extremely important conceptually. We can begin by discussing it from this point of view and then describe some of the problems one confronts in its application to "real world" problems.

Stated in formal terms, the rational decision approach specifies maximizing an objective function subject to a set of constraints. It will be recognized that, in form, this is similar to the decision framework of the firm which seeks to maximize profits (its objective function) subject to the constraints prescribed by costs and by techniques available for combining plant, equipment and labor to produce a product. However, the substance of the framework for environmental planning is quite different.

The objective function is a rule which allows one to add and subtract the various benefits and costs that result from a proposed project, policy or program. The constraints may comprise all the real world limitations, physical, social, political and biological, within which the project must operate.

Still speaking in conceptual terms, one can postulate three general objectives which can make up the objective function of environment planning:

(1) Physical and mental health;
(2) Esthetic pleasure;
(3) Wealth (national, regional or group income).

The objective function is that rule which allows one to add the benefits and subtract the costs associated with these three diverse objectives. A common approach to such rule is to express all these benefits and costs in terms of money, so that maximizing the objective function corresponds to maximizing the net value of the proposed project or program.

The constraints reflect the limitations of the environment within which

the maximization of the objective function must take place. In practical terms these constraints may be budgetary constraints (an upper limit on project cost), technological constraints (representing the techniques by which real resources may be combined to produce the project benefits), resource constraints (reflecting upper limits on real resources available for application to the project) or political constraints (such as an upper or lower limit on the scale of the project).

THE USE OF STANDARDS IN ENVIRONMENTAL PLANNING

This rational decision-making approach which we have outlined above has important implications for the use of standards in environmental planning. First let us note the way in which standards may be viewed as constraints in this formal framework. An example will serve this purpose. Suppose a public health administrator establishes a standard for water quality in a stream. This represents a typical problem of traditional environmental management. The problem for this decision maker, in terms of our rational decision model, may be: Given the techniques available, minimize the cost of achieving this standard. The objective function (here to be minimized) is the cost of the water quality program. The constraints are (a) the technology available for such a program and (b) the standard of quality which is to be achieved.

Clearly, the problem could have been stated differently. For example, we could have considered the water quality of the stream as an objective. Then we have the problem as one of maximizing the quality of the water given two constraints: (a), again, the available technology and (b) some upper limit on the cost of such a program.

In the latter case, what we have called a water quality standard is represented as an objective or goal, while in the former case the water quality standard was a constraint to be honored in the process of cost minimization.

This interchangeability of objectives and constraints is an important aspect of the decision model we are dealing with. In solving such constrained maximum problems (either by Lagrangian analysis or linear programming) one can obtain an indication of the marginal cost of honoring a particular standard. In the event a Lagrangian solution is possible, the Lagrangian multiplier obtained represents the marginal opportunity cost of attaining a prescribed standard. When solution of the problem by one of these methods is possible (i.e., where the variables are defined and measurable), computation of this cost can assist the decision-maker in assessing the reasonableness of the standard in light of all the objectives of the community and all the costs involved in meeting them.

METHODOLOGICAL PROBLEMS

We have very briefly discussed a rational decision-making approach to environmental planning and illustrated the operations of such an approach by means of a traditional public health problem—that of attaining a standard of water quality. It should be recognized at this point that to carry out this kind of optimization we need to define the following relationships with respect to the relevant environment of the program or project:

(1) The benefit-output function;
(2) The cost-input function;
(3) The objective function;
(4) The production function.

Any approach to environmental planning which claims to be comprehensive in scope will have to find solutions to these problems of methods. The problems involved will be discussed in a little detail. However, in summary form it can be said that objective function is inherently a political or ethical problem, the production function and the benefit-output function involve the most sophisticated ecological consideration and even the cost-input function, which at first glance seems to be a simple engineering economic problem, is far from solved.

Derivation of the *benefit-output relationships* for public investment and management programs is generally recognized as a difficult task and, in many respects, still an unsolved problem. Recent literature on public investment economics reflects the increasing concern with this problem of valuation, but as yet offers few answers for the field of environmental management. The problems of evaluating benefits of programs to improve the environment have two aspects:

(1) Measurement of the actual effect of an environmental change on the well-being, physical and mental, of individuals;
(2) The subjective valuation of this effect by individuals, in terms of changes in welfare, as measured by market or voting behavior, or by response to interviews.

The relationship between these two aspects can be illustrated by an example. Suppose a severe case of air pollution in a community is improved significantly by regulation of emission from factories. But the effects on health of the original condition and the improved situation are both difficult to measure; many health effects of air pollution are subtle and are revealed only after years of exposure. In general, man's adjustment to the stresses of pollution, intense crowding and monotonous, ugly, depressing environments has pathological effects, often delayed and extremely indirect. In the case of moderate air pollution, the subjective valuation of individuals of both the original and improved conditions may also be difficult to come by. Willingness to pay for air pollution control is more likely to be a function of the social and economic composition of the community rather than the physical degree of pollution.

Compared with the difficulties it offers in deriving the benefit functions, *the cost-input function* appears to offer fewer difficulties in estimating the cost of various levels and mixes of inputs to investment and management projects and programs. Money costs can be estimated in a straightforward fashion by using standard procedures of engineering economics and cost accounting. However, even here there is a consistent underestimating of money costs for large and complex projects, such as those which characterize many environmental systems. The total cost and the money costs may be significantly different because of external effects of a project which impose costs on others, or because resource costs may diverge from money costs when resources, such as labor, are underutilized.

Wreckreation in Our National Forests

Robert B. Ditton

Recreation is usually considered an unlimited opportunity, the economic backbone of many states, the frosting on the American Dream, and rarely a problem. Yet the impact of providing for peoples' recreation activities has left and continues to leave its mark on our already beleaguered environment—often with the official blessing of the government agencies involved.

First, many recreation resources have been acquired by the federal government with little thought as to how they will sustain the massive human impact to which they are being and will continue to be subjected.

Second, we find that many federal resource development schemes sold on their recreation values are in fact ecological disasters. The true recreation values of many of our natural resources are being misused today in the brutal process of project justification. As a result, regional grassroots organizations are springing into existence to prevent further destruction of the environment in the name of leisure and recreation.

It may be difficult to consider recreation as a pollutant, because we have been saying all along that recreation is the first to suffer from water pollution and other environmental degradations. But the increasing numbers of recreators engaged in diversified recreation pursuits (many with a high environmental impact such as camping, snowmobiling, all-terrain vehicle use, powerboating, and trail-bike use), together with many of the developments specifically planned for their use, are actually furthering the deterioration of natural resources.

LOVING OUR NATURAL RESOURCES TO DEATH

Madison Avenue advertising organizations, ecologically-insensitive resource planners, communities bent on economic windfalls from our public lands, conservation groups with narrow self-satisfying objectives, and the development-minded public are all actively promoting the leisure misuse of our natural resources. They are unknowingly encouraging over-use or improper use. In everyday language, we are encouraging people to love our natural resources to death. This was first recognized and reflected in the policy of the American Waterworks Association—a

Reprinted with permission from National Recreation and Park Association. Official publication *Parks and Recreation*, June, 1971.

group of water supply administrators who restrict the recreation use of water supply reservoirs, regardless of treatment and enforcement levels. They recognize the leisure impact on water quality, but do not have the means to mitigate the impacts.

In his 1970 State of the Union message, President Nixon proposed new financing methods for purchasing open space and parklands "now before they are lost to us." In light of present "pork barrel" management of the public domain, the mere allocation of more recreation resources, or making those lands now in public ownership more accessible, is not the answer but often the beginning of the problem. Our nation's 200 million-plus population with more leisure on its hands is beginning to exert physical pressures on our natural resources that are beyond the comprehension of many resource planners.

In the past, federal acquisition has helped to spare many of our natural resources from exploitation by private enterprise. But this is only part of the story. A number of areas have been spared defilement at private hands only to endure exploitation by the public resource management agencies to whom they have been entrusted. While unanimously supporting public acquisition, environmental protection groups have nevertheless become disheartened with many of the development and management activities being carried out by federal agencies. The U.S. Army Corps of Engineers has probably received the greatest attention in the past because of its impoundment procedures. The emerging trend of the National Park Service toward mass recreation development has been recognized. Court actions have involved the Federal Power Commission and the U.S. Department of Transportation. The seemingly always-distant Bureau of Land Management is even beginning to come under scrutiny.

TRUST IN FOREST SERVICE IS MISPLACED

But what of the U.S. Forest Service? Until recently, this agency has not received the attention accorded the other agencies. Through this agency's historic beginnings with Gifford Pinchot to its present day use of such altruistic images as Smokey Bear, the friendly Forest Ranger, and the Lassie television program, people have been led to believe that the Forest Service is the ultimate protector of our public lands, woods, and waters. But recent experience has shown that such thinking is naive and the trust misplaced. Because of their inability to predict and eliminate the environmental destruction of their holdings, environment protection groups have brought several federal court actions against the U.S. Forest Service.

If we are to sustain the magnificence of the public domain, federal management of recreation resources must insure that they survive the onslaught of being too accessible to humans. The Forest Service misses this point altogether and counters with "you are to humans. The Forest Service misses this point altogether and counters with "you are trying to lock up our resources for a few people." Rather than locking up our delicate resources, they need to be managed in such a way that unique ecologies are sustained. (The word "preserved" is avoided here because of the recognition that unique ecologies are naturally dynamic.) Resources can be sustained by determining the human carrying capacity of each natural area. Regulation of these human carrying capacity levels can be done, hopefully, through a management plan that recognizes man's collective impact on our natural resources—or the hard way, by restricting the number of users to an area and closing it daily when this limit is reached. The latter approach is particularly unsatisfactory in light of the dramatic increase in outdoor recreation predicted for the future. But we may have to endure this approach because many planners lack the imagination and tools to correlate numbers of people with the environmental qualities of our natural areas.

In addition to these increasing physical impacts, the Forest Service has shown little concern for the impact of their development and management decisions on peoples' recreation experiences. Many of these decisions are gradually reducing the number of recreation alternatives that can be pursued. Many management and development procedures have been conveniently tied to the wishes of majority interests rather than the maintenance of a wide number of user-groups, each with predictable recreation experience requirements. The results indicate that the public domain is being slowly fitted solely for those recreation pursuits involving the greatest numbers of people. The impact of these majority-focused management decisions on the recreation experiences of particular user-groups, such as wilderness users, has not been recognized to date.

POPULARITY VERSUS VALUE

Popularity of an activity should not be confused with its value. The fact that several federally funded studies indicate that driving for pleasure is the number one recreation pursuit in the country does not mean that we need more roads in our National Forests. Many planners, however, rely too heavily on these national trends as their development barometers. Providing facilities for the most popular recreation activities is in itself a safe guarantee that they will be used. Even more so, it is a crass promotion of these very pursuits. With more demand generated, there must be further development. Not only is much of pres-

ent recreation development closing environmental alternatives but, just as importantly, it is narrowing the breadth of peoples' available leisure opportunities. Many people are having to conform to the recreation developments provided because of lack of diversity. The impact of this "leveling process" on peoples' leisure opportunities is yet to be fully determined.

Federal agencies must interpret recreation and their authorized responsibilities for providing recreation opportunities for a variety of user-groups, e.g., hikers, snowmobilers, primitive campers, convenience campers, nature enthusiasts, hunters, canoeists, picnickers, motorboaters, fishermen, etc. These user-groups cannot be lumped together in the site planning process if resource management agencies expect to provide quality recreation experiences for any *one* group. Areas need to be planned for complementary user-groups if recreation is indeed to be a human outcome of resource use. With the United States rapidly becoming a nation of congested, frustration-ridden urban centers, it is imperative that our recreation resources maintain their ability to provide people with satisfying recreative experiences.

The provision of open space and recreation lands is not a sufficient goal for the federal government. They must insure through user-resource planning that 1) a balanced variety of human recreation needs are met, and that 2) environmental degradation of these resources is minimized if not totally prevented.

A review of ill-conceived federal recreation resource development projects reveals the growing role of the U.S. Forest Service in environmental destruction:

● While not necessarily thought of as a reservoir builder the Forest Service has warmed to the task because "the need for water-oriented recreation opportunities is important in providing essential benefits to the public." But in providing for the public well-being, we should know what is being sacrificed. In the Shawnee National Forest (Illinois) the U.S. Forest Service has development plans which would sacrifice the unique ecology of Lusk Creek, a cool, clear free-flowing stream which contrasts sharply with the many other murky bottomland streams found in this locale. Lusk Creek is presently used for a number of recreation pursuits, mostly of an environmentally compatible low impact nature. With the wide variety of recreation lakes in Southern Illinois, it is incomprehensible why one more unique stream and woodland resource need be inundated to provide the same recreation experience that is now a common commodity. The future of Lusk Creek is presently in the hands of the Forest Service, but more importantly, Congressional appropriations.

- In 1968 the U.S. Forest Service seriously considered a Disney-inspired resort area in the Mineral King Valley in the Sequoia National Forest. Planning was carried out in anticipation of 1.7 million visitors annually. To place this in perspective, we should note that Yosemite Valley in Yosemite National Park receives about 1.7 million visitors annually—only Yosemite Valley is seven times larger. With problems of environment impact readily apparent in Yosemite, the Sierra Club brought legal action against the proposed resort development—and won. Recently, however, the Sierra Club's right to bring this suit against the Forest Service has been challenged by a California Federal Court of Appeals decision and the battle continues.

- With pressure from a number of national conservation organizations, the Sylvania Tract in Michigan's Upper Peninsula was acquired in 1965 by the U.S. Forest Service because of its wilderness qualities and its ability to provide people with a unique experience. Today the tract is knowingly or unknowingly being developed for high impact recreation pursuits with little concern for the environmental implications of access and resulting human impact. Ecologically inappropriate and uncontrolled use is being encouraged creating further enforcement problems. Development is threatening the habitat and solitude of a rare but reproducing population of bald eagles in Sylvania. Even with partial restrictions instituted, remaining use (and management) of snowmobiles and all-terrain vehicles threatens to negate all previous conservation efforts in behalf of the vanishing bald eagle in the north country. Timber is being cut on the tract by the Kimberly Clark Corporation of Neenah, Wisconsin—further detracting from the quality of the wilderness experience. The uniqueness of Sylvania is being destroyed by the very thing it is capable of providing—recreation opportunities. It is being destroyed by the access roads that not only have led to the silting of boglands, but also make it overly accessible. Sylvania's destruction is entangled with the political process which places high priority on development for the public and low priority on wilderness.

It is not enough to merely consider the recreation resource planning activities carried out singularly by the U.S. Forest Service. There are a number of other federal agencies who seek to sell their public works projects to the great silent majority on their incidental ability to satisfy leisure needs:

- Federal roadbuilding efforts have recently sought to bring people to unique areas with little realization of the ecological dangers accompanying the roadbuilding process. Roads have a way of reducing uniqueness rapidly—you have seen a hundred examples of roads which swallow up the views you were supposed to see. The Department of Transportation is cooperating with the U.S. Forest Service in the construction of the Ellis Loop Road that will render the Sandia Crest Recreation Area in the Cibola National Forest (New Mexico) more accessible. The present low-standard road to the Crest follows a less objectionable path than the proposed road and also serves as a buffer against over-use of the area. If the proposed road is constructed, recreation use of the Crest will certainly increase and it is highly likely that more roads will be needed. Secretary of Transportation John Volpe justifies the construction of this super-blackway through the northern Sandias with simplistic wisdom: "In the early 1960s the President's Advisory Council on Recreation conducted an intensive nationwide study of recreation activities of the American public. This study revealed that driving for pleasure is the nation's most important outdoor activity." If the road is to be built, it will be done over the documented objections of a number of conservation groups.

• In 1936 the Secretary of Agriculture dedicated 3,800 acres of virgin forest in Western North Carolina to the memory of Joyce Kilmer, author of the well-remembered poem "Trees." The area was "to be preserved in its natural state and to include only the simplest recreation facilities." But today this forever-wild designation is threatened by the bulldozer and bureaucratic doubletalk. Working with the U.S. Department of Transportation, the Forest Service has proposed the construction of a scenic highway through the Joyce Kilmer Memorial Forest. Originally the highway route was scheduled to run south of the Memorial Forest; but many of the local constituency want the road to cross the high peaks in the northern part of the Forest because of the extra-scenic view and the promise of added tourist dollars. The proposed intrusion involves more than unsightly road cuts, turbid waters, and the destruction of a virgin forest; it violates a 1936 commitment to all Americans to maintain this tract in its natural state amid development and urbanization pressures whatever they may be. Probably an easy commitment to make in the thirties; it is seen today as a landmark decision in the wilderness-short eastern United States. If the commitment is broken, the future security of many of our other recreation resources, however designated, is uncertain.

• Even the U.S. Navy's proposed Project Sanguine is being billed by its leading Congressional proponent as potentially one of the greatest tourism and recreation attractions in the country. What is Project Sanguine? The project is described by the Navy as an ultra low-frequency antenna buried six feet underground to transmit one-way messages to Polaris submarines at sea. The antenna will underlie the northernmost 21,000 square miles of Wisconsin, a 26-county area. Once again, the U.S. Forest Service is involved; this time with the U.S. Navy. The project, if completed, would require that 30-foot swaths be cut in a grid pattern every two-to-six miles throughout the Chequamegon National Forest (Wisconsin). Aside from Sanguine's not-too-apparent tourism value, planning authorities are quick to point out that the project will conveniently create snowmobile trails and more deer browse. Concurrently, environmental studies conducted by the Hazelton Laboratories of Falls Church, Virginia, have demonstrated substantial environmental impact at power levels far below what the proposed 1.5 million dollar project will ultimately require. To date, the Forest Service has demonstrated little public response to these environmental study findings. Aside from the development damage involved, can we expect our National Parks and Forests to be openly vulnerable to defense hardware testing and military fortifications in the future? Sanguine's disposition will give us a clue to the answer in so far as the U.S. Forest Service is concerned.

RECREATION PLANNING CLOSELY TIED TO ECONOMICS

Why does much recreational resource development continue to be ecologically dysfunctional? Why? It appears that an answer lies in the fact that much federal recreation planning is more closely tied to economics than ecology. Ecological disasters begin with the nationwide trends projected for leisure activity. Improperly so, these national participation projections guide the extent and type of development at *local* development projects. Regardless of delicate or atypical natural conditions, a site's development plan is usually geared to meet these projections and then justified on the basis of their attendant economic benefits to the immediate region. With economic justification a prerequisite, recreation resource planners must play the "numbers game" . . . even if the "numbers game" disregards good ecological savvy. Maximum recreation resource development is much easier to justify economically than optimum develop-

ment because the value of sustaining a resource in high quality condition is difficult to express in dollars and cents.

This dysfunctional planning process has a number of inherent weaknesses: 1) Concepts of human ecology are generally ignored; 2) There is usually more concern with bringing large numbers of people to an "attraction" than there is in sustaining its environmental quality; 3) Little consideration is given to such nonproduction oriented intangibles as aesthetics; and 4) There is failure to conceptualize all the factors involved in environmental quality and the related quality of human life.

Management plans are needed that will keep open recreation alternatives for the future, and that will insure a sustained yield of high quality indigenous recreation. Working counter to this goal, however, are the economic incentives encouraging increased development which return 25 percent to all National Forest production (including recreation) receipts to local county government. Many resource economists, therefore, support a system whereby local government units are compensated for losses in their tax base due to government purchase of recreation lands with in-lieu-of-tax payments for an agreed upon number of years. Without such legislation, recreation resource planning, based entirely on economic impact, will continue with critical repercussions for our National Forests. The singular planning concept of economic impact or a "local-get-rich-quick" philosophy stands to be rejected by federal agencies. They must begin to believe that a good ecological decision will, in the long pull, be good economics. A typical example of such thinking already employed by the U.S. Forest Service is the decision to employ sustained yield production rather than the uncontrolled clearcutting of yesteryear.

MORTAL MEN ARE
PREOCCUPIED WITH PRESENT

Why can't the Forest Service perceive the potential environmental degradation that may result from their plans and actions? Such agencies are staffed by mortal men who, along with most other Americans, are preoccupied with the present. Concerns for the quality of tomorrow are not only difficult to express, but difficult to put into practice in today's government maze that places high-priority on project justification in short-term economics. "Planning for today" is also encouraged by the irrational pressures of many "conservationists" with narrow objectives who argue for maximum development as a means of "making areas public." While these "conservationists" are familiar with concepts of ecology and use them freely when concerned with water and air pollution, they generally ignore this man-environment concept in dealing with recreation planning. In catalytic fashion they play into the hands of resource planners who are more concerned with the politics of placating local interests than the maintenance of unique ecosystems.

All federal agencies involved in recreation planning and development have a clear responsibility to predict and be sensitive to the environmental consequences they may initiate. To wait for resource deterioration to begin before taking remedial action to restrict or modify use pressures is no longer acceptable. Many of the over 200 university departments specializing in recreation are preparing professionals capable of this prediction responsibility. Yet their graduates are still excluded from employment by the U.S. Forest Service. A new set of employment qualifications for recreation resource planning positions (Series GS-023) has been developed by the U.S. Civil Service Commission. But these are only qualification standards. They are as yet no assurance that recreation graduates will be employed along with foresters and landscape architects to deal comprehensively with the ecological complexities of recreation planning.

The American people must also become more sensitive to the intricacies of environmental quality management if the environmental 70s is to be more than a decade. We need to respond to more than the popular and easily visualized environmental degradations depicted by the media if we are to expect recreation resource planners to do so. With increasing population, more abundant leisure, and subsequent user-resource pressures, the public as well as their congressional representatives must begin to recognize that recreation resource development (when over-developmental or when incompatible recreation pursuits are promoted) can be as great an exploiter of the environment as industries that dump their wastes into our nation's rivers. Just as industry needs to be curbed, so too must the U.S. Forest Service lose its taste for pork and begin to recognize and respect the long-term public interest.

In doing so, they will genuinely demonstrate that "they are as concerned as we are."

Toward the Park and Recreation Professional

Pasadena Recreation Department, Pasadena, California

WILLARD W. BROWN "A Parks & Recreation Essay"
Parks and Recreation, National Recreation and Park Association, June 1971.

DONALD A. PELEGRINO "A Profile of the Municipal Recreator"
California Parks and Recreation, California Parks and Recreation Society, Inc., October 1970.

LOUIS F. TWARDZIK "The University's Commitment to the Parks and Recreation Profession"
Parks and Recreation, National Recreation and Park Association, March 1968.

DAVID E. GRAY "New Values, New Mission, New Role, New Preparation for Recreation Personnel"
Journal of Health, Physical Education, and Recreation, AAHPER.

LOREN E. TAYLOR "Let's Get the Elephants Out of the Volkswagen"
Parks and Recreation, National Recreation and Park Association, February 1967.

H.D. EDGREN "How to Build a Strong Community Image: Do's and Dont's for Recreators"
Parks and Recreation, National Recreation and Park Association, April 1962.

Toward the Park and Recreation Professional

The decade of the sixties has brought with it an important change in the intellectual climate throughout many parts of the world, evidenced by a new attitude toward the future that has become apparent in public and private planning agencies and municipal recreation departments. The effect has been to extend customary planning into a more distant future and to replace haphazard intuitive gambles, as a basis for planning, by well-educated professions.

The changes in attitude toward the future is manifesting itself in several ways: Philosophically, in that there is a new understanding of what it means to talk about the future; pragmatically, in that there is a growing recognition that it is important to do something about the future; and methodologically, in that there are new and more effective ways of in fact doing something about the future.

"Recreation cannot be limited; it embraces all phases of a person's being—the mental, physical, social, emotional and spiritual."

Leisure time becomes more abundant as years progress. Technology, scientific developments, and the desire for more free time is providing man with additional time in which he may socialize with other individuals or become involved in activities of his own choosing. Because man now has more free time than ever before in history he will utilize facilities and request the services of those individuals being employed by park and recreation departments. These individuals employed are park and recreation professionals.

The word "profession" is a widely used term employed in very diverse ways. In one sense it implies only that one is paid for his services. Thus we speak of professional baseball players or professional writers. But in the stricter sense in which we often use the word professional it implies a more precise definition. In this stricter sense a professional is one who has: (1) a relatively long period of specialized training; (2) possession of a specialized body of knowledge; (3) opportunity to personally apply his skill or art; (4) life membership in the service in which he practices his skills; (5) ethical principles and ideals of service.

Within this definition some individuals who occupy park and recreation administrative positions could qualify as professional. Whether the position of park and recreation administrator is a profession is still debatable.

In the past a recreation professional has been viewed by the general public as one who distributes equipment at the playground, coaches a

"... No profession can be truly great unless its practitioners have the vision of the greatness possible in that profession—and the skill and imagination to relate its service to the strongest of man's motivations."

particular sport, or one who takes all nonacademic courses in college. The recreation profession has also been looked upon with very few social benefits such as prestige, status, or those which can make a worthwhile contribution to human life. These are fallacies of the past. They can remain as beliefs for present and future generations or they can be changed into attitudes which depict the recreation professional as an individual who contributes and offers fulfilling experiences for mankind.

Recreation professionals have now reached the stage where they must educate the general public about their profession. This task is not only for the individual working in the field but also for educational institutions and agencies whose goals are to provide recreation and its services.

Life styles are changing. The recreation professional must learn some new ways and be aware of the problems and changes that are taking place in our society. He must be able to relate or make a concerted effort to relate with individuals who are products of life styles which could be completely different from those to which he is accustomed. He must be aware of the community in which he is working.

By knowing what is taking place in the community and having specific knowledge about the individuals and their life styles, he will be able to more effectively plan and operate a program that will be worthwhile for the community being served. He can no longer devote himself to "Locking the gates" and issuing equipment. The role is changing. Organized sports, arts and crafts, games and skills will be coupled with involvement in humanity and aimed at social goals. Training has now reached the level where it must involve interacting with other individuals.

"The recreation movement has not escaped this torrent of social change. So far we have not adapted very well to the realities of our current society. If we do not adapt we are destined to be a social fossil of historical interest only."

Educational institutions can also be effective in helping to change the image of the recreation professional. The type of course content used in educating must be relevant to needs that are being expressed in our society. Course content which was once geared toward physical aspects of getting people to participate is not always relevant. Educational institutions or other service agencies can no longer view recreation as something that can be executed by individuals who have had little recreational experience. Educational institutions can further help realize the importance of recreational outlets for developing a well-balanced human being.

Educational institutions should take a close and evaluative look at recreation programs of the past in determining the type of training and professionalism that is to be offered for potential recreation personnel of the present and future. Recreators should be aware of the needs of our society.

In establishing a curriculum, traditionalism is not always a sound basis for planning worthwhile programs. The needs of recreation program participants change as society changes. Park and other recreation facilities which were once used exclusively by the young child are now used by adults who, because of their increased leisure, may want to receive benefits from recreation experiences. Educational and in-service training programs will have to be devised which will offer training and experience for professionals in working with the adults in our society.

"The university today is an increasing complex institution called upon to serve as the searcher, preserver and dispenser of knowledge in a wide variety of disciplines."

The recreation person will also need training in dealing with communities. In helping the community to develop, it is important to be considered as part of the community—as someone that has been placed there to understand the community, provide it with recreation services, and help it prosper. To help individuals of the community find outlets for their frustrations and help with day-to-day problems is not a minor task.

Traditionally park people and recreation people have had dissimilar educational backgrounds. Park people pursue, in college, an educational program centered in the physical and biological sciences including agronomy, horticulture, architecture, landscape architecture, and the like. The recreation people follow a program based in the social sciences and the arts including sociology, cultural arts, journalism, psychology, and education. Each of these is a full program.

There is, apparently, some subtle selective device which we do not understand that operates when education and vocational choices are made that leads one into one curriculum or the other. It is very rare for one individual to have equal and comprehensive educational background in both curricula or equal experience in both fields.

The list of variables to be considered in planning a course of instruction are endless. Certain models have been preestablished. One may work better than the other to provide instruction and guidance that will prepare the recreation person for situations he will face. Judgments must be made about the acceptability of the risks to be encountered. Who is to say that once a program has been put into effect to deal with these things it will provide a working model to follow. Not only administrators but students as well must be willing to work diligently to change the image of the recreation professional.

"In the argot of the day, those that do not change are no longer relevant."

"The image the administrator establishes in any community is determined by his actions within his department and the part he plays in all aspects of community life."

The image of the park and recreation professional will also be reflected in the way he handles and delegates responsibilities. His position will not only be centered around activities at his own agency; it will also include developing a working relationship with other public and private service agencies. Through these agencies he can become aware of programs being provided by other organizations and prevent duplication of programming and avoid gaps in services.

The recreation professional should also learn to evaluate his programs on quality and the benefits being provided, rather than depending entirely on the number of participants who utilize his facilities as a criterion of success. The quality and processes by which a program is executed may be a

"All too often the number of participants has been our only criteria of evaluation. We count numbers—and after a while only numbers count."

better indicator of benefits for the recreator than one which is deemed successful entirely on the basis of the number of individuals involved.

"A world in which everyone is in touch must have people in touch with themselves."

Through recreation man can be helped to attain self-respect and self-discovery. By self-respect he can reestablish his identity as an individual. Here he is no longer placed in categories or treated as only a number to be put on file with the use of a computer. He is viewed as one who can contribute and show others the respect that he feels for himself. By self-discovery his ability to become aware of his physical environment, intuitions, and his relationship with nature can be expressed. He can learn to live and cope with the problems which an expanding society creates.

"To contribute to the enrichment of the quality of life and the basic culture of communities throughout the nation through the gifts of self-discovery and self-respect, park and recreation professionals must teach the average man how to survive in a society whose institutions have become for him so big, so impersonal, so unresponsive, and so inhuman."

The role of the recreation professional in the future may in no way relate to those of today. As a society changes so does its people. With these changes will come new ideas and values. The needs of the people will be reflected by the life styles that they pursue. The recreation person will again be faced with the challenge of trying to meet these needs and to strive and maintain happiness among as many individuals as possible. Meeting those needs being expressed by society will determine whether recreation, on an institutional level, will survive.

The role of the recreation professional will also be determined by his eagerness, creativity, and willingness to continue in his chosen tasks even though he will sometimes meet with failure. If things do not go as planned, he should not abandon his task.

There are no guarantees for the future. Every year guidelines will have to be devised which will create a program that can meet the needs and take care of current interests of society. A profession such as recreation grows by not only providing service to its clients, but also by evaluating programs and improving the effectiveness of services.

A Parks & Recreation Essay

Willard W. Brown

The broad, diverse changes which mark the American scene today are assuming epochal proportions as the country shifts from a predominantly scientific impulse to a more humanistic one. The "Golden Age of Science" with its historic successes in the splitting of the atom and the landing on the moon is itself in eclipse. The shadow of the Russian bear may grow, but no longer can science claim the top dollar. We have discovered that the price of this "scientific progress" has been a growing inhumanity in the bigness and remoteness of our institutions and an accelerating erosion of the sense of identity and self-respect of the individual. We may have learned to dominate our universe, but now we have elected to learn more about ourselves.

I believe that the most casual observer must sense that for the park and recreation profession—its time has come; that the opportunities for the application of its outstanding, unique public services are at hand.

The profession is, however, highly diverse in experience and modest in its own awareness of where it stands and where its future lies. No profession can be truly great unless its practitioners have the vision of the greatness possible in that profession—and the skill and imagination to relate its service to the strongest of man's motivations. Perhaps by reference to some of the lessons of history and the laws of human nature, we can see in the park and recreation profession and its commitment not only the timeliness of its relevance but its potential greatness, a profession that does offer to one's fellowman basically two great services, two great gifts—that of self-discovery and of self-respect.

THE GIFT OF SELF-DISCOVERY

Man is a bundle of paradoxes, a delicate balance between antagonistic forces. He is highly individualistic, but he is also a gregarious animal, dependent for life and well-being upon mingling with others of his kind. Like the porcupines, we are keen on huddling together for warmth on a cold day, but even then we "keep our distance."

"No man is an island" and "All men are brothers" may have been theoretical statements before, but in this age of specialization, interdependence, and population density, they are cries for self-preservation. A

Reprinted with permission from National Recreation and Park Association. Official publication *Parks and Recreation*, June, 1971.

world in which everyone is in touch must have people in touch with themselves. Where the actions of one can drastically affect the lives of others, it is critical that each person master the skill of empathy, of feeling that which others feel. But such empathy is possible only in one deeply aware of one's own feelings.

Our park and recreation facilities and services serve as a bridge between our human resources and our natural resources. "I feel, therefore I am." To discover and understand oneself, one must be cognizant of one's heritage of the ages, one's intuitions and instincts, one's "humanness," an interplay between man's nature and his environment, an inextricable bond between man and the laws of Nature. The ultimate deprivation of man is his sequestration from or denial of a periodic exposure through our park system to the natural life or wilderness from which he came.

The riots of 1967-1970 were shocking because they represented conflict outside the civilized process, outside the two great institutions of the city—the forum and the market place. For centuries, these have been the primary instruments of communication, of social, economic, and political conflict. With the development of the automobile, the telephone, and the scattering of our leadership throughout the suburbs, there has been a breakdown in communication and the loss of the living person-to-person contact amongst people of many diverse disciplines and ethnic backgrounds, so indispensable to human understanding and creativity.

It is on the ceiling of the Sistine Chapel in the Vatican that one sees the "Creation of Man" by Michelangelo, creation being the act of the personal, human "touch." Our parks and our centers of recreation have replaced the forum and the market place as the stages upon which the essential function of person-to-person communication and creativity is taking place.

THE GIFT OF SELF-RESPECT

The great confrontations in history have been between the "haves" and the "have-nots." In this Age, the real "have-nots" are not only the poor, but the disenfranchised elements in our modern technological society—those too young to be allowed a voice in our government or in our economic system; and now, most significantly, those unable to participate in a meaningful way in the society they feel they help build or in the economy of which they are a part.

After continental expansion had been achieved, after the U.S. world power had been demonstrated, after economic growth came to be assumed, it was not surprising that Americans, especially the young, should seek a new challenge. It was not surprising that this search should turn upon such nonmaterial values as those represented by civil rights, the moral aspects of the war in Vietnam, and the attainment of a "good life" expressed more in terms of the full creative and moral development of the individual man than in any increase of the Gross National Product.

The unpleasantness of a job has nothing to do with whether it is repetitive or not. It depends solely on a man's sense of involvement—on how many parts of the man are used and how well they are being used. If only a part of a man is being used, the salvation of his sanity depends on what he himself does with the unwanted parts. It is the horror of emptiness, of lack of purpose, far more than economic privation or political injustice, that drives people to seek revolutionary change.

"Pride in work" and "Pride in self"

have lost much of their relevance now that the forests are hewn and the frontier swallowed up. "Hard work" has become "efficiency," and "success" has become "bigness." We live in a big society, and there seems to be no way to run a big society with a big economy except by big institutions where work must be simplified and specialized so that it will be easier to plan, control, and direct. This has meant managing people by procedures, reducing individuals to categories, and purring decisions about them through the computer, turning our institutions into faceless bureaucracies. When people are shut off, treated like numbers, excluded from the decisions that affect their lives and they feel that they cannot influence the organization or bureaucracy that is running things, they no longer count as individuals. They lose their self-respect, their self-esteem.

One of the remarkable facts of human nature is that we really love our neighbors as we love ourselves. In turn, he, who has no respect for himself, has none for others. He hates in others what he hates in himself. It is not the love of self but the hatred of self that is the root of the troubles that afflict us.

In the growing acceptance of the four-day work week, and in the ever increasing use of our parks and recreation centers, Americans see work not as an end, but as a means to earn enough to achieve the sense of fulfillment, identity, and self-respect in their avocation that has been denied them in their vocation.

History has shown that only through the experience of self-discovery and the attainment of self-respect can man effect a constructive balance between society and self, a balance that is the foundation of any culture and the inspiration to man's appetite for continuing self-education.

At a graduation exercise where Albert Schweitzer gave the Commencement Address, he concluded with the statement: "I don't know what your destiny may be, but one thing I do know, the only ones among you who will be really happy are those who have sought and found how to serve." To contribute to the enrichment of the quality of life and the basic culture of communities throughout the nation through the gifts of self-discovery and self-respect, park and recreation professionals must teach the average man how to "survive" in a society whose institutions have become for him so big, so impersonal, so unresponsive, and so inhuman. Such a professional service is of outstanding significance and should enjoy the highest priority in public understanding and support.

A Profile of the Municipal Recreator

Donald A. Pelegrino

For several decades, the field of recreation and parks has been steadily gaining ground with the American public and in all segments of the community. The facilities, buildings, and grounds of our federal, public, and private jurisdictions are staffed by what is known as "the recreation and parks professional," but who is commonly referred to as the "recreator," "recreationist," or, in its simplest form, the "playground director."

In the field of medicine we have doctors, in the field of education we have teachers, and in the field of human welfare we have social workers. Each of these professionals has had certain education and training which was early surveyed by sociologists, psychologists, and others interested in learning and building an empirical base regarding their profession, and is now readily known by the general public. Very little is known, however, about the recreation professional.

With this thought in mind, and with some prompting by my professional colleagues, I was encouraged to take on an independent study about the recreation professional: namely, the recreation professional who is employed by a city or other municipal department. For the sake of clarification and for purposes of definition, I have termed him "the municipal man." For purposes of this study it is a man or a woman who is employed in the field of parks and recreation by a city or county governmental agency.

THE SAMPLE

The construction of a questionnaire which consisted of 45 questions and 110 items was the principal instrument used for the determination of a profile of the municipal park and recreation man. The questionnaire was sent to a national sample consisting of every tenth name in the American Park and Recreation Society Directory and the California sample of every tenth name in the California Park and Recreation Society Directory. A total of 557 questionnaires was mailed. A return of 35 percent (192) was received from respondents throughout the United States.

The construction of the questionnaire focused upon such pertinent

Reprinted with permission of California Parks and Recreation Society, Inc., *California Parks and Recreation*, October, 1970.

areas as personal background, education, and training, leisure-time classes, professional responsibilities, cultural and leisure pursuits, tenure on the job, type of position, economic areas of interests, credit cards, home ownership, etc. To obtain such information, the questionnaire had to remain anonymous and confidential. Some of the information elicited is the kind that the professional would only relate confidentially and anonymously, which is perhaps one of the reasons for such a good and reputable return.

The purpose of this research investigation was *not* to find the characteristics of a good administrator such as decision-making, consistency, knowing one's abilities and limitations, keeping informed, creating participative environment, being circumspect and realistic, having the courage to take risks based on sound decision-making, being a man of action, and so forth.

It was also *not* the purpose of this study to find out if an administrator was a good communicator and used clear, accurate, and complete communication within his administrative responsibilities. The purpose of this study was also *not* to find out if the administrator was a good planner, or if he had knowledge of and an inclination for research to keep informed of current developments in this field.

The study *did seek* answers to such questions as:

1. Who is a municipal recreation man— what is his background, what is his training, and what is he all about?
2. What is his economic status—how much money does he make, how does he spend his money, what is his credit card position, and does he own his own home?
3. What is his religious affiliation and his political affiliation—in what category does he consider his political leanings?

4. How does the municipal recreation man feel about the profession in which he is presently working—with respect to such factors as status in relation to other traditional professions, public acceptance, compensation, and professional preparation?

With the above questions in mind, I attempted to put together and construct the profile of a municipal recreation man. From the data gathered in the survey of municipal recreation employees, it was possible to draw such a profile.

THE PROFILE

The municipal man is generally an optimistic, Caucasian male between the ages of 30 to 39. He is married and has two children. His religious affiliation is Protestant, but his political choice is Republican. He considers himself moderate in his political attitude and leanings. He is not going to school for any credit, or attending classes in his leisure to increase his professional competence; however, he is taking classes primarily because of personal interest or some other non-professional reason. He possesses a degree awarded as a result of a four-year college education. His major was recreation.

The title of a municipal man's position ranges from such descriptive job headings as park superintendent, superintendent of planning, chief operations director of harbors, beaches and parks, to area supervisor, supervisor of concessions, director of athletics and playgrounds. He may be called regional director, service club director, assistant professor of recreation, or recreation specialist. He is employed in a city with a population of 25,000 to 50,000 people.

He has over twenty years in the park and recreation field, at least five years in his present position, and has not changed his employer within the last five years. His work schedules average over 45 hours per week for which he receives approximately $10,000 per year. As fringe benefits he has some form of group insurance, a retirement plan, two weeks' vacation per year, and the use of a public car for business (he does not receive a mileage allowance). He considers this compensation only satisfactory, but thinks his position affords him the security equal to comparable employment with other public service fields and with the voluntary social service field.

The municipal man does not want any more decision-making power than is available to him in his present position, and he believes that his authority is commensurate with his responsibility. He has not considered changing jobs at all. The municipal man thinks that he is ranked as competent by his clientele as a recreation activity leader. His coworkers rate him as a good recreation executive.

He is a member of the local PTA; belongs to at least three trade or professional organizations and *at least* one service club (such as the Junior Chamber of Commerce or Kiwanis); spends up to $10 per month on business-related entertainment and between $10 and $15 on professional dues.

He sometimes supplements his income by engaging in employment in a related field. His spouse sometimes works, but only part-time.

The municipal man owns his home, the value of which is between $20,000 and $29,000. He owns one car (1½) and possesses at least two credit cards, one of which is an oil company account and the other a department store account.

In his free or leisure time the municipal man spends between 1 to 3 hours per week reading books; 1 to 3 hours per week reading magazines; 1 to 3 hours per week reading trade or professional journals; and over ten hours per week reading newspapers.

As a participant he regularly engages in swimming, beach activities, social dancing, golf, and fishing. He seldom participates in dramatic productions, square dancing, modern dance, painting, drawing, and tennis. As a spectator he attends regularly football and baseball games, motion pictures, track and field meets and other sporting events. He very rarely attends the opera, ballet, modern dance recitals, classical and/or folk music concerts.

The University's Commitment to the Parks and Recreation Profession

Louis F. Twardzik

The university has historically had various objectives but never has it deviated from the idea of furthering knowledge and teaching it. The professions generally look to the university to train their specialists. Not in every case, however, were the universities interested in or able to further the professions. Indeed, the idea of serving the professions by training their specialists and thereby meeting the changing needs of the community is relatively new to the universities, dating back to the Morrill Act of 1862.

This is the situation today. Professionals in parks and recreation are now looking to the universities to advance their cause but the universities are only reluctantly accepting the challenge.

One reason why the universities do not accord a whole-hearted interest is the still incomplete evolution of the profession. It has not made a decision on the direction it wants to go; in other words, it has not defined its goals as yet. It is unlike the barber profession of days gone by when the value of specialization in surgery was recognized. This profession eventually split into two groups, one whose members became the disciples of Aesculapius, while the other group, interested in cutting and dressing hair, remained barbers. The present status of the park management profession is one of a combination of barbers and surgeons. How effective we are in either is a moot question, but if a judgment is not made soon, others will make it for us.

PROGRESS MADE

There has been some progress made in this process of professional evolution. The history of parks and recreation in this country has some important milestones. It includes a park conceived, designed and developed for public use and administered by a professional. Of course, this is Central Park, in New York City, considered by many to be the first public park, with the first professional—the designer and superintendent, Frederick Law Olmsted. His profession was landscape architecture.

The concept of a free local public pleasure ground spread fast, faster than landscape architecture. The people who were responsible for these

Reprinted with permission from National Recreation and Park Association. Official publication *Parks and Recreation*, March, 1968.

areas in cities and towns throughout the country became known as "park men" or "park superintendents." As their work gained public acceptance, individuals with professional, scientific backgrounds in horticulture, floriculture, civil engineering, botany and forestry were attracted to the field. They became designers, managers and maintainers of urban lands and waters called parks. They were dedicated to the concept that certain parts of the community should be areas of natural beauty. Although art was permitted to permeate the early parks in the form of statuary and fountains, the emphasis was on greens, flowers, trees and waters. Quite often they were arranged in formal fashion indicating continental European influence but more often they followed the natural design of English parks and gardens. They served primarily as places of beauty, guarded carefully against abuse by the public. This gave rise to the "keep off the grass" signs so prevalent until the 1950's.

At the same time, in the 19th century, the National Park movement was launched with the establishment of Yellowstone. Its dominant concern for enjoyment through preservation carried over to the state parks when they emerged as another level of public recreation.

THE RECREATION LEADER

As a result of the park man's lack of interest in what the people needed or wanted in recreation, together with the evils of industrialization, crowded, dirty tenement living, another type of professional, the recreation leader, came into being. He offered pleasurable opportunities for all people where they lived. These new professionals started as volunteers caring for children, but eventually

municipalities realized that their work could serve a broader social purpose.

Inevitably, there occurred the confrontation between the park man and the recreation leader. The park people controlled the open, public spaces that the recreation leaders wanted to use for games, sports and playgrounds. The inability of both groups to join successfully in a common cause during the past century is largely responsible for parks and recreation not being represented by a recognized profession. It was only two years ago that the nation's five major park and recreation organizations including the National Conference on State Parks joined in a common organization known as the National Recreation and Park Association.

Philosophic Differences

If it can be said that park management and recreation held similar purposes basic, then it must be admitted that at least they viewed them from different perspectives. The sciences that contributed to the growth and maintenance of plant life and soils were well established. The park man, knowledgeable in these sciences, made a unique contribution—instead of creating an economically useful product from natural resources, he wrought the miracle of beauty. His ultimate art suffered only because he was expected to share the approbation of the public with his creation. But unlike other creative persons he did not bother to consult with his patrons on what they wanted. He believed that "what is good for the resource is good for the people." He, of course, being the judge.

The recreation leaders found their cause in people. They did not need anything beautiful or unique to brighten and enrich the lives of tenement dwellers. They cleared dirty lots and made playgrounds of them. They taught people to ignore their squalor and find beauty and fun in the midst of a miserable existence. People could brighten their lives if they only knew how. An empty room, a quart of paint— and they could square dance, sing and play games. From this social effort emerged the opposite principle of resource development, "what is good for the people is good for the resource."

The University's Interest

Similarly, as some universities became interested in these fields they gravitated quite naturally to the faculties of established departments.

Earth science courses were usually in the Agriculture College which was the first to become interested in park management. The social phases of recreation became the concern of the Schools of Education. The wise use of leisure was early a major objective of educators.

Park management was accepted as a special curriculum in only a few universities. Although the demand for park men was equal to that for recreation leaders, the discipline in which it found itself trying to survive was not as amenable to its growth as was the College of Education for recreation leaders. The proliferation of colleges and universities offering degrees in phases of recreation jumped after World War II from a few to between 150 and 200. Park management has not been seriously pursued in more than a half dozen schools over this same span of years.

With few exceptions, faculty in park management or recreation leadership was seldom composed of more than a few full-time teachers. The situation is improving due to the increasing number of Ph.D. programs available to those who want to devote themselves to teaching or research. Generally, however, the number of qualified teachers throughout the country remains low. For instance, in one of the older and more respectable university curriculums in parks and recreation the teaching staff remains at 2 half-time teachers and 3 visiting lecturers for 50 undergraduate and 25 graduate students while the Soil Science Department in the same college has 35 staff members for a total of 65 students.

A new and significant plateau has been reached during the past decade and consumated in the formation of the National Recreation and Park Association. This was the merging of recreation and parks into a more understandable grouping of social and natural resource interests on a national level. By effectuating this long needed merger, the profession was able to advance some needed concepts including recognition that the professional competency of the field was in philosophy, principles, techniques and practice of parks and recreation and not in allied fields. This was the long missing element in the search for professionalism, the one unique and significant contribution it offered. It meant that now landscape architects could practice their profession and educators theirs and foresters theirs and the same in horticulture and all other recognized fields and disciplines who for so long were the fountainhead for university offerings in the practice of parks and recreation.

VOCATIONALISM AND PROFESSIONALISM

To the scholar, vocationalism and professionalism are synonymous with specialization. Any student studying outside the humanities and the liberal arts is in a specialization. The classical scholar considers the study of a specialty as something which could take place elsewhere than the university. But through the Morrill Act of 1862 and subsequent legislation, land-grant colleges were established to teach skills that could contribute directly to the agricultural and industrial expansion of the country. Later, private colleges and universities began to train the specialists required by a changing society.

Universities often respond to demand. The days of demand for people with specialized training in parks and recreation has arrived. The difficulty with this demand, however, is that the universities have had a taste of educating specialists in this field according to professional requirements. It has left much to be desired. The universities are becoming, or should be, reluctant to any longer offer their prestige, time and financial resources to training at the levels of professional requirements which have generally overstated their case; we can no longer justify the requirement of a baccalaureate to carry on maintenance responsibilities in a park or recreation leadership for games and sports.

JUNIOR COLLEGE PROGRAMS

Fortunately there are now prospects of programs at Junior Colleges and similar institutions which provide training of technicians competent to work at these levels. The universities are now advancing this view while many professionals are accepting it with reluctance. The reason for the universities making professional training determinations is the obvious failure of many traditionalists still in the profession to move ahead with changes in concepts and service for a changing society. The profession has fallen short in many phases and at all levels of parks and recreation management. The public demand for outdoor recreation after World War II caught us all flat-footed, despite the protestations of insufficient funds. Today, new federal

programs bring college students without professional training to cities to discover the need to provide recreation areas and programs for minority groups to congregate and play. Similarly, the reawakening of the need for public outdoor recreation came from a variety of professional groups and academic disciplines in the natural and social sciences as did the programs for open space and natural beauty. We who consider ourselves professionals in parks and recreation played a small, if any part in this.

Small wonder that the universities see a need to change the training for this field. The universities are no longer interested in training people for skills in park maintenance or playground crafts; and they should not be. Those are technical skills, needed skills, but to be taught elsewhere. NRPA is undertaking a study with funds from the U.S. Office of Education to prepare a new publication "Guidelines for Developing a Two-Year Junior College Curriculum in Recreation Program Leadership." It is hoped that this work, when completed will be immediately followed by a companion study for a two year junior college curriculum in park management.

"Is park management a recognized profession?" If park management is considered to be a bunching of techniques on how to maintain a park the answer is no; it is no longer, if it ever was, a recognized profession in the universities.

But there is a profession in parks and recreation and until someone finds a more appropriate term, it can be named, at least for the time being, Parks and Recreation Administration.

Professor Charles E. Doell, superintendent emeritus, Minneapolis Park Commission, put it more clearly when he stated at the 1964 National Conference on Professional Education for Outdoor Recreation that "Education for administrators and total recreation services must be on the professional managerial plane with required background in recreation philosophy and an appreciation of the sciences, techniques, and skills necessary for resource development and management in the field of recreation services. There will be demand for more highly skilled technicians and recreation leaders, and better educated scientists in many fields as time goes on, but the education of the top administrator must not be ignored and left only to the vagaries of experience."

This profession should be based on its own principles which in turn should reflect a high level of intellectual pursuit and academic achievement. The park and recreation administrator today need not be a trained researcher, but he should know about new research techniques and what they can do for him or how they can assist him in making his decisions. He has to understand recreation as an indispensable ingredient in man's aspiration for a quality of life and then be able to defend it as a high priority objective of public service.

To accomplish this task universities are making some progress not only in improved physical facilities, but in the number and quality of faculty. The percentage of faculty with doctorate degrees is increasing as is the breadth of their competencies and interests. The faculty is now more prepared to understand and formulate theory and sophisticated research. It does, however, retain the proper perspectives for the practical exposures and experiences which are indispensable to a student's training.

The university today is an increasing complex institution called upon to serve as the searcher, preserver and dispenser of knowledge in a wide variety of disciplines. It is also asked to address itself to specific social needs. One of these is the training of specialists in park and recreation administration. You can be sure that the new professional the university is grooming is one who is first an educated person and then a specialist, a person who will concern himself with the significant and far-ranging policies and problems of a people living in a leisure age as well as with day-to-day operational responsibilities.

It is well to remember that the profession that addresses itself solely to current operations loses the basis for its future. The university refuses to train barbers.

New Values, New Mission, New Role, New Preparation for Recreation Personnel

David E. Gray

It is a cliche to say the world is changing but it is a fundamental truth of our time that rapid technological change is remaking our world. In the process, social institutions and social movements change or become organizational fossils, of historical interest, but no longer significant in the living world. In the argot of the day, those that do not change are no longer *relevant*.

The recreation movement has not escaped this torrent of social change. So far we have not adapted well to the realities of our current society. We *must* adapt or become increasingly irrelevant, destined to be a social fossil of historical interest only. To say we must change is also a cliche but to say *how* we must change is not. There are few guidelines and almost no literature on the subject. This article sets forth my analysis of existing, impending, or needed changes in recreation services and speculates on the impact such changes may have for our curriculum designs.

In undertaking development or revision of a recreation curriculum, several questions must be answered before the curriculum can be designed. Among such questions are these.

1. *What will the new graduate at the entering professional level be asked to do? What will he need to be prepared to do after five years service, after ten years?*
2. *How much of current practice in the recreation field should be reenforced and perpetuated?*
3. *What new goals, what new tasks, what new methods will the recreation movement embrace in the next few years; what values will guide recreation practice?*

The following assumptions with respect to such questions should also be considered when curriculum development is undertaken:

1. *How will recreation services be distributed in the community?* In the earliest days of the recreation movement, playgrounds were located in what was then called "underprivileged" neighborhoods. Gradually as the movement matured and public acceptance improved, the idea grew that any neighborhood which lacked public recreation service was, in a sense, underprivileged and that youth services and centers ought to be

Reprinted with permission from the American Association of Health, Physical Education and Recreation Journal.

provided throughout the city. In some cities where residents of the more affluent neighborhoods employed their power to articulate needs and influence political processes, a preponderance of new facilities often went into the developing suburbs and what inequalities in distribution of facilities existed favored the more affluent population. In the future this may change. Although a basic level of service is likely to be available everywhere, there is growing recognition of the fact that people are unequal in their need for community supported recreation services. It requires substantially more effort to get similar results in a culturally deprived area of the city than it does elsewhere. It appears that in the future we may take this into account in the construction of facilities and the deployment of recreation personnel. This could result in a disproportionate expenditure of resources and effort in culturally deprived neighborhoods.

2. *How will professional recreation personnel be deployed and employed?* The questions of what constitutes professional work, what is the entering level for professional personnel, and how professional recreation personnel should be deployed are important and difficult ones. The answers which evolve will condition the way our enterprises are operated, but the answers are not clear. The traditional responses are (1) that professional work consists mainly, or initially at least, of personal leadership of recreational groups, supervision of grounds, management of facilities and equipment, and related tasks; (2) that the entering level for professional personnel is the recreation leader (or director); and (3) that the new professional will be deployed on a school staff or as a member of a community center staff. Deployment of a college educated, career recreator as a full-time leader in this way is a luxury only the largest agencies

can afford even today. It appears possible that in the future, the entering level for professional recreation personnel may be the supervisor or center-director level with recreation leadership, ground supervision, equipment control, and related tasks assigned to subprofessional and part-time personnel.

We operate now on what I have come to call a "chain link fence" philosophy which binds recreation personnel to a school or center. Such a philosophy holds that the primary concern of the staff is to operate the center. It identifies the primary tasks as surveillance of grounds to assure compliance with rules, safety, proper use of facilities and control of equipment; development of a schedule for use of the facility; planning and execution of a program of activities with the staff in face-to-face leadership roles; coordination of maintenance activities to insure the readiness and sanitary condition of the premises. Such a philosophy rewards facility managers. The most deleterious effect of this philosophy is on the deployment of staff.

In contrast to this view, there is a concept of the professional recreation personnel's role which perceives them as *community* figures. This concept identifies as central, the development of people, human interaction, improvement of the community, preservation of the virtues of urban life, and concern for the social problems of our time.

A really good creator working within this concept can operate in a community without *any* facility and earn his salary. He can become a person of stature in his community for the contributions he can make to community living and the growth of people, without ever throwing a light switch, taking in a flag, or locking a gate. His job would be to generate events that would look for a place to happen, not to fill up a facility that he was hired to manage. This vision of the recreator as a community organizer raises serious questions about the way we recruit, educate, and deploy staff and about the nature of professional work. There is no doubt that most "professional" recreators do much work that is sub-professional. Such tasks are easily identified. The challenging undertaking is to identify and describe the character of professional service.

The difficult professional task in these times is the role of community catalyst. In this role, the job of the recreation leader assumes proportions as organizer, moderator, stimulator, interpreter, adviser, and teacher. Using recreation content and method, such a figure seeks to improve the social climate of his community. There is no precise model for this kind of professional. The task may be accomplished in one community by an outstanding minister, in another by a particularly able school principal or an effective YMCA secretary. Most communities lack such a person; they are the poorer for it.

3. *What will be the major concerns of recreation and park agencies in the future?* In the matter of who shall lead the attack on the social ills of our nation we have no choice; government will lead the attack. In the matter of which among the several agencies of local government shall be used as an instrument, there is a choice. Such choices are being made and recreation agencies are seldom chosen.

We have narrowly defined our services in the past. In the future will we be concerned about contributions to the education of our people, the welfare of the elderly, maintenance of domestic tranquility, the quality of American life, beauty and conservation of the urban environment, the design of our cities, improvement of community life, development of the young, and cultural affairs? If we are not, which agencies in

local government will be? These are much greater concerns than scheduling and staffing activities and management of recreation and park properties. They represent a major involvement in contemporary affairs. We currently lack expertise in many of these areas, but who is expert in the management of contemporary urban life? Shouldn't we be attempting an enlarged contribution to the solution of enlarged urban problems? The central question is not, "is that our job?" It is what does the society need done and how can we do it? Whether it falls within the traditional role of the recreation agency is irrelevant.

4. *Who will be the clientele of municipal recreation departments in the future?* We have traditionally drawn many of our participants from the children of the middle and lower-middle class strata of society, but under way now or on the horizon are revised school programs which include longer school days, increased academic performance, summer school for half or more of the school population, and lengthened school years. In the great middle stratum of society, children are no longer a leisured class. In addition we have rising affluence, improved commercial recreation services, rising expectations, increased vacation leisure among adults, and a host of other changes which suggest our traditional clientele might choose to do something else with their leisure. Homes are being developed to provide more recreational opportunities—paperback libraries, television and radio, records, swimming pools, billiard tables, and other equipment are commonplace. Groups with the most leisure and the least money, who are therefore most dependent on municipal recreation and park services and the schools, are the poor and the elderly. It appears they may become a larger proportion of our

clientele in the future than they have been in the past.

5. *What values will we espouse in our agencies?* The recreation movement was born with a social conscience. It grew up with the settlement house movement, the kindergarten movement, and the movement that fostered the great youth agencies of the nation. Its earliest practitioners had a human welfare motivation in which the social ends of human development, curbing juvenile delinquency, informal education, cultural enrichment, health improvement, and other objectives were central. Gradually the social welfare mission weakened and a philosophy which sees recreation as an end in itself was adopted. This is the common view in public recreation agencies throughout our country. Agencies which embrace this view express their goals as "providing a program of activities for the entire community," or they say "we provide recreational activities for all the people."

I do not think we can divorce ourselves from the great social issues of our time. When we seek to make a contribution to the solution of social problems we will rediscover our social consciousness and begin to define our goals in terms of human welfare. Our ends then will not be activity, that will be the means. Our ends will be the development of human potential in all its richness and variation.

6. There is another and difficult question. *What is the most feasible division of responsibility for the learning required assuming the requisite skills and knowledge necessary to be successful on the job can be identified and agreed on?* Clearly, all of the education involved cannot be undertaken within the college curriculum. How much and what specific kinds should be accomplished in the elementary and secondary schools; how much in college; how much in in-service

education conducted by the employing agency; how much by the individual himself as a result of a rich recreational life and his own intellectual curiosity and professional commitment?

All of these matters much be considered in curriculum design. If recreation personnel are going to undertake different tasks, occupy a different community role, help provide a broader kind of service, deal with unfamiliar clientele, and embrace a different set of values, clearly the recreation curriculum cannot follow traditional patterns and be relevant to the needs of the field. What kind of an education is needed to perform well under these new conditions and what part of the necessary learning should we attempt in the college program? In reaching these decisions there is no model; we are groping for the kind of curriculum we need.

Lacking such a model one must make judgments and start out. When I make these judgments and start out, the minimum essentials of the recreation portion of such a curriculum appear to be—

1. the nature of the recreation experience
2. the history and philosophy of the recreation movement
3. leisure in America
4. community organization
5. leadership of individuals and groups
6. program appreciation, planning, and skills
7. supervision
8. administration
9. the nature of urban and rural environments
10. field experience

This year we have been considering these problems and debating these issues at California State College, Long Beach, in the process of making a major revision of our undergraduate recreation curriculum. When all the points of view had

PROPOSED BACHELOR OF ARTS DEGREE REQUIREMENTS
FOR THE RECREATION MAJOR

Lower Division			*units*
Recreation	211	The Recreation Program	3
Recreation	241	Community Recreation	3
Fine Arts	211	Cultural Arts in Recreation	3

Upper Division			
Ed. Psych.	301	Child Growth and Development	3
Ed. Psych.	302	Adolescent Growth and Development	3
Recreation	312	Recreation Leadership	2
Recreation	318	Outdoor Recreation Resources Mgt.	3
Recreation	330	Recreation in the Urban Community	3
Recreation	340	Leisure in Contemporary Society	3
Recreation	421	Supervision in Recreation	3
Recreation	425	Organization and Administration of Recreation	3
Speech	434	Communication in Organizational Settings	3
Journalism	470	Public Relations	3
Recreation	475	History and Philosophy of Recreation	3
Recreation	484	Fieldwork in Private Recreation Agencies	3
Recreation	485	Fieldwork in Public Recreation Agencies	3
		Specialization in two program areas: Creative arts, performing arts, or physical recreation activities	16

been heard, when all the issues had been discussed, when all the realities had been confronted, and all the compromises had been negotiated, we evolved the above curriculum.

At first glance, this curriculum may appear undistinguished, but it is based on a rationale that departs from tradition. Among the underlying assumptions the following are worth noting.

1. The changes enumerated earlier in this article will influence substantially the way recreation personnel are deployed and what they will be asked to do.
2. Students ought to have a substantial amount of control over their own educational programs.
3. Students need an early exposure to field conditions.
4. The "recreation method" is an amalgum of leadership, supervision, administrative, basic encounter, group work, communication theory, parliamentary procedure, and other techniques.
5. Community organization, politics, demographic conditions, ethnic background, social interaction patterns, and other elements of the urban environment condition recreation services.
6. Leisure and its role in contemporary society are changing rapidly.
7. The development of a program generalist with strong personal skills in many areas is not feasible.
8. The learning required is far greater than can be accomplished in college alone. In choosing what is to be attempted in college, that learning which can best be undertaken in college should have priority.

These are the new values, the new mission, the new role, and the new preparation for recreation personnel in the first half of the 1970's.

Let's Get the Elephants Out of the Volkswagen

Dr. Loren E. Taylor

"Are you with the University?" asked the man.

"Yes," answered the professor.

"What department?"

"Recreation."

"Oh." The man became interested. "What do you coach?"

"Well, I don't coach," answered the professor. Then on second thought, "Well, yes. I do coach dramatics."

"Dramatics?"

"Yes."

"But—but that's not recreation. Don't you help with football?"

The above is an account of an actual conversation overheard between a well-dressed man and a professor of recreation education at a large midwestern university. It is typical of the confusion regarding recreation throughout the country. This confusion needs to be clarified.

RECREATION AND PHYSICAL EDUCATION

No one would condemn a Volkswagen because it is not a suitable vehicle to haul an elephant. It wasn't built to haul elephants. Likewise, the objectives of physical education, however noble, are not broad enough to include recreation.

Physical education is more important today than perhaps it was at any other time in history, but physical educators seem to be more concerned with recreation, outdoor education, safety, health, and other related areas. The department has lost its identity and has become a dumping ground for any innovation in the modern curriculum. As a result of this burden, physical educators are helpless and ineffective in achieving their own goals. A good program of physical education can contribute to recreation, and, in fact to many disciplines; but it cannot administer these areas without weakening its own structure and becoming a catch-all for academic innovations.

Physical Education departments too often serve as an academic haven for athletes who are neither interested in nor qualified for teacher education; and for students whose primary interest is in health, safety, outdoor education or in recreation. Physical education is losing

Reprinted with permission from National Recreation and Park Association. Official publication *Parks and Recreation*, February, 1967.

its battle to gain recognition in the curriculum of the public schools and universities. The burden of administering the related areas leaves no time for teaching physical skills and for promoting the objectives of physical education.

America needs once again to know the value of physical fitness and the importance of a "sound mind in a sound body."

The nation needs the leadership of outstanding physical educators who know the objectives of their field and who are willing to devote full time to the promotion of physical education.

RECREATION AND FORESTRY

Since World War II, there has been an increasing demand for park facilities and outdoor recreation areas. Both the Federal and state governments are trying to meet this demand by (1) land acquisition and (2) a multiple-use program. Government agencies with land under their control, particularly the U.S. Forest Service, have been asked to open their holdings for recreation purposes. Operation multiple-use is the order of the day.

Land set aside for forestry purposes cannot be opened to hoards of people without proper supervision and management. Multiple-use can quickly result in multiple-abuse. Several forestry departments, realizing this, are requiring their majors to complete courses in recreation philosophy and park management.

The Forestry Department, however, is not the place for housing the recreation curriculum. Webster defines forestry as the science of planting and taking care of forests, an act of establishing and managing forests; whereas recreation is concerned with the education and management of *people* during their leisure hours. The graduate with a degree in forestry may expect a job as forest ranger, district forester, district fire warden, forest fire patrolman, timber scaler, and timber sales marker.

The graduate with a degree in recreation may expect a job as park executive facility planner, park and recreation superintendent, and executive or leader in special areas and services, such as industries, hospitals, student unions, schools, commercial recreation, and private agencies. A professional forester is not qualified to offer courses in recreation, just as the recreation profession cannot pretend to know forestry. Forestry cannot provide leadership for the majority of the above-named recreation positions. It, like physical education, cannot afford to get into the recreation business. To do so would be an injustice to both the forestry profession and to the recreation profession. The forester is concerned with the welfare of the forest because the forest contributes to the welfare of man. Operation multiple-use makes it imperative that the recreator and the forester get together both for the benefit of people and for the protection of the forest. However, courses in forestry should remain in the Forestry Department and courses in recreation should remain in the Recreation Department.

RECREATION AND SOCIOLOGY

At first thought, sociology may seem the logical department for the recreation curriculum. Further consideration, however, eliminates this possibility. True, recreation involves human association and may be considered a social institution, but the same can be said for education, religion, government, and the social aspects of psychology, anthropology and other social sciences. Sociologists have neither the time nor the desire to provide a curriculum for any of these fields of study.

Sociology is the science or study of

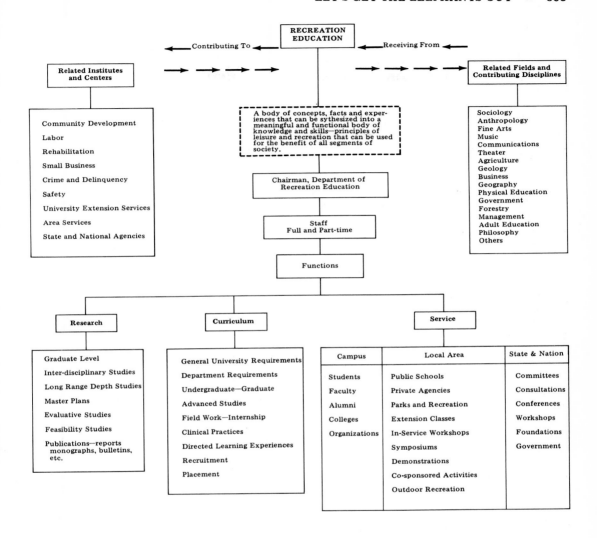

RECREATION
EDUCATION

← Contributing To ←   → Receiving From →

Related Institutes
and Centers

Related Fields and
Contributing Disciplines

A body of concepts, facts and experiences that can be sythesized into a
meaningful and functional body of
knowledge and skills—principles of
leisure and recreation that can be used
for the benefit of all segments of
society.

Community Development

Labor

Rehabilitation

Small Business

Crime and Delinquency

Safety

University Extension Services

Area Services

State and National Agencies

Sociology
Anthropology
Fine Arts
Music
Communications
Theater
Agriculture
Geology
Business
Geography
Physical Education
Government
Forestry
Management
Adult Education
Philosophy
Others

Chairman, Department of
Recreation Education

Staff
Full and Part-time

Functions

Research

Curriculum

Service

Graduate Level

Inter-disciplinary Studies

Long Range Depth Studies

Master Plans

Evaluative Studies

Feasibility Studies

Publications—reports
monographs, bulletins,
etc.

General University Requirements

Department Requirements

Undergraduate—Graduate

Advanced Studies

Field Work—Internship

Clinical Practices

Directed Learning Experiences

Recruitment

Placement

Campus	Local Area	State & Nation
Students	Public Schools	Committees
Faculty	Private Agencies	Consultations
Alumni	Parks and Recreation	Conferences
Colleges	Extension Classes	Workshops
Organizations	In-Service Workshops	Foundations
	Symposiums	Government
	Demonstrations	
	Co-sponsored Activities	
	Outdoor Recreation	

the origin, development, organization, and functioning of human society. Sociology focuses upon the patterned regularities of social behavior wherever they may exist in society. Since most recreation activities involve human associations and group interaction the sociologist is interested in recreation because it helps him to understand and to explain the processes of social interaction. The recreation professional must keep abreast of the findings of the sociologist; the sociologist has neither the time nor the inclination to keep abreast of the changes in recreation except for his own leisure pursuits.

RECREATION AND EDUCATION

The introduction of an abundance of leisure time into the American social structure has exploded many of the traditional beliefs about leisure and has given new status to recreation.

Recreation cannot function in a watertight compartment any more than education can be effective if it is confined to the schoolhouse. A good education system cannot ignore the home and the community; a child is educated by his total environment. Both education and recreation are partners in the community and as such must be intimately related to all aspects of community life. Recreation today has become a vital part of daily living in all communities. Indeed, it is a basic human need and, therefore, must be related to education.

As early as 1918, the "worthy use of leisure time" was listed as one of the now famous Seven Cardinal Principles of Education. Unfortunately, two world wars and a crippling economic depression accompanied by a nineteenth century philosophy of education has given little support to this objective. It is yet to become a goal.

Schools have always been selective.

Early schools were for men. Many years were to pass before it was thought that women should be educated. Traditionally schools have been designed for bright students; no one worried too much about dropouts. In many sections of the country, it was not important to educate the Negro.

Today, however, the character and scope of education is changing. Pressures both from society and government are broadening the definition of education. Schools are offering programs for all segments of the population—to parents and adults, the retarded, the handicapped, the culturally and economically deprived, and the pre-school children. Flint, Michigan, boasts a community program where "everyone goes to school," and her citizens draw no sharp distinction between their education and their recreation.

Leading thinkers in the field of education and recreation tend to agree that in an age when education for leisure is fully as important as education for vocation, the schools must assume the responsibility for educating children for intelligent and creative use of leisure time.

Education is a prerequisite to the worthy use of leisure as a state of mind and recreation as an expression of man's self lifts him to higher levels of enriched community life. Through education in science and technology, America has mastered the art of saving time; through recreation education, America must now be concerned with the art of using leisure time.

THE RECREATION CURRICULUM

Recreation has too long been associated with the playing of games, with physical education, and even with the coaching of athletics. This came about because early leaders in recreation were physical educators who, because of their background, saw but one channel through which people could recreate—the physical.

Even today, many specialists working in recreation view the problem from their own personal education and experience. The dancing teacher recommends dancing, the librarian recommends reading, the dramatics teacher likes dramatics, the forester likes the forest, the art teacher prefers art, and the music teacher sees music as the ideal media for recreation.

All these areas and many more are important to both education and recreation, but they have their own excuse for being and their objectives are much more limited in scope. The major differences between physical education, forestry, art, music and dramatics on the one hand and recreation on the other rests in (1) motivation and (2) range of pursuits. Actually each of these areas, and many more, can make a contribution to recreation, but to confuse the whole with its parts is illogical and indefensible.

Recreation cannot be limited; it embraces all phases of a person's being—the mental, physical, social, emotional, and spiritual. It takes many forms and differs with the interests of each and every individual. The recreation program is built up on activities which cover the entire field of human interests. Although it includes sports and games, it may also encompass arts, crafts, dramatics, reading, gardening, swimming, hiking, nature loss, camping, hobbies, community services and countless other aesthetic and cultural pursuits.

Since World War II, the American society has undergone rapid and intense changes as a result of scientific research and technological improvement. One of the most dynamic and challenging, and yet most perplexing, of these changes is the leisure revolution.

With the ever-increasing leisure and continuing dehumanization of work, the average American is finding that leisure rather than work is becoming the factor which integrates and gives meaning to his life. Today, for the first time in history, man, en masse, has available disposable time, energy, and money which are unused in the process of making a living and which can be used for the enjoyment of his leisure hours. Such a change coming as it does in the context of an economy of plenty constitutes a primary revolution in which man takes his leisure as seriously as he once did his work.

Colleges and universities are faced with a sudden demand for recreation leaders. Because of the great demand, much leadership must come from the more narrowly trained special field leaders, such as forestry, physical education, music, dramatics, and other related fields. It is better to have a university graduate in an allied field than to have a person with no background in recreation at all.

Offering a recreation program in the church basement does not make the preacher a recreation leader. Moving the program to the hospital does not mean that the M.D. must be involved, and moving recreation to the woods should not demand that the forester serve as recreator. The professional recreator should be able to work in any setting wherever people come together for recreation. The minister, the physician, the forester, the physical educator and so on does not have time to prepare both in his own field and for the new and challenging profession of recreation.

A great need exists for a department of recreation, inter-disciplinary in nature and free to draw from every other department and area of the university. It is past time that colleges and universities provide leadership for recreation management positions.

Recreation must have a broad approach; like education, it must be general. The manager, leader or superintendent of recreation must see the value of all disciplines. In serving all the people, he cannot afford to stress one interest over another. His job is to promote fun and enjoyment, individual fulfillment and creative self-expression, and a sense of service to his fellowman and to his community. He must make these objectives attainable to every individual possible in the community in which he works.

The piece-meal approach to recreation education in the academic structure—that is, placing it in existing departments (usually physical education, sociology, or forestry)—has hampered both the unfortunate department and recreation itself. It has brought about confusion as to the meaning and the importance of recreation, and it has created the impression that all one need do is get a college degree in order to become a recreation leader.

In order to provide leadership for the age of leisure, colleges and universities must add departments of recreation to their academic structure. With America becoming more urbanized each day, forestry is hardly the place to house recreation. With the new concept of recreation, physical education is too limited in scope to provide the broad interdiscipline background needed by those who will manage man's leisure activities. Many other components, such as art, music, drama, sociology, psychology, geology, zoology, and geography can all make a contribution to recreation leadership; but each discipline alone does not have the broad objectives needed for educating the professional. The confusion and distortion regarding recreation will continue; and when the recreator says, "I teach recreation," the question will still be "What do you coach?"

How To Build a Strong Community Image: Do's and Don'ts for Recreators

H.D. Edgren

The belief that Qualified Professional Leadership is basic to effective programming and administration is a well established fact in the field of Recreation. The image the administrator establishes in any community is determined by his actions within his department and the part he plays in all aspects of community life.

He is recognized in the community as exemplifying the professional in Recreation, just as the doctor represents the medical profession, the Lawyer—Law and the Teacher the teaching profession. The extent to which he represents the best characteristics of our profession will be the image of recreation to the citizens of a given community.

The effective administrator giving the best image of professional leadership to the community will be characterized by the following:

1. In all areas of his administration he is guided by principles: (that is—accepted practices based on valid experience). Guas, White and Dimock in their book, *The Frontiers of Public Administration* give support to this when they say, "The difference between a great executive and a mediocre one is that the former will follow principles, whereas the latter relies upon precedent. The former will be progressive, inventive, original; the latter's actions will be stodgy, unimaginative, shot through with red tape."

2. He not only delegates responsibility to subordinates, but also the authority to go with it.

3. He is a cooperator with other municipal departments and other agencies in the community.

4. The program of his department is determined by objectives and goals sought for the life of the participant.

5. He is an efficient and accurate administrator of finance and the budgetary aspects of his job.

6. He believes in working with people rather than for them. Involvement of others in all aspects of the program is part of his philosophy.

7. He is familiar with all aspects and areas of the community in which he works.

8. He recognizes the importance of good public relations and uses all

Reprinted with permission from National Recreation and Park Association. Official publication *Parks and Recreation*, April, 1962.

of the best means of communications to promote his program and to keep the public informed.

9. He has a written policy which is the framework which governs all practices and programs.

10. He has a definite plan of selection, training, and supervision of all staff including volunteers.

In the development of an effective and positive community image of an administrator, I want to elaborate on six concepts which in my mind would go a long way in producing a noteworthy image.

I. LEISURE & RECREATION

The many communication media, books, magazines, newspapers, radio and TV have made a great contribution in identifying the importance of Leisure and of stimulating individual recreation pursuits. In this background of readiness on the part of the public, the time is right for the professional to make a case for the additional values of *organized recreation with professional leadership*. We need to stress the fact that recreation has become a significant function in our society and like other functions such as Health, Education, and Government, must have well qualified leadership. With this kind of leadership, recreation can make a "quality" kind of contribution to individuals and to society.

We will need to be more specific in the objectives and goals of recreation in terms of the values to the participants. General purposes such as *Fun* and *Happiness* are not enough. Fun is a result of the kind of experiences individuals may have had, that have met their needs. "Fun" may well be the goals of the participant but is not a professional objective. Many of our leaders have been too long content with claiming they have

the "know how." They have been experts in knowing *what* to do and how to do it, but have been unable to identify *why* they do it. The truly effective administrator of Recreation will know the *what, how,* and *why* of his program. Such an administrator is a professional.

II. COOPERATION FOR GOOD OF THE COMMUNITY

A major frontier waiting to be explored is the area of cooperation by public recreation with other Leisure Time Agencies, and self-motivated groups in our various communities. The public recreation director in particular has in my mind a unique opportunity of working with planning commissions, community welfare councils and other community groups. The alert recreation executive will see and use the opportunity of sharing his knowledge, insight and skill with other groups as an aid to total community betterment.

A national voluntary agency expressed a desire to establish a program in a city in my home state of Indiana. This request came to the attention of the Welfare Council. The City Recreation Director being a member of this Council was in a position to indicate the nature and scope of his program. The other members of this Council also indicated the scope of their program. As a result of this total picture of the community recreation program of this city, the Welfare Council recommended to the City Planning commissions that "A new agency would only duplicate what was already being adequately done and would make additional, unnecessary financial demands on the citizens of this city." As a result, this new agency was not invited to start a program in this city, Membership of this Recreation Executive on a Welfare Council added valuable knowledge to this group in viewing the needs of the entire community.

III. HUMAN BEHAVIOR

We will never know all there is to be known about the total behavior of individuals. The effective executive needs to be alert by constant study of new insights being developed in the areas of human development. With this knowledge, he will be concerned with what makes the individual act as he does and will spend more time in trying to understand the cause rather than the symptoms of aggressiveness, timidity, oversensitiveness are often indications of unmet needs and can be thought of as "The Language of Behavior." He will need to develop the ability to translate this knowledge and understanding about human behavior and motivation in all areas of his administration. This understanding can be part of his image."

IV. LEADERSHIP

We all agree I am sure that adequate and effective leadership is the key to successful program and administration. Recent studies cause one to question whether qualifications and traits are the same for all leaders. Ross & Hendry in their new book *New Understandings of Leadership*, give considerable evidence that the situation and needs of the group determine the leader. What is needed at a particular time in the life of a group, has a big effect on the type of leader who will be needed. This should prompt us to recognize that many individuals have qualifications for leadership and can serve in the role of leader at various times in the life of a group. It supports the belief that, "Leaders are made and not born."

We have too long magnified and belabored the need for motor and activity skills as a requirement of the recreation profession and have failed to magnify the need for the skills of the creator, the stimulator, the organizer, the promoter, the cooperator, the evaluator and the skills of democratic leadership. These it seems to me are the skills which make for the successful executive and will help the public to recognize and accept organized Recreation with professional leadership.

We must move from a belief that volunteers are only poor substitutes for paid workers to a concept that "being a volunteer" is "program" for the volunteer. Using them is justified for the value that comes to the volunteer as well as to the leadership of the department. Being related to some cause like organized recreation is a way of giving life, meaning and significance to the volunteer.

V. AGENCIES AND RECREATION

The effective administrator of Recreation can play an important role in delineating and clarifying the lines between the many different agencies in the leisure time field. He will be concerned with identifying common concerns as well as avoiding duplication of efforts. He will help to identify contributions that each can make to the other for the betterment of the total community. Some of us have belittled informal education as expressed in the volunteer agencies. All of us ought to appreciate the insights gained from those in this field who have magnified the significance of interaction between individuals and that they respond to recreation because of who is going to be present as well as because of the activity itself. Acceptance of this concept would influence the methods of promotion of our program.

It seems to be that we need to give

attention to and help clarify the distinctive and unique roles of both the public and voluntary agencies. The lack of of understanding of these agencies of each other has contributed to conflicts, rivalry and competition. In many communities the development of "Community Councils" has been an attempt to coordinate the efforts of all of the leisure time agencies. The recreation executive is in a unique position to stimulate and further the development of community councils so that agencies might better relate their particular contribution to the common community good.

A very significant study of relationships was made in 1946 entitled, *The Y.M.C.A. and Public Recreation, Informal Education and Leisure Time Programs.*" Many very important findings for us resulted from this study. A major generalization is, "The clear implication of Dr. Davis' study is that Y.M.C.A.'s should encourage the development of public recreation in their communities, that they should cooperate fully with those agencies and that they should seek the coordination of all public and private agencies to the end that the recreation needs of all the people might be met adequately." This I am sure is what we believe, but I am afraid we must admit we have not done very much to implement this concept for in many communities rivalry, competition, and jealousy are more prevalent that cooperation,

sharing and support of one another for the community good.

VI. EVALUATION

All too often the number of participants has been our only criteria of evaluation. We count numbers—and after a while only numbers count. Some leaders refer to other values as the "intangibles" of our program and they are thus relieved of considering them further. This has served as a screen to excuse leaders from pursuing evaluation.

In reality it must be the objectives and goals in the life of the participant that must become the basis for evaluation of any program.

As a significant fact of administration, we need to remind ourselves that "Whatever exists at all, exists in amount—and anything that exists in amount can be measured." Adequate tests and techniques are available for evaluating the many objectives of recreation.

Frequent evaluation should become the basis of modifying, refining, and upgrading our programs and administrative practices.

I have tried to identify some of the main areas in which each of us need to function in today's world if recreation is to make its all important contribution to our society and give a community an effective image of a professional Recreation Administrator.